Archaeology in the Holy Land

Kathleen M. Kenyon

Archaeology in the Holy Land

Fifth edition

Thomas Nelson Publishers
Nashville • Camden • New York

Published in the United States by Thomas Nelson, Inc., Nashville,
Tennessee and distributed in Canada by Lawson Falle, Limited, Cambridge, Ontario. First American printing in paperback: 1985.

First published 1960 by Ernest Benn, Limited, London
Second edition 1965
Third edition 1970
Fourth edition 1979

Library of Congress Cataloging in Publication Data

Kenyon, Kathleen Mary, Dame.
    Archaeology in the Holy Land.

    Reprint. Originally published: London: E. Benn, 1979.
    Bibliography: p.
    Includes index.
    1. Palestine--Antiquities. 2. Excavations
(Archaeology)--Palestine. I. Title.
[DS111.K4 1985]   933   85-13733
ISBN 0-8407-7521-0 (pbk.)

Contents

71998

Preface

This new edition was revised by Dame Kathleen and nearly ready for press just before her untimely death in August 1978. It was her intention, as stated in the Preface to the Third Edition (1969), to be able to incorporate into the Fourth Edition new material which had become available since the First Edition was published in 1960. Those familiar with past editions will note that this new one has been completely redesigned, the textual matter extensively rewritten, and new photographs and figures added to present the most up-to-date information concerning the archaeology of Palestine. This edition has therefore admirably fulfilled Dame Kathleen's intention.

The inclusion of the most important archaeological discoveries made within the last twenty years adds considerably to our knowledge of the cultural and historical problems of Palestine. The discovery of Pre-Pottery Neolithic B sites, for example, in both Syria and Palestine at Tell Ramad and Beisamun contributes valuable information for interpreting the seventh-millennium settlement at Jericho, a site which stood in isolation for its remarkable finds when Dame Kathleen's excavations were in progress from 1952 to 1958. Not only do these sites confirm that the PPNB newcomers at Jericho came from the north, but they also yielded plastered skulls comparable to those from Jericho which reveal to some extent the artistic achievement of these early settled communities.

Although Jericho remains one of the outstanding sites for the study of the pottery repertoire at the beginning of civilization in Palestine, recent excavations at Teleilat Ghassul provide pottery links with the final stages of Pottery Neolithic Jericho. The finds from Bab edh-Dhra', located on the east shore of the Dead Sea, offer evidence for interpreting the succeeding Proto-Urban Period which, at present, is best illustrated by tombs at Jericho, 'Ai, and Tell el Far'ah.

Excavations continue to produce so much material concerning the city states of the Early Bronze Age that most books are out of date by the time they reach the press. However, results of the most exciting and recent discoveries made at sites such as Bab edh-Dhra', Tell Arad, 'Ai, Ras el 'Ain (Tel Aphek), and Tell el Far'ah are presented to fill out the picture we already have from a number of well-known Palestinian sites. 'Ai, in particular, has provided material for Carbon-14 determinations which, studied in conjunction with well-defined Egyptian contacts, gives a good chronological framework for a great part of the Early Bronze Age.

The intermediate period of history in Palestine between the Early Bronze Age and the Middle Bronze Age, known as the EB–MB Period, was hardly known to exist forty years ago. Dame Kathleen's excavation and publication of the EB–MB Jericho tombs in the 1960s well illustrate some of the material remains of this period, but much more material has accumulated. Finds from the Dhahr Mirzbâneh tombs, Gibeon (el-Jib), the Beth-shan Northern Cemetery, Ma'ayan Barukh, and El-Huṣn shed much light on the origins and customs of the EB–MB people.

Even though the Middle Bronze Age is fairly well documented, Dame Kathleen offers new insights into urban development, burial practices, pottery sequences, and fortifications during this period of history. Almost all of Chapter 8, 'The Late Bronze Age and the Coming of the Israelites', has been rewritten to demonstrate how pottery chronology based upon the Jericho and Tell Beit Mirsim evidence, in particular, can clarify the periods of occupation assigned to the sites described in this chapter. Dame Kathleen's reinterpretation of the Megiddo evidence is of great importance as are her conclusions on temple architecture and Canaanite religion. The scanty archaeological evidence for the entry of the Israelites into Canaan is treated in detail.

Much new information has been forthcoming concerning the Philistines and the beginnings of the Early Iron Age. This period is well illustrated with the latest discussion bearing upon the excavations at Ashdod, Tell Qasile, and Deir el-Balah in relation to sites already known to have Philistine material.

Due to brilliant archaeological detective work on sites and a critical examination of published excavations by scholars in recent years, Dame Kathleen has been able to present us with a much clearer picture of the vast building operations carried out under King Solomon's leadership during the period of the United Monarchy at famous sites such as Megiddo, Hazor, and Gezer as well as corroborative evidence for the use of Phoenician-type masonry. The archaeological details of the Kingdoms of Israel and Judah have vastly increased because of renewed excavations at Megiddo, Gezer, and Lachish (Tell Duweir) and with recent publication of material from Jerusalem, Tell Arad, and Beersheba. In describing the fall of the Hebrew Kingdoms, Dame Kathleen draws heavily upon results of her own 1961–67 excavations in Jerusalem which are important for understanding the problems discussed in the final chapter.

The appendix, Excavated Sites and Bibliography, has been greatly expanded to include descriptions of the most important sites excavated with fairly comprehensive bibliographic references which contain useful information for both layman and scholar.

I am confident the reader will agree with me that Dame Kathleen has fulfilled the wish recorded in her first preface 'that this book will be of interest to the wide general public which regards the Bible as the greatest literary document in the world, and which likes to be able to understand it as the record of an actual people against a factual background'. Those with whom I share the privilege of having been closely associated with Dame Kathleen both in the field and on the publications of her scholarly endeavours will deeply appreciate the great effort it took on her part to complete this work in the midst of trying to bring to fruition the final publication of the magnificent excavations at Jericho. Everyone interested in the Holy Land will find much food for thought in these pages which reflect the culmination of a lifetime devoted to a greater understanding of the Bible through archaeological excavation and research.

Oxford   *T. A. Holland*
September 1978

List of Plates

51   Middle Bronze Age plastered rampart at Jericho. The vertical face in the foreground represents the position of the original revetment at the foot, from which the stones were removed for use in subsequent stages

52   Revetment wall at base of the third and final Middle Bronze Age rampart at Jericho. The wall is built on rock. The wall in the foreground belongs to the Iron Age, after débris had silted up against the face of the earlier wall

53   Middle Bronze Age plastered rampart at Tell Duweir. *Lachish* IV, Pl. 5.2

54   Air view of Hazor. In the foreground is the tell, on which Iron Age occupation was concentrated, in the background the plateau defended by the Middle Bronze Age rampart. *Hazor* I, Pl. I

55   Gaming pieces from Tell Beit Mirsim. *AASOR* XVII, Pl. 21b

56   Lower part of Stela from Tell Beit Mirsim, probably representing a serpent-god. A serpent appears to be coiled round the figure's robe. ibid., Pl. 22

57   The lower part of the Jericho street shown on Pl. 58, showing the drain beneath it, in Square H III

58   A street in Middle Bronze Age Jericho, in Square H II. On the right is the door of a house opening on to the street

59   Storage jars filled with grain in a Middle Bronze Age house at Jericho. The grain was burnt and the jars crushed when the town was destroyed, probably *c*. 1580 B.C.

60   A typical Middle Bronze Age tomb, G 73, at Jericho. The latest burial is in front, the earlier ones pushed to the rear

61   Jericho Tomb H 18; the principal burial lies on a wooden bed, beside which is a wooden table with a wooden platter on it; the food with which the table was loaded when found, has been removed; in the left-hand corner is a basket

62   Jericho Tomb H 22, with mass simultaneous burials; at the rear is a table loaded with food

63   Reconstruction of a room in a Middle Bronze Age house at Jericho, based on the evidence of furniture found in the tombs

64   Altar of Fosse Temple I at Tell Duweir. *Lachish* II, Pl. II

65   Fosse Temple Structure III at Tell Duweir. On the right is the altar; the benches were for the deposit of offerings; in the side wall are cupboards in which vessels were stored. *Lachish* II, Pl. IV.6

84   The outer enclosure wall at Samaria, with typical Israelite bossed masonry. *Samaria* I, Pl. XXXII.1

85   The first enclosure wall of the royal quarter at Samaria, illustrating the fine masonry (lower ashlar) of the earliest Israelite periods. ibid., Pl. XIII.2

86   The hill of Samaria from the east. ibid., Frontispiece

87   Ivory plaque from Samaria. The carving is in Egyptian style. *Samaria* II, Pl. II.2

88   Ivory plaque representing a palm tree, from Samaria. ibid., Pl. XX.1

89   Ivory 'bed-head' from room SW7, Fort Shalmanezer, Nimrud. *M.E.L. Mallowan, Nimrud and its Remains*, Pl. 390

90   The tunnel of the Megiddo water-system, leading from the base of the shaft to the spring. View taken looking back to the foot of the shaft. The bulge on the left indicates a very slight correction that had to be made in the alignment. *Megiddo Water System*, Fig. 48

91   Wall of the later monarchy at Jerusalem

92   Crest-mount of an Assyrian helmet from Tell Duweir. The reconstruction on the right shows the holes by which the flowing crest was attached. *Lachish* III, Pl. 39.1 and 2

93   Street of Level III at Tell Duweir. ibid., Pl. 15.2

94   Overflow channel from Pool of Siloam in Jerusalem

95   Cult centre outside walls of Jerusalem

96   Wall of Jerusalem on western ridge during the later monarchy. *IEJ* 20:3–4 (1970), Pl. 29

List of Illustrations in Text

Acknowledgements

Acknowledgement for kind permission to reproduce photographs is made to the following, to whom the copyright belongs:

'Ai expedition, Professor Joseph A. Callaway, director: 43, 44
American Schools of Oriental Research: 55, 56, 68
British School of Archaeology in Egypt: 72
British School of Archaeology in Jerusalem: 7, 8, 9, 10, 11, 12, 13, 14, 15, 16, 17, 18, 19, 20, 21, 22, 25, 36, 37, 46, 47, 50, 51, 52, 57, 58, 59, 60, 61, 62, 63, 69, 75, 76, 77, 91, 94, 95
Professor H. de Contenson: 26
Hebrew Union College, School of Biblical Archaeology, Jerusalem: 83
Institute of Archaeology, the Hebrew University of Jerusalem: 34
Israel Exploration Journal: 27, 30, 31, 79, 80, 96
Israel Exploration Journal and Mr S. J. Schweig: 32, 33
Mrs Diana Kirkbride-Helbaek: 28, 29
M. E. L. Mallowan, *Nimrud and its Remains*: 89
Oriental Institute, University of Chicago: 35, 40, 41, 48, 49, 70, 71, 73, 74, 82, 90
Oxford University Press: 1, 2, 3, 4
Palestine Exploration Fund: 84, 85, 86, 87, 88
University of Pennsylvania: 42
Pictorial Archive (Near Eastern History): 38
Rockefeller Museum, Jerusalem: 5, 6, 23, 24, 39, 81
James de Rothschild Hazor Expedition: 54, 66, 67
Professor C. F. A. Schaeffer-Forrer: 78
The Wellcome Trust: 45, 53, 64, 65, 92, 93

1 Introduction:
The Setting of Palestine in the History of the Near East

When the Palestine Exploration Fund was founded in 1865, its aims were defined as 'the accurate and systematic investigation of the archaeology, the topography, the geology and physical geography, the manners and customs of the Holy Land, for biblical illustration'. The essence is in the last two words. In the mid-19th century there was in England a great awakening of interest in the ancient history of the Near East. From Mesopotamia and Egypt were coming spectacular finds that demonstrated that these countries must be placed beside Greece and Rome as the homes of major ancient civilizations. But to God-fearing Victorian England, the Land of the Bible was a potential source of interest exceeding the still rather shadowy empires of Assur-bani-pal and Sargon or Thothmes and Rameses. The Palestine Exploration Fund was indeed the first of the societies to be formed for the study of the ancient past overseas, older by nearly twenty years than the Egypt Exploration Society and by fourteen years than the Society for Hellenic Studies.

The study of the background of the Bible was therefore the motive force behind the earliest exploration of Palestine. In the ensuing hundred years, many great discoveries have been made in the course of this exploration, and much patient work has supplemented the more spectacular finds. As a result, a connected history of Palestine for the period covered by the books of the Bible can now be written. But while this work has been going on the study of the ancient history of the other countries of the eastern Mediterranean and western Asia has made enormous strides. It would be true to say that early in the 19th century the Jews were the one nation in the ancient Near East with which the European was familiar. Now, partly owing to the decipherment of their texts and partly from the excavation of their cities and shrines, the history of the Egyptians, the Sumerians and other inhabitants of modern Iraq, the Hittites,

1

the Hurrians, and others is almost equally well known, and the position of the little Jewish kingdoms can be seen in a much better perspective as part of the whole great civilization of the Near East.

This is one aspect of our present understanding of Palestinian history and archaeology. The other is equally far-reaching. In Palestine and in the rest of the Near East, archaeology has pushed back our knowledge of places and people to thousands of years before the beginnings of written history. The decipherment of the Rosetta stone in the 1820s and of the Behistun inscription in the 1850s had given the key to the reading of the many documents of, respectively, Egypt and the Mesopotamian empires, which has carried back the beginnings of written history into the fourth millennium B.C. Pure archaeology without any help from documents provides our evidence for what went before.

Though the earliest interest in the archaeology of Palestine was in any association which could be established with the Bible, and though the interest in Egypt and Mesopotamia was in the spectacular monuments and written documents of their great periods of civilization, the earlier periods can now be seen to be of equally compelling interest, for this area is recognized to be the ultimate cradle of all European civilization. It is generally agreed that it was in the Near East that took place the first steps in the long process by which man ceased to be a savage, a hunter, and collector of wild foods, and became the inhabitant of a civilized community. We can now say that Palestine was at least one of the places in which some of these first steps were made. In order to appreciate the significance of the finds in Palestine, and to see in perspective the story that is told in the following chapters, a brief outline must now be given of what is known or deduced of the early steps in man's progress towards civilization, and thus of Palestine's setting in the general background of Near Eastern history.

Our earliest human ancestors, the first representatives of *Homo sapiens,* as well as those other species of man that for some reason died out in the evolutionary struggle, lived in what is known as the Palaeolithic stage. When the 19th-century archaeologists were trying to introduce some system of classification into the remains of ancient man, they used for the purpose the artifacts believed to be typical of the different stages, giving a primary classification of Stone, Bronze, and Iron Ages. The Stone Age was subdivided into the Old Stone Age, the Palaeolithic, in which implements were mainly made by a chipping technique, and the New Stone Age, the

Neolithic, characterized by polished stone axes. These distinctions were broadly valid for the area, western Europe, on the material of which the the classification was made. Nowadays our knowledge of man's way of life in the various stages has enormously increased. As a result, when we now speak of the Palaeolithic stage, we mean not only, and even not necessarily, that the typical implements are chipped stone hand-axes, but that the men of the period were dependent for their existence on the food they could gather by hunting, fishing, and other natural sources; they were food-gatherers. This stage is roughly co-terminous with the later stages of the Ice Age of Europe. Between the Palaeolithic and the Neolithic it is now recognized that there was an intermediate stage, the Mesolithic, in Europe belonging to a time when the Ice Cap had receded, and men were having to adapt their food-gathering methods to new environmental conditions.

The great development from the Palaeolithic and ensuing Mesolithic came when man started to produce food instead of gathering it. The importance of this is that it made it possible for him to settle down on one spot. The food-gatherers had to move about following their sources of food, the seasonal movement of the animals or the periods of growth of the herbs and grasses, and the resources of these foods meant that only a limited population could be supported in one area. Men lived, therefore, in nomadic family groups. The discovery of the possibility of cultivating wild grains, and thus of greatly increasing their yield, and of domesticating wild animals, and of thus keeping them within their owners' control, is basic to further progress. The cultivators of fields were not only enabled to settle in one spot because the yield of crops was sufficient to support them there, but they were in fact tied to that spot for at least part of the year while they waited for their crops to ripen.

Progress in tracing the origins of agriculture and of the domestication of animals has developed greatly in the last decades and new discoveries are still being made. Professor Gordon Childe was led from his investigation of the origins of European civilization to its background in the Near East. Since he wrote the last edition of his brilliant study of the ancient Near East,[1] the facts of the development of cultivation have become much more firmly established.

The claim of the Near East to be the place where settled life based on agriculture and stockbreeding began, and whence it spread to Europe, is based on the fact that it is in this area that are found wild

3

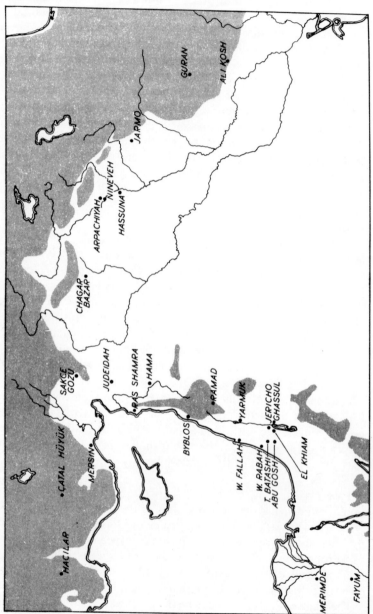

Fig. 1. Map of Near East showing principal Neolithic sites

the grains that man in due course cultivated and the animals he domesticated.

We now have a fairly clear picture of the distribution of the wild wheats and barleys that were the ancestors of the cultivated varieties.[2] The important early wheats were emmer, *triticum dicoccum*, which was considerably the more important, and einkorn, *triticum monoccum*. The wild ancestor of emmer, *triticum dicoccoides*, has a limited distribution, in the mountains of the Syro-Palestinian coast and the hill slopes of north-eastern Iraq. Since its cultivated descendant had such preponderant importance, it must be accepted that this area played an important part in the genesis of agriculture. *Triticum aegilopoides*, the ancestor of einkorn, had a wider distribution, covering the same area and most of Asia Minor. The wild ancestor of barley, *hordeum spontaneum*, is again found in this area, but its extension is even wider, in a broad band stretching to the region south and east of the Caspian. Since the wheats, emmer and einkorn, and barley are the basis of cultivated grains, it is reasonable to deduce especial importance in the beginnings of agriculture for the area in which all these are found.

The first food animals to be domesticated were goats and sheep. Their natural habitat corresponds closely with that described for the first grain-producing plants. There is considerable difficulty in deciding at what point domestication has taken place. Ultimately, the domesticated animals become smaller than their wild progenitors. But it requires many generations for morphological changes resulting from domestication to be reflected in the skeletons, which are in any case usually only fragmentarily recovered in excavations.

There is still much to be learnt about the early stages. The process is not a tidy one of nomadic or semi-nomadic Mesolithic food-gatherers settling down and developing agriculture to the extent of creating the artificial domesticated forms of grains. There are suggestions that in favourable circumstances a year-round settlement could be supported by harvesting wild grains, while at 'Ain Mallaha (Eynan), a year-round settlement with houses was apparently still dependent on a hunter-fisher economy. Much more evidence is still required.

In due course, the year-round settlement dependent on cultivated grains or stockbreeding became standard, with a fully-established settlement at Jericho by 8000 B.C., with evidence of many other sites in the next two thousand years. Progress thereafter was a rapidly

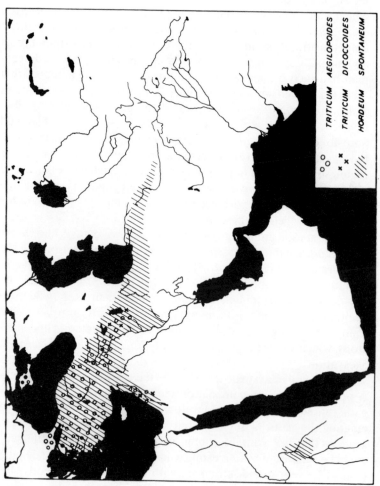

Fig. 2. Map of Western Asia showing distribution of wild grain.

accelerating phenomenon. The Palaeolithic stage, from man's first emergence from the beasts, may have lasted half a million years, the Neolithic some five thousand, the Bronze Age two thousand, and the Iron Age only five hundred or so before the Mediterranean classical civilizations emerge. Once man is settled in one spot, the rest follows. He has leisure to develop skills, and a sedentary life means that he can burden his household with their products, with the results of his handicrafts and his arts. A community life grows up, which is the basis of civilization. It is no longer a case of one family group against nature, including other family groups; man gains the security of living in an increasingly large group, and in the give and take of group life he sacrifices some of his primitive freedoms in turn for this security; the give and take becomes systematized into the regulation of customs and ultimately laws, and a communal organization emerges.

The investigation of the process of this transition of man as a savage to man as a member of a civilized community is thus of fascinating interest even to people living as far away as England or the United States from its first centres in the Near East.

Excavations since *c.* 1950 have shown that there are many variations in the rate and direction of development in this stage of fully established Neolithic settlements. Palestine will be dealt with in the next chapter. In at least three other areas there were other independent developments. On the Iraqi foothills of the Zagros Mountains a technological succession has been found of a terminal food-gathering community in the cave-shelter of Karim Shahir and a settlement at Jarmo, at first camping and followed by year-round occupation in which both forms of wild wheat and their domesticated descendants are found. Another important step is the appearance of pottery. The date is approximately 6000 B.C. The second area is in Anatolia, where at Hacilar and Çatal Hüyük remarkable examples are found of towns *c.* 6500 B.C., with fully domesticated wheat. There again, pottery appears in the later stages. Thirdly, there appears to be an independent North Syrian group with the most important site at Ras Shamra. A Pre-Pottery (or aceramic) stage here is followed in *c.* 6000 B.C. by the appearance of pottery, and a number of other Pre-Pottery sites are known in Syria, to which further reference will be made in connection with the Palestinian evidence.

This evidence acquired in the last two decades has provided us with a framework for the beginnings of settlement, of villages and towns, in western Asia. It has shown us what lay behind the point reached by research by about 1950. At that point it was taken that the string of villages running round the Fertile Crescent in which primitive pottery was found represented the beginning of the Neolithic. We now know that in fact they represented the last stage of the Neolithic way of life. We also know that there was not one area where this way of life emerged and that a comparable evolution took place in a number of areas.

One of the stimuli that caused communities to develop beyond the Neolithic stage was the discovery of the uses of materials, chief among them copper, which could not be provided by each group for itself. As the advantages of copper over stone for tools and weapons became apparent, communities had to enter into trade to secure it, and therefore had to produce extra foodstuffs or other natural products to pay the traders and also the smiths who made the implements, and who, as specialists, no longer had the time to provide their own food. Thus the self-sufficiency of the small units began to break down, and the complex structure of civilized communities began to develop.

Up to this stage there was apparently more or less parallel development over much of the Fertile Crescent, including, as we shall see, Palestine. But in subsequent stages, dating from approximately the beginning of the fourth millennium B.C., the two tips of the Crescent began to outstrip the rest. The reason for this was the opportunity provided by the great rivers which watered the two valleys. The rivers provided the fertility that rendered possible the accumulation of surpluses of food which could be traded for other goods, and at the same time the necessity of controlling irrigation and flooding called forth the development of organization and leadership. Also, the river valleys lacked stone for making tools or for building, so the communities early had to develop the enterprise necessary to obtain these materials. Thus the villages of the river valleys began to outstrip others less favourably situated, and in the course of the fourth millennium proceeded to develop into towns and city states. Early in the third millennium the process was in each case completed by one of the city states taking the lead, and uniting the rest into an empire. Connections between these two river valleys had begun to be established by the end of the fourth millennium, and the interplay between the two empires was to be the main theme of Near Eastern history for the next three thousand years. From each end of the Fertile Crescent the influence of the developing civilizations spread back into the rest of the Crescent, stimulating the more backward areas, and the rivalry between the two empires, later supplemented by other great Powers in Asia Minor and its fringes, inevitably affected continually the fate of countries such as Palestine which lay on the connecting route.

Such, in very brief outline, is the background against which the history of Palestine develops. Situated as it is towards the south-western end of the Fertile Crescent, it shared in the development towards civilization of the people of the Crescent. When the great empires at the extremities of the Crescent began to assert themselves, it absorbed influences from them, primarily of course from its nearer neighbour Egypt, but Mesopotamian contacts can also be traced; it fell under their sway at times of their political expansion, and it formed the route they traversed in warfare against each other.

The degree to which different parts of Palestine were influenced by her neighbours was largely modified by the geography of the country itself. Like Syria to the north, which forms a physical unit with it, Palestine is divided into four sharply distinguishable belts running north and south: first, the Coastal Plain, secondly the Central Range, running down from the Lebanon through Galilee and the mountains of Samaria and Judaea, and then dropping to the table-land of the Negeb, thirdly the Jordan Valley, with its continuation the Wadi 'Arabah stretching down to the Gulf of Aqaba, and finally the Eastern Range running down through the Hauran and the mountains of Gilead and Moab to Edom, while to the east it slopes away into the plateau of the Arabian Desert. The Central Range rises fairly gradually from the Coastal Plain, by way of the Shephelah or low hill-country, but to the east, from an average height of 2,400 feet above sea level in the mountains of Judaea, it drops abruptly to the Jordan Valley, which at the Dead Sea lies 1,290 feet below sea level, and the Eastern Range rises almost as abruptly to about 2,000 feet.

This physical conformation has had two important historical results. In the first place, the easiest lines of communication are inevitably north and south, and among these routes the Coastal Plain provides the principal. Connected with the Coastal Plain is another physical feature of historical importance, the Plain of Esdraelon, which breaks across the Central Range and forms a connection between the Coastal Plain, the Jordan Valley, and the uplands of Transjordan. This provided in fact the principal route between the extremities of the Fertile Crescent, for in Syria the

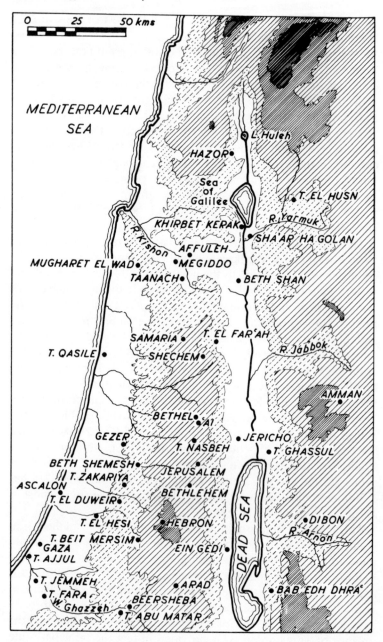

Fig. 3. Map of Palestine, showing principal ancient sites

Coastal Plain is much constricted and inconvenient, and it was by this Esdraelon route that passed the great armies of Egypt and her enemies. The Coastal Plain was also naturally open to influences from the sea, though its harbours were few and poor. Thus the flat country along the coast and the Plain of Esdraelon were especially affected by foreign influences and its cities were liable to destruction by foreign enemies.

On the other hand, the uplands of the Central Range, though by no means inaccessible even from the east, tend to lie to one side of the main currents. Foreign influences penetrate slowly, while foreign armies may pass by without affecting it, unless they are bent on subduing the country and not merely using it as a route.

But though most of the civilizing influences throughout its history have come to Palestine along the Fertile Crescent, another equally important influence must not be forgotten. The Fertile Crescent encloses the plateau of the Arabian Desert, which from the dawn of history has served as a vast reservoir of nomadic raiders upon the riches of the surrounding Crescent. The history of each of the countries of the Crescent has been profoundly modified by a whole series of incursions of these nomads, sometimes raiding and returning, but more often overrunning and settling down. These nomads each in their turn destroyed much of the pre-existing civilization, but also absorbed much, and, by the introduction of new blood, revitalized the population and in their turn produced a new civilization. A study of the archaeology of Palestine will show evidence of a succession of waves of newcomers, many no doubt originating from the desert. Of these waves, two, those of the Hebrews and the Arabs, are well known to us, but they are only two among many.

Though Palestine is the home of the most famous book in the world, our knowledge of by far the greater part of its story, in terms of time, is dependent upon archaeology. Written history, or at least written documents upon which history can be based, are available at a date some fifteen hundred years earlier in the valleys of the Nile and Tigris—Euphrates, but even in these areas archaeology both carries the story back into earlier millennia and does much to supplement it even after the periods from which written documents survive in considerable numbers. Since much of the story to be told in the following chapters is based wholly or in part on archaeology, it is desirable at this stage to consider what archaeology can do, and what are its limitations.

Given reasonably favourable conditions, archaeology can

11

recover from a site on which man lived those structures and those objects which have survived the passage of time. That is the first major limitation. Many materials, for instance wood, textiles, basketry, in fact almost all untreated organic materials, do not survive the passage of time, and one has only to consider one's own surroundings to see how incomplete the picture would be if all objects of organic materials had disappeared. Even solid structures, when abandoned, comparatively soon start to crumble under the effects of time and weather. One can see the process going on in abandoned crofters' houses in the Highlands of Scotland. The roofless walls stand up from heaps of débris derived from the collapsed roof and crumbling superstructure, and each year more stones from the walls add to the débris, until nothing but a mound remains, and vegetation completes its burial. The archaeologist would be able to recover the plan of the house from the stumps of the walls, and from the objects left behind by the inhabitants, as being not worth taking away when they evacuated, he would gain some impression, but a one-sided one, of their culture. From the traces of their outbuildings, he might obtain an impression of the area of land they cultivated and how they cultivated it. From stray coins, or from objects which could be associated with a particular period, say part of a bicycle, or a muzzle-loading fire-arm, he could make an estimate of when the building was first occupied and when abandoned.

In some cases, of course, conditions are more favourable. If a building, or a town, is overwhelmed by a great catastrophe, and the inhabitants have to leave all their possessions behind, there is much more to tell the archaeologist how they lived, particularly if the nature of the catastrophe is such as to preserve large portions of the buildings. The supreme examples of this are Pompeii and Herculaneum, where volcanic dust and mud respectively buried the houses to a great depth, so that sometimes even their upper storeys are preserved.

This then is the basic material upon which an archaeologist examining a house or town site has to work, the plans of the structures (and of course the architecture if there is enough preserved) and their contents. Sometimes these contents will include objects of art; sometimes only common household goods. Sometimes they will include written material, a dedicatory inscription of a Roman temple, or a centurial stone commemorating the building of a military structure, with attendant details of the Emperor and the responsible officials, while in western Asia archives or literary documents written on clay tablets may survive. In these cases, the association of the structures with known history, within a chronological framework, is easy.

In the excavation of a single, one-period building, or of a village or town of short duration, the archaeologist's *problem* is a relatively simple one, though considerable manual skill may be required to recover delicate objects. He has merely to trace the buildings and find and preserve (and of course interpret) the objects. But very often even a single building may have a complex history of rebuildings and alterations. In order to discover the full history of the building, these must be recognized and interpreted, and the objects found associated with the correct phase. Sometimes the interpretation may be relatively easy. To return to our example of the crofter's homestead. If after the original homestead had crumbled into a mound a second crofter had come and built his house on top of the mound, the two houses would be separated by the débris derived from the earlier. There should not be much difficulty in differentiating between the objects belonging to the two periods, except that the foundations of the later walls might have been cut down some distance into the earlier débris. More often, however, the position is much more complex. An original nucleus may have a whole series of additions made to it, converting a simple cottage into an elaborate farm or even mansion. Successive houses may have cut into earlier ones, on almost the same level, or even terraced down below the absolute level of the earlier floors. If the picture of the social and economic development is to be correctly interpreted, one must be able to say which objects are to be associated with which stage; otherwise one might date the original building much too late, or, if the evidence seemed to point clearly to its being of a certain period, one might ascribe objects erroneously believed to be associated with it to too early a date. One might, for instance, say that one had evidence that bicycles were in use in the Highlands in A.D. 1800, because one found a bicycle frame outside the front door of a homestead dated by coins to that date, whereas really it was in the cellar of an overlying homestead built in A.D. 1910.

The position in the Near East is usually much more complicated. For one thing, settled life has been going on there for far longer than it has in the West. Moreover, the tendency is for villages and towns to remain on the same site for hundreds or even thousands of years, usually because the site is favourable either for military or for economic reasons, such as proximity to a good water supply. From natural decay or from destruction by enemies, by earthquakes, or by accidental fires, houses and public buildings have succeeded one another time and time again. Each has risen on the ruins of its predecessor, sometimes a few inches higher only, sometimes upon feet of débris. Though deliberate cutting down or terracing into earlier buildings has sometimes taken place, the general tendency has been for the town level to rise. Much of the Near East is therefore covered by mounds marking the site of ancient towns or villages, sometimes with a modern settlement on top, sometimes abandoned. In the Arabic-speaking areas these artificial mounds are known as *tells*. Ancient Jericho is thus Tell es Sultan, Megiddo Tell el Mutesellim, and the central mound of Ur Tell el Muqayyar. The growth of these tells is particularly characteristic of those areas in which the local building material was mud-brick, for a destroyed building of mud-brick disintegrates into mud again, which cannot be used again in the same way that stone from a stone building can be. The growth of the tell is therefore more rapid. The job of the archaeologist is to excavate these tells in such a way that from the surviving remains he can reconstruct their history.

This is completely dependent on recognizing the different layers in the soil and correctly associating them with the successive build- ings. In this way, one knows which objects are on, or in, the floors of a building, and which belong to the débris of the building under- neath. As long ago as 1890, Sir Flinders Petrie established for Near Eastern archaeology the main principle of the succession of building levels in his excavation of Tell Hesi in southern Palestine. But the full refinement of this stratigraphical excavation is a product of western European archaeology, especially British, German, Scan- dinavian, and Dutch. The remains of ancient structures in these countries are mainly so slight, and the finds so relatively scanty and commonplace, that the development of refinements in excavation technique was essential to extract any information at all. Excavation in the Near East had big potential prizes—temples, palaces, and royal archives—and also a large and cheap labour force available, and therefore minutiae of archaeological observation were ignored. In Palestine the greater part of results of the major excavations before the First World War on sites such as Gezer, Samaria, and Jericho cannot be relied upon, and much revision is required of the results of the excavations between the two wars, though improve- ments in technique did result in sufficient information being provided for the necessary reinterpretation. Reference to some of these reinterpretations will be made in the following chapters.

By the proper technique, therefore, the archaeologist should be able to produce the story of the sequence of events and cultures of the site with which he is concerned. But this is only the beginning. The site must be fitted into a regional and a chronological framework. Even at very early periods, in the Palaeolithic stage, fashions of technique in the making of stone implements provide evidence of regional cultures, and their succession provides a broad chronological framework, which can be tied in with phases in the Ice Age and the geological features connected with it. In the early post-glacial phases, flint techniques, and also techniques in making bone implements, are still the basis of establishing cultural relationships. But once the manufacture of pottery becomes common, this becomes much the most important means of diagnosis. The usefulness of pottery vessels ensures their presence in every household, their comparative fragility ensures the presence of great numbers of potsherds on all occupied sites, and the practical indestructibility of a potsherd ensures for the benefit of archaeologists the survival of evidence of what kind of pottery was in use. Moreover, conservatism and imitativeness as human characteristics have resulted in the widespread use of similar forms of vessel among allied peoples, and of the almost contemporary spread of newly introduced types. We can therefore say that groups of people in, say, Early Bronze Age Palestine, using the same types of pottery, are approximately contemporary, and that the appearance of a new type on different sites marks a definite chronological point. By stratigraphical excavation we can associate this same chronological point with a structural phase in the history of the different sites. Other objects also can be shown to have regional and chronological significance, for instance types of bronze daggers and pins, but pottery is relatively so much more common that its importance transcends all other finds.

Between the two wars a reasonably complete and accurate knowledge of the sequence of the pottery forms of Palestine was built up. But a sequence is not a chronology. Chronology in Palestine cannot stand on its own feet until one is dealing with a relatively late epoch. Until the first millennium B.C. it must rely on links with neighbouring countries. Earlier in this chapter mention was made that by the end of the fourth millennium the towns of the great river valleys of the Nile and Tigris—Euphrates began to outstrip the settlements of the rest of the Fertile Crescent. The increasing complexities of town and state organization involved, among other things, the working out of a calendar. The first true calendar was established in Egypt, perhaps as early as *c.* 3000 B.C., and a combination of literary sources and archaeological evidence makes it possible to date dynasties and phases in Egypt and Mesopotamia reasonably accurately back to about that date. We have no early literary sources or king-lists for Palestine. Even in the period covered by the biblical record the genealogical evidence is not reliable (a point which is discussed in a later chapter) until the period of David, *c.* 1000 B.C., and no true calendar is used at all. Events are recorded as taking place, for example, 'in the thirty and first year of Asa King of Judah', and though the chronology of the various kings of Judah and Israel can now be fixed within close limits, this is only because their reigns can at certain points be linked with Egypt.

Archaeological remains, however, must still be linked with the reigns of these biblical kings, and it has so happened that there is very seldom much direct evidence for this. An exception is Samaria. It was founded by Omri on a virgin site in the sixth year after his accession, which can be fixed, ultimately by links with the Egyptian calendar, to 880 B.C. The destruction of Samaria in 720 B.C. by the Assyrians, and of other cities, such as Lachish, by the Babylonians in 596 and 588 B.C., can also be fixed, and be associated with archaeological levels. Otherwise, even in these comparatively late periods, it is mainly a matter of establishing a sequence and fitting it in as closely as possible with known events. It is true that a certain amount of epigraphic material of the period of Hebrew kingdoms has been found. None in itself, however, provides dating for a phase in the history of a site, for it so happens that none providing exact chronological data has been found *in situ* on a site,[3] and the knowledge of ancient Hebrew epigraphy is not yet exact; the epigraphic material has to be dated from its find-spot, and not vice versa.

For the earlier periods, both those preceding the biblical period and those for the period in which the biblical record is in the form of a traditional account rather than of a contemporary chronicle, the archaeological sequence is the only framework, and this can only be given a broad chronological significance by relation to Egypt and, occasionally, to Mesopotamia. In the late fourth and third millennia there were occasional imports into Palestine which serve to tie in the Palestinian periods with those of those countries that had already entered the historic period. Moreover, it is clear that the fortunes of the Palestinian and Syrian littoral became broadly linked with those of Egypt once the Old Empire was established *c*. 3200 B.C.[4] Under the Old Empire, and even earlier, contacts were established at least as far north as Byblos, just north of Beirut, and some control may have been exercised over the coastal lands. In Palestine such links as we have provide reasonable evidence that the period of settled and urban development of the Early Bronze Age is approximately contemporary with the Old Empire. The Intermediate Early Bronze—Middle Bronze period in Palestine, marked by nomadic invasions, corresponds with the interruption of civilization of the First Intermediate of Egypt, due to the same reason and possibly to the same groups of people. The restoration of civilization in the Middle Bronze Age of Palestine corresponds with the Middle Empire of Egypt, and numerous imports reflect a close connection. The evidence of the Hyksos invasion of Egypt *c*. 1730 B.C. can be traced in Palestine, as can the events when the first kings of the Eighteenth Dynasty in Egypt threw the Hyksos back into Palestine *c*. 1560 B.C. The archaeological sequence in Palestine from *c*. 3000 B.C. can thus broadly be linked with the fixed chronology of Egypt, but only broadly, and any attempt to assign exact dates in years within these broad limits can be guesswork only.

A chronology based on an ancient calendar, however, can take us no farther back than *c*. 3000 B.C. Until very recently, that was all that we had. Anything earlier was a sequence only and dates in years assigned to any phase were also only guesswork. Since 1944, however, a new method, first developed by Dr Libby in Chicago, has been introduced. This is usually known as the Carbon-14, or radioactive carbon, method. It is based on the fact that all living organisms, human beings and other animals, trees and plants, absorb radioactivity while they are alive, and after they are dead give it up at a rate which can be established. The surviving amount can be measured in organic materials recovered on archaeological sites. For various technical reasons charcoal, and to a lesser extent shell, is the most satisfactory material. By comparison of the surviving amount of radioactivity and the established annual rate of loss, the date at which the organism died, for instance the date at which the tree was cut down, can be established.

The method is still being adjusted. In the early stages it was taken that the strength of radiation from the sun had been constant. By comparison of radio-carbon dates of Egyptian material, especially of the third millennium B.C., to which a historical date could be given, it became apparent that some radio-carbon dates were too young. A

17

means was found by checking radio-carbon dates by dendrochrono-
logy, the counting of annual growth rings of trees, using specimens of
an extremely long-lived tree, the bristle-cone pine. The results suggested a curve of variation of radioactivity could be established by
which radio-carbon dates could be more closely adjusted to calendar
dates. The degree of variation is still not firmly established, and
archaeologists are advised to continue to use the Carbon-14 dates,
with the recognition that there may be a divergence of several
hundred years from the calendar dates.

There is, however, always a standard margin of deviation, usually
of about 150 to 200 years on either side of a central date. Therefore
for the periods after *c*. 3000 B.C., the Carbon-14 method is unlikely
to give as exact a result as evidence based on other archaeological
grounds. But for the earlier periods it is our only source. As will be
seen, we already have dates going back to *c*. 9000 B.C., and as
evidence accumulates from additional observations we shall both
gain assurance whether or not these comparatively isolated results
are reliable, and be able to fit other phases and cultures into the
general scheme.

Notes

1. *New Light on the Most Ancient East*, rev. ed. (London, 1958).
2. See especially H. Helbaek, *Science*, vol. 130 (August 1959), no. 3372.
3. The Siloam inscription, which can reasonably be associated with the work of
   King Hezekiah (see pp. 290-3), dates the Siloam tunnel, but not any phase in
   the history of the town of Jerusalem itself. The Moabite stone was a casual
   discovery. The Samaria ostraca by the regnal years of the king provide limits for
   the reigns of the king to which they refer, but their find-spot was not accurately
   recorded with reference to the structural phases of the town.
4. Egyptian chronology itself is still not quite firmly fixed for these early dates, and
   different authorities suggest initial dates for Dynasty I between *c*. 3200 B.C. and
   c. 2900 B.C. The revised *CAH* favours 3100 B.C.

2 The Beginnings of Settled Life

On the seaward slopes of Mount Carmel are a number of caves that have provided evidence of human occupation covering tens of thousands of years during the Palaeolithic period (Pl. 1). Hunters, resembling those of Europe both in physical type and in the implements they used, made these caves their headquarters. Overlying these Palaeolithic levels are others belonging to the Mesolithic, the period in which in Europe the Ice Cap was retreating, and in which the descendants of the hunters of the Palaeolithic were adapting themselves to their changed environment. In the Mount Carmel caves, there is evidence that in Palestine too man adopted a new way of life.

Above the layers containing Palaeolithic implements is the evidence of the appearance of a new group. The flint industry does not seem to be derived directly from any Upper Palaeolithic culture, and its ancestry has not yet been traced. It seems, however, to have been an indigenous Palestinian culture, found only as far north as the mid-Lebanon, and in the south there is an outlier at Helouan in Egypt. The name Natufian has been given to this culture, after the Wadi en-Natuf where it was first found. Like the Mesolithic industry in Europe, the flints include great numbers of microliths, small flakes of various shapes, many of them probably used as part of composite tools. Most characteristic of all are the lunates, very fine little flakes with a straight edge and a crescent-shaped back. Over four thousand of these were found in one of the Mount Carmel caves (Pl. 6).

The Natufians of Mount Carmel, and of rock-shelters on the eastern and western slopes of the Judaean hills, lived mainly by hunting. In the Mount Carmel caves were found enormous quantities of gazelle bones. Gazelles live in open country and fairly dry conditions, indicating that as conditions in Europe were changing as the Ice Cap receded, so in the Mediterranean area the contemporary pluvial period was passing away. Fishing was also a means of subsistence, for both bone harpoon-points and bone fish-hooks are found.

One type of implement among the equipment of the Natufians is of special interest. This is a sickle. Large numbers of sections of blades were found with the cutting edge showing a broad band of lustre from use, and with, as a rule, the back trimmed to a ridge to fit into a V-shaped groove in a haft. Portions of bone hafts with flints still in position have been found, and also two complete hafts, each of which has an animal head or figure carved on the end of the handle (Pls. 2, 5).

The presence of sickles is not a proof that agriculture was practised, for the sickles might be used for gathering wild grains. Many authorities do, however, accept the view that the Natufians of Mount Carmel had begun to cultivate grain. Some claim that wild grasses cannot be harvested with such sickles, since the heads are too brittle and the seeds would be lost. It is, on the other hand, compellingly argued that since so much care was lavished on the fashioning of the sickles and since such a high proportion of sickle blades was found, they represented something of considerable importance in the life of the community. Certainly, too, the Natufian group inhabited the Mount Carmel area for a very long time, so something probably tied them to the spot. A case can therefore be made out for some first experiments in agriculture in Palestine in the transitional stage following the end of the Ice Age. There is not, however, any clear evidence of the domestication of animals.

What would appear to be a later stage in development is found at 'Ain Mallaha, on the edge of Lake Huleh in the Jordan Valley. Here the occupants lived in huts rather than caves. The huts were circular, semi-subterranean, paved with flat slabs and surrounded by stone walls up to 1·20 metres high, above which there was presumably a superstructure of reeds and clay. The huts had a single room, and it could be calculated that there were about fifty contemporary structures, with a population of two hundred to three hundred individuals. The material equipment was Natufian, resembling that of the Mount Carmel caves, but the inhabitants apparently lived by fishing in the waters of the Lake rather than by gathering grain.

Another settlement not associated with a rock-shelter, in which there were also traces of huts, was Beidha, east of the Arabah, and about 6 kilometres north of Petra. The Mesolithic deposit was found beneath a fill of *c*. 2 metres of sterile sand, above which was a Pre-Pottery Neolithic village. The number of Natufian sites now known in Palestine covers a wide area, and it is clear that there were widespread groups belonging to this transitional stage of progress towards a fully-settled way of life.

The other main point of interest about the Natufian people is their burial practices. The dead were buried beneath the area inhabited by the living. At the Mugharet el Wad, on Mount Carmel, more than sixty individuals were buried in the cave or on the terrace in front of it. The earlier burials seem to have been communal, with the bodies tightly flexed, the later individual, with the bodies less tightly flexed. The communal burials in particular give evidence of the taste of the Natufians for personal ornament. In each group one skeleton, presumably that of the most important member of the family, has a quite elaborate adornment of shells and pendants. The most common ornaments were made up of *dentalia* shells, little tubes which can be picked up on the shore of Palestine today. These would of course be readily accessible to the inhabitants of the Mount Carmel caves, but they are also found on sites on the eastern slopes of the Judaean hills, showing that objects even at this early date could be collected or traded from an appreciable distance. The most elaborate use of these shells for adornment was in a head-dress consisting of a fan-shaped arrangement on either side of the head (Pl. 3). The bodies also had necklaces of pendants, made of pierced teeth or the toe-bones of gazelle, or carved in bone and arranged in pairs rather like opposed heads of wooden golf-clubs (Pl. 4).

The burial of the dead was apparently a matter of some cere-mony. At the Mugharet el Wad, a wall, pavement, and some basins hollowed out of the rock were apparently associated with a group burial, and at Erq el Ahmar a similar group was also covered by a pavement. At 'Ain Mallaha, on the shores of Lake Huleh in the Jordan Valley, a burial closely resembling that of Mount Carmel, with a crown of *dentalia* shells, was made in a pit lined with plaster, covered by a pavement above which was an arrangement of stones in circles.

In the period following the end of the Ice Age, Palestine therefore was inhabited by a group of which the way of life resembled that of Mesolithic groups in Europe in many ways, particularly in its reliance on hunting and fishing and in its use of microlithic imple-ments. The ornaments worn are peculiar to the group, but neither these nor the carvings in bone and stone would be out of place among similar European communities. It is in the probability that these people were experimenting in agriculture that they are unique. The finds from Mount Carmel are the earliest suggestion of the cultivation of food that have so far been found.

The Natufian on Mount Carmel and other sites had a long life. A Middle and Upper Natufian can be identified from developments of the types of implements. On the whole, these represent deterioration, particularly in the bone implements made. A new introduction in the Upper Natufian is a recognizable arrowhead. A claim that there is evidence in a Middle Natufian level for the domestication of dogs has recently been queried.

But it now becomes probable that the sequence from Lower Natufian to a Middle and Upper Natufian of a similar but poorer character is not the only line of development. In 1957 Professor Dorothy Garrod could say 'there is no trace of Natufian occupation at the base of any of the Palestinian tells'.[1] This position has now been changed by the latest finds at Jericho.

Ancient Jericho is today represented by a mound about 10 acres (4·05ha.) in extent and about 70 feet (21·34m.) high, on the outskirts of the oasis of modern Jericho. It owes its existence, as indeed does modern Jericho, to the magnificent perennial stream that wells up at its foot. The stream must draw its source from some underground reservoir fed by the rains on the uplands of Judaea, and it is vital to the life of Jericho. Rainfall in the Jordan Valley may be violent in winter, but in summer the great heat of this area, at Jericho *c.* 900 feet below sea level, dries everything up. Only in areas within reach of the waters of some permanent source such as that of the spring of 'Ain es Sultan at Jericho can the rich soil of the valley be made truly productive.

The mound of ancient Jericho (Pl. 7) is an emphatic witness to the importance of the spring. The whole of its 70 feet is the result of human occupation, covering a period of over eleven thousand years. The spring today emerges at the eastern side of the tell, forcing its way out of the ground over a fairly wide area. The original source, perhaps a cave in the limestone, must lie buried beneath the débris of occupation, and has not been found. But it is clear from the evidence of the various areas excavated to bedrock that before there was any human occupation the surface of the rock sloped gently down from the west, from the ultimate foothills of the cliff-wall bounding the Jordan Valley, and that the spring must have

22

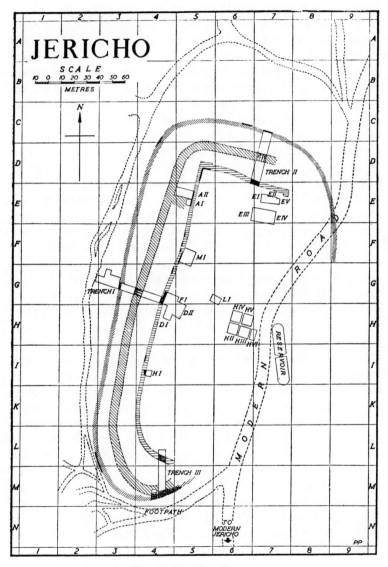

Fig. 4. Plan of Jericho, showing Bronze Age walls and excavated areas

broken out to the surface just at the point at which the hill slopes flatten off into the alluvial plain of the valley-bed.

Hunters may have visited the spring from the very earliest stages of the Palaeolithic, as no doubt did the animals they hunted. One Palaeolithic hand-axe was indeed found in a Neolithic level, but there is no means of telling whether it was derived from the vicinity or from farther afield. The first definite evidence on the site concerns the Mesolithic period. On bedrock towards the north end of the tell (Site E on Fig. 4) excavations in 1958 revealed a curious structure (Pl. 8). In this area basic limestone was in its natural state covered by a layer of clay about a foot thick. Over most of the area excavated this clay had been removed by man, and the surface of the limestone exposed. But at the west end of the excavated area, a rectangle of the clay, 3·50 metres broad and more than 6·50 metres long, had been left, and had been enclosed by a substantial wall of stones, with wooden posts set in the wall at intervals. This structure was quite unlike any dwelling-house found on the site. Moreover, there were two other noteworthy features. Built into the wall were two large stone blocks, which had had holes bored right through them, the total depth of the holes being about 2 feet 6 inches (0·75m.). A third block, broken in half, lay beside them. They had obviously been intended to hold posts, and from their resemblance to flag-pole sockets, one is tempted to suggest that they held totem-poles, the primitive equivalent to flag-poles. Secondly, though the adjacent rock surface was covered with débris and rubbish, the surface of the clay platform had been kept scrupulously clean throughout the time it was in use. It is therefore possible that this curious structure was a sanctuary or some kind of holy place.

The interpretation of the structure is hypothetical, but its cultural setting is certain. From the associated débris were recovered a collection of objects which are certainly Natufian. Among the numerous microliths was a beautiful little lunate, and, most characteristic of all, there was also a bone harpoon head. This is particularly important, since at Mount Carmel harpoon heads were found only in the Lower Natufian levels. Therefore it is certain that the first structure at Jericho was built by people allied to the first Mesolithic group in the Mount Carmel caves. Thus one can reasonably interpret it as a sanctuary established by Mesolithic hunters beside the source of the Jericho spring. Water sources have been held sacred by primitive people throughout the ages. Beautiful little votive objects have been found at the source of the Seine; many fine

Romano-British objects have been found in the well of Coventina on the Roman Wall in Britain; and even today, in the Orient, rags will be attached to a tree beside a spring as a propitiation of the spirit of the spring.

Most fortunately for archaeologists, this structure was eventually burnt down. The surrounding area was covered by charcoal from the beams that had been incorporated in it. The first Carbon-14 dating from this charcoal was 7800 B.C. ± 210. A corrected date from the same apparatus gave a date of 8840 B.C. ± 180. A date from Philadelphia (using the same basis of calculation) gave a date of 9216 B.C. ± 103 or (on a different basis) 9687 B.C. ± 107. Further refinements may make it possible to say which is the probable date, but for the time being it looks as though a date of *c*. 9000 B.C. is probable for this first record of human activity near the spring of 'Ain es Sultan.

The general background of the Mesolithic builders of this structure is certainly that of hunters and food-gatherers. But as we have seen, the inhabitants of the caves on Mount Carmel may have already been experimenting in agriculture, the prerequisite of any full settled occupation. The finds at Jericho show that these experiments laid the basis of success. Towards the centre of the tell (Site M on Fig. 4) a highly significant discovery was made. Here was found a series of the Neolithic structures which are described below. But between them and bedrock was a deposit of 13 feet (3·96m.) which produced no traces of any solid structure. A close study showed that this 13 feet was made up of innumerable floors bounded by slight humps which were all that remained of slight, hut-like structures. Therefore, for a very considerable length of time, people were living beside the spring of Jericho; living on the same post, but still living in the sort of habitation suited to a nomadic, hunting type of life. Only after a length of time which, judging from the number of floors which went to the building-up of this nucleus of the tell to 13 feet, was considerable, did they start to build solid structures.

Ultimately some genius led the way in building a solid house, and one can say that the first Palestinian architecture appears. These first houses have an obvious derivation from the primitive shelters, for they are round or curvilinear in plan, and the inwards-inclination of the surviving portions of the walls suggests that they had domed roofs (Pls. 9-10). They are a translation into a solid medium of the impermanent huts of a nomadic population. Each has a projecting porch, in which is a stepped or sloping entrance leading down from a

25

higher external level (Pl. 11). The walls are constructed with hand-moulded bricks, of the type known as plano-convex, with a flat base and a curved top, which often has a hog-backed silhouette. Sometimes wooden posts and wattling are incorporated in the walls.

The extent of the transitional, or Proto-Neolithic, settlement which produced the 13 feet of deposit without any substantial structure was apparently not large, for the deposit was found only in the one area. But the stage in which solid architecture was evolved was followed by a major expansion. The round houses have been found from end to end of the tell, covering an area which may be estimated at about 10 acres (4·05ha.).[2]

The Proto-Neolithic settlers who developed their habitations from slight shelters to solid houses were in fact making the transition from a nomadic, Mesolithic-type, way of life to a settled, Neolithic-type, way of life. Their equipment develops nicely into that of Pre-Pottery Neolithic A (Pls. 14-15). Yet it does not derive directly from the equipment of the Mesolithic of Jericho, as was at first thought. The connections of the Proto-Neolithic people with their Mesolithic predecessors have still to be worked out.

After the settlement had expanded to its full size, it was surrounded by massive defences, and assumes an urban character. The town wall was a solid, free-standing, stone affair 6 feet 6 inches (1·98m.) wide. At the north and south ends as found it had been destroyed to its lower courses, but on the west side it was preserved to a height of 12 feet (3·66m.). At this point the excavated area coincided with the position of a great stone tower built against the inside of the wall, still surviving to a height of 30 feet (9·14m.) (Pl. 12). It is to be presumed that it was for the purpose of defence, and provision was made for manning the top by a passage entering from the eastern side, and leading to a steep flight of twenty-two steps climbing up to the top of the tower. The whole comprises an amazing bit of architecture.

The tower and defences had a long history. An occupation layer soon after the construction of the first phase of the defences is dated by Philadelphia to 7825 B.C. ± 110 and by the British Museum to 7609 B.C. ± 63. The date of the construction of the defences is therefore likely to be soon after 8000 B.C. Three main building phases in the tower and town wall can be traced. With the second town wall goes a rock-cut ditch, 27 feet (8·25m.) wide and 9 feet (2·75m.) deep. Philadelphia dates for a destruction late in the second stage of the defences are 7677 B.C. ± 104 or 7734 B.C.

± 232. There are other higher dates given both by Philadelphia and the British Museum, which seem improbable. The third and final stage of the town wall is that shown in Pl. 13. By the time it was built, the internal level had risen considerably, and on its inner side its lower part was not free-standing, but built against a fill. It still survives to a height of 25 feet (7·62m.). Subsequently a series of houses, of the usual curvilinear plan, was built against the tower and wall. The latest certain dates for subsequent occupation while the defences were still operative are 7276 B.C. ± 76; one dating of 6850 B.C. ± 210 should perhaps be looked at with suspicion. Pre-Pottery Neolithic A Jericho must have lasted down to *c.* 7000 B.C.

The descendants of the Mesolithic hunters who had established their sanctuary by the spring at Jericho had therefore made remarkable progress. In the course of a period which Carbon-14 evidence suggests is about a thousand years, they had made the full transition from a wandering to a settled existence in what must have been a community of considerable complexity, for the imposing defences are evidence of an efficient communal organization. When these finds were made at Jericho, the earliest villages known elsewhere were dated more than two thousand years later, and the pyramids of Egypt, the first great stone buildings of the Nile Valley, are four thousand years younger than the great tower of Jericho. The reasons for this development are obviously of great interest.

It may be inferred with a high degree of probability that this Pre-Pottery Neolithic A settlement of Jericho was based on a successful system of agriculture.

Examination of the plant evidence has shown that cultivated grains are found in the Pre-Pottery Neolithic A levels at Jericho, though the number of all specimens recovered from this period is small. Examples of emmer wheat (*Triticum dicoccum*) and two-row barley (*Hordeum distichum*) were found, both of which are cultivated forms. It is interesting that so far examples of the respective wild ancestors, *Triticum dicoccoides* and *Hordeum spontaneum*, have not been identified. Both are at home in Palestine, but their usual habitat is in the upland ranges. It would be quite in keeping with the trend of archaeological evidence that the first experiments in agriculture were made by the Neolithic Natufians of, for instance, the Mount Carmel caves, and that the migrants to the Jordan Valley brought with them grain that had already produced the mutations that made them more suitable for agriculture. It can thus now be said that this first Neolithic stage at Jericho had an economy in which there was a definite element of food production.

It is probable that in this area the appearance of agriculture preceded that of animal domestication. The main source of meat in Pre-Pottery Neolithic A Jericho was gazelle. There is no evidence that these were herded, or in any other way organized by man. The source of food second in importance was the fox. In Pre-Pottery Neolithic B, evidence of domesticated animals appears, so we have at Jericho evidence that in this area (but certainly not necessarily everywhere) agriculture took precedence over animal domestication. Such an economy of a combination of food production and hunting could clearly support a sedentary population grouped in large units.

An inference can also be made from the size of the settlement. A closely built-up area of about 10 acres (4·05ha.) might, by modern oriental standards, house a population of about two thousand people, and such a population could not have been supported on supplies of wild grain and wild animals obtainable within reach of the settlement. At a stage in the occupation of the site, which one may presume to be coincidental with the development of the nucleus-tell of 13 feet (3·95m.) of deposit, the first experiments in agriculture, ascribed to their cave-dwelling predecessors on Mount Carmel and elsewhere, were developed by the Natufians at Jericho into the practice of regular food production. This produced sufficiently reliable supplies of food to enable them to settle permanently on the site and build the long succession of hut-like shelters. But the waters of the spring in its natural state would only have reached a limited area. Today, the widespread oasis is based on an elaborate system of irrigation. A further inference on the economy of Pre-Pottery Neolithic A Jericho can therefore be made. At a stage when the expanding population required a large area of fields, irrigation channels must have been constructed to carry the waters of the spring farther afield.

This inference has important implications. The successful practice of irrigation involves an elaborate control system. A system of main channels feeds subsidiary channels watering the fields when the necessary sluice-gate is closed. Therefore the channels must be planned, the length of time each farmer may take water by closing the sluice-gates must be established, and there must be some sanction to be used against those who contravene the regulations. The implications therefore are that there must be some central communal organization and the beginnings of a code of laws which the organization enforces. It has long been recognized that a major influence in the development of the villages of the valleys of the Nile and the Tigris–Euphrates into towns and states was their depen- dence on irrigation, which both brought them great wealth and stimulated the evolution of urban characteristics.

The inference is that something of the same sort developed at Jericho. As regards evidence of the actual irrigation, it can never be more than inference, for all the area concerned is now covered by modern fields and irrigation channels. But the evidence that there was an efficient communal organization is to be seen in the great defensive system. The visual evidence that this provides links with the chain of reasoning based on the size of the settlement. The expansion of the settlement precedes the building of the defences, and thus the need for irrigation had called into being the organiza- tion of which the defences are evidence.

A further interesting feature in connection with Pre-Pottery Neolithic A Jericho is the evidence that some form of trade had already developed. Progress has recently been made in the identifi- cation of the sources of obsidian used for tools on ancient sites. An appreciable quantity was found in Pre-Pottery Neolithic A levels, and the nearest known site for this particular type is near Kayseri, in Anatolia, about 500 miles away. So far we have no evidence of how such trade was organized, but the probability is that there were a series of middlemen. It is at least certain that there must have been fairly widespread contacts among groups.

There were thus the greatest possible contrasts between the urban Natufian settlement at Jericho and the other settlements in which evidence of the stages developed from the Lower Natufian have been found. It looks as though there were two lines of development. One Lower Natufian group settled down at Jericho, and it is surely to be presumed that other groups established settle- ments in comparable positions. It is difficult to believe that Pre- Pottery Neolithic A Jericho developed in isolation; there must be comparable sites, but they have escaped observation, perhaps because they are not so large. But the cousins of the settled groups, living mainly in the hills, in areas less favourable for agriculture, continued in a Mesolithic way of life, still living as hunters and food-gatherers. The caves and shelters in which they lived have produced the implements which have been classified as Middle and Upper Natufian.

On the western slopes of the Judaean hills sites have also been found which can be identified as Neolithic villages. The most interesting is that in the Wadi Fallah (Nahal Oren), low on the slopes leading down to the Mediterranean, south of Haifa. Above evidence of occupation in the Upper Palaeolithic and Mesolithic periods, there was found a village of at least fourteen houses, terraced into the slope. The houses were round or elliptical in plan with dry-stone walls surviving to the height of a metre. This may have been the maximum height of the stone walling, with a lighter superstructure as at 'Ain Mallaha, and the style of building could be derived thence. There is also a clear connection with Pre-Pottery Neolithic A Jericho, both in the style of architecture and in material equipment. Dating evidence has not yet been published, so it is not yet clear if the Wadi Fallah settlement marks an early stage of Neolithic village settlement, from which Jericho developed, or whether it represents a more humble contemporary way of life.

A similar stage is found at El Khiam, near Bethlehem. It is not now generally accepted that here there was a transition to the next Neolithic culture, in which the flint industry is known as the Tahunian. As will be seen, this culture appeared at Jericho after a complete break, and so far the evidence from the lesser contemporary sites is similar.

Wherever the Pre-Pottery Neolithic A town of Jericho has been examined along the edge of the mound, the layers have suffered considerable erosion. In Trench I, on the west side of the tell, it is clear that the upper part of the town wall ultimately collapsed. The layers representing the successive houses built up against its inner side were eroded, as was the top of the tower, and the resultant débris filled up the ditch and piled up against the base of the town wall. By the time the débris had reached its angle of rest, the town wall was completely covered. In Site I, and in Trench II, both towards the north end of the site, a corresponding phase of erosion is represented by stream beds, which cut down into the house levels in three successive phases before it finally silted up. Elsewhere the evidence is similar.

It is impossible to tell how long a period of time is covered by this phase of erosion. It may have taken place very quickly, or it may have covered a period of years or centuries. What is quite clear is that it marks the end of the occupation of the Pre-Pottery Neolithic A people. They may have been driven out, and their town destroyed, by their successors, or some disaster, such as an earthquake temporarily diverting the water-supply and destroying the irrigation system, may have caused them to abandon the site.

These successors were an entirely different group, to which the name Pre-Pottery Neolithic B is given, and their flint industry is Tahunian. Almost all their other equipment also was different, for instance even the shape of the querns and of the grinding stones used with them. But most striking of all is the difference in architecture, which is described below, with large, many-roomed houses of rectilinear plan.

Historically, the most important point is that the newcomers arrived with this architecture already fully developed. Immediately above the layers of erosion appear houses of a remarkably stereotyped plan which lasts throughout the Pre-Pottery Neolithic B period at Jericho. This means that the newcomers had already behind them a sufficiently long period of settled occupation to develop an architecture, and even a detailed house plan, which was to serve their needs for a thousand years or more at Jericho.

The houses of the Pre-Pottery Neolithic B phase are of very surprising architectural development. The rooms were mostly large, with wide doorways, sometimes flanked by timber posts. The plan of these rooms was rectangular, with slightly rounded corners, and the walls were straight and solid (Pl. 16). The bricks of which the walls were constructed (Pl. 17) were made by hand (not in moulds as is usual later), in shape rather like a flattened cigar, with the surface impressed with a herringbone pattern by pairs of prints of the brick-maker's thumbs, thus giving a keying for the mortar such as is provided by the hollow in modern bricks. Such bricks again are entirely different from those used by the A people. The floors were covered with a hard lime-plaster, often reddish or cream-coloured, carried also up the walls, with its surface finished with a high burnish. The main rooms were flanked by small chambers, some of them apparently used for storage, and rain-water was conserved in plastered vats built against the walls. The houses were built round courtyards, in which most of the cooking seems to have taken place, for the floors were found covered with thick charcoal layers.

The only utensils belonging to these people which have survived are stone bowls of various forms, the majority in a white limestone, finely worked and carefully finished. These vessels no doubt would have been supplemented by others of materials which have perished, probably of skin, and possibly of wood, though it is a curious fact that the tools found included very few suitable for heavy woodworking. The tools (Pl. 18) are mainly of flint or chert. The great majority are blades formed from flakes, which would have served as knives of all varieties and sizes. Some of the blades have been given fine serrated edges, and from the characteristic gloss that most of them bear it is clear that they were used as sickles to cut corn or grass; most are short sections which would have been set in a wooden haft; longer ones may have been provided with handles in the same manner as a knife. Other implements are borers and scrapers for use on skins. But again in contrast to the A group, there are hardly any heavy tools which could have been used as axes, adzes, or hoes, and it is difficult to see what implements were used to cut down trees; the use of some timber is attested by the sockets of posts in the walls, but it seems probable that wood was not extensively used. In addition to the cutting implements, there are innumerable hammer stones, pestles, and polishing stones of all sizes (Pl. 19).

Evidence of agriculture is provided by the sickles already mentioned, by the find of large numbers of querns and rubbers (Pl. 12c), and by the find of actual grain. The querns are of a standardized form, sub-rectangular, with a wide, flat rim round three sides, and the grinding hollow running out to the edge at one end. Cultivation of the ground was probably carried out by digging-sticks, pointed sticks weighted by stones, of which the evidence survives in the form of heavy stones pierced by a hole.

The number of specimens of grain recovered is not very great, but the present evidence is that it was in Pre-Pottery Neolithic B that einkorn wheat (*T. monococcum*) appeared. This is one important point. The ancestor of emmer wheat (*T. dicoccum*), which was the only wheat found in Pre-Pottery Neolithic A, is found in Palestine, though probably in the Galilean hills rather than in the Jordan Valley. The ancestor of einkorn is to be found to the north, in Anatolia and north Syria, suggesting that the Pre-Pottery Neolithic B people had northern connections.

The implements found include arrowheads, some of them finely worked, but they do not form a high proportion of the total. Hunting therefore was an element in the economy of the inhabitants, but probably not an important element. Large numbers of animal bones found on the site, however, show that they were certainly meat-eaters. Gazelles certainly continued to be an important source of food and were probably still wild. There is, however, a marked change in the meat supply. In Pre-Pottery Neolithic A, bones of sheep and goat were very rare. In Pre-Pottery Neolithic B, they constitute almost half the number of bones and teeth recovered. There is evidence, particularly in the shape of the horn core, that some of the goats were domesticated. On the whole, however, the size of the bones suggests that the animals were still wild, though they may be in the early stages of domestication before morphological changes had developed. The same considerations apply to the remains of cattle and pigs.

The economy so far revealed is that typical of a Neolithic community, consisting of self-sufficient farmers, with some domesticated animals, but still obtaining some of their food supply by hunting. The self-sufficiency was not quite complete, for a few of the tools were made of obsidian, which was probably obtained from Anatolia. Some small lumps of turquoise matrix have also been found, which must have come from the Sinai Peninsula, and cowrie shells may have come from the Mediterranean. Such exceptions are quite usual in many Neolithic communities, for even in those early times a few luxury articles seem to have been obtained from distant sources.

The evidence of agriculture, the elaborate architecture, and the comparatively lavish equipment (even though it did not include pottery) show that these early inhabitants of Jericho formed a prosperous and highly organized community. There is also some evidence as to their spiritual and aesthetic development.

The principal concern of such a community would no doubt be the fertility of their fields and flocks. A number of little clay figurines of animals have been found, which were probably votive offerings to a supernatural power which was believed to control these things. More striking is a figurine of a woman only some 2 inches high, an elegant little lady with flowing gown gathered at the waist, her arms akimbo, and her hands beneath her breasts; unfortunately her head is missing. In attitude, the figure is typical of representations of the Mother Goddess common in much later cultures, and it is evidence that our early inhabitants already imagined a personified deity.

Another aspect of their approach to the deity is provided by a small shrine in a private house. The shrine was formed by blocking openings in the walls of one of the large rooms. In one of the walls of the small room so formed was a semicircular niche, at the base of which was set a rough stone to serve as a pedestal. In the débris of the house, not far away, was found a remarkable stone which exactly fitted the niche. It was of volcanic rock from the neighbour-hood of the Dead Sea. It had been elaborately flaked into a pillar of pointed oval section 18 inches (·45m) high. The unusualness of this object, and its probable association with the niche, strongly suggest that it had a cult significance, probably as a representation of the deity. It thus foreshadows the *mazzeboth* of the Canaanite religion of many centuries later, the stone pillars which are found on the sites of so many Semitic sanctuaries.

Another structure that might serve a religious purpose was a building with a central room 20 feet (6·08m.) long and more than 12 feet (3·66m.) wide, in the centre of which was a carefully plastered and moulded rectangular basin. At each end of the main room were annexes with rounded walls. The size, elaborateness, unusual plan, and central basin all suggest some ceremonial use.

The most remarkable finds of all at Jericho have implications both for the religion and the artistic capabilities of the Neolithic inhabitants. In 1952 a find was made which suggested that special reverence was paid to human skulls. This could be deduced from the skull of an elderly man which had been set carefully upright beneath the floor of one of the rooms, in the angle of two walls. The find suggested that his spirit was intended to remain in the house, and his wisdom to be preserved for its inhabitants. In 1953 a find was made which gave even greater evidence on the importance attached to skulls.

In the débris beneath the floor of one of the houses of the Pre-Pottery B stage there came to light a deposit of seven human skulls. Later two other similar skulls were found in another room of the same house. The lower part of these skulls had been covered with plaster, moulded into the likeness of human features. Each head has a most individual character, and one cannot escape the impression that one is looking at real portraits. The eyes are inset in shells. In the case of six of the heads, the eyes are made of ordinary bivalve shells, with a vertical slit between two sections giving the appearance of the pupil. The seventh head has cowrie shells, and the horizontal opening of the shells gives him a distinctly sleepy expression. The moulding of the features, mouth, nose, ears, and eyelids is fine and delicate, giving the impression that the people whose portraits we here see had small and well-fashioned features. The top of the skull is always left uncovered, though in one case the skull is painted with broad bands of dark paint, perhaps to represent a head-dress. One curious fact is that in only one instance is the lower jaw present. In the rest, the chin is moulded over the upper teeth, and the heads have therefore a somewhat squat appearance (Pls. 20, 21).

These heads give an amazing impression of the technical skill and artistic powers of their creators, totally unexpected at such an early date. They are not the oldest representations of the human form, nor even possibly the oldest portraits, for representations exist in Palaeolithic and Mesolithic art. But they are far more lifelike than any earlier examples. Moreover, it can be claimed that they are the earliest human portraits directly ancestral to modern art. The art of the earlier epochs is divided by a gap of some thousands of years from subsequent developments, whereas from the Neolithic period onwards civilization develops in an unbroken line, and the line of artistic achievement through the ancient Sumerian and Egyptian leads on to the Hellenic and so to the modern world.

The artistic importance of these heads is clear. But their cultural significance is more obscure. When found, the original seven were in a tumbled pile, obviously discarded when the house in which they had been treasured was ruined and succeeded by the next, beneath the floor of which they were buried. There was nothing in the part of the lower house that was uncovered to show whether they had been set in a shrine, or simply preserved in a dwelling-house. The practice of removing crania from bodies was strikingly illustrated in a slightly subsequent level. Beneath the floor of this house was found a large number of burials.

Burial beneath the floors of the houses seems to have been the normal practice. What was exceptional was the very large number of individuals in the particular place, some forty or more within quite a small area. In some cases the skeletons were intact. In others the skull had been removed, leaving the lower jaw behind. In still others, the disturbance was much greater but again hardly any skulls were found, and it looked as if a pile of partly decayed bodies had been searched through for the particular purpose of removing the skulls. It was first thought that the plastered skulls had been derived from these mass burials, but this proved not to be the case. The treatment of the mass burials is, however, striking evidence of the importance attached to skulls.

Modern anthropological parallels would suggest that the heads preserved were either those of venerated ancestors or of enemies, kept as trophies. The only possible light on this is that such a mass of burials suggests some disaster. When the bodies were buried, there was at the same time built the first of the town walls belonging to the Pre-Pottery Neolithic B period; previous to this the town of the B people had apparently not been defended. This might suggest that a massacre by enemies had shown the necessity of providing defences. The heads, on which too much loving care had been spent for it to be likely that they were enemies, might be those of import-ant people killed in a massacre. But the evidence is slender, and is not borne out by any signs of injuries on the skeletons.

In 1958 another plastered skull was found far away at the north end of the tell. Moreover, as successive layers were excavated in all the different areas, skeletons were found from which the cranium had been removed. Though a corresponding number of plastered skulls was not found, it is clear that the removal of crania from burials was a regular practice; it is possible that they were removed to some central repository or shrine, which has not been located. It is therefore clear that the Jericho skulls are those of venerated ancestors and are not trophies.

From this practice of making portrait heads with an actual skull as a basis, there seems to have been a stylistic development. In the 1930–36 excavations, a very different kind of human represen-tation was found. This consisted apparently of three almost life-sized figures of plaster, but of them only the head of one could be preserved. This head (Pls. 23-4) resembles the plastered skulls in the use of shells to represent the eyes, but in almost nothing else. The head in profile is a flat disk, and is thus a very stylized represen-tation. There was some uncertainty as to whether these figures came from the Pre-Pottery Neolithic B levels or the succeeding Pottery Neolithic levels. Finds in 1958 make it probable that they belonged to the Pre-Pottery phase, for the 1959 finds represent a further degree of stylization, and they came from the very top of the Pre-Pottery levels. They also may have been representations of complete, life-size figures, for many fragments were found. But the only one of which a substantial portion could be recovered extended only as far as the bust (Pl. 22). The head (and numerous other fragments of heads) is now completely stylized, a spade-shaped disk without any attempt to render any features, and painted completely schematically. The shoulders and bust, however, are moulded com-paratively realistically. The three types of figures are most interest-ing evidence on the developments of primitive art.

The first Pre-Pottery Neolithic B settlement at Jericho was apparently not defended. The houses extended well down the slopes of the mound which the earlier settlement had already built up to a height of about 24 feet (7·32m.) above the plain, and in Trench I, where the sequence could best be studied, there was a succession of ten house levels without any trace of an enclosure wall. The need then apparently arose for defence. It may be of significance that this immediately followed the multiple burials already referred to (pp. 35-6), but, as is there pointed out, the skeletons did not provide any evidence of wounds which would prove death at the hands of enemies. The defensive wall which was then built was a massive affair, not so regularly built as the Pre-Pottery Neolithic A walls, nor surviving to so great a height as the final wall of that phase, but employing much larger stones. One, visible in Pl. 25, was a great orthostat nearly 5 feet by 3 feet (1·52 by 0·91m.) in surface dimensions, and one in what is probably the continuation of the wall 140 feet (42·56m.) to the north (in Square M I), was nearly 10 feet (6·08m.) by 6 feet (1·83m.). The wall was, to the height to which it survived, free-standing only on the outer side. It was constructed by cutting it back into the house levels on the inner side, removing the corresponding levels on the outer side, and piling the soil so derived on the inner side to form a terrace. On this terrace, houses were built right up to the inner side of the wall.

This wall has been located only at the two places on the western side already mentioned, Trench I and Square M I. In Trenches II and III, at the north and south ends of the tell respectively, the houses of the period run to the extremities of the trenches, where they are truncated by the great Middle Bronze Age revetment (pp. 162-4). It therefore cannot be proved that it was a town wall and not a citadel wall, but the contours of the tell suggest that it was a town wall enclosing the whole area of the town, which was therefore considerably greater than the area of the largest Bronze Age town, for the Middle Bronze Age revetment was the base of a band of defences at least 130 feet (39·52m.) wide, and the dimensions of the Neolithic town exceeded those of the Bronze Age town by at least that amount at the north and south ends.

This wall may not have had a very long life. In Trench I it seems to have collapsed, possibly owing to the weight of soil in the terrace behind it, and to have been succeeded by a similar wall about 40 feet (24·32m.) in advance. There may even have been a third stage, on the evidence of further advancement of the house levels, but if so, this has disappeared in subsequent denudation.

The Pre-Pottery Neolithic B settlement of Jericho has therefore all the urban characteristics of its predecessor in long-continued occupation, size, and evidence of communal organization. The possible temple in Trench I may be evidence also of the public buildings which are one of the features suggested as necessary[3] to support a claim to the title of a town. The domestic architecture, with its large and rectilinear plans, is obviously much more sophisticated than that of the A phase. Carbon-14 datings for Pre-Pottery Neolithic B are not yet numerous enough to give a complete or consistent picture. Samples from levels early in the sequence of levels give dates in the first half of the seventh millennium B.C., and it is probable that the greater part of the Pre-Pottery Neolithic B occupation comes within that millennium.

At the time of the excavation of Jericho, between 1952 and 1958, nothing comparable had been discovered, either in Palestine or in neighbouring countries. Subsequently, excavations in Anatolia, especially at Çatal Hüyük, have shown that here too there was remarkable progress towards town life in the Neolithic and, as already noted (pp. 7, 30), there were certainly a number of different centres in which this progress took place.

Of more importance for Palestinian archaeology, we now know much more about background and setting of Pre-Pottery Neolithic B Jericho. Jericho remains the outstanding site, but it is no longer in isolation. The complete break between Pre-Pottery Neolithic A/B Jericho has already been emphasized. An alien culture had supervened on the indigenous A group. A hint that the newcomers came from the north was given by the appearance of einkorn wheat (p. 32). This is now confirmed by the discovery of Pre-Pottery Neolithic sites in Syria with clear links with Jericho.

The most striking is Tell Ramad about 12 miles (19km.) south of Damascus. The site is a large one, of which only a small part has so far been excavated. The lowest level, dated by Carbon-14 to the last centuries of the seventh millennium B.C., has definite affinities with Pre-Pottery Neolithic B Jericho. The houses had plastered floors turning up the face of the walls, some of the flint tools are in the same technique, and the trough querns are similar. The grain included emmer, einkorn, and club wheat, but there is not reported to be any evidence of domesticated animals or even of sheep, goats, and cattle in process of domestication. The striking link is the preservation of plastered skulls (Pl. 26), found clustered in nests near the huts. With them were found clay statuettes, on which the skulls may have been set, though the statuettes were of a much smaller scale. In addition to these are links with coastal sites in Syria such as Ras Shamra Level Vc.

The line of contacts with these Syrian sites is continued down into Palestine by the site of Beisamun, adjoining the site (which now has disappeared in modern drainage) of Lake Huleh.[4] Neolithic remains were revealed beneath modern fish-ponds, and stretch over a considerable area. The structures were rectangular, with plastered floors which had a plastered surface. In one of the rooms were found two plastered skulls (Pl. 27). Technique is not quite the same as in the Jericho examples, but the connection is clear. There is no definite dating evidence. The general conclusion is that this second stage of Pre-Pottery Neolithic in Palestine is derived from the north, basically from Syria. It superseded the indigenous Pre-Pottery Neolithic A culture, though for what reason and how quickly is not yet clear.

Jericho in the Pre-Pottery Neolithic B stage shows, however, that the site could still generate an exceptional development. To what extent it can be compared with the known great Pre-Pottery sites of Syria, especially Ras Shamra, is not yet clear. There is, however, enough evidence to show that it was outstanding in Palestine.

On the other hand, research in the last twenty years has shown that it does not stand in the isolation which made it so remarkable when the excavations were in progress from 1952 to 1958. The identification of the characteristics of the buildings, equipment, and economic development at Jericho has enabled other sites, both those excavated earlier and in more recent work, to be assigned to this period. The list is long, including stages at El Khiam, Wadi Fallah, Abu Gosh, and Munhatta. All are village settlements, important as evidence of the general development, but in no way comparable with Jericho.

A special mention must be made of Beidha, a site on the slopes of the Wadi Arabah, which continues the depression of the Dead Sea to the Gulf of Aqaba. This is an area which is today within the orbit of the Bedouin tribes of Transjordan; they are not fully nomadic, but they have connections with the nomadic tribes of the area, and are utterly different from the villages of the settled area of Palestine and Transjordan. Yet in this area, a few miles north of Petra, was found a Pre-Pottery Neolithic village, on a site on which there had been a Mesolithic settlement, though there was no direct connection. There were six Neolithic levels, from which Carbon-14 dates of 6990 b.c. or 6760 b.c. ± 160 were obtained from the lowest level and 6600 B.C. for the fifth stage. Agriculture was extensively employed, especially of a cultivated form of wild barley. Emmer wheat was also found, but not its wild ancestor, and it was presumably brought by the settlers from its habitat further north.

The earliest houses were circular (Pl. 28), with stone walls supported by wooden posts. There is in them a transitional stage of rectangular rooms with rounded corners, followed by fully rectangular rooms (Pl. 29) with plastered floors. There is thus a transition from the Jericho Pre-Pottery Neolithic A-type house to the Pre-Pottery Neolithic B-type. There is also not the same clear-cut distinction in the tools and utensils, with a preponderance of B types. Chronologically, the earliest occupation comes within the B stage at Jericho. A possible interpretation is that an A group retired south when the B people arrived in central Palestine, and either in due course were culturally influenced by them or actually mixed with them.

Notes

1. *Proc. of the British Academy*, XVIII, p. 214.
2. This can only be an estimate, since the limits on the east side are uncertain, owing to the encroachment of the modern road.
3. V. G. Childe, *Antiquity* (March 1957).
4. *IEJ* 16 (1966), 271–2; 19 (1969), 116–17.

3 From the First Settlements to the Beginnings of Civilization

Palestine, as represented by Jericho, can therefore put forward a good claim to be one of the places in which there took place the transition from a nomadic way of life to the settled existence that is the prerequisite of all development towards civilization. We must, however, be careful *not* to claim that it was the only area and the only site in which this development took place.

In the last chapter, reference has been made to the growing number of Pre-Pottery, or aceramic, settlements that have been discovered in Syria. These are followed, sometimes on the same site but sometimes as new foundations, by others in which pottery appears. It is simple and handmade, with many local varieties. The map (Fig. 1) gives an impression of these villages stretching right round the northern part of the Fertile Crescent from the Iranian foothills to the Mediterranean coast. Their culture and economy vary considerably, but all are of modest size and firmly established.

The first manufactured vessels to appear are known as white ware or pozzalanic ware, which is really moulded plaster. It appears on a number of sites, and at Tell Ramad can be dated to *c*. 6000 B.C. True pottery, fired clay, appears in Syria soon after, and in Anatolia, at Catal Hüyük, may appear as early as the mid-seventh millennium. A type of pottery, known as dark-faced burnished ware, is found on a large number of Syrian sites, as early as 6000 B.C. at Ras Shamra, and provides a useful link with related ware at sites such as Byblos, though there it only seems to appear *c*. 5000 B.C.

Developments in Palestine seem to lag behind those to the north, for reasons that are not yet clear. When pottery does appear, the settlements seem considerably more primitive than those in Syria, and they do not develop direct from the Pre-Pottery settlements as do many in Syria. Again, most of the evidence comes from Jericho.

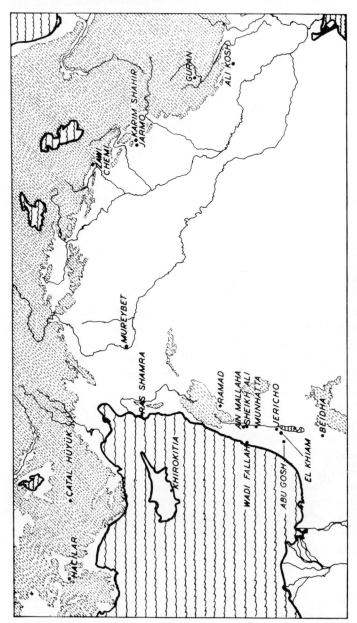

Fig. 5. Map of Near East, showing principal Pre-Pottery Neolithic and Chalcolithic sites

Like its predecessor, the Pre-Pottery Neolithic B town of Jericho comes to an abrupt end. Its destruction was much more disastrous to progress, for the succeeding occupation marks a great retrogression. The newcomers brought with them the use of pottery, but in every other respect they were much more primitive than their predecessors. As in the case of the end of the Pre-Pottery Neolithic A town, the destruction of the final B town is followed by a period of erosion, with the familiar wearing-away of the levels on the edges of the mound until the débris reached a natural angle of rest. Above these ruins, again after a time interval which it is impossible to estimate, appears the evidence of the newcomers. This evidence is of a very curious sort. Everywhere the first pottery appears in pits cut into the ruins of the earlier town. These pits literally honeycomb the mound wherever it has been excavated. In the earlier seasons of the excavations, it was thought that the pits were quarry pits to obtain materials to make mud-bricks, at a stage in which a camping existence was being succeeded by one with permanent structures. Further examination has shown that this was a misinterpretation. The pits are really pit-dwellings. In them are a series of floors, and the edges of the pits are revetted by slight walls of pisée and stone. The newcomers were therefore almost troglodytes; wherever there appear to be layers belonging to the period which are not in pits, they consist of surfaces and hearths only, and no solid structures. Such a way of life is very surprising, but has been made less so by the discovery of the subterranean settlement of the Chalcolithic period near Beersheba (pp. 59 ff.).

The most notable product of the newcomers, the Pottery Neolithic A people, is their pottery. They certainly arrived at the site already possessing the art of making it. The vessels divide themselves into two main classes, coarse ware and fine decorated ware. The shapes in both classes are approximately the same, and are simple and primitive (Fig. 6). The most common vessels are saucer-bowls with flat base and splaying wall, of varying sizes. There are also a few bowls with gently curved walls. The jar form has a flattish base with globular body, slight shoulder, high neck contracting upwards, and no moulding on the rim. Usually there are two small lug handles at the base of the neck; ledge and knob handles, however, also occur both on jars and bowls.

The ware of the coarse vessels is crude in the extreme, and certainly suggests that the craft of pot-making had not progressed very far. It has many grits, perhaps derived from the clay employed,

43

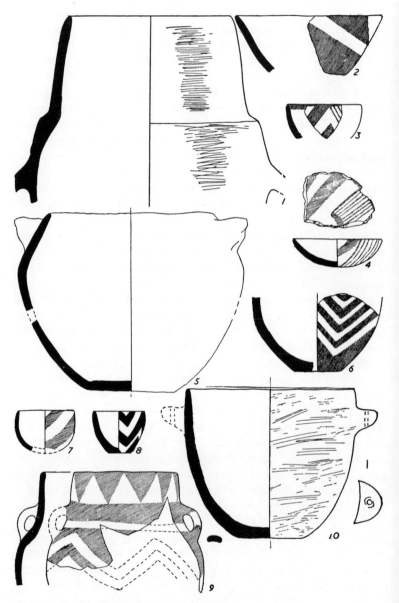

Fig. 6. Pottery of the Pottery Neolithic A period at Jericho. ⅕

and, to provide the necessary cohesion, straw has been added in considerable quantities. The firing was obviously at a low temperature, and as a result the ware is soft and crumbly. The surface has often been smoothed over with a handful of grass.

The finer pottery is very different in appearance. It is still friable and has considerable straw in it, but it is distinctly better fired and of cleaner clay. But the chief difference is in the finish. The surface is comparatively smooth, and is covered as a rule by a cream-coloured slip. This slip in turn is partially covered by a red slip, so that the reserved portions of the cream slip form a pattern, usually in some combination of chevrons or triangles. To heighten the contrast, the red slip is finely burnished with a beautifully lustrous finish. Altogether, it is a most attractive ware and contrasts strongly with the coarse pottery.

Not only were the Pottery Neolithic A people distinguished from their predecessors by their use of pottery, but their other equipment was quite different. The fine grinding querns, pestles, and stone bowls disappear, and only crudely worked stone vessels seem to have been used. The flint industry also was quite different, the most notable change being the use of a sickle blade with a coarse denticulation instead of the finely serrated edge of the blades used in the Pre-Pottery B phase. This type of sickle blade continues in use in Palestine throughout the Early Bronze Age, and it is therefore probable that the descendants of this group formed one element of the Bronze Age population.

What the antecedents of these people were we do not yet know. This distintive pottery has only rarely been found elsewhere, a single sherd from a cave at Tell Duweir in southern Palestine,[1] two sherds from the Wadi Rabah on the west slopes of the central upland zone, near the head-waters of the River Yarkon,[2] a few probable sherds from the lowest levels at Megiddo[3], and sherds from Abu Gosh, El Khiam, and Tell Batashi, south of Lydda. Though these finds are scanty, their wide geographical distribution may be an indication that the Pottery Neolithic A people of Jericho will eventually be found to have been established in a considerable part of Palestine. The finds at Tell Batashi are of particular interest. Not only were they made in pits resembling those at Jericho, but they included sherds that could be related to the dark-faced burnished ware of Syria, which at Byblos could be as late as 5000 B.C.

The conclusion at present seems to be that between the flourishing Pre-Pottery Neolithic B stage in Palestine, with Jericho as the outstanding site, but, on the evidence of recent discoveries, many other subsidiary sites, and the next stage at Jericho there is a gap of many years. No other Palestinian site has suggested anything to fill this gap, and we are left with a hiatus between *c.* 6000 B.C. and 5000 B.C. It is inconceivable that there was a complete lack of occupation in Palestine during this period, but we do not yet know how to fill it.

The pits containing the Neolithic pottery are found all over the tell at Jericho, and the population was therefore numerous. But throughout their period of occupation at Jericho, the Pottery Neolithic A people seem to have built no solid, free-standing structures. They were succeeded by another group, the Pottery Neolithic B people, who, at least to begin with, seem to have been almost equally primitive, for they seem to have built their huts in the upper levels of the pits occupied by their predecessors. How sharp the break between the two groups was is not yet certain, for the evidence has not been fully worked out. At any rate, a new and considerably more sophisticated pottery appears, brought by newcomers who either superseded, or more probably mingled with, the A group. This pottery is much better fired, the ware is thinner and has not the large amount of straw in it that is found in the early sherds, and the forms are more advanced. Notable characteristics are jar forms with rims which are concave internally, to which the name 'bow-rim' has been given, and the jar handles which splay out at their attachment to the vessel. The burnished, red-on-cream decoration of the earlier finer ware disappears, but many of the vessels are covered with a deep red slip, sometimes burnished, sometimes matt. The most characteristic decoration, found both on jars and bowls, is in bands of herringbone incisions. The bands are usually delineated by grooves, and very often they are covered by a band of cream slip, with the rest of the vessel covered by a red slip (Fig. 7).

The Pottery Neolithic B people do not seem to have brought the practice of solid architecture with them. But in due course they started to build free-standing houses. These have stone foundations, with a superstructure of mud-bricks. These bricks are still hand- and not mould-made, but they are quite different from those used in the Pre-Pottery phases. They are planoconvex, and can be described as bun-shaped, round in plan and humped on top. The structural remains that survive of the period are comparatively slight, for the levels suffered some denudation after the end of the period. Some of the buildings seem to have been rectilinear, while

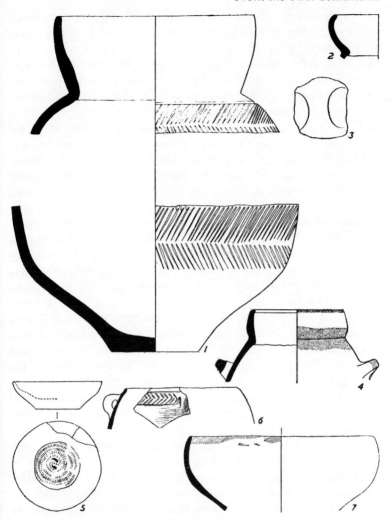

Fig. 7. Pottery of the Pottery Neolithic B period at Jericho. $\frac{1}{5}$

some of the walls were curved, but no complete house plan has been recovered. There were several building stages, and belonging to the second of them was a wall, 2·25 metres broad, which has been traced for a distance of 19 metres, which is certainly an enclosure wall, and might even have been a town wall. At a later stage, buildings with substantial, rectilinear stone walls were constructed, but again little of the plan survived.

47

The great importance of this stage is that at last it provides us with a link with other sites. Another site in the Jordan Valley has produced closely similar pottery. This is near a settlement called Sha'ar ha Golan, at the junction of the River Yarmuk with the Jordan, just south of the Sea of Galilee. The finds came not from an archaeological excavation but from the digging of an anti-tank ditch and subsequent agricultural cuttings. The material was derived from a layer of dark earth overlying river gravel with Palaeolithic implements. No structural features were recovered, but great quantities of pottery, flint implements, and animal bones were found. The inhabitants of the settlement certainly harvested grain, but it is not clear whether this was wild or cultivated, and they apparently relied to a considerable degree on wild animals for food. The culture and economy of the group would not appear to have been of an advanced type. Some of the pottery is very close to that of Jericho Pottery Neolithic B, particularly vessels decorated with bands of herringbone incisions (Pl. 30). The total range of forms at the two sites, however, is not the ·same, so the groups are related but not of identical composition. A very distinctive class of find at Sha'ar ha Golan is the large number of very schematic figurines made trom pebbles (Pl. 31); the pebbles from which these were made were, however, a natural feature of the area, whereas they do not occur in the neighbourhood of Jericho, so their absence at Jericho is not necessarily significant.

This connection between the Yarmuk site and Jericho is interesting. But more important is the fact that the pottery with the bands of herringbone incisions also occurs at Byblos. The ancient town of Byblos was one of the most famous of those on the Syrian coast. Its harbour was the principal route by which the natural resources of the Lebanon, especially its renowned cedarwood, were exported to the rest of the Mediterranean. This was of particular interest to treeless Egypt, and there is definite evidence that trade relations existed between Byblos and the Nile Valley in Predynastic times, that is to say, in the fourth millennium B.C. For many years the painstaking excavation of the mound by the beautiful little natural harbour has been in progress, and at the base two layers have been found, to which the description Éneolithic (or Chalcolithic) A and B has been given. The lowest, Éneolithic A, consists of a settlement of houses approximately rectangular in plan, with well-made plaster floors. These floors have a resemblance to the Pre-Pottery Neolithic B houses at Jericho in that their surface was polished, but the resemblance stops there. The superstructure of the houses was apparently flimsy in the extreme, possibly little more than a tent of branches, covered with skins. The pottery from this level includes a surprisingly large number of quite different types of ware. Perhaps this suggests that the population of Byblos was already cosmopolitan, and that a number of different groups had already been attracted by the natural advantages of its position. One type of ware with incised decoration, often in herringbone pattern, does seem to have definite affinities to the ware of Sha'ar ha Golan and the Pottery Neolithic B of Jericho. A further link is that at Byblos the pebble figurines of Sha'ar ha Golan are also found, which adds much weight to the pottery evidence.

One of the other groups of pottery at Byblos was the dark burnished ware which has already been mentioned (p. 45) as occurring in the Neolithic villages stretching right round the northern part of the Fertile Crescent. This is a point of great importance. For the first time an approximate chronological link, independent of any question of Carbon-14 dating, can be established between Jericho and the rest of the northern Fertile Crescent. It would seem that a way of life had grown up which spread from the foothills of the Iranian plateau right round the fringes of Anatolia and down into Palestine. It was a way of life with comparatively simple characteristics, small villages, permanent but unelaborated structures, and a modest agricultural economy. The interesting thing is the divergencies and the links. As has already been suggested, the divergencies indicate that the route the ancestors of the village communities had traversed on their journey from a nomadic to a settled existence had not been a single one. But by a date probably in the mid-fifth millennium (or possibly earlier if the most recent Carbon-14 datings are to be accepted) the various routes had begun to come together. A similar way of life was growing up, and the similarities were stimulated by the contacts which the villagers apparently had with each other.

This way of life was undoubtedly a retrogression as far as Palestine, as represented by Jericho, was concerned. Nothing on the scale of the Pre-Pottery Neolithic A and B towns of Jericho is found. For some reason, the light of progress seems to flicker out. It is possible that the town-dwellers had become decadent, and fell victims to more barbarous elements, descendants of their relatives who had continued to pursue a nomadic existence, or adventurers from the less progressive area to the north. Alternatively, something may have happened to upset their economy, a deterioration of climate to which they failed to adapt their agricultural methods, or at Jericho some interference with the course of the spring. At any rate the drab villages which were the highest achievement to date of the rest of the Fertile Crescent succeed the far higher achievements of eighth-to sixth-millennium Jericho.

But though as far as Palestine is concerned this stage is a retrogression, it is nevertheless an interesting stage, just for the reason that all these various lines of progress towards a settled life were beginning to converge. Progress is also both competitive and imitative, and this growth of a generally similar way of life over a wide area was a stimulant to progress. The next stage was that of the Chalcolithic. The term Chalcolithic implies that a metal, copper, was being used as well as stone. The significance of this goes far deeper than the mere fact that more efficient tools and weapons were available. It lies in the fact that the sources of copper are geographically restricted. Regular trade to supply the new material gave a great stimulus to the breakdown of isolation and the spread of cultures and ideas. Side by side with it went the change in economy involved in the necessity of specialists to deal with the new material, which is referred to in Chapter 1.

The difficulty in deciding where to place the transition from the Neolithic to the Chalcolithic is reflected in the existing confusion in nomenclature. Sometimes the one and sometimes the other name is given to allied groups. The transition is in fact a gradual one. The dawn of the new era is not marked by the sudden appearance of copper implements on a site, but by the gradual breakdown of isolation and the resultant spreading of ideas and cultures over a considerable area. In Palestine, in fact, as far as our evidence goes, metal seems to have played a relatively small part among the materials employed until quite a late date, about the end of the third millennium. But in spite of this, the change in outlook is reflected in the gradual growth of widespread cultures, and the eventual amalgamation of isolated groups into a cultural whole.

In the northern part of the Fertile Crescent, this stage is marked by the appearance of a widespread culture, called Halafian, after Tell Halaf in northern Syria where it was first found. Site after site, from Mesopotamia across to the Mediterranean coast, has shown that after the stage of the Neolithic villages with all their diverse ways of life, a remarkably similar economy appears, with, as a characteristic feature, a type of pottery with geometric decoration in red on a light background. This is usually dated to the late fifth millennium, and in Mesopotamia the phase is succeeded by the stages which lead up to the evolution of the city states to which the name 'Proto-Literate' has been given.

The Halafian culture does not extend as far south as Palestine. Twenty years ago one would have thought that there was nothing to correspond with it. But each year now is bringing new discoveries which have to be fitted in in the period between the Pottery Neolithic B Jericho and the beginning of the Early Bronze Age. There is still much that is uncertain. We know a number of isolated facts, and we know that there are a number of communities with distinctive cultures, which have to be fitted in in this twilight of prehistory before we reach the dawn of history, with reasonable illuminated landmarks, round about 3000 B.C. In trying to fit into place the cultures these communities represent, we should learn a lesson from the progress of research in European prehistory. Earlier European scholars tried to place each culture observed into a regular sequence. Now it is recognized that many cultures represent regional developments, and several may have existed side by side. The older sequence-method tended to produce very inflated chronologies, which have had to be considerably reduced now that the picture has become more coherent. This we should bear in mind in trying to piece together the jigsaw puzzle which our present state of knowledge in Palestine represents, and in fact some of the new pieces of the jigsaw which almost every year emerge from the ground do suggest that the whole picture will eventually portray a number of groups of people living side by side each with their own distinctive culture, but with just enough links with other groups to suggest contemporaneity.

The first discovery of a group which seemed to belong to this period was at Teleilat Ghassul, which has given its name to the Ghassulian culture. The pottery on this site has some affinities with that of Jericho Pottery Neolithic B. A form of jar, of a simple, bag-like shape with incurved rim, called a hole-mouth jar, is found on both sites. At both the potters often made their vessels by setting them on a mat. A peculiar vessel found at Ghassul is shaped like an ice-cream cornet, and some fragments of these have been found at Jericho; and there are a few other similarities. But many highly individual forms found at Ghassul are not found at Jericho, and we do not yet know whether the reason is difference of period or difference of group. It may be that Ghassul belongs mainly to a period when there was a gap in occupation at Jericho, probably after the Pottery Neolithic B stage, or is the site of a settlement of a different group. The present weight of evidence does suggest that the Ghassulians were newcomers from outside Palestine, and the fact that nearby Jericho shows only slight evidence of connection with them may suggest the idea of a gap there covering most of the period of occupation at Ghassul.

Teleilat Ghassul, like Jericho, lies in the Jordan Valley, a little north-east of the Dead Sea and about 3 miles east of the Jordan. The site is not an impressive one. You can search for a long time through the scrub-covered sandy waste until you locate the low hillocks, only about 6 feet (1·83m.) high, which mark the site. The district does not seem to be particularly inviting, for today most of the immediate neighbourhood is uncultivated, and the only signs of life are Bedouin encampments. But water is not far off, coming down from the precipitous hills of the east side of the Jordan Valley, and the excavated remains show that the resources of the neighbourhood in antiquity were well able to support a settled population.

The excavations, carried out between 1930 and 1938 by the Pontifical Biblical Institute, revealed a settlement covering a total area of about 850 yards by 475 yards (777 by 434m.), but divided into three hamlets which each built up its own little mound during the period the site was inhabited. The excavation showed that there were four main layers of occupation, each marked by a rebuilding of the houses, apparently after a destruction by fire, and a raising of the level of the site on the ruins of the earlier houses.

Only the top layer of houses was excavated in any completeness. The evidence from this layer suggests that we have a firmly settled farming community. The houses are of moderate size and closely built, giving each the appearance of a closely knit unit, but there was no evidence of any enclosure wall. The houses are irregular in plan, and the rooms vary from approximately rectangular to trapezoidal. The walls have solidly built foundations of stone, with a superstructure of hand-moulded bricks or in some cases of *terre pisée*. One might perhaps think that the general appearance was of somewhat simple, crude structures, if it were not for the fact that some fragments of remarkable painted wall plaster were recovered. One fragment shows a spirited representation of a bird somewhat resembling a pheasant. Other fragments could be reassembled to form an extraordinary futuristic-looking composition with stylized human forms, sunrays, and an impression of some religious ritual (Fig. 8).

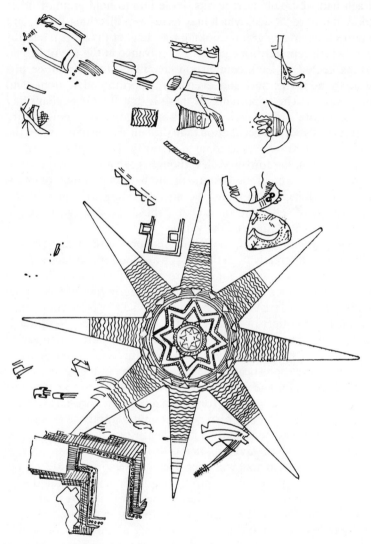

Fig. 8. Painted wall-plaster from Teleilat Ghassul

The equipment of the houses seems to be almost standardized. Each had well-built storage pits, large jars to hold grain or other food, flat paved spaces which may have been threshing-floors, and querns for grinding grain. Cooking was done both on open hearths and, which represents a considerable advance in the use of fire, in ovens heated by sunk combustion chambers. In the storage pits were found corn grains, and, even more important, date stones and olive stones. The importance of these is that the Ghassulians had access to orchards, which implies a necessarily very much more permanently settled occupation than the cultivation of grain, for the trees require long years to come to maturity. Today, the olive does not flourish in the Jordan Valley, though it can grow, and it may be that the olives were traded from some orchard-cultivating community in the hills, which would be an interesting inference of the breakdown of self-sufficiency. Date palms, of course, grow well in suitable irrigated areas of the valley.

The household goods, tools, and weapons of the inhabitants of Ghassul differ greatly from those of any of the Jericho stages. Even the querns are different, for they are of the common saddle-quern type, a plain block of stone with a concave grinding surface, quite unlike those of Jericho described above. The few points of contact between the pottery of Ghassul and that of the Pottery Neolithic B of Jericho have already been mentioned, but in ware and in varied repertory of forms the Ghassul pottery presents a much more advanced and sophisticated appearance. Many of the vessels are of quite hard, thin, and well-fired ware. The forms are surprisingly elaborate. One vessel was given the name of the bird-jar. It had a handle at either end of a body which might remind one of a sitting hen, and a central neck, and for it the suggestion has been made, on the basis of modern Arab use, that it was a churn for making butter by suspension and rocking. Two types of decoration are found. There is a frequent use of applied bands, mainly decorated with crescentic impressions, sometimes in the form of snakes, and incisions on the body of the vessel are also common. The second class has painted decoration, of a dark colour, usually red, on a light background, cream or pink. The designs are simple and geometric.

The stone vessels are also elaborate. There are many finely ground stone saucers, and a remarkable type is a brazier-like vessel with a pierced conical base, the cutting of which out of a hard basalt must have been a skilled operation.

The flint industry is rich (Fig. 11). The most striking form is

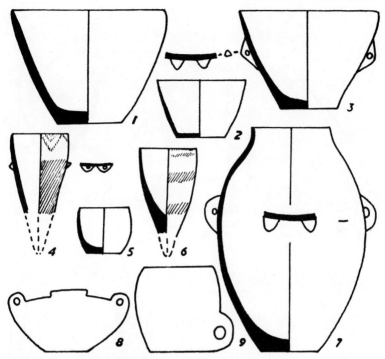

Fig. 9. Pottery from Teleilat Ghassul. ⅕

a fanscraper, a large thin flake with one semicircular edge, struck from a block of tabular flint, so that the cortex (or outer crust) of the block is often left on the implement, and the semicircular edge then finely flaked. Knife blades and toothed sickle blades are common, as are also efficient-looking picks or adzes, which according to their varying sizes would have served as woodworking tools or hoes for agriculture. Only a few arrowheads were found, showing that hunting did not constitute an important part of the economy.

An interesting find was that of two copper axes of simple form, which would show that this culture is correctly assigned to the Chalcolithic phase, when metal was beginning to make its appearance.

In 1966 and again in 1976–77, excavations were resumed at Ghassul under the auspices of the British School of Archaeology in Jerusalem and the University of Sydney. These excavations penetrated in places to the base of the occupation deposits, and have shown that there was a long and complicated succession. An

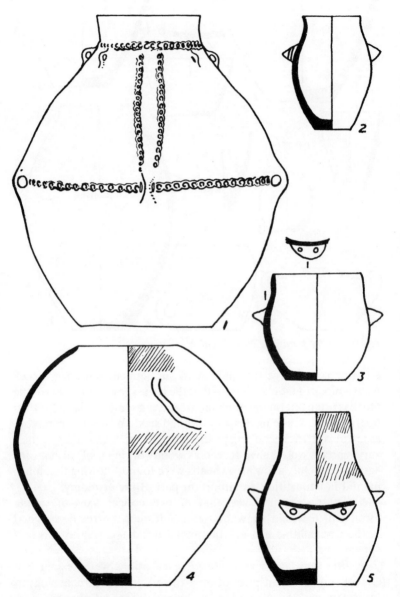

Fig. 10. Pottery from Teleilat Ghassul. $\frac{1}{5}$

interesting phenomenon was the evidence of earthquake cracks and subsidence, to the extent that one section of floor might have dropped as much as 2 feet below that of the other part of the room, a phenomenon which causes considerable archaeological confusion if not observed.

At least ten successive building periods were identified, with a uniform architectural style, though developments in the pottery style can be suggested. Beneath the lowest of these buildings, there were remains of occupation in circular or oval pits, and in this level there was pottery linking with that of Pottery Neolithic B Jericho. The study of all the finds from these excavations is in early stages, but the grain, vegetable, and animal remains suggest a prosperous settled community. Evidence of sanctuaries found in the earlier excavations was confirmed. An interesting result of the 1977 excavations was to show that the impression of a group of little mounds was erroneous. Originally there had been one mound, which had been cut into by erosion at a period of high rainfall. The settlement was therefore on a considerable scale.

Charcoal from what was probably an important sanctuary gave dates of *c*. 3700 B.C. The charcoal came from the destruction of the building, but there is not yet evidence that this marks the desertion of the site.

These excavations have provided a clear link at the base of the site with the final stages of Pottery Neolithic Jericho, but it remains certain that the main occupation of Ghassul is subsequent to the end of the Pottery Neolithic stage at Jericho. The problem of whether the Ghassulians were an incoming group, or evolved from the late Pottery Neolithic inhabitants of Palestine, under the influence of changing climate and environment, is still argued. To me at the moment the arguments seem to favour some new arrivals.

When the excavations of the Pontifical Biblical Institute first revealed the culture of the inhabitants of Ghassul, it appeared to represent an isolated phenomenon, which might be contemporary with one of the other main cultural phases, and the elaborateness of much of the equipment suggested that it might be as late as the Early Bronze Age in the third millennium. But subsequent discoveries, and the reassessment of some earlier ones, show that people sharing the culture were widespread over Palestine. Finds of the characteristic pottery have been made in places as far apart as a site near Jericho, at 'Affuleh in the Plain of Esdraelon, on the Coastal Plain, and in the neighbourhood of Beersheba in the south, to mention a

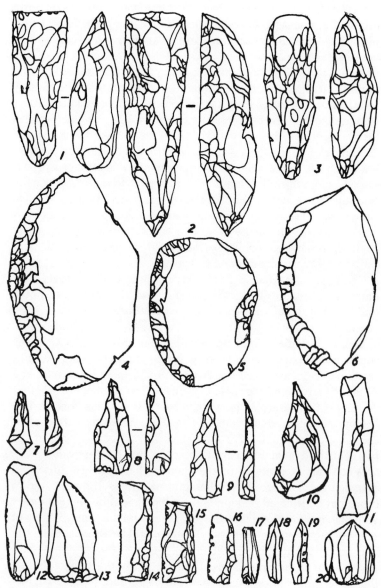

Fig. 11. Flints from Teleilat Ghassul. ½

few only. Interesting finds at Ḥederah and Azorea in the Coastal
Plain, associated with Ghassulian pottery, were of a number of
pottery ossuaries to hold the bones of the dead. Some were in the
form of model houses, with either slightly rounded or gabled roofs,
which give valuable evidence of the form of contemporary houses,
and show that the dead were considered to need their dwellings as in
lifetime.

A group of sites which are interesting for another reason lies in
the Wadi Ghazzeh in southern Palestine, not far from Gaza. Here
Sir Flinders Petrie excavated a number of sites. Many of the finds
are almost identical with those at Ghassul. There are such
specialized pot forms as the 'bird vessel' or churn, the cornet, and
the same types of decoration. The stone vessels include the same
elaborate brazier type, and the flint industries the fine fan-scrapers
and the characteristic hoes. But these finds, instead of coming from
a site with all the evidence of long-established settlement such as
Ghassul, come from a number of settlements which give no evidence of substantial structures and are in fact clearly camping sites.
We have here, therefore, to do with nomadic groups, possibly
practising a seasonal agriculture which the sporadic rainfall of the
area allows, but never settling long enough in one spot to find it
worth while to build themselves permanent houses. With such a
nomadic way of life, one difference between the equipment of these
people and those of Ghassul, the presence of far more flint arrowheads, would fit in well.

A more recent find of a settlement related to that at Ghassul is at
Tell Abu Matar, just south of Beersheba. This is a most remarkable
affair. The site was a natural mound made up of a layer of alluvial
loam and a layer of loess to a combined depth of about 14 feet
(4·27m.) above bedrock. In these layers had been constructed a
series of artificial cave-dwellings. Some were entered by horizontal
passages from the edge of the mound, some by vertical pits, in the
sides of which hand- and foot-holds were cut, giving on to horizontal
galleries. The dwelling-caves were of an average size of about 14
feet by 10 feet (3·05m.), and they were connected by galleries into
groups of five, six, or seven chambers. Along the walls of the
chambers were pits, some of them lined with plaster, presumably for
water storage, and in the middle of the chambers, or in the connecting galleries, were bell-shaped silos with a capacity of 40 to 55
bushels. On the surface of the mound were associated pits and fireplaces. The main dwelling-chambers showed numerous occupation

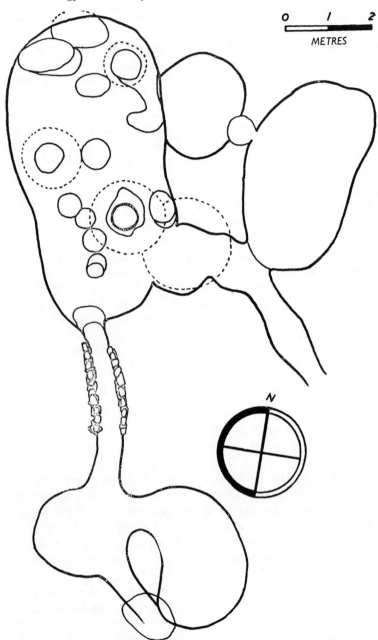

0   1   2
METRES

N

Fig. 12. *Subterranean dwelling at Tell Abu Matar*

layers, with spreads of ash and occupation material separated by deposits of sand, and pits and silos could be assigned to the successive layers. There was also a succession of structural phases. The comparatively soft material into which the caves were cut tended to crumble and the roofs to collapse. The dwelling might then be superseded by another, or a new dwelling be established in the pit formed by the collapse of the cave, presumably with a superstructure partly above ground. Altogether, three main phases of subterranean dwellings could be traced. The fourth phase on the site represented a major change, for above the filled-in pits of the earlier stages were found rectilinear houses with walls built on stone foundations.

This curious troglodyte community, which the twenty houses found suggest might have numbered about two hundred persons, seems to have lived primarily by agriculture. Their flint industry included no arrowheads, and they were therefore not hunters, while the numerous silos show that they had abundant supplies of grain, in spite of the semi-arid neighbourhood. But the most striking thing about them was that they were copper-workers. Evidence of the whole process was found. The preliminary reduction was carried out in open fireplaces. Then the ore was smelted in specially constructed ovens, circular basins about a foot to 18 inches (0·46m.) in diameter, with thick walls of earth mixed with straw; as found, the interior of these chambers was glazed from a combination of the melted metal, silica, and residual matter. Then the ore was refined in crucibles, and finally it must have been cast in moulds, though these were not found. This represents the earliest undoubted impact of the metal age upon Palestine. The nearest source from which the ore could have been obtained is 60 miles (96·5km.) away to the south; a regular trade in raw materials must therefore have existed, and the inhabitants of Tell Abu Matar must have been able to produce sufficient supplies of food material to finance expeditions to fetch it, or to buy it from itinerant merchants. Moreover, the working of the metal was a specialist's job, and he also had to be supported by the food production of the rest of the community. We have here, therefore, evidence of an important stage of transition from a self-sufficient Neolithic way of life to that of a complex community. But the evidence shows that the use of metal had not yet become a dominant factor. The tools and implements of the inhabitants of Tell Abu Matar were still of flint. The manufactured copper objects found were mace-heads (which probably had a ceremonial rather than a warlike significance), pins, rings, ornamental cylinders, and handles. The metal was still regarded as far too precious for rough, everyday use.

To this evidence of the processing of copper ore at Tell Abu Matar can now be added evidence concerning its mining. At Timna, about 17 miles (30km.) north of Eilat at the north end of the Gulf of Aqaba, were found extensive traces of smelting and habitation. Nearby, among mine shafts belonging to later periods, especially the Late Bronze Age, were found the mines of the Chalcolithic period, comparatively shallow shafts from the base of which radiated galleries following the ore-bearing strata, so incredibly narrow that they can only have been worked by pigmies or children. It was not for another two thousand years that this area was again so thoroughly exploited for metal.

There is no doubt that these people have some connection with the inhabitants of Ghassul. Their flint industry is not identical, since most of the implements were rough choppers made from pebbles locally available; there were only a very few of the fine fan-scrapers so common at Ghassul, but they did use the hump-backed Ghassulian picks. Their stone vessels included basalt bowls with brazier-like bases, which were very characteristic both of Ghassul and of the sites in the Wadi Ghazzeh. The pottery again is not identical, but includes a number of similar forms, especially the peculiar 'bird-vessel' or churn.

Another group of Ghassulian sites was in caves in the high cliffs of the Judaean mountains flanking the Dead Sea, and the finds from these sites included the most spectacular of all. It may be no coincidence that many of these caves contained pottery and other objects of two periods, the Ghassulian and those of refugees from the Romans in A.D. 135 after the Second Revolt of the Jews. The Ghassulians, like the Jews of the 2nd century A.D., may have taken refuge in these barren and almost inaccessible spots in the face of an approaching enemy. In one of the caves in Nahal Mishmar was found a hoard of objects that can almost certainly be interpreted as an attempt to preserve precious objects.

In all 429 objects were found, wrapped in a straw mat and hidden beneath a boulder. Some were in stone, including beautifully worked mace-heads, others in ivory or bone. The most exciting objects were in copper, with in addition to many maceheads, chisels, and axes, objects which most certainly can be identified as ceremonial, crown-like cylinders with elaborately moulded birds and other objects on the rim (Pl. 32), and a great variety of wands or sceptres (Pl. 33). They provide astonishing evidence of the skill of the Ghassulian metalworkers.

An interesting suggestion has been made as to the source of this hoard. Down near the shore of the Dead Sea, about 6 miles (9·65km.) north of the cave where the hoard was found, a building standing on a projecting rock terrace can be identified as a Ghassulian shrine, consisting of a courtyard with buildings against its wall. One of these was certainly a shrine, a long narrow room entered by a door on the long side, and opposite the door the site of the altar, with ashes of offerings and the probable base of a cult object; pits in the floor contained the remains of offerings. A circular structure in the courtyard was used for liquid offerings.

This building as found had been stripped of all its equipment. Only broken potsherds mixed with the offerings indicated its date. The suggestion has therefore been made that the Nahal Mishmar hoard is in fact the cult equipment and offerings from this shrine, hidden for safety in the hills at the approach of an enemy. We can so far only guess at who this enemy was. It could have been the Proto-Urban people described in the next chapter, or it might have been the campaign of the Egyptian king Narmer, *c.* 3100 B.C.

There are, in fact, three inferences that can be drawn from our present knowledge of the Ghassulian culture. The first is that it is intrusive and not indigenous in Palestine. Its highly developed and specialized pottery is not derived from anything which, as far as we know, went before in Palestine. The flint industry, especially at Ghassul itself, is also very individual. Attempts have been made to find parallels for both the pottery and the flint industry, but without any real success. Some parallels can be traced in Egypt, but they are so general that one must conclude that the group was not derived from that direction. The conclusion is that they must have come from the east or north-east, but there material of the period is almost unknown owing to lack of exploration.

The second inference is that there were a number of groups only rather loosely connected. There is no identity in equipment and way of life between the inhabitants of Ghassul, of the Wadi Ghazzeh, and of Tell Abu Matar. It is suggested that these groups were all inhabiting marginal areas. But the potential fertility of the Jordan Valley, when water supplies are controlled by a settled population, is undoubted, and as one approaches the Beersheba neighbourhood from the south in spring, one realizes why the Israelites considered

Palestine a land flowing with milk and honey. On the other hand, the area of the Wadi Ghazzeh is the real desert-fringe. The contrast of economy between the settlements there and those of Ghassul and Tell Abu Matar is emphasized by the high proportion of arrowheads found in the former, while they are practically absent in the other two sites. Allied settlements are also found in the north, at 'Affuleh on the fringes of the Plain of Esdraelon and Hederah in the Plain of Sharon, comparatively rich agricultural areas. Immigrant groups therefore settled all over the country, though on present evidence more in the south than the north, and adapted their way of life to their environment.

The third inference is that though on the Tell Abu Matar evidence these groups had an economy which was transitional towards the great advances of the metal ages, they directly contributed surprisingly little to the ultimate civilization of Palestine. So far, evidence of Ghassulian occupation has never been found in the lower levels of any of the sites which subsequently became a town. Their settlements seem simply to have died out. The recognizably Ghassulian forms of pottery and flint implements do not have their descendants in the forms of the Early Bronze Age. The origins of the town-builders of the Early Bronze Age must be sought elsewhere.

There are now a number of Carbon-14 dates for Ghassulian settlements, Safadi 360 B.C. ±350 and 3310 B.C. ±300, Horvat Beter 3325 B.C. ±150, and Nahal Hever 3409 B.C. ±125. The straw mat in which the Nahal Mishmar hoard was wrapped gave a date of 3429 B.C. ±150 and 2919 B.C. ±250. A date of the last third of the fourth millennium B.C. is thus indicated. We are, however, now getting near to the historical period, and in particular to that in which there are connections between Palestine and historically fixed dates in Egypt. One must therefore take into account the adjustments the scientists are finding it necessary to make in interpretation, due to increased understanding of solar variations. It is probable that all these dates have to be placed some five hundred years earlier.

There is still not enough evidence of trade to provide firm cross-links between Palestine and the rest of western Asia. The Ghassulians, in fact, seem to have been very self-centred; a suggestion made earlier that there was some connection between the Halafian pottery of the widespread Chalcolithic culture of the northern Fertile Crescent is not now generally accepted. The present evidence from Carbon-14 dates leaves us in Palestine with a nasty long period to fill. Even if one brings down the appearance of Pottery Neolithic to *c*. 5000 B.C., one cannot reach firm dates until the Proto-Urban which, on historically linked evidence, must be the last quarter of the fourth millennium. Within this comes the Ghassulian.

They were, as has been stressed, undoubtedly immigrants. They certainly do not account for all the groups that exploration is gradually bringing to light, which must be fitted in between the Neolithic and the stages preceding the full Bronze Age. Some of these are probably to be regarded as indigenous descendants of the inhabitants of Sha'ar ha Golan and Pottery Neolithic B Jericho. The lowest levels at Beth-shan and Megiddo, and some so far unrelated deposits at Jericho, suggest something of the sort, while a recent survey of the Jordan Valley shows that there are a number of ancient sites which must fall into the general period. Palestine in the early fourth millennium must be visualized as settled by a number of groups of diverse origins, living side by side.

Towards the end of the millennium we reach a period for which excavation has provided much clearer evidence. We reach the period in which many of the subsequent towns seem to have been founded. It has already been pointed out that occupation of a Ghassulian character has not so far been found at the base of a tell. The new material does occur in the lower levels of a number of important sites, and from it a direct succession to the full Bronze Age can be shown. We are therefore at the dawn of a new period.

Notes

1. *Lachish* IV, Fig. (1) and p. 300, Cave 6019.
2. *IEJ* 8, Fig. 4.
3. *Megiddo II*, Pl. 2. 30, 31, 34–6.

4   The Proto-Urban Period

The new period is ushered in by the invasion of a number of new groups, that recurrent theme in Palestinian history. They arrive as migrant tribesmen, probably from different areas and with varying equipment, and they do not bring with them a ready-made urban civilization. But, as was pointed out in the last chapter, the settlements they established grew into the city states of the Early Bronze Age. These invasions took place in the last third of the fourth millennium B.C. For reasons which will be discussed later, the best name for the phase in which they took place seems to be the Proto-Urban period.

The first evidence of the new groups comes from tombs. Their presence in some considerable numbers and over a wide area in the north and centre of the country is attested by their burials, but so far the evidence of their actual settlements is slight. On a number of sites which were subsequently to grow into towns, for instance Megiddo, Jericho, Beth-shan, Tell el Far'ah, pottery and occupation levels are found at the base of the layers of the city-mounds, but little in the way of structures. At other sites, for instance Tell Nasbeh, a few miles north of Jerusalem, and Samaria, traces of occupation are found, but the sites are subsequently deserted, in both cases until the Iron Age; the first village population was perhaps absorbed into a town elsewhere.

The appearance of the tombs is of interest in itself, and is strong additional evidence, over and above the new types of pottery, of the arrival of entirely new groups. For the first time in Palestine, tombs are cut in the rock, or natural caves are used, and in them multiple burials of up to three or four hundred individuals were made over a long space of time. At Jericho the contrast is very marked. In all the large area searched for tombs, not a single one has been found of an earlier period. The Pre-Pottery Neolithic people of both groups buried beneath the floor of their houses. There is no evidence as to how either of the Pottery Neolithic groups disposed of their dead; from this it can probably be deduced that they were not formally buried at all, but the bodies simply exposed, unless they were buried in simple graves, without grave goods, in the cultivated land to the east and south of the tell, which is not very likely. There is a suggestion that the Ghassulian burials are associated with megalithic monuments, but the evidence is not yet clear. With the newcomers in the last part of the fourth millennium comes the new practice of multiple tomb-burial, and, to the great benefit of archaeologists, this is associated with the practice of offerings to accompany the dead. Presumably the offerings were originally of food and drink, or perhaps scents and perfumes, but what survives is the containers of pottery. These vessels provide us with evidence to define the culture of the group that used the tomb. Since vessels found in tombs are often reasonably intact, whereas on occupation sites only broken sherds are found, the tomb deposits are a very important element in our knowledge of the pottery. It must, however, be remembered that not all types of vessel were placed in tombs (for instance cooking-pots are always rare), so there may be differences between finds in tombs and those from contemporary occupation deposits.

It is probable that the newcomers came from the north and east, for so far little evidence of their presence has been found in south and west Palestine except at Gezer, easily approachable from the coastal plain; in this area it may be presumed that the descendants of the Ghassulian people continued to live side by side with them. To groups arriving from the east, Jericho would be a natural point of entry, and the evidence suggests that some of them did in fact come in that way.

Some half a dozen tombs at Jericho contain pottery of the same new types. The tombs are cut into the soft limestone of the slopes surrounding the settlement. The roofs of all the tombs of this period that have so far been discovered have disappeared, which is an indication that there has been a considerable subsequent erosion of the rock, a point which will be referred to later. What survives are the bases and walls of large chambers, about 4·50 metres by 3 metres, with the lower parts of the entrance shafts that gave access to them. In general construction they appear to have been similar to later tombs, which have a roughly circular vertical entrance shaft, from the base of which an entrance leads into a tomb chamber, at this period, judging from the surviving height of the walls, about 2 metres high.

The burial practices in these tombs were strange. They all contained the remains of a very large number of individuals, in one case of about a hundred and forty, in another of over four hundred. But though we can say that four hundred individuals are represented, we have nothing like the complete remains of four hundred bodies. The count is made on the skulls. These we find for the most part entirely separated from the bodies, and neatly ranged round the edge of the tomb. In the middle of the tomb is a jumble of the other bones, mostly completely disarranged, but sometimes one finds a complete limb, a leg or an arm, in articulation, though separated from the rest of the body. In one tomb these bones in the central area were cremated; a few of the nearest skulls round the edge were scorched, though not included in the cremation, but there was no sign of fire in the other tombs. Another remarkable fact is that there are not nearly enough long bones to go with all the skulls. All this points to the fact that the burials as we find them were secondary. That is to say, the bones were only placed in their present position after the flesh had largely decayed. It is very difficult to decide what were the first stages. Was the process a lengthy one, with continuous burials in each tomb, and, as the bodies decayed and new burials were made, the skulls placed round the edge and the rest of the bones left in the centre? Or, at intervals, were skeletons collected up, from other tombs or simply after exposure, and the skulls and some of the other bones placed in mass ossuary-tombs? A consideration of all the evidence suggests that the burial practice was that of multiple successive burials in large communal tombs. As the bodies decayed, the skulls were carefully removed and stacked around the wall of the chamber. It is the care with which the skulls were moved, ensuring the preservation of delicate nasal bones, that shows that the skeletons could not have been collected up from primary burials elsewhere and transported to the tombs in which they were found. As the tombs became full, the skulls were carefully removed from the bodies and stacked, and most of the other bones were disposed of, in the case of Tomb A 94 by cremation. A recent study suggests that the same process can be deduced concerning Cave Tomb 2 I at Gezer. There is also evidence at Jericho that successive phases in the Proto-Urban A pottery can be identified. In Tomb K2 the second phase is succeeded by one containing Proto-Urban B pottery, associated with a new burial custom involving the use of stone

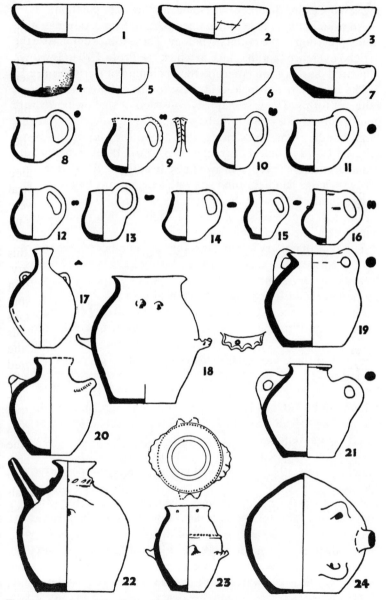

Fig. 13. Pottery of the Proto-Urban period from Jericho Tomb A94. ⅕

platforms. Some pottery forms of Proto-Urban A types continued in use, suggesting that there was some mixture of population.

An examination made of the allied pottery from 'Ai brings additional precision to the pottery typology. These tombs emphasize the Jericho evidence that the stage at which the Proto-Urban B people appeared does not long precede the beginning of Early Bronze I.

The pottery vessels placed in these tombs did not cover a great range of forms. The vast majority consisted of shallow bowls with gently curved sides and little bag-shaped juglets with a relatively large handle, sometimes rising well above the rim of the vessel (Fig. 13.*10–11*); some, both of the bowls and of the jugs, have a very crude decoration in red or brown lines. In addition there were some jars with ledge handles, some jars with a high projecting spout, and in one tomb, A94, which may be taken as a representative of this group, a very odd vessel of beehive shape, with a spout and two handles on one side (Fig. 13.*24*).

This type of pottery is found in tombs at a number of other places. At Tell Nasbeh the range of forms in Tombs 32, 52, and 67 seems to have been very similar, and the same group of people may have pushed on from Jericho into the central uplands.

On the evidence of the pottery from two burial caves at Azor,[1] the same group of people would appear to have reached the coastal area. Most of the Azor material belongs to the Proto-Urban A period, but there are some items belonging to the Proto-Urban B period as well. The pottery assemblage is similar to Jericho tombs A 94 and A 114A as well as Tombs C and G at 'Ai; Tombs 5, 12, 32, 54, 66, and 67 at Tell Nasbeh; and Tombs 1, 3, 5, and 8 at Tell el Far'ah. But at Tell Nasbeh, Cave Tomb 5–6, and at the site of 'Ai, not far from Tell Nasbeh, in Tombs B, C, and G, the same pottery appears in conjunction with a quite distinct type, not found in Jericho Tomb A94 and the allied group. This type is characterized by decoration in fairly elaborate patterns of grouped bands, quite different from the crude drip-lines which are all that is found on the other group. The forms, with deep bowls, basket-handle vessels with vertical spouts, and round-based bottles, are also different.

The distinction is made more clear by the fact that in Jericho a single tomb, A13, was found in which, above lower levels containing pottery like A94, this other pottery is found, unmixed with the A94 pottery. On the ceramic evidence, therefore, we have two groups of people, and we may label the A94 people Proto-Urban A and the A13 people Proto-Urban B. At Jericho and in some of the

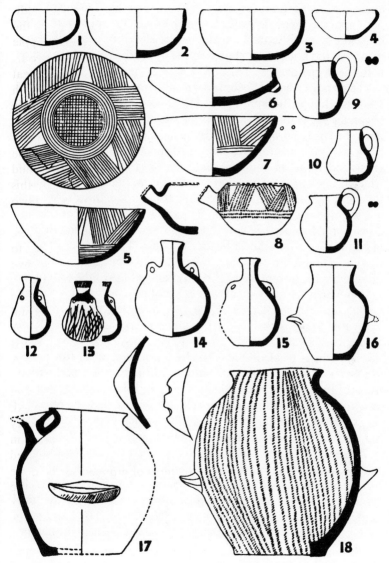

Fig. 14. Pottery of the Proto-Urban period from 'Ai Tombs G and C(10). ⅕

Tell Nasbeh tombs they are distinct, but they must have been living side by side, and on the evidence of Tell Nasbeh Cave Tomb 5–6 and of the 'Ai tomb they must in due course have mingled. The pottery of the B people is also found on Ophel, the spur south of the present city of Jerusalem which was the site of the earliest settlement, but it is not quite certain whether or not they were here mixed with the A people.

The Proto-Urban A people were also found farther north. In 1946 the École Biblique of the Dominican Fathers in Jerusalem began the excavation of the imposing site of Tell el Far'ah. This site, not to be confused with the site of the same name (referred to in this book as Tell Fara for the sake of distinction, though this is an anglicized form) in southern Palestine, lies in the Wadi Far'ah, which is one of the main valleys that cut down into the west side of the Jordan Valley from near Nablus. It has a long history, though not without interruption, from the period we are now considering down to the Iron Age, when it has a position of especial importance in connection with biblical history (Chapter 11). Besides lying on this important route between the central highlands and the Jordan, the site has the advantage of two excellent springs at the foot of the hill on which the settlement was established.

Only quite a small area of the very large tell has been so far excavated to bedrock. The first occupation is called by Père R. de Vaux, its excavator, Middle Chalcolithic. Above it is a level which he calls Upper Chalcolithic. The structural remains of this period are not very substantial, but indicate a firmly settled occupation. Most of the finds of the period come from tombs in large natural caves in the surrounding hill slopes. The tombs seem to be typical of the period in containing multiple burials, similar to those of Jericho, but they were much disturbed by subsequent re-use.

These tombs contain pottery closely allied to that found in the Proto-Urban A tombs at Jericho. There are the same innumerable little bag-shaped juglets, the same shallow bowls with curved walls, the same jars with high curving spouts, and even an almost identical beehive-shaped jar with side spout. There are, however, some differences. The forms are rather more elaborate, the loop-handles of the juglets higher, some of the bowls have developed an odd conical knob in the centre, and there is a type of jar that has been compressed laterally at the mouth (Fig. 15.22). Another difference is that a fairly high proportion of the vessels have a burnished red slip, which is rare at Jericho; this may suggest that the Far'ah tombs

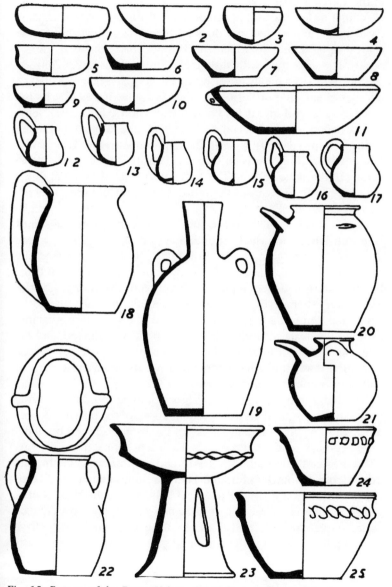

Fig. 15. Pottery of the Proto-Urban period from Tell el Far'ah. $\frac{1}{5}$

are somewhat later, since it is a practice that becomes very common in the Early Bronze Age.

A final difference is more important. With the Proto-Urban A pottery is found a type that does not occur at Jericho nor in the central upland sites in which the Proto-Urban A and B groups occur. This is a type with distinctive forms (Fig. 15.*23–25*) and characterized by a highly burnished grey slip. It has been found on a number of sites in northern Palestine, and since it was first recognized in a group of sites in the Plain of Esdraelon, it is usually known as Esdraelon ware. At Tell el Far'ah all the tombs containing Proto-Urban A pottery contain Esdraelon ware as well, as do the Upper Chalcolithic levels on the tell; it was therefore presumed to belong to the same culture. The Jericho evidence shows that this is not necessarily so. We can therefore identify a third group, which we can designate Proto-Urban C.

The most spectacular finds of this period come from the site of Bab edh-Dhra', to which attention was drawn in 1965 by the appearance of large numbers of attractive pottery vessels on the market in Jerusalem; as a result excavations were carried out there by the American School under the direction of Paul Lapp. The site is on the east shore of the Dead Sea, on low hills just above the Lisan, the peninsula that projects out into the sea. Here is a large fortified town site, which has been only slightly examined, and the finds came from an adjacent cemetery of enormous size. It has been estimated that it must have contained twenty thousand tombs, in addition to later burial structures.

The shaft tombs belong to the Proto-Urban period. They provide most interesting parallels to and explanations of the burial practices at Jericho. At the latter site, rock-cut tombs approached by shafts have been presumed, but the evidence has been lost in erosion. At Bab edh-Dhra' the shafts survived to *c.* 2·10 metres, possibly the original height. At Jericho, intensive continuous use complicated the interpretation of burial practices. The Bab edh-Dhra' people were much more energetic in digging new tombs, and only eight or so individuals were buried in the tombs excavated (admittedly a very small proportion). The general practice in the two places seems, however, to have been similar. The skulls were detached, and carefully ranked round the edge of the chamber. The long bones were piled in the centre of the chamber, usually on a mat. Not all the long bones were present, but those that were were intact, and the flesh must have been removed by boiling rather than exposure.

With the bodies was placed a liberal provision of pottery vessels, stacked in such a way as to suggest that they did not contain food, though they may have been used in a funeral feast. Some objects of organic materials survived, such as a wooden staff and a pair of sandals. The pottery has a distinct resemblance to that from the Proto-Urban tombs at Tell el Far'ah. It is not, however, identical. There is not the multiplicity of round-based juglets with handles to the rim, nor of the shallow, round-based bowls. The greater number of them resemble the Proto-Urban C vessels which at Tell el Far'ah (though not Jericho) are mixed with the Proto-Urban A vessels, but instead of having a burnished grey slip like the typical Esdraelon ware, most of them have a well burnished red slip, which at Tell el Far'ah was found on the Proto-Urban A vessels.

An enormous number of tombs was found with this mixture of pottery. In addition were found two tombs with the typical decoration of grouped lines of the Proto-Urban B group. Proto-Urban A pottery was also found in an above-ground burial place, aptly named a charnel house, which was the burial method characteristic of the Early Bronze Age at Bab edh-Dhra'. There was some stratigraphic evidence that at Bab edh-Dhra', as at Jericho, the Proto-Urban B tombs were later than the Proto-Urban A tombs. It would also seem that these later arrivals were associated with the settlement which was to become a walled town, but in all the areas excavated it was clear that this pottery appeared in the layers that were earlier than the town walls.

The finds at Bab edh-Dhra' add considerable supporting evidence to the conclusion that at this period there were a number of groups in Palestine with markedly different characteristics, at least as far as their pottery was concerned. They share with other newcomers a thousand years or so later the characteristic that nearly all the evidence concerning them comes from tombs. However, pottery of the various types is found at the base of many of the mounds which subsequently became the walled towns of the Early Bronze Age, and this is a justification for describing them as Proto-Urban. It must, however, be noted that the number of the Proto-Urban A + C tombs at Bab edh-Dhra' is enormous, and it must represent a central burial place of a large semi-nomadic or pastoral group unconnected with the town.

At this stage we first come to the great site of Megiddo, where the same combination of Proto-Urban A and C is found. The ancient city, several times mentioned in the Old Testament, today is

75

represented by perhaps the most impressive tell in the whole of Pales-, tine (Pl. 35), a great oval mound looking out northwards over the Plain of Esdraelon. In historic times its great importance lay in the fact that it guarded the pass that cut across the low neck between Mount Carmel, jutting out towards the sea, and the central mountain range. This pass formed part of the route of age-long historic importance between Egypt and Syria, and the interest of Egypt in the control of Megiddo recurs at many stages in the Egyptian archives. Excavation, however, has shown that the first occupation of the site dates back to well before the Egyptian Empire began to be interested in foreign contacts.

Megiddo, like Jericho, has been the subject of interest to more than one archaeological expedition. The most ambitious attempt to investigate was the excavations begun by the Oriental Institute of Chicago in 1925. The plan was to excavate it completely from top to bottom. But the mound of Megiddo covers at its summit 13 acres (5·5ha.), and its depth in the centre of the mound is some 55 feet (17m.). The scheme proved beyond the powers even of the Oriental Institute. With the financial depression of the 1930s, a much-reduced plan had to be adopted, and the base of the mound was, in the sequel, only investigated in a very limited area.

In this small area beneath the mound, and also on the slopes of the hill on which it is situated in an area which was cleared before the dumping on it of spoil, evidence was found of periods long before Megiddo became a walled town. The very earliest occupation of all was rather curious. It was found in a cave in the rock surface. The deposits contained only flint and bone implements, with no pottery at all. But the flints are of the same type which in the occupation on the surface of the rock are associated with pottery of, as we shall see, the second half of the fourth millennium, and are therefore probably not much earlier than this phase. By this time, of course, the fully pottery-using cultures just described were found widely spread over Palestine, and it seems strange that there was still a group at Megiddo in the pre-pottery stage. There may be an explanation in some specialist use made of the cave, or it may be a further illustration of the separate groups living in Palestine, each progressing towards civilization at a different rate.

Though these earliest inhabitants at Megiddo apparently lived in caves, and though in the area excavated there are no structures that can be ascribed to them, they were by no means entirely primitive in their equipment. Among the flint or chert implements found were javelin heads, which showed that hunting played a part in their economy, but there were also a number of sickle blades, which suggests they were agriculturists. What were apparently two complete sets of teeth of sickles showed that these had cutting edges about 32 centimetres long. Still more interesting are a number of long 'wands' of bone, carefully shaved down from the long bones of animals, which are pointed at one end and pierced by a circular hole at the other. It is suggested that these were used as needle shuttles for weaving, and also to beat up the weft. The textile made must have been light, since the tools are slender, and may have been of a material like flax. Similar tools were found at Ghassul, where a fragment of textile was probably of some plant fibre.

The succeeding people who lived in the surface of the rock had still a distinctly primitive culture. All that survives in the way of structures are some slight, irregular, and disconnected foundations, suggesting only flimsy buildings. Besides these there are a number of pits cut into the rock, some of which no doubt correspond in function as silos (storage pits) with the brick- or stone-lined pits of Ghassul. Others may have served for some purpose such as pressing olives for oil, for two adjacent pits are often joined by channels. The occupation of this period must have been widespread, for the area in which it was found spreads well down the slope of the hill.

The published material from the lowest levels of the tell proper is a mixture,[2] for the stratigraphical deposits were not properly analysed. It contains material allied to both Jericho Pottery Neolithic A and B and Chalcolithic sherds with some contact with Ghassulian. With this mixture, and also in the lowest layers of the early occupation that spread down the slopes of the hill before the later nucleated settlement was defined,[3] are published (though they are certainly not truly associated) vessels of Esdraelon ware and Proto-Urban A material. Some of the occupation of the period was in caves, for in Tomb 903[4] and elsewhere the same pottery is found in occupation levels underlying burials of a later period.

Other sites in the Plain of Esdraelon at which the Proto-Urban C ware is found are 'Affuleh and Beth-shan. At 'Affuleh the evidence is slight , owing to the nature of the excavation. At Beth-shan the lowest levels beneath the great tell, representing the town that was to rival Megiddo in importance at a later date, were only examined in a small sounding. The lowest levels, deposits in pits and Level XVIII, contained material which may be related to Jericho Pottery Neolithic B, and may represent the indigenous Chalcolithic which

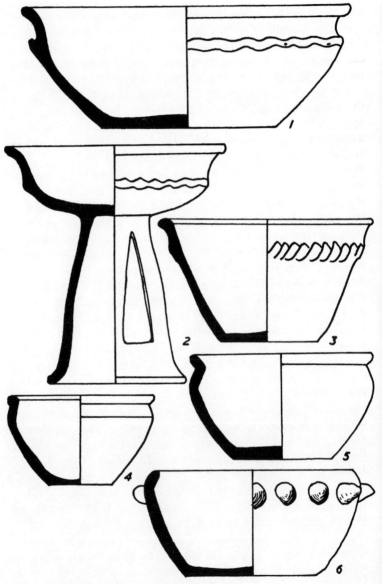

Fig. 16. Forms of Esdraelon ware vessels. $\frac{1}{5}$

probably existed side by side with Ghassulian, and in which in the earliest stage pit-dwellings were also customary. In Level XVII Esdraelon ware appears, and is more common in XVI.[5] At this site, however, the published material does not suggest any mixture with Proto-Urban A, but rather with the preceding indigenous Chalcolithic. This is an additional indication of the separate identity of the Proto-Urban C group.

The Proto-Urban C ware is completely lacking at Jericho, both in the tombs and on the tell. But curiously enough it is found in appreciable quantities in a deposit beneath Herodian Jericho, about a mile to the south of Tell es Sultan.[6] The published evidence is not very clear, but none of the characteristic Proto-Urban A forms are illustrated, and the accompanying material may again belong to the indigenous Chalcolithic. Since the Tell el Far'ah evidence shows that the two groups must have been approximately contemporary, the complete contrast between two sites so close together may suggest hostility between them in this area.

The interlocking of the three Proto-Urban groups and of the presumed indigenous Chalcolithic shows that a complex intermingling was going on. The process may of course have been a slow one. Efforts have been made to work out a sequence of forms in the Esdraelon bowl shapes and from this to deduce a chronology. This is not generally accepted, and the fact is that there is not enough evidence of sequence on any one site.

So far, we have mainly discussed the different elements in terms of different groups of pottery types. Accumulated archaeological experience has shown that a distinctive group of pottery types in fact is the evidence, sometimes the only evidence, which survives of a distinctive group of people. Therefore, we can translate our A, B, and C pottery types into three groups of people who appear in Palestine at this time. They come in as independent groups, as the Jericho evidence shows, and as they penetrate into the country some of them intermingle. Perhaps, as the Jericho tombs show that there the A and B groups were separate, Jericho was actually the point of entry of these groups, indicating that they came from the east, as so many groups did in the later history of Palestine. Thence they may have penetrated almost due west into the highlands, where, at Tell Nasbeh and 'Ai, some of them settled down together. Others of the A group may have turned north up the Jordan Valley, and then west up the Wadi Far'ah, where they met the C group. The latter almost certainly came from the north, either direct down from the Lebanon highland zone or perhaps from inland Syria to the north-east, crossing the Jordan Valley, near the Sea of Galilee, into the Plain of Esdraelon. Unfortunately, the homeland of none of these groups can be satisfactorily identified, since we cannot point to the same pottery elsewhere. But there is little doubt that eventually we shall be able to do so, when the lower levels of the great occupation sites in countries bordering on Palestine have been more fully examined. Until we know more about their homeland, we shall have to be content to leave them anonymously designated by letters of the alphabet.

So far nothing has been said as to the date of this phase. For the preceding one, that of the third stage of Jericho and Ghassul, the first half of the fourth millennium has been tentatively suggested. There is no doubt that the period shortly precedes and eventually merges into the Early Bronze Age and at that point Palestinian stages can be linked with Egyptian chronology. It is generally accepted that Palestinian Early Bronze Age II is contemporary with the First Dynasty of Egypt, of which the date accepted in the revised edition of the *Cambridge Ancient History* is 3100 to 2900 B.C. This would place the Proto-Urban period in the second half of the fourth millennium B.C. This would fit the discovery at Megiddo of a number of sealings impressed on jars which are usually considered to be of the Jemdet Nasr period in Mesopotamia, which again belongs to the second half of the fourth millennium. Jericho Tomb A 94 has produced a Carbon-14 date. The original result gave 3260 B.C. ± 110. But further research in recent years has shown, as has been explained on p. 64, that dates have to be adjusted to take into account variations in the sun's radiation, and samples giving dates of the late fourth millennium have to be read as being some seven hundred years earlier. On Palestinian evidence, this made nonsense. However, further material from the same sample has now been tested, and the date when adjusted gets us back again to 3200 B.C. This all seems very odd and rather shakes one's faith. However, the general picture of groups of newcomers entering the country in the last half of the fourth millennium B.C. is probably correct.

A further Carbon-14 dating from the upper levels of Safadi, certainly contemporary with the Proto-Urban cultures, is 3160 B.C. ± 310. A study of the connections between Palestine and adjacent countries[7] has emphasized the length of the Proto-Urban period, especially at Tell Gath, and shown that there is a clear chronological overlap with the First Dynasty of Egypt, certainly to the time of Narmer and probably overlapping that of his successor Menes. On the chronology adopted in the revised version of the *Cambridge Ancient History*, this would give a terminal date of *c.* 3050 B.C. Other datings would place the end of the period a hundred or two hundred years later, which in many ways would fit the Palestinian evidence better.

Therefore, in the last centuries of the fourth millennium we have coming into Palestine a number of groups of people, of which three can now be identified, and it is very probable that further research will add to their number. Of their way of life we know very little, for most of the evidence about them has been recovered from tombs. But this fact in itself tells us something. Traces of their houses have been found at Megiddo and Tell el Far'ah, and at Jericho there is evidence, from pottery finds in the earlier excavations, that they lived on part but not the whole of the site. Everywhere their houses were slight, nowhere is there any evidence that they lived in walled towns. They were villagers, not town-dwellers. Apart from that, we know that they deposited the dead in great multiple-burial tombs, with rather strange rites, but little else.

At Megiddo there is a little additional evidence, but this is again connected with ritual rather than how they lived. This is the construction, in the second level above bedrock, of a substantial building which is probably a shrine. It included a room, 4 metres by more than 12 metres in size, with a doorway in one of the long sides. Opposite the door was a low altar, 0·50 metre high, of mud-brick, covered with plaster, rectangular in shape, with a low step on one side. A number of flat stones set in the floor were probably too slight to carry columns supporting the roof, so they too may have had some religious significance. Subsequently the altar was enlarged, and its base then overlaps the line of stones in the centre of the room. We may take the appearance of this building as showing a development in community life, and also of increased architectural experience, but the inhabitants were still probably villagers.

A very surprising discovery has recently been made at Jawa in Transjordan, in the basalt wilderness north-east of Mafraq. Here Svend Helms has excavated what is apparently a walled town covering an area of 25 acres (10ha.) of the Proto-Urban period. Such a large settlement was made possible by an elaborate water conservation system with substantial dams across the adjacent wadis. Such an establishment is infinitely more advanced than the contemporary settlements farther west. It is a most intriguing problem, but its discovery is so recent that the details available are scanty.

Knowledge concerning this stage in Palestinian history has been gradually accumulating over the last twenty years or so. When G. E. Wright made his pioneer study of the early material,[8] he classified the Esdraelon ware as Chalcolithic and the decorated pottery found at 'Ai, Ophel, and Gezer as Early Bronze Age Ia. Père de Vaux at Tell el Far'ah classified his material as Late Chalcolithic. It can now be shown that all the groups are at least in part contemporary. Wright would therefore now prefer to call them all Early Bronze Age, as he feels there is no break between this stage and the full Early Bronze Age, whereas de Vaux would prefer still to call A and C Chalcolithic and B Early Bronze Age, as he feels that it is from that more southerly group that the Early Bronze Age spreads over Palestine. My original view would have been to call them all Chalcolithic, for they would seem all to represent the same type of occupation, of comparatively recently arrived migrants, living in non-nucleated settlements, with little evidence of their architecture, and certainly no walled towns, such as are the characteristic of the full Early Bronze Age.

Such diversity of nomenclature would obviously be a great source of confusion. This is one reason why the term Proto-Urban has been suggested. The other reason is that it suggests the actual economic stage of development. It is from the component groups of this stage that emerges the population which developed the urban civilization of the Early Bronze Age. The stage of development corresponds to those which preceded the Old Empire of Egypt and the Early Dynastic period of Mesopotamia. In Egypt this is designated the Proto-dynastic Period, and in Mesopotamia the term Proto-Literate Age has recently come into use.[9] In Palestine neither a dynastic nor a literate period succeeds, but one which is characterized by urban development. Like the Proto-dynastic Period and the Proto-Literate Age, and covering, like them, the last centuries of the fourth millennium, the period is a formative one for an advance in civilization, and a comparable designation seems appropriate.

Notes

1. A. Ben-Tor, *Qedem* 1 (1975), 1–53.
2. *Megiddo II*, Pl. 1–2, 92–95.
3. R. M. Engberg and G. M. Shipton, 'Notes on the Chalcolithic and Early Bronze Age Pottery of Megiddo', *SAOC* 10 (Chicago, 1934, Stages VII-IV.

4. *Megiddo Tombs*, Pl. 3.
5. *Museum Journal*, Philadelphia, XXIV, Pl. III.
6. *AASOR*, XXXII-XXXIII, Pl. 37.
7. J. B. Hennessy, *The Foreign Relations of Palestine during the Early Bronze Age* (London, 1967).
8. *The Pottery of Palestine* (New Haven, 1937).
9. *Relative Chronologies in Old World Archaeology*, ed. R. W. Ehrich (Chicago, 1965).

5   The City States of the Early Bronze Age

The third millennium marks the first appearance of the great empires of the ancient world. It also marks the beginning of the historic period in which written records supplement archaeology. The two developments are interrelated. As communal organization developed, the need was felt for some means of recording contributions required by the central authority, of decisions which were binding on the community, and of events of importance to the community. By the beginning of the third millennium a system of writing was in use in both the Nile and the Tigris–Euphrates valleys. Allied with this was the establishment of a calendar by which events could be recorded and further events given a time-scale. This invention took place in Egypt, probably somewhere about 3000 B.C., under the stimulus of the necessity of calculating the annual beginning of the inundation of the Nile. The Egyptian calendar is the parent of our modern one, and on correlations with Egypt depend all archaeological datings.

These various developments are a measure of the progress by which the towns of the two great river valleys were outstripping those in the rest of the Fertile Crescent. It is generally agreed that two major factors were responsible for this progress, both environmental. A complex society, as distinct from one in which each family produces enough food and artifacts for its own use, depends on a proportion of the community being able to produce enough food to support those craftsmen, traders, exploiters of natural resources such as quarries or mines, who do not produce their own food. The alluvial plains of the river valleys made production of food surpluses possible, so the potential of developing a complex society was greater in those areas. But the alluvial plains could only be fully exploited if the waters of the rivers could be controlled to supply enough and not too much water. Irrigation was therefore an essential. Irrigation requires a controlling organization. It must be planned, the channels constructed, regulations made and enforced as to the use of the water. Power over all aspects of the community life tends to become concentrated in the controlling organization, including that of intercession with the gods to ensure that the agricultural operations are fruitful. Thus control becomes concentrated in the hands of priests or of princes with divine attributes, and the production surpluses tend to come into their hands.

The second environmental factor is that the river valleys lacked many of the other raw materials. Timber, metals, building stone, even flint for making stone tools, had to be brought from a distance, often from considerable distances, such as timber from the Lebanon and copper from the Sinai Peninsula to supply Egypt's needs. These materials had to be bought from agricultural surpluses, or food had to be provided for the traders who went to fetch them. There was thus in the river valleys an exceptional stimulus for the provision of surpluses.

Towards the end of the fourth millennium the areas that lacked this stimulus and this opportunity began to be left behind. In Palestine we have been able to trace the build-up of a sedentary, agricultural population, making parallel progress to that in Egypt and Mesopotamia. The people of the Proto-Urban stage settled themselves down successfully enough for their villages to start growing into towns somewhere about the end of the fourth millennium. The origins of many towns of importance in the historic period can be traced to this stage, on sites that first acquired a sizeable population in the Proto-Urban period. But as far as we can tell, they did not progress beyond the town stage. Until David united the Hebrews about 1000 B.C., under the short-lived United Monarchy, Palestine remained a country of city states. Presumably each of the Bronze Age towns was surrounded by its agricultural lands, with perhaps dependent villages. The agricultural surpluses were enough to provide for modest needs in the way of trade and specialists. Archaeological finds show how modest those needs were. Copper or bronze is rare in the Early Bronze Age, and not really common until the second half of the second millennium. In the third millennium any imported goods are rare, and the demand for specialist craftsmen of any sort cannot have been great. The town lands produced enough food for the population, but could never produce great surpluses to put power in the hands of the local leaders, and no leader ever became powerful enough to establish a hegemony.

Most of this is a matter of inference, based on the interpretation of the archaeological record. Just because the towns of the Mediterranean seaboard did not have the stimulus and opportunity of the river valleys, they did not develop a form of writing for another fifteen hundred years or so. We can only deduce that there was no outstanding political power in Palestine, because if there had been, it would presumably have been mentioned in the Egyptian records. With the establishment of the Old Empire, Egypt became sufficiently powerful to expand its interests beyond its borders. From this time onwards, Palestine was of interest to Egypt as the route connecting the Nile Valley with the rest of the civilized world. The age-long route between Asia and Egypt passed up the Palestine coast and thence inland by the Plain of Esdraelon across the Jordan Valley. Palestine towns, at any rate those fringing the international route, were thenceforward kept under some sort of control at all times at which Egypt was powerful, and their names, or the names of their chiefs, occur in Egyptian records. At no time, however, did Egypt really rule the whole country. Garrisons might be maintained, for instance at Beth-shan, but for the most part selected chiefs were induced to become client-rulers.

Between the different towns and their chiefs there was no doubt rivalry and even warfare. This we can deduce because the towns were protected by walls. An additional reason for this, however, may have been that the whole of the narrow strip of relatively fertile land which makes up Palestine was always to some extent a frontier zone between the Desert and the Sown. As we have seen, the immigrants of the Proto-Urban period were ex-nomads, and though their descendants built up a compact area of permanent settlement, the semi-desert to the east and north-east was populated by their relatives, still nomadic pastoralists, who at intervals cast covetous eyes on the easier and richer life of the coastlands. During the Early Bronze Age they were kept at bay; the unbroken culture of the period shows that there was at least no major incursion, and that if there were any infiltrations, they were absorbed.

Excavations over the last twenty years have produced striking, and largely unexpected, evidence concerning the Early Bronze Age towns in Palestine. As will be seen, the famous sites tend to reach full development towards the end of the Early Bronze Age. We now have evidence of urban development to fully walled town from other sites. It may be relevant that much of this new evidence comes from sites to the east and south of the main development area in

Palestine; certainly these sites are evanescent in archaeological terms, though their life-span may have been some five hundred years.

Simply because the well-known Palestinian sites dominate the conventional archaeology, I refer to these sites as fringe sites. The results from recent excavations are exciting. The site of Bab edh-Dhra' has already been mentioned in connection with the very large Proto-Urban A + C population which buried its dead in an enormous cemetery near the town site. There were far fewer tombs belonging to the Proto-Urban B group, but these were apparently the people who founded the town. Their pottery was found in the levels that preceded the town walls. The town itself has been only slightly investigated, but it has been established that there were two stages of town walls, the earlier constructed of mud-brick, the later of stone; the mud-brick wall had attached towers, and it is possible that towers also existed in the later period. In the cemetery, a new type of burial belongs to the period of the town, though there may be a typological predecessor belonging to the Proto-Urban B group. The dead were deposited in brick-built structures up to 11·50 metres by 5·50 metres in size, only slightly sunk into the ground. The plan was very similar to that of houses of the beginning of the Early Bronze Age, with the entrance on one of the long sides. Within these charnel houses were piles of disarticulated bones and pots, in some cases the piles being up to a metre high. One building contained the remains of about two hundred individuals and more than nine hundred complete pots. The charnel houses were definitely stratified over the Proto-Urban shaft tombs, and the contents covered the whole of the life of the walled town, in period from Early Bronze I (EBI C in American nomenclature) to Early Bronze III. A crescentic axehead resembles one from Jericho Tomb A 114 (p. 104), and though only one sherd of Khirbet Kerak ware (p. 109) was found, this scarcity may be on regional rather than chronological grounds. In at least some cases, the last stage before the door of the chamber was sealed was the lighting of a fire on top of the bones.

The second of the important newly discovered sites is Arad. This lies in the Negeb about 18½ miles (30km.) east-north-east of Beersheba. The area is arid, and until the intensive irrigation with water from Galilee carried out by the Israelis, agriculture must have had many difficulties. Agriculture was, however, certainly carried out by the early inhabitants, for grain and storage silos have been found. It must, however, have been chancy, and the site would not have been chosen purely on its agricultural potential. There are no springs or wells, and the inhabitants must have depended solely on cisterns, for which the rock is well-suited, with possibly a larger general reservoir. These difficulties did not deter the inhabitants of the late fourth millennium from building a walled town covering an area of about 25 acres (10·18ha.). As at Bab edh-Dhra', the site was first occupied before the walls were built. The pottery from this first level is described as Chalcolithic, but it has not been published, and it is not clear whether it is related to the Ghassulian culture or to the Proto-Urban; the latter is more likely, since there is said to be no break between this level and the second, to which the walls belong, which is certainly Early Bronze I.

Only a small area of the town has so far been cleared, but it shows a full urban development. The encircling walls have semicircular towers, and their line can be followed for most of the circuit of the site. The houses are solid and well-built. The plan is stereotyped, a long, narrow room, entered on one of the long sides, with a bench round the walls of the room. Adjacent are subsidiary cook and storage houses and courtyards. Twin temples were found of the same broad-house plan, calling to mind the Ghassulian temple at Ein Gedi (Pl. 34), and the plan will also be seen at 'Ai and Megiddo.

The occupation of the town dates from Early Bronze I (I C) and continues to the end of Early Bronze II. It is of special interest that Egyptian vessels are found in all the occupation levels, and the comparisons are sufficiently close to show that Arad flourished during the period of the first Egyptian Dynasty, c. 3100 to 2890 B.C. The Carbon-14 dates, however, suggest dates some two hundred years later, and we may have to wait for further information. The dates on the pottery seem to carry conviction. This strong Egyptian connection also probably gives us the reason for the existence of such an imposing town in such an inhospitable area. Arad is an important staging-post on the road from the mouth of the Nile, along the south-eastern fringe of the Mediterranean, across the northern Negeb via Beersheba to the Dead Sea. One of the products needed by the Egyptians from the Dead Sea was asphalt, and many lumps of asphalt were found in the Arad houses. It could also be the route by which copper from the Arabah was carried to Egypt, though the main source of supply was Sinai.

The town was destroyed towards the end of Early Bronze II and never rebuilt. Its *raison d'être* may no longer have existed. We do not

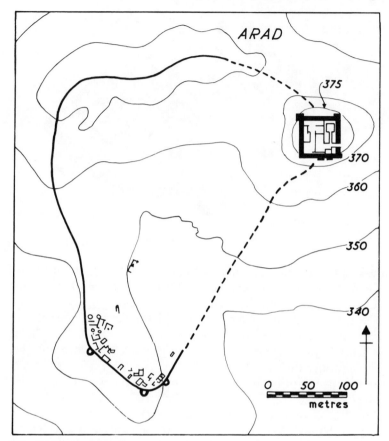

Fig. 17. Plan of Arad

yet know enough about the internal history of the Early Bronze Age to say why some towns disappear before Early Bronze III and others appear only to have been founded then. However, the amount of evidence is growing.

From these fringe sites, we turn to the main central sites. The gradual infiltration of groups from the east and north-east towards the end of the fourth millennium has already been mentioned. Bab edh-Dhra' may well have been a major site of newcomers from the east. Arad may also owe its origins to such a group. Of the main central sites, Jericho was especially in danger for until in 1958 a great new road was cut down through the eastern mountains bounding the Jordan Valley to cross the valley just north of the Dead Sea,

89

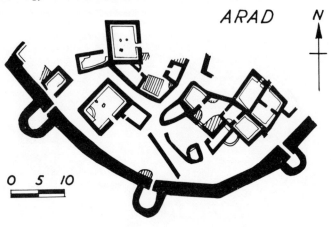

Fig. 18. Houses, streets, and town walls at Arad

Jericho lay on the best route from the east to the central uplands. The Israelites under Joshua were following this route when Joshua sent his spies with the instructions 'go view the land, and Jericho'. The recent excavations have shown what importance the inhabitants of Jericho placed on their defences.

The walls of Jericho on the north, west, and south sides crown the mound which the successive Pre-Pottery Neolithic towns had built up to a height of nearly 50 feet (15m.). On the west they almost exactly overlie the line of the Pre-Pottery Neolithic town walls, though separated from them by a thick layer of débris. On the north and south they recede to the brow of the mound, respectively 100 and 84 feet (30·5 and 25·5m.) within the line of the earlier walls. This was no doubt to obtain the advantage of a steep exterior slope. Much of the east side of the circuit has been destroyed by the modern road which cuts into the foot of the mound. The line of the walls is, however, indicated by a large oblong tower excavated by Professor Garstang, and by a chance cutting made in connection with a military water-point. This lies just south of Square H V on the plan (Fig. 4), and runs on an oblique line which passes beneath the road just east of Square H V. It is therefore apparent that even at this stage the tell had a pronounced tilt downwards to the east, almost certainly because the buildings always sloped down towards the spring. There is no means of establishing where the spring issued from the ground at that period, whether inside or just outside the walls. A gate almost certainly must lie somewhere

here, for it would be needed for access to the cultivated fields to the east.

At Jericho the town walls are built of unbaked mud-bricks, for this is the natural building material in this neighbourhood, used even today. The bricks are in fact very like those used today, and are quite different from those used in the successive Neolithic periods. The latter were hand-made, in shapes that vary for the different periods. From the Early Bronze Age onwards, they are rectangular slabs made in moulds, usually about 2 inches (·05m.) thick and about 14 inches (·36m.) by 10 inches (·25m.) overall. The bricks are set in mud mortar with fairly thin joints and care is as a rule taken to break the joint. The brickwork rests on a foundation of one or more courses of stone. In the earlier stages, the wall is about 3 feet 6 inches (1·07m.) thick.

Such a wall can make a solid and impressive barrier. It does, however, need constant attention to keep it in repair. The top must be kept solid to prevent water percolating in, erosion of the face must be prevented by plastering, and no denudation allowed to undercut the foundations. In addition to the dangers of deterioration, there was at Jericho a special danger from the forces of nature. The whole of the Jordan Valley is an area of seismic disturbance, and major earthquakes happen on an average four times a century. The excavations have revealed clear evidence of collapses from an earthquake with the face of the wall fallen straight forward on to the contemporary ground level. A rather curious feature in the structure of the walls is possibly intended as an anti-earthquake device. At intervals in the course of the wall, apparently in almost all phases, were cavities about 3 feet (·91m.) wide, and therefore not large enough to have been towers, running almost the whole thickness of the wall. The effect certainly was to localize the collapse, for in places a section would be found to have collapsed to its foundations, while the immediately adjacent section, beyond a cavity, would be standing 10 feet (3·05m.) or so high (Pl. 36).

Finally, the walls of Jericho undoubtedly suffered on occasion from the attacks of enemies. In all the sectors examined, the walls had at least once been subjected to a violent conflagration. It is probable that these fires were not all contemporary, for the walls so affected do not seem to come at the same point in the constructional sequences. More than one attack must have taken the form of setting fire to the walls. The clearest example of this, and the clearest evidence that the firing was the intentional act of an enemy, came from the south end of the tell. Against the outer face of the wall was a layer of ash 3 feet (·91m.) thick, derived from an enormous pile of brushwood (Pl. 37). The town wall at this stage was 17 feet (5·18m.) thick, and the fire had burnt the bricks red through the whole thickness, aided by the fact that the bricks of the wall had been tied together by timbers, again possibly an anti-earthquake measure, and these had been set on fire. The purpose of the fire can hardly have been simply the destruction of the wall, for in actual effect it hardened and strengthened it by burning the bricks. The disastrous effect was undoubtedly on the town inside. Everywhere where the inner face of the wall had been cleared, houses have been found to be built up against it. The firing of the wall would therefore set these houses alight, and the fire would no doubt rapidly spread to the rest of the town, for much timber was used, and the roofs seem often to have been made of reeds.

The walls of Jericho therefore had a chequered history. On the west side of the tell seventeen successive phases of building and rebuilding could be traced. This does not of course mean that the whole circuit was rebuilt this number of times, for some collapses were undoubtedly local. It is not possible to tell how many building phases are present without cutting right through the wall. Sometimes the rebuilding took the form of a thickening wall built against the interior or exterior of the earlier wall. Sometimes the collapsed wall survived in the shape of an inverted U, and the rebuild consisted of a capping which might have foundations on the same level as the original wall, thus completely masking it. To establish the complete history would therefore require a very large number of cuts.

A number of interesting features emerged from the various clearances made. On the west side there was found to be a semicircular external tower, as substantial as many medieval towers. This is a very unexpectedly early occurrence of this type of addition to a town wall, and its purpose is not very clear, since at a period in which projectiles were not in use it would not seem to add to the strength of the defences; archery was certainly not in use then, and there is not even any evidence of sling-stones. At the north end of the tell there was also an external tower, at one stage rectangular and at another semicircular. Here it is possible that it was associated with a gateway. The slope of the mound is more gentle here than on the west side, and protecting the main town wall was a claw-like projection, overlapping the tower, but with a possible entrance way between the two. The plan is like the clavicula which protects the gates of Roman forts, but the town wall of the period could not be fully excavated to see if in fact there had been an entrance here.

The most unexpected feature discovered was that at a number of places the wall had been protected by an external ditch. This was the case even on the steep western side of the mound, where four separate re-cuttings of the ditch could be traced. They belonged apparently to the later stages in the history of the wall, but it is possible that later re-cuttings removed the evidence of earlier phases.

The connection between the history of the defences and that of the town inside has not yet been fully established. It was not possible to excavate an appreciable area immediately adjacent to the walls, so the correlation of the wall phases and those of the building sequence inside is dependent on the associated pottery, which has not yet been worked out. It is likely that three points will emerge. It seems probable that there is a stage of fully developed occupation before the town was actually walled; on the south side there appear to be substantial structures stretching farther down the slope than the subsequent wall, and the same may be true at the north end, but there is always the possibility that walls on the edge of the mound have been completely removed by denudation.

The second point is that there is a very marked change in architecture in the course of the period. The earliest houses are very substantial, the rooms larger and the walls thicker than in the case of the later ones, but they are much less regularly built. The rooms themselves often have rounded ends, or in some cases are wholly circular, but there seems to be no accepted town-planning system; the buildings lie at all angles, and there are changes in axis in successive building stages. The occupation also seems to have been rather more sordid, for there are thick levels of midden deposit in several places, indicating that rubbish was allowed to accumulate in the courtyards and streets.

The later stage of occupation was probably considerably the longer. In it, in each of the areas excavated, the houses assume a much more regular plan, and are consistently orientated on a north–south axis. Though the walls are less substantial than those of the earlier period, they are nevertheless solid and well built. A feature of this later stage is the large number of brick-built silos which were associated with the houses. In them grain would have been stored from one year to the next, and they are evidence of a flourishing agricultural community. The inhabitants of this stage did not apparently allow the rubbish to accumulate around the houses, but threw it over the town walls, particularly at the north-west angle. This practice may have been more sanitary, but it cannot have been conducive to the efficiency of the defences.

There was a considerable use of timber in the buildings. The evidence of this mostly came from burnt beams lying on the floors of rooms, and the timber was therefore used in the roofs and ceilings. A number of post-holes could be traced, but there does not seem to have been a consistent use of roof supports on the central axis. The rooms on the whole were not large enough to require this.

The third point is that the buildings seem to follow the slopes of the pre-existing mound, with little attempt at levelling up. On the east side in particular, above the spring, the buildings of the later stage (the earlier one was not reached in this area) slope down very steeply from west to east, probably allowing for an approach to the spring. On the summit of the mound, however, there was also a distinct slope outwards towards the walls, with the buildings stepping down in a series of terraces.

The picture of Jericho in the Early Bronze Age is therefore of a flourishing town, closely built up of solid and substantial houses. The general plan seems to have remained consistent, at any rate in the second phase, and the town wall seems to have followed approximately the same line. There were, however, some slight alterations in size. At the north end the wall was at one stage advanced some feet down the slope, but appears to have receded to the original line at a later period. On the west side, the earlier walls were all on the same line, but the fifteenth building stage was advanced 22 feet 6 inches (6·86m.) down the slope, and an appreciable area was thus added to the later stages of the town.

Tell el Far'ah, like Jericho, grew into a town early in the Early Bronze Age, developing out of the Proto-Urban settlement. The site is one very suitable for an important town. It lies on a hill that rises steeply on the north and south, and fairly steeply on the east; only on the west is there a gentle slope joining the hill to the main mountain range. At its foot to the north and south are excellent springs, of which the valleys curve round the foot of the hill and join to form the Wadi Far'ah. The site itself commands the Wadi Far'ah, which is the only wide pass leading from the Jordan Valley into the heart of Palestine, and which is continued by a narrower valley up to Shechem, lying on the main north–south route along the backbone of the hill country. Another road leads north from Tell el Far'ah to Beth-shan. The surrounding hill slopes and valleys provide good agricultural land. Strategically and environmentally the site is excellent.

The Early Bronze Age levels have been examined at two fairly widely separated points. The town was therefore large, though its full extent is not known. The completion of the excavation shows that from the beginning of the Early Bronze Age the settlement was defended by a town wall.

The wall of Period I was of mud-bricks on stone foundations, and, like the first houses, it was built directly over the remains of the Proto-Urban (or, as Père de Vaux preferred, Pre-Urban) period. It is to this first stage in the defences that belongs the gateway on the west side, with its two very well preserved brick-built towers projecting outwards from the wall. The wall has been traced almost the complete length of the west edge of the summit plateau, with some evidence that there was a projecting tower at each extremity. The remains of the wall peter out at the north end, and the line of the north wall was not established; it lay, however, appreciably to the north of the later rampart. To the south it is suggested that no defences were required, owing to the steepness of the slope, and the eastern perimeter has not been investigated. These defences date to early in Early Bronze I. It seems probable that the people who built them came from an area in which building in rectangular, form-made, mud-bricks was already fully established. At Far'ah, urbanization certainly seems to be imposed by newcomers and not to develop out of the preceding period. The later stone wall, with which the brick-built gate continued in use, comes at the beginning of Early Bronze II. To the north, it was set back from its predecessor.

Within the town the rooms were rectangular, many of them of considerable size. The surviving parts of the walls were mostly of stone, but some at least of them were carried up in mud-brick. In the larger rooms there was often a row of slabs which must have carried uprights to support the roof; in other cases uprights apparently stood on slabs against the side walls. In several cases a low bench runs along one or more sides of the room. Five successive building levels were found, closely linked in plan and in the associated finds. The first two can be dated to Early Bronze (EB) I, the last two to EB II, and the third comes about at the transition between EB I and II. In the northern area excavated, the EB I houses were destroyed by fire, but this does not occur in the western site, so it may have been only a local catastrophe.

The greatest change came with the fourth period, at the beginning of EB II. For the first time, the defences of the town achieved massive proportions. On the northern side, these consisted of a great stone rampart, over 27 feet (8·23m.) wide and surviving to a height of 6 feet (1·83m.), with the exterior protected by a glacis of beaten earth. On the west side, it is even more imposing. There, it was built of mud-brick, of considerable width, surviving in places to a height of 13 feet (3·96m.), in which the earlier gateway continued in use. One can presumably infer that at the beginning of EB II conditions were becoming unsettled. This may be because of pressure from nomadic tribes from the east, for the Wadi Far'ah route would lay the town open to such incursions, but more probably it is due to increased competition and rivalry between the growing number of city states.

One extremely interesting find, in the buildings of Period 3, transitional from EB I to EB II, was a pottery kiln (Pl. 96). This is a type in which the fire is in a lower chamber, and the pots are stacked on a floor through which flues penetrate from the combustion chamber beneath. The method is a great improvement on firing pots with the fuel stacked round them, which was apparently the method up till now. It is in fact the type of kiln which remained in use until the Roman period.

The town of Tell el Far'ah was completely abandoned before the beginning of EB III. The brick rampart on the western site collapsed at the end of the Period 5 occupation, its ruins spilling over the houses of the period. On top of the ruins, some more houses of the same type were built, but their life was apparently not long. They were abandoned, and there is then a complete gap in the occupation of the site for some seven hundred years. As far as one can judge from the history of other sites, this is not due to political causes. It may simply be that the site was subject to malaria. Until very recent health measures, the population of the villages in the vicinity was strongly infected with this disease, and it was perhaps for this reason that such a particularly important site was abandoned at a period when other towns were flourishing.

At Megiddo, as at Jericho and Tell el Far'ah, a Proto-Urban occupation was succeeded by an Early Bronze Age town. The mound at Megiddo is immense, and the air photograph (P. 35) shows what a very small proportion Area BB, the only area of the city proper cleared to the lower levels, forms of the whole town. Only an indication is therefore given of the history of the site during the period. The picture is unfortunately rendered less clear than it might have been by the somewhat summary methods of excavation.[1] It would appear that there was an occupation during EB I and II, which was probably of fully developed urban type, but of which only rather scanty and confused remains survive.[2] There is no evidence as to whether there was a town wall at this period. In EB III there was a major town-planning development. Hitherto, the buildings had followed the natural slope of the rock. In EB III some very massive retaining walls were built, behind which flat terraces were built up, and an elaborate new town plan laid out (Fig. 19). On the lower terrace is a monumental building with large rectangular rooms. On the upper is a road flanked by buildings, of which only the fringe was excavated. Among them is a very interesting feature. It is a conical stone structure, surviving to a height of 1·40 metres, and 8 metres wide at this height. A flight of steps leads up to the top (Pl. 41). This is undoubtedly to be interpreted as an altar, and the overlying débris was full of animal bones and fragments of pottery, presumably derived from sacrificial offerings. The lower terrace wall was interpreted by the excavators as a town wall. Though it was certainly massive enough for this purpose (Pl. 40), house walls are built against its lower side, which would obviously not be the case if it were a defensive wall. The massiveness is to be accounted for by the fact that the terrace fill behind it was about 5 metres thick. It is highly probable that a town with such an elaborate layout was in fact walled, but the excavators did not locate the line; the edge of the buildings below the great terrace wall is destroyed by erosion, and the town wall may have disappeared in this process.

The other great city of the Plain of Esdraelon is Beth-shan, a site represented today by a mound as imposing in size as that of Megiddo (Pl. 42). A prolonged campaign of excavations was carried out here by the Museum of the University of Pennsylvania, starting in 1921. The main clearance only reached the level of the Middle Bronze Age town. Beneath this, a sounding, 24 metres by 16 metres, was sunk to virgin soil, revealing Neolithic, Chalcolithic, Proto-Urban, and Early Bronze Age levels. The site therefore had as prolonged an occupation as that of Megiddo, and like Megiddo was probably a town of importance in the Early Bronze Age. The area cleared did not of course reveal much in the way of details of the successive stages, and no detailed report on the finds has ever

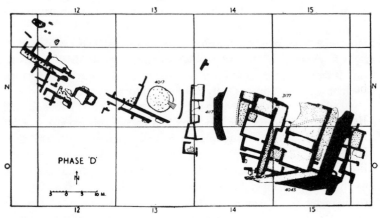

Fig. 19. Plan of Megiddo area BB in EB III

appeared.[3] As at the other sites already described, the Early Bronze Age town developed direct from the Proto-Urban occupation, in which the excavation evidence suggests that brick-built houses had already appeared. The transition to the Early Bronze Age would appear from the pottery to come in Stratum XIV, when the scattered houses of the earlier levels were replaced by buildings with closely built rooms of rectangular plan. These, as at Jericho and Tell el Far'ah, were associated with brick-lined storage silos. The succeeding Level XIII also contained well-built houses. It is to be dated to EB II, and was destroyed by fire, though there is no means of telling whether this was a general catastrophe or merely a local incident. Levels XII and XI were not interesting architecturally, for the houses were small and insignificant. They are marked, however, by the sudden appearance of a particularly beautiful imported pottery, known as Khirbet Kerak ware from the site south of the Sea of Galilee where it was first found in quantity. It is discussed below (pp. 109–11); there is no doubt that it represents a foreign influence, but there is nothing at Beth-shan to suggest it was brought by invaders, for side by side with it the native wares continue, and there is no significant change in architectural features.

Level XI is the last of the EB levels at Beth-shan. It is difficult to judge with certainty, since only a selection of the pottery is published, but it does not seem to last to the end of the Early Bronze Age; the EB pottery is not, for instance, as late as that from 'Ai. Mixed with the material published from both Strata XII and XI are

98

vessels belonging to the following Intermediate Early Bronze–Middle Bronze period, and even some Middle Bronze Age vessels, so there were clearly intrusions, but it would appear that the Early Bronze Age town came to an end midway through EB III for some unexplained reason, and, like Tell el Far'ah, Beth-shan did not become a town again until Middle Bronze II.

Another town in northern Palestine important in the Early Bronze Age is Khirbet Kerak. The site gave its name to the beautiful red and black burnished pottery that appears in Palestine in EB III (pp. 109–11), for many sherds were picked up on the surface by Professor Albright in 1925, before it had been encountered in excavations. The site lies just west of the place where the Jordan issues from the Sea of Galilee, and its remains appear to cover an area of some 50 acres (22·5ha.). Only two small areas have been excavated, at the north and south ends of the site, but as thick Early Bronze Age occupation layers appear in both, it is probable that the town of this period extended over the whole site. The first settlement, founded on virgin soil, dates from the Proto-Urban period, with pottery including the grey burnished Esdraelon ware of Proto-Urban C. What other elements it includes is not clear as the material is not fully published. Occupation was in huts half sunk into the ground, as in other sites of this and the preceding period.

This Proto-Urban occupation was succeeded by houses associated with EB I pottery, and we would thus appear to have another example of the direct development of an EB town from a settlement first established in the Proto-Urban period. Above these houses were others dated by the pottery to EB II. Belonging to one or other of these settlements (the report is not clear on this point) was a town wall of mud-bricks about 8 metres wide. The final Early Bronze Age stage was apparently the most important of all, with deposits more than 2 metres in depth. These deposits were characterized by the presence of many vessels of Khirbet Kerak ware, and the phase therefore belongs to EB III. A stonebuilt town wall was at first ascribed to the period, but it subsequently became apparent that it probably belonged to the Middle Bronze Age. The most important building was a remarkable one, some 30 metres square, obviously a public building, but of uncertain use. Set in exceedingly massive outer walls were eight circles in an average diameter of 8 metres. Radiating from their walls like spokes of a wheel were four partition walls, which, however, did not reach the centre of the circles (as it were leaving the hubs of the wheels missing). Within this massive outer wall was an oblong hall paved with pebbles, and a court 25 metres long, to which a gateway in the outer wall gave access. Finds of ovens, figurines, and burnt animal bones inclined the excavators to identify the structure as a shrine, but they put forward an alternative suggestion that it was a public granary.

With the exception of Jericho, all the sites so far discussed lie in northern Palestine. This is largely due to the chances of excavation, which has directed the attention of archaeologists in recent years to the great upstanding mounds in that area, and sites in the hill country, most difficult of excavation, have been neglected. An important site in the hill country to be excavated comparatively recently is that of 'Ai, identified in the imposing remains known as Et Tell covering a hill some 10 miles (15km.) north of Jerusalem. This was excavated by Madame Marquet-Krause on behalf of Baron Edmond de Rothschild between 1933 and 1935. Unfortunately, Madame Marquet-Krause died before she could make a full publication of her results, and the volume recording the work is little more than that of an undigested field register. The site is of peculiar interest, since, according to the biblical account, 'Ai was captured by Joshua after the fall of Jericho. The excavations showed, however, that the site was abandoned at the end of the Early Bronze Age, and was not reoccupied until well on in the Iron Age. One explanation suggested is that confusion has arisen between the history of 'Ai and that of the nearby site of Bethel.

From the point of view of the history of the Early Bronze Age, the remains at 'Ai (Pl. 43) are, however, interesting on their own account. Recent excavations under the direction of Professor J. A. Callaway have shown that 'Ai can provide full and dramatic evidence of the history of Palestine in the Early Bronze Age. Reference has already been made (p. 70) to the evidence of Proto-Urban occupation on the site, mainly from tombs, but also from a village on the summit of the hill. This was unfortified, and its occupants were certainly related to the Proto-Urban B group at Jericho, whence they may have come. The next stage was the construction of a planned walled city enclosing 27.5 acreas (10·93 ha.). The focal area of that town was where the hill rose to a rocky knoll on the west side, bounded by steep slopes from north-west to south-west. From this the town walls sloped down to enclose a less steeply sloping area to the east. The rocky knoll or acropolis (Pl. 44) is dominated by a long, narrow building, with an entrance in the centre of a long side. This was certainly a temple at a later stage, and probably should be so interpreted in the first stage; reference has already been made to buildings with similar plans in the Chalcolithic and Proto-Urban periods (pp. 63 and 81). This building and the accompanying defences which included four gates, are dated to Early Bronze I (EBIC on the American scheme), and correspond well with Jericho Tomb 108 and the first Urban stage at Bab edh-Dhra', with connections with the early First Dynasty of Egypt. Callaway believes that the formative force in the creation of this town came from the north, from coastal Syria and Anatolia.

This phase came to an end *c*. 2860 B.C. with a violent destruction, and in Early Bronze II the acropolis and walls were rebuilt with some modifications. This city was also violently destroyed by fire, probably as the result of an earthquake, and Carbon-14 tests suggest a date of *c*. 2720 B.C., near the end of the Third Dynasty of Egypt. The succeeding Early Bronze III A city is of particular interest because of the evidence of Egyptian influence. This is most strikingly shown in the temple. The rebuilt wall was constructed in neatly hammer-dressed stones set in mud-mortar giving the impression of bricks, an Egyptian style belonging to the time of the Third Dynasty, and the stone bases of the roof-supports trimmed to careful rectangles with the use of a copper saw, again a technology found only in Egypt. The whole building was finely finished with plaster. In the building were cult vessels in Egyptian alabaster.

The EB III A city was destroyed *c*. 2550 B.C. by enemies coming from the north, who brought with them Khirbet Kerak ware. After the destruction, again with evidence of burning, the defences were repaired, resulting in a wall 8 metres wide and still standing 7 metres high. The change of culture is shown especially strikingly in the temple. The adjacent ruler's house was left buried in débris, and the temple building was taken over as the ruler's residence. The cultic centre was transferred to a nearby building against the so-called citadel wall, which was remodelled to serve this purpose, with a tripartite plan ancestral in conception to that of later Semitic sanctuaries, including Solomon's temple. To it were transferred cult objects from the original sanctuary, and with these were mixed Khirbet Kerak ware and other northern-orientated cult objects. The Egyptian-orientated shrine was not only displaced from its original centre, but the religion of which the new sanctuary was evidence became a composite affair. The Early Bronze III B city was destroyed, perhaps by avenging Egyptians, *c*. 2400 B.C.

The evidence from 'Ai, therefore, is of great importance for a number of reasons. Events covering the whole of the Early Bronze Age have been studied in some detail, and the number of sweeping destructions have produced evidence of clearly defined stages. The finds provided material for a number of Carbon-14 tests and these, with evidence of well-defined Egyptian contacts, have given a chronological framework for much of the Early Bronze Age.

For many of the other great sites of central Palestine our information is meagre, for none of them has been excavated in recent years and older archaeological techniques could not disentangle the difficult and scanty evidence. At Jerusalem itself, there was certainly occupation in the Proto-Urban period, for some of the most beautiful specimens found of Proto-Urban B pottery come from a tomb discovered on the slopes of Ophel,[4] the spur to the south of the present city which was the nucleus of the pre-Israelite site. Excavations on the slopes and summit of the ridge have produced Early Bronze Age pottery, but only fragments of occupation levels. It cannot yet be said if there was an actual town. The widespread area over which finds have been made makes it quite possible. Gezer was also excavated many years ago, and the finds cannot be satisfactorily interpreted. The site, however, was certainly occupied from the Proto-Urban period on through the Early Bronze Age, on the evidence of finds in the tombs. Tell Nasbeh and, farther north, Samaria were not occupied during the Early Bronze Age, though there had been Proto-Urban villages on both sites.

A site that has for long been known to have Early Bronze Age occupation is Ras el 'Ain, identified as the biblical Aphek and now known to Israeli archaeologists as Tel Aphek. It overlooks the coastal plain near Tel Aviv, and is situated near the source of the River Yarkon. Early Bronze pottery was first found here in excavations connected with water works in 1935–36, and archaeological exploration was carried out in 1961 and 1972. Occupation began in the late fourth millennium, and the town, 30 acres in size, was walled in Early Bronze I. Not much of the town of the period has yet been cleared, but the town lasted until Early Bronze III.

It is only when we come to southern Palestine that we have satisfactory evidence again, though it is still scanty. Tell Duweir, identified as the biblical site of Lachish, is the mightiest mound in Palestine (Pl. 45), the 18 acres (7·29ha.) of its summit being equalled by Gezer and exceeded only by Hazor, which has a later origin, and its height of 40 metres probably surpasses the man-made deposits of any site. Occupation in the neighbourhood goes back to the Chalcolithic period, but the Proto-Urban groups of the north do not seem to have penetrated to this region. In the course of the Early Bronze Age, occupation began to be concentrated on the site of the city mound. Unfortunately, excavations had to be suspended before the lower levels were reached, and knowledge of the remains of the early periods only comes from caves and tombs, and from a single cutting into the side of the mound.[5] From the available evidence, it would appear that the history of Tell Duweir as a town begins fairly late in the Early Bronze Age. None of the material is characteristic of EB I, so it may be that the Early Bronze Age civilization did not penetrate into southern Palestine in the first stages. In EB II some of the inhabitants still lived in caves, for instance Caves 1519 and 1535, but the excavation of the lowest levels of the tell was insufficient to say whether the town site also began to be occupied at this period. In the succeeding period, these caves were used for burials, which in itself is significant of a change of dwelling habits, and the lowest excavated levels on the edge of the tell show that occupation was now being concentrated in that area. In the section cut into the edge of the mound, pottery types found elsewhere at the end of EB II and the beginning of EB III occur in the lowest levels, and Khirbet Kerak ware occurs on bedrock, so the spread of the settlement to the full extent of the later town certainly did not take place until the beginning of EB III. There is no evidence as to the size of the settlement, or whether it was walled. None of the tomb groups published belongs exclusively to the last stages of EB III, but the evidence is too scanty to establish whether at Tell Duweir, like Beth-shan, occupation was interrupted before the end of the Early Bronze Age.

Tell Beit Mirsim lies, like Tell Duweir, in the fringes of the hill country, in a semi-arid area which could be fertile in years of good rain, and, like Tell Duweir, could obviously support a sedentary population, since it was the site of a settlement from the later stages of the Early Bronze Age until the end of Early Iron II. It did not, however, attract settlement until late in the Early Bronze Age, and the remains of the period are slight. The pottery published is scanty, and it is not easy to relate it to finds elsewhere, but it must certainly come late in EB III. No traces were found of any town wall, and the architectural remains were fragmentary.

The history of Tell Hesi, in the same general neighbourhood as Tell Duweir and Tell Beit Mirsim, is probably similar. The excavation of the site was begun as long ago as 1890 by Sir Flinders Petrie, and it was in fact at Tell Hesi that the foundation was laid in Palestine of stratigraphical excavation and of the recording of pottery in relation to the building sequence. The records therefore require much reinterpretation. But one important fact emerges in connection with the earliest occupation. A group of copper weapons is recorded from the lowest levels.[6] These include an axehead of crescentic form which can be exactly paralleled by an axehead from a fairly late EB III tomb at Jericho (Fig. 20.*1–2*).[7] This serves to place the earliest occupation of Tell Hesi in EB III, and is also interesting evidence of the increased use of copper weapons at this period, for hitherto they had been rare.

The extension of the Early Bronze Age culture to southern Palestine does not, however, seem to have been on a large scale. At Tell Fara and Tell Ajjul, sites at which considerable excavation has taken place, no traces have appeared of a settlement at this period, though they became important towns in the second millennium.

This outline of the history of the various sites will have suggested that much of the history of Palestine in the Early Bronze Age has still to be recorded. In all the sites which give indications of having been important towns at this period, only limited areas have been examined, or else the excavation methods have not been able to produce a clear picture. But stray finds and surface exploration have

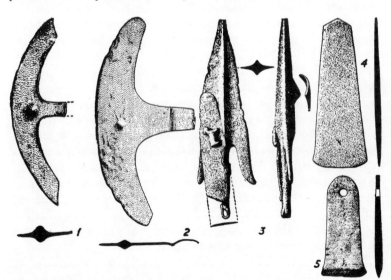

Fig. 20. Copper weapons from Jericho (1) and Tell Hesi (2–5). ⅕

added emphasis to the widespread nature of the culture. In Trans-jordan in particular surface exploration has located many sites of the period, but none of them has been examined with the exception of Bab edh-Dhra'. In Palestine proper the scantiness of the evidence is in part due to the very nature of the culture. In very many cases the Early Bronze Age towns are the ancestors of the later ones, and their remains therefore lie buried deep beneath the later accumulation.

As the picture is outlined at present the major towns, and those starting earliest and lasting longest, are in the north and centre with the towns of southern Palestine only growing up later. This is partly due to the earlier history of the areas. The preceding Proto-Urban cultures, described in the last chapter, do not occur in southern Palestine, where the Chalcolithic of the Ghassulian and allied groups may have continued later. On the pottery evidence, it is out of the Proto-Urban cultures that that of the Early Bronze Age was evolved. The Ghassulian groups seem to have lacked the necessary impetus to develop into towns, and it was from the north that the habit of town-dwelling spread to the south, perhaps not much before EB III. The other factor stimulating development in the north was probably contacts with the towns of coastal Syria. The seaports of the Phoenician coast early tended towards urban development, for they were dependent on trade rather than agriculture, and contacts with Egypt were established at a very early date. The first town at Byblos is dated to *c*. 3100 B.C., and there are many similarities in form and technique between the Byblos pottery and that of Palestine at this stage. The impulse towards urban development may have come from the same direction.

In this generalization, the fringe sites of Bab edh-Dhra' and Arad have been left aside, for they seem both in distance and character to be extraneous. They are walled cities of great size set in the desert. Both start from the very beginning of the Early Bronze Age but hardly last into EB III. In due course evidence will probably be found as to how they are to be integrated into the general plan.

The summary of the evidence from the sites excavated will have shown that it is not possible to gain a very clear picture of the way of life of the people of Palestine at the time. In no single instance have we enough of a town plan to say if the houses were all on a similar scale, or whether some exceeded others in size sufficiently to indicate markedly different wealth and social status. On the whole, the evidence suggests reasonable prosperity but no very great wealth. The population was apparently mainly agricultural, and there is little evidence of trade. There were some contacts with Egypt, which will be referred to in connection with the pottery, but most of the objects found were probably home produced. The most striking evidence of this is the relative scarcity of metal. The period is conventionally known as the Early Bronze Age, but in fact there is no certain evidence that bronze was used, and even copper is not very common. As has already been described, copper was worked in Palestine in the Chalcolithic, and occasional implements are found from then on. Copper beads are found in EB III tombs, and the weapons found at Jericho and Tell Hesi suggest that at this stage it was coming into more common use. But the population was certainly not dependent on it for everyday use, and flint remained much the most common material for tools and weapons.

Not much evidence survives as to religion, though gradually some information is being recovered about sanctuaries or temples. The most interesting is that at 'Ai, with an original building of the broad-room type in which there were suggestions of Egyptian influence in the cult objects, which in the second building stage was emphasized by a distinctively Egyptian building style. The cult and its appurtenances were, however, rudely displaced in Early Bronze III, and were moved to a converted dwelling-house. The new sanctuary had a tripartite plan, with an innermost Holy of Holies. The cult objects of the earlier sanctuary were transferred to this new one, where they were found with other objects suggestive of northern influence.

The twin temples at Arad were of the same general form, and adjacent to them were other rooms and objects possibly connected with religious usage.

In 1959, a sanctuary was identified at Tell el Far'ah. It lasted throughout the Early Bronze Age, but the most convincing remains belong to the first period, early in EB I. A large room had an open front at the east end. Its area was divided into two by a somewhat oblique kerb of bricks on which there stood a rectangular stone structure, perhaps an altar. To the west of this kerb, the walls were flanked by benches 25 centimetres high, widening into a platform in the north-west corner. It is suggested that this area formed the *cella* of the sanctuary. The plan is clearly very different from those at 'Ai and Arad, but we have so little comparative material that we cannot interpret the significance. This sanctuary belonged only to the first period; its successors had less distinctive features, but could also have been sanctuaries.

The burial practices do not seem to indicate any complicated belief in a life after death, though the dead were considered to have some needs. The best evidence on this comes from a series of tombs at Jericho which covered almost the whole of the Early Bronze Age. Throughout the period the dead were buried in tombs with multiple interments, twenty or so in the earlier tombs, rising to fifty or a hundred in the later ones. With them were placed bowls and jugs, presumably containing, or symbolizing, food and drink, and little juglets presumably for oil or scent. The only personal ornaments seem to have been beads, of carnelian, bone, shell, stone, or frit. The tombs were large rock-cut chambers, but in every case the roof and most of the entrance shaft had disappeared in subsequent erosion, so little could be established about their form. The burial practices were strange. Apparently the bodies were originally placed in the tombs complete. But when the available space became full, many of the bones of the earlier burials were thrown out. Most of the bones are found completely disarticulated; even if a trunk is complete, it may lack some limbs, and though large numbers of skulls were found, sometimes placed together against the wall of the tomb, the number of long bones are quite insufficient to account for the rest of the body. It would seem that even before the flesh had completely decayed, it was no longer felt necessary to treat the body with any reverence. The skull alone remained worthy of care, and it alone was left with any consistency in the tomb.

Much of the evidence of the distribution of the Early Bronze Age towns, and of their relative dates, comes from the pottery, which is very abundant on all sites of the period. Technically, the better-class ware is of quite high quality, and very attractive in appearance. The attractiveness is due more to the surface finish than to the forms, which are relatively simple. The especial characteristic of the period is a burnished slip, usually red, but occasionally black. The burnishing, always by hand, is sometimes continuous, and sometimes in criss-cross or other patterns, and the ware is a pleasure to handle. This practice of burnishing was coming in during the Proto-Urban period. It was hardly found in the Proto-Urban A pottery of Jericho, but almost half this pottery in the Tell el Far'ah tombs was treated in this way and it is also found at Bab edh-Dhra'. It does not, however, reach its full development until the Early Bronze Age. Another type of surface treatment, found mainly on jars, is decoration in bands of red or brown. In the north the bands show veining, as if from the hairs of the brush, and is known as grain-wash; in central and southern Palestine the bands are solid, and the technique is derived from the Proto-Urban B pottery.

One reason for the improved technical quality of the pottery is due to a factor already mentioned in connection with the finds at Tell el Far'ah. This is the use of a proper kiln for the firing of the pottery, with a separate combustion chamber. Most of the pottery of the period is well and evenly fired. The second reason is the increased use of a potter's wheel. The first tentative beginnings of the use of a tournette or primitive wheel are found in the Proto-Urban period, when many of the bowls have a smooth and regular rim. The body of the vessel was apparently first made by hand, for the lower part is quite noticeably irregular, and then it is placed on some form of turntable, and the rim is smoothed. This practice was developed during the Early Bronze Age. The form of wheel was probably improved and became faster, though it was never a true fast wheel. For a long time, however, the practice continued of making part of the vessel by hand. Only in EB III were some of the smaller bowls made entirely on the wheel, and throughout the period the larger vessels were hand-made except for the rim. In spite of this, vessels were made of a very great size, so large that intact vessels hardly ever survive. The type of jar known as the hole-mouth jar, neckless with a simple in-curved rim, which was used for cooking and for storage, may be as much as 3 feet (·91m.) in height, and the storage jars, with short necks, usually collar-rims, and ledge-handle, may be equally large.

The development of the pottery is the basis for the evidence on which the history of the various sites has been outlined earlier in this chapter. The degree of definition is not yet very close, for the number of closely stratified groups is not yet great. In Figs. 21–3, 25–6 are shown selected forms from tomb groups at Jericho which seem to belong to EB I, EB II, and early EB III and mid-EB III. In the first group, some of the forms, such as the bowl (Fig. 21.*4*) and the juglet (Fig. 21.*8*), are derived from Proto-Urban A, and the juglet (Fig. 21.*12*) from Proto-Urban B. In the next group the same forms continue, and other forms derived from Proto-Urban A, the bag-shaped juglets and jars (Fig. 22.*11–14*), are also found, as well as later forms such as the bowls with inverted rim, and the first appearance of the piriform juglets (Fig. 22.*20–21*). In the early EB III group, the early forms such as the round-based juglets and the

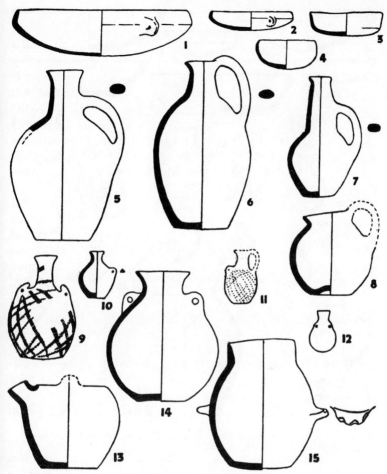

Fig. 21. Pottery from early in the Early Bronze Age from Jericho Tomb A108. ⅕

bag-shaped juglets have disappeared, the piriform juglets have become very common (Fig. 23.*20–28*), while the early types of bowl are rare and devolved (Fig. 23.*1*) and the new types of jug (Fig. 23.*15–19*) appear. A small, round-based bowl, often used as a lamp, is common (Fig. 23.*5–6*), and a flat-based saucer, also used as a lamp, is just appearing (Fig. 23.*10*). Side by side with the native wares are vessels of Khirbet Kerak ware (Fig. 23.*12*), to which reference has already been made (Fig. 24). These vessels are

109

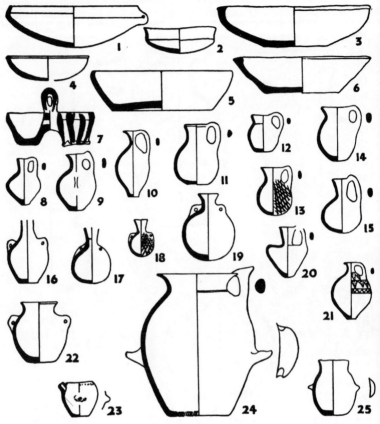

Fig. 22. Pottery of the middle of the Early Bronze Age from Jericho Tomb A127. ⅕

hand-made, and have a most striking highly burnished finish, on a slip with sharply defined zones of red, black, and light brown colour. The surface of the vessels is sometimes decorated with flutings. This type of pottery is also found in northern Syria, but, as in Palestine, it is intrusive there. Its home appears to be in north-eastern Anatolia.[8] In Syria its appearance is accompanied by disturbances, suggesting actual invading groups. In Palestine there is no clear evidence of disturbance, so it may be deduced that at most there was some infiltration or perhaps trade. The sites at which the greatest quantities are found, Beth-shan and Khirbet Kerak, are both on the route crossing the Jordan from Syria, and the amount becomes steadily less farther west and south, though a little is found as far south as Tell Duweir.

In the mid-EB III group, the earlier forms have completely disappeared. The number of round-based bowls is decreasing and that of the flat-based saucers increasing. The place of the earlier bowls seems to be taken by flat-based platters. Round-mouthed jars with side spouts, which have antecedents in earlier groups, become common. A later stage in EB III is represented by the pottery from the 'Ai sanctuary (Fig. 27), and by Tomb 351 from the earlier excavations at Jericho.[9] In these groups the flat-based saucers and platters have entirely superseded the earlier forms, and both the native Khirbet Kerak types of burnished pottery have disappeared.

The sequence of Palestinian Early Bronze Age pottery can be established on internal evidence. But absolute chronology can only be established by contact with Egypt. Fairly adequate links can be shown. On Fig. 23, No. 15 is a type of jug of hard, thin ware, with a fine burnished red slip, which is usually known as metallic-ware. It is found at Megiddo, Tell el Far'ah, Jericho, and other sites. The Megiddo evidence as to its associations is not clear, but at Tell el Far'ah it appears in the EB II levels;[10] at Jericho it occurs in a group which continues into EB III. This type of jug is also found in Egypt, being probably imported from Syria or Palestine. In Egypt, it is found in tombs of the First Dynasty. It follows that EB II in Palestine must date from about the same period. The link of the 'Ai sanctuary with the Fourth Dynasty of Egypt has already been mentioned, and the pottery from this sanctuary seems to come late in EB III.

A thorough examination of the contacts between Palestine and Egypt has recently been made.[11] Egyptian objects of the First Dynasty date are found in Palestine both in Proto-Urban and Early Bronze I assemblages. If the *Cambridge Ancient History* dates for the First Dynasty of 3100–2900 B.C. are accepted (which is unwelcome to Palestinian archaeologists), this would imply an initial date for EB I of *c.* 3050 B.C. The whole of EB I would seem to come within the period of the First Dynasty, for EB II also seems to overlap with that period, and may start *c.* 2950 B.C. EB II again covers a comparatively short period, for EB III has links with the Second Dynasty (*CAH,* 2900–2686 B.C.), and may start about 2700 B.C. These correlations accord not only with the finds of Egyptian imports, but with the amount of evidence concerning the different

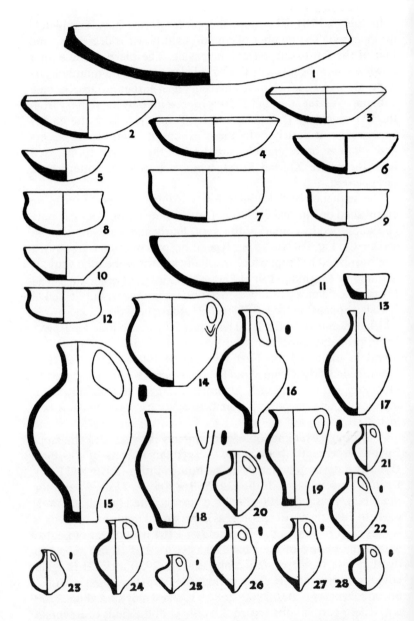

Fig. 23. Pottery of the beginning of EB III from Jericho Tomb F4. ⅕

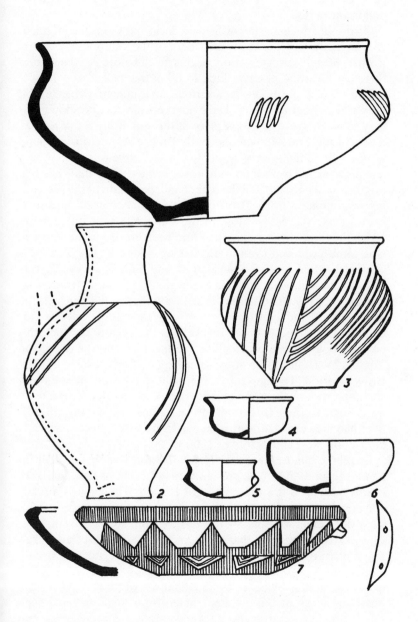

Fig. 24. Khirbet Kerak ware from Beth-shan. ⅕

periods. There is no doubt that EB III is the longest and most important period.

On present evidence it is difficult to decide how long it continued. It is unlikely that the next main period, the Intermediate Early Bronze–Middle Bronze period, begins much before 2300 B.C., and there seems at the moment little to fill in the gap.

This may be partly due to a serious environmental change that took place about this time. The evidence from Jericho shows that very substantial erosion took place at the end of the Early Bronze Age. All the Proto-Urban and Early Bronze Age tombs as found were roofless, though the beginning of the curve of the roof, and fallen fragments from it, in most cases make it clear that they had originally been roofed. On the other hand, the tombs of the succeeding Intermediate Early Bronze–Middle Bronze period had their roofs intact. Six feet or more of the soft rock of the hill slope in which the tombs are cut had therefore been eroded in the interval. One tomb produced even more striking evidence. The Tomb K2 belonged to the Proto-Urban period, and had, as always, lost its roof. Its contents were all set in a deposit of concrete-like hardness, formed of gypsum. Gypsum is deposited by a lowering of the water-table,[12] and a lowering of the water-table is naturally associated with erosion. A lower bracket for the period at which this erosion took place is provided by the fact that into the deposit in Tomb K2 was cut a tomb of the Intermediate Early Bronze–Middle Bronze period. The deposit was already so concrete-like that the shaft and roof of the tomb chamber could be cut in it as if it were rock. Since all the EB III tombs were roofless, and all the EB–MB ones had intact roofs, the erosion must have taken place some time after 2600 B.C., and before *c.* 2300 B.C.

Erosion is almost always the result of deforestation. On environmental grounds, it is to be presumed that the hills of Palestine were once wooded, as are those of the Lebanon. Timber was already scarce in Palestine in the time of Solomon, since he had to obtain his supply of timber for building the Temple from Hiram king of Tyre. The evidence suggests that very considerable deforestation had taken place during the Early Bronze Age, with resultant erosion. This seems very probable on two grounds. Both at Jericho and Tell el Far'ah there is evidence of abundant use of timber. At Jericho many instances of burnt timber fallen from the roof have been found, and in several stages of the town walls numerous horizontal lacing-timbers were employed. At Far'ah in most of the rooms there

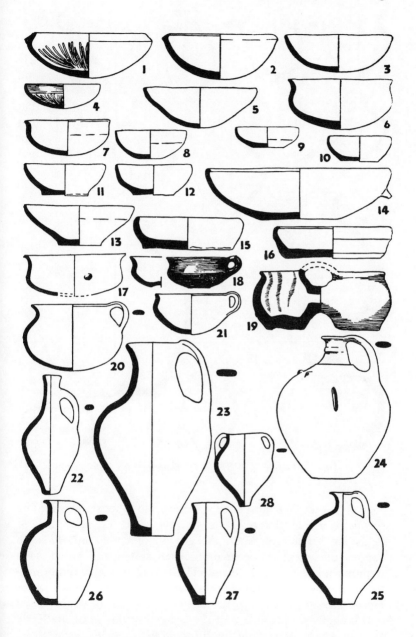

Fig. 25. Pottery of the middle of EB III from Jericho Tomb F2. $\frac{1}{5}$

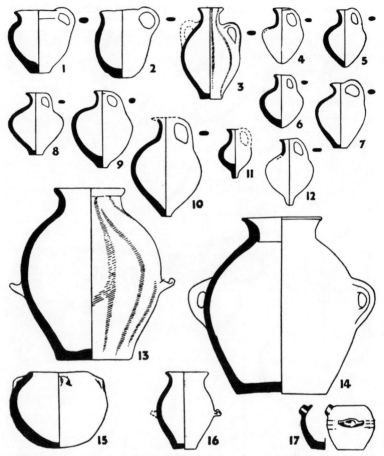

Fig. 26. Pottery of the middle of EB III from Jericho Tomb F2. ⅕

were slabs on which must have stood posts to support the roof. The second reason for deforestation would have been the clearance of fields for agriculture. With the growth of comparatively large centres of sedentary occupation, each settlement would have required a large area for crops. The two factors apparently produced an effect from which the countryside of Palestine has never recovered.

It is therefore possible that the last century or so of the Early Bronze Age marked a decline in town life as fields began to be affected by denudation, and that as a result some towns were

116

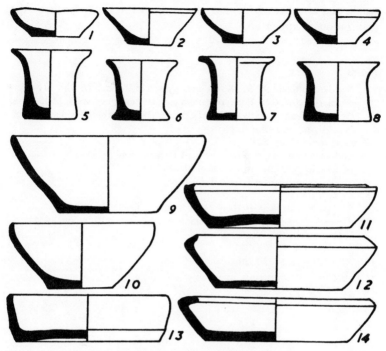

Fig. 27. Late EB III pottery from the Sanctuary of 'Ai. ⅕

abandoned, or the occupation was restricted and therefore the evidence of it has not been found. It may be that some of the population migrated to Transjordan, where surface exploration suggests that there was considerable occupation late in the Early Bronze Age, and where types of pottery are found that do not occur in Palestine.

The final end of the Early Bronze Age civilization came with catastrophic completeness. The last of the Early Bronze Age walls of Jericho was built in a great hurry, using old and broken bricks, and was probably not completed when it was destroyed by fire. Little or none of the town inside the walls has survived subsequent denudation, but it was probably completely destroyed, for all the finds show that there was an absolute break, and that a new people took the place of the earlier inhabitants. Every town in Palestine that has so far been investigated shows the same break. The newcomers were nomads, not interested in town life, and they so completely drove out or absorbed the old population, perhaps already

117

weakened and decadent, that all traces of the Early Bronze Age civilization disappeared.

Notes

1. The description of the levels and finds is given in *Megiddo II,* with an earlier summary in *SAOC* 10. For a critical analysis of the evidence, see K. M. Kenyon, 'Some Notes on the Early and Middle Bronze Age Strata of Megiddo', in *Eretz Israel* V, and in *Levant* I.
2. *Eretz Israel* V, pp. 52-3.
3. Interim reports were published by G. M. Fitzgerald in *PEQ* (1934), and, on the pottery, in the *Museum Journal* of Philadelphia, XXIV.
4. L. H. Vincent, *Jerusalem sous Terre* (London, 1911).
5. *Lachish* IV.
6. F. J. Bliss, *A Mound of Many Cities* (London, 1894), pp. 36–7.
7. *Eleventh Annual Report of the Institute of Archaeology* (London, 1955).
8. S. Hood, *Anatolian Studies* I.
9. *LAAA* XXII, Pl. XXXIV.
10. *RB* LXII, Fig. 14. 23, 29.
11. Hennessy, op. cit.
12. The interpretation is that of Professor F. E. Zeuner.

6   The Arrival of the Amorites

In 2185 B.C.[1] the Old Empire of Egypt fell before the attacks of Asiatic invaders, and the period known as the First Intermediate began. Such a period ranks with the Dark Age of Europe which followed the collapse of the Roman Empire in the face of the attacks of the northern barbarians in the fifth century A.D. Civilization suffers an eclipse, history becomes misty and indefinite, literacy almost disappears. It is at such periods that archaeology becomes once more the only means of tracing the course of events, as it had been in the prehistoric period. Just as the Dark Age of Europe is gradually being illuminated by archaeology, and the events recorded in poetic sagas are being given precision, so in the Near East events during this intermission in civilization are gradually being traced by excavation and other archaeological methods.

It is only comparatively recently that it has been recognized that there was in Palestine between the two periods of civilization of the Early Bronze Age and the Middle Bronze Age a stage comparable with the First Intermediate of Egypt. The picture of the period has for long been blurred by the attempted assimilation of features in it into either the Early or the Middle Bronze Age. The first to recognize that there was an entity to be distinguished was Sir Flinders Petrie. At Tell Ajjul in 1931 he found a number of tombs of distinctive character, which he ascribed to the Copper Age. The ascription was reasonable, since many of the tombs were characterized by the presence of copper weapons. But more recent work has shown that these tombs belong to a phase between what have long conventionally been called the Early Bronze and Middle Bronze Ages, and it is therefore confusing to give it a name suggesting an earlier technological stage. It is in fact an intermediate phase, just as is the First Intermediate of Egypt, and it is therefore more apt to call it the Intermediate Early Bronze–Middle Bronze period, and, as will be seen, it corresponds in date approximately to the First Intermediate of Egypt.

It must, however, be pointed out that neither American nor Israeli archaeologists accept this nomenclature. Some would prefer to assign at least some of the groups described below to an EB IV period, accepting the evidence of a break in the rich urban culture of EB III, but emphasizing the continuation of some EB characteristic.[2] In opposition to this view, the characteristics associating these groups with the other ones must also be stressed, and I would prefer to describe them all under the new designation of EB–MB. For the other groups, the designation Middle Bronze I, first employed by Albright at Tell Beit Mirsim, continues to be used,[3] in spite of the clear evidence of complete lack of continuity with what they call MB II A. Lapp [4] has proposed as an alternative to the admittedly clumsy Intermediate Early Bronze–Middle Bronze period, the term Intermediate Bronze, which seems unobjectionable, but EB–MB is well established among British archaeologists, and is retained here.

At most sites our evidence consists of the abrupt appearance of a new type of pottery. The most characteristic form is a tall, ovoid jar with flat base and flaring rim (Fig. 38.*2–3*). Smaller pots with lug handles at the neck and bowls either barrel-shaped or slightly waisted (Fig. 37.*2–3*) are also common. The typical decoration is incised, usually a combination of straight and wavy lines, or else a series of stabs. The burnished finish of the Early Bronze Age vessels and the painted decoration also typical of that period are never found. The ware is usually brittle and not well fired, but the actual making of the pots, with remarkably thin walls, is skilful. A striking characteristic is that though the bodies of the jars are made by hand, the rims are usually made on a fast wheel. This combination of a hand-made lower part and a wheel-made rim is also found in the Early Bronze Age, but the contrast and differentiation are not nearly so marked.

There is rarely any difficulty in distinguishing this pottery from that of the Early Bronze Age, and there is none in distinguishing it from that of the Middle Bronze Age, when the shapes of the pots are quite different, and they are completely made on a fast wheel. On this evidence alone, therefore, it is safe to postulate an invasion of a new group. Some broad similarity between their pottery and that of the Early Bronze Age people, such as the flat bases of the jars in contrast with the pointed bases of those of the Middle Bronze Age, and the use of ledge handles, though in quite distinct forms, may suggest some links; they are probably, however, only those of a remote common ancestry. As will be suggested at the end of the chapter, there is good reason to believe that these newcomers were the Amorites.

The differences extend over a far wider field than merely that of pottery; in way of life, in architecture, in burial customs, in weapons, in social organization. These differences are illustrated particularly clearly at Jericho.

As has already been described, the latest of the Early Bronze Age town walls at Jericho was destroyed by fire. With this destruction, town life there came to an end for a space of several hundred years. Newcomers, who were presumably the authors of the destruction, settled in considerable numbers in the area, but they did not build for themselves a walled town. They spread all down the slopes of the mound and over a considerable part of the adjoining hillside. But on the town mound the only evidence of the earlier stages of their occupation is a considerable spread of their characteristic pottery, mingled with household débris. Similarly, on the adjacent hillside, occupation débris and pottery are found, but no structures. It was only after the ditch of the Early Bronze Age town had silted up to a depth of 2·50 metres that the first structures appear. The newcomers therefore were essentially nomads. They destroyed existing towns, but did not create their own. It is perhaps one of the clearest instances in the long history of Palestine of the temporary triumph of the Desert over the Sown.

The evidence from the tombs of these newcomers throws considerable further light upon them, and emphasizes both their differentiation from their predecessors and their nomadic organization. The tombs of the Early Bronze Age had all contained multiple burials. In the Intermediate Early Bronze–Middle Bronze period, the burial practice is essentially that of single burials, though occasionally there are two bodies. As a result there are enormous numbers of tombs of this period. All energy and constructive ability seem to have been directed towards habitations for the dead instead of the living.

Though the practice of single burials is so characteristic, the burial customs in other respects show many variations, and these variations are probably to be explained as evidence of a tribal organization, each group maintaining its own burial customs. The tombs can be classified in five types.

The first type is the Dagger-type tomb. In this type the tomb is

121

small and very neatly cut (Pl. 46). In the tomb chamber is found the intact skeleton, lying in a crouched position necessitated by the small size of the tomb chamber. If the burial is of a man, he has with him a dagger (Fig. 28.*1–5*), if of a woman, there is usually a pin and beads. The whole burial custom is simple and austere, and the prominence given to weapons suggests a group of warriors.

Pottery-type tombs form the second category, so called because always pottery and never daggers comprises the funerary offerings. A further difference between this group and the last lies in the form of shaft and chamber. The shaft is very wide and deep, the chamber large in area, though only about 3 to 4 feet (1·22m.) high; both chamber and shaft are very roughly cut. The final difference is that the body was put in literally as a bag of bones, disarticulated and lying in disorder, apparently dumped in in some sort of textile or matting container (Pl. 47). The labour of excavating such enormous tombs to contain these disordered bones seems a remarkable proceeding. The reason may lie in a nomadic habit of transporting bodies of those who had died during the course of the seasonal migrations of the tribe to a tribal burying-place. The pots placed with the burials seem to have been made especially for funerary purposes, for they are not found on the habitation sites. They are ugly, clumsy little things, showing the same combination of hand-made bodies and wheel-made rims as others of this period (Fig. 29). Another characteristic find is a four-spouted lamp, usually placed in a niche cut in the wall of the chamber. The rock of the niche is often blackened by smoke, showing that the lamp was in fact intended to light the habitation of the dead.

In the third group there is to some extent a combination of features of the Dagger-type and Pottery-type tomb. Shaft and chamber are of medium size, nearer, of the two, to that of the Pottery type, but not so large as the majority, and not so roughly cut. The burials are of intact skeletons, and with them are placed both weapons and pots. A new feature is that the weapons may include a javelin, a short copper weapon with a small spear-shaped or poker-shaped head and a curled end to the tang (Fig 28.*6–7*). The most striking differentiation of the group from the others is that the tomb shaft is approximately square in plan, and for this reason they have been called the Square-Shaft-type.

Group four can only be called the Outsize-type, for everything about these works is on a grand scale. Like the Square-Shaft-type, they may contain both pots and weapons, and the skeleton is intact.

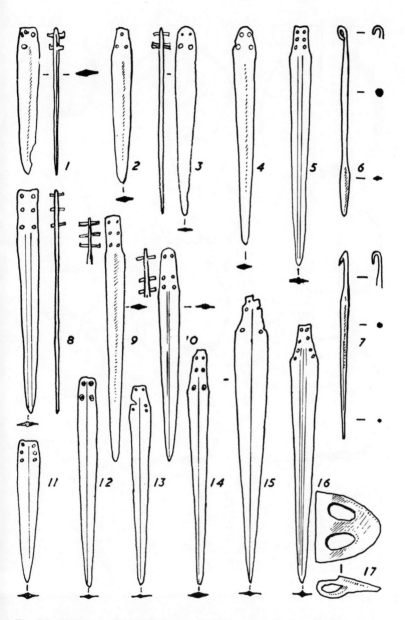

Fig. 28. Weapons of the EB–MB period from Jericho (1–10), Tell Ajjul (11–16), and Megiddo (17). $\frac{1}{5}$

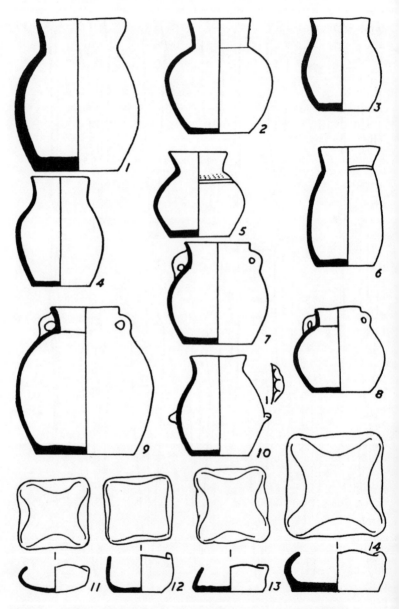

Fig. 29. Pottery of the EB–MB period from the Pottery-type tombs at Jericho. $\frac{1}{5}$

But the chamber and shaft are of enormous dimensions. Particularly in the height of the chamber they contrast with the Pottery-type. The largest chamber was 11 feet 3 inches (3·43m.) in diameter and nearly 8 feet (2·44m.) high, and the largest shaft 11 feet 9 inches (3·58m.) and 22 feet 9 inches (6·93m.) deep. The pottery offerings too are on the grand scale both in numbers and in the size of the vessels, which are large plump jars in place of the universal dumpy little pots of the Pottery-type (Fig. 30).

The final type is less interesting, for the offerings were so paltry. The tombs were usually not cut very deeply into the rock, and therefore have often lost their roofs in denudation. The skeleton was dismembered, as in the Pottery-type, and the sole objects placed with the bodies were some beads or a pin, or fragments of bronze studs, possibly all simply belonging to articles of apparel or adornment. As beads were the most constant find, this class was called the Bead-type.

There was almost nothing to show what was the relationship of these five tomb-types to one another. One instance did occur of a Pottery-type tomb cutting into a Dagger-type chamber, but that is not enough to show that all Pottery-type tombs are later than the others. For the rest, the Dagger-type tombs are so distinct from the Pottery-type that there can be no possibility of one having developed from the other. In view of the general character of these newcomers to Palestine, especially their lack of interest in town life, the habit of the Pottery group in burying collections of disarticulated bones, which may suggest a nomadic background, and the emphasis on weapons in the case of the Dagger group, which suggests that they were warriors, the most satisfactory explanation seems to be that the difference in burial customs is due to a tribal organization. The newcomers would thus be nomadic tribesmen, uniting as a predatory band to invade the richer lands of the coastal fringe, but still retaining individual tribal habits.

It is on the distinction between the Dagger-type and Pottery-type tombs that tribal distinctions can most confidently be argued. The Square-Shaft-type of tomb also seems to introduce new features, notably the shaft plan which has been used to designate the group, and the placing of both weapons, with a javelin as a new feature, and pottery, with the burials. The Outsize group adds entirely new pottery forms, as well as the feature of their enormous size. These differences are not, however, as great as those between the Dagger-type and the Pottery-type tombs, and it is not impossible

125

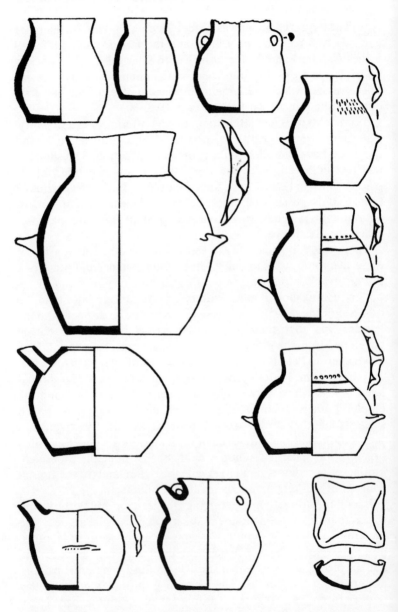

Fig. 30. Pottery of the EB–MB period from the Outsize-type tombs at Jericho. $\frac{1}{5}$

that they are evolutionary. Another group of tombs does in fact seem to combine features from most of the other classes. It may therefore be that, after the arrival of a number of tribal groups with separate burial customs, there was some mingling of characteristics, but this has yet to be proved.

It is interesting to find that at two other sites, Tell Ajjul in the south and Megiddo in the north, there is evidence of a similar organization. The evidence is again from burial customs. Petrie excavated at Tell Ajjul two separate cemeteries, the 100–200 Cemetery (the tombs being numbered within this series) to the east of the tell, and the 1500 Cemetery to the north of the tell. In the 1500 Cemetery the tombs have (with one doubtful exception) surface openings which are rectilinear and approximately rectangular in shape. They are thus like the Square-Shaft-type at Jericho. A notable feature is a central nucleus of three rows of three tombs of which the chamber was lined, and probably originally roofed, with stone or brick. The tombs of the 1500 Cemetery contained, with very few exceptions, single intact skeletons. In over a third of the tombs a dagger was included among the offerings, in some cases as the sole offering. The pottery vessels were very restricted in type. They consisted entirely of jars with extremely vestigial ledge handles and sometimes with a spout; a few lacked the ledge handles (Fig. 31.*4–6*).

In the 100–200 Cemetery most of the tombs have a rounded shaft and contain disarticulated skeletons. There are more varieties of pottery than in the other group. The majority of the vessels are again jars, but none of them have the vestigial ledge handles; in addition there were some dishes and bowls. There were only two daggers in the cemetery, but on the other hand there were two javelins. A minority of the tombs were similar in plan to those of the 1500 Cemetery, and in a few cases there were intact burials.

As a general summary it may be said that Cemetery 1500 was exclusive and homogeneous in its tomb types, method of burial of body, and predominance of daggers, but borrowed some of the pot types, the jars without ledge handles, from the other cemetery. Cemetery 100–200 borrowed some examples of tomb type and burial method, and the occasional dagger-offering, but has its own pottery type.

These Ajjul groups do not correspond exactly with any of those at Jericho. The single, intact, crouched burial is for instance found in tombs with the rectangular shaft. Others of these tombs with the

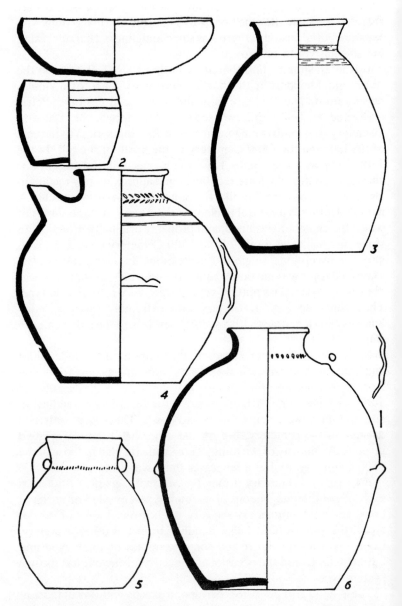

Fig. 31. Pottery of the EB–MB period from Tell Ajjul cemetery 100–200 (1–3) and cemetery 1500 (4–6). ⅕

rectangular shafts may contain intact burials with both dagger and pots, and to this extent resemble the Square-Shaft-type at Jericho, but the pots are different. The Jericho pottery which most resembles the Ajjul type comes from the Outsize group, but the repertory is not identical, and the Ajjul tombs do not approach those of Jericho in size. The tombs at Ajjul with disarticulated skeletons have not the characteristic plan and section of the Jericho ones, and the pottery is quite different.

The characteristic the tombs of the two places have in common is the practice of single burial. There is also the same emphasis on weapons, and the occurrence of the peculiar practice of disarticulated burial. Though the pots of the two sites are largely different in form, in character of manufacture and ware they are similar, and it cannot be doubted that they belong to the same general phase. How the groups at Jericho and Ajjul are related, as indeed how those at the same site are related between themselves, must remain uncertain. At Ajjul, as at Jericho, arguments for a chronological succession, from pots with ledge handles, for instance, to those without, or from rectangular-plan shafts to rounded shafts, are not really satisfactory, though such a succession remains a possibility. The merging of characteristics at Ajjul which fall into separate groups at Jericho, and the fact that at Ajjul the differences between the groups are less sharp cut, might suggest that a gradual amalgamation was going on, which would be quite in place in a site which represents a further penetration into the country of groups certainly originating in areas to the north and east. Alternatively, the Ajjul burials may be those of yet further tribal groups. It is a subject that needs further investigation.

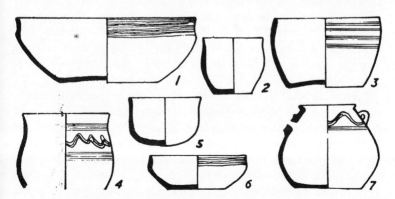

Fig. 32. Pottery of the EB–MB period from Tell Duweir. ⅕

129

At Tell Duweir, a cemetery (the 2000 Cemetery) resembles in many respects the 100–200 Cemetery of Tell Ajjul. It lies on a hill spur some 700 metres north of the tell. About a hundred tombs were located, closely grouped on the edge of the hill. A minority of the tombs were approached by square shafts, but the great majority had either round shafts and chambers, or else no shafts at all, possibly as the result of erosion. Unfortunately no evidence was recovered as to the position or condition of the bodies, perhaps because all the skeletons were dismembered. All the tombs contained pottery vessels. The range of forms is not unlike that of the Ajjul cemetery, except that there are greater numbers of bowls and cups, and that the jars tend to be narrower and taller. A very few, of a fatter form and with vestigial ledge handle, resemble those from the Ajjul 1500 Cemetery, and there are some spouted jars which also occur in that cemetery. Two tombs have a dagger, of which one also has a javelin, and two others have a javelin. It would appear that this group is allied to the group burying in the 100–200 Cemetery at Tell Ajjul; the differences in the material might be accounted for by a later date, with a typological development of forms and a slight mingling with features characteristic of the other Ajjul group. As always, interpretation is difficult, as one never finds different combinations of characteristics in stratigraphical relationship.

Considerable additional material related to these EB–MB groups has accumulated in recent years. The most important is perhaps that in the hills to the east and north-east of Jericho, from the crest of the hills to halfway down the arid slopes to the Jordan Valley. Material from Khirbet es-Samiyeh, from early unrecorded excavations and now in the Institute of Archaeology in London, had suggested some of the closest parallels to the small jars characteristic of the Jericho Pottery-type tombs (Fig. 29. *1—6*), as did vessels also in the Institute described as from 'Cave East of Olivet', probably excavated by Warren on the slopes of the Mount of Olives at Jerusalem. There is now additional information about both these areas.

It appears that there is a whole group of cemeteries in the neighbourhood of 'Ain es-Samiyeh about 7 miles north-east of Beitin, in desolate, rocky, hill-country. At one of them, Dhahr Mirzbâneh, Dr Paul Lapp excavated thirty-six tombs.[5] In plan and section, they are closely similar to the Pottery-type tombs at Jericho. Like these, they contain only disarticulated bones; some even contain none, and it seems more reasonable to interpret them as tombs prepared and not used than as 'burials without bones', which seems a very strange

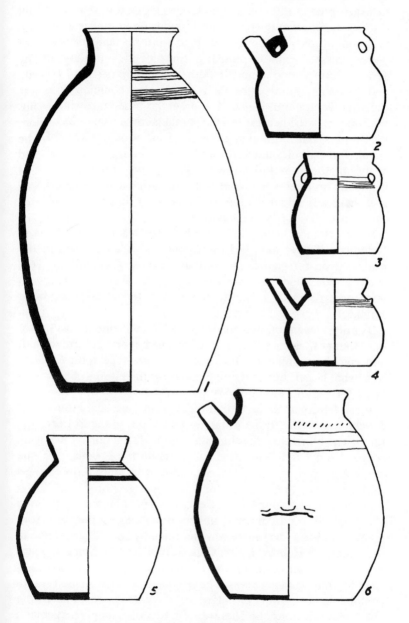

Fig. 33. Pottery of the EB—MB period from Tell Duweir. ⅕

description; cenotaphs would be a better one if this interpretation is to be accepted. A difference from Jericho is that four shafts had two distinct chambers at the base, only found in one instance at Jericho in a composite-type tomb, and there were no lamp niches. The pottery vessels again are similar but not identical to those of the Jericho Pottery-type tombs. In both, the small jars (Fig. 29. *1—6*) and the four-spouted lamps are by far the most common finds, but the Mirzbâneh tombs include the large, flat-based jars with flaring rims, to which the nearest Jericho parallels come from the Outsize-type tombs, but more akin to those of the southern sites of Tell Ajjul, Tell Duweir, and Tell Beit Mirsim. A dagger and a javelin, again not found at Jericho in the Pottery-type tombs, were also included. An interesting point about the Mirzbâneh cemetery was that there was evidence of adjacent camping sites, suggesting seasonal visits of a pastoral community.

Similar tombs, with similar finds, were made at el-Jib, near Ramullah. There, many of the tombs had been re-used in the Middle Bronze Age, but the contents of those that had not been, and the finds left in the re-used tombs, had just the same range, with large pots distinctly closer to those from the Outsize tombs at Jericho.

Thirdly, eleven tombs were excavated in 1965 on the east side of the Mount of Olives.[6] They introduce a new type—in form of shaft and chamber similar to the Jericho Dagger-type tombs though somewhat larger, but containing pottery with features of that from Pottery-type tombs, but also other forms.

It can hardly be doubted that these groups are allied to those at Jericho, especially to the group burying there in the Pottery-type tomb. The blurring of the sharpness of the distinctions could again suggest some amalgamation or intermarriage which is one hypothesis put forward in connection with the Ajjul groups (p. 129).

A fourth large group has been excavated near Hebron. Attention was directed to it by finds, mainly pots, coming on the antiquities market in 1967. The source was identified by Dr William Dever of the American Hebrew Union College Biblical and Archaeological School in Jerusalem, and proved to be a place some 12 kilometres west of Hebron. There was a large cemetery area of shaft tombs containing one or more burials of disarticulated bones. There were also some cairn burials. There were traces of a simple settlement, mainly in caves, but few structures. The pottery is closely linked with that from Tell Ajjul, Tell Duweir, and Tell Beit Mirsim, all only a few miles away.

Megiddo adds yet other details. A number of tombs were excavated on the rock surface sloping down from the foot of the tell on the east. Included among them were two groups which must fall in the Intermediate Early Bronze—Middle Bronze period.

The first group was in Tomb 1101–1102B Lower. This locality was part of a complex of interconnecting rock-cut chambers, cave-like in form, entered from the slope of the hill. Their final use was in the Early Iron Age (the 'Upper' deposits) after there had been considerable roof falls which covered the remains of the early periods. The 'Lower' deposits in themselves represented several successive uses.[7] The first falls in the Proto-Urban period, when there was domestic occupation. A second phase of domestic occupation, with stratified layers of household rubbish, was in the Early Bronze Age, probably entirely EB III. Lying on top of some 0·50 metres of these deposits were burials accompanied by the vessels shown on Fig. 34 and a group of copper objects (Pl. 48). The burials, representing fourteen individuals, were regarded by the excavators as disturbed, for though a few bones were in articulation, most were in no order at all. In the light of the evidence from Jericho, and the inference therefrom as regards Tell Ajjul, it is probable that once again we have to do with burials after the flesh had disintegrated from exposure. Some of the bones had been blackened by fire; this was on the upper sides only, so the fire was clearly after they had been placed in their present position, and must represent a funeral ceremony. This is a feature not found so far in other burials of the period.

The pottery placed with these burials (Fig. 34) has clear connections with that of Jericho, particularly in the folded or envelope ledge handles. The copper objects (Pl. 48) include a dagger resembling those of Jericho and Tell Ajjul, spearheads, and a swollen-headed toggle-pin, a most useful object, to which reference will be made later (p. 145). But though there are these resemblances to material from Jericho and Tell Ajjul, there is no identity between the finds and burial customs of any of the sites.

To the second group of tombs at Megiddo the excavators gave the title of Shaft Tombs, thus emphasizing the fact that rock-cut tomb chambers approached by entrance shafts were unusual there. But though such tombs are the normal type at Tell Ajjul and Jericho, this particular type at Megiddo has a most unusual and elaborate

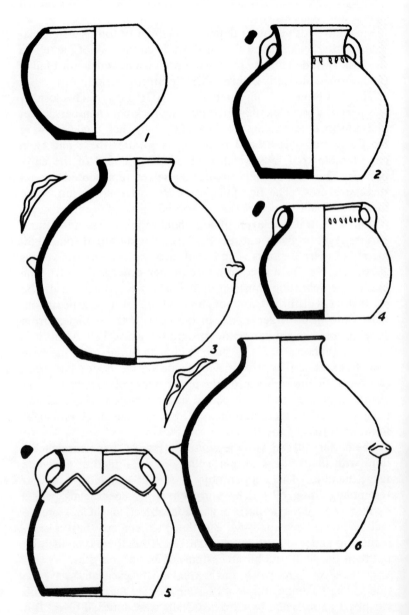

Fig. 34. *Pottery of the EB–MB period from Megiddo Tomb 1101–1102B Lower.* ⅛

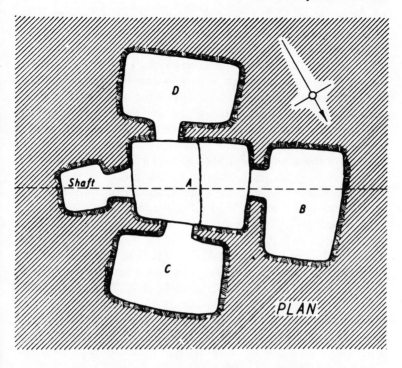

PLAN

SECTION

METERS

R.S.L.

Fig. 35. Typical Shaft Tomb at Megiddo

form. The shaft is square in plan, about 2 metres deep, with foot-holes in its vertical sides. At its base a very small doorway, closed by a blocking stone, leads into a central chamber. From this chamber small entrances led to three others on a slightly higher level, one on the axis of the shaft, the others on either side of the central chamber. The cutting of the tomb had been carried out with copper tools, 5 centimetres and 12 centimetres broad, and sometimes they were finished with a coat of plaster or whitewash. The plan was a stereotyped one, though some variations occurred.

Many of these tombs had been re-used at a later date. But the excavators were puzzled to account for the disordered state of the bones, even in the case of those which had not been disturbed in this way. They suggest that gold or other precious objects must have been placed close to the bodies and that the disturbance is due to robbers, even though the blocking-stone was often found in position. The Jericho evidence makes it quite clear that here again at Megiddo there was the practice of burying dismembered bodies.

Some of the pottery from these tombs (Fig. 36) resembles that from other EB–MB groups. It includes small jars with lug handles at the neck (Fig. 36.*10*), which are found at Jericho and Tell Ajjul, and in Megiddo Tomb 1101–1102, the jar (Fig. 36.*1*) is a common form at Jericho and Beth-shan, and is close to vessels found in the 1500 Cemetery at Tell Ajjul (though these have more vestigial ledge handles), and a bowl is close to forms found at Jericho and Tell Beit Mirsim. In addition, there are great numbers of little spouted jars which are the lug-handled jars with a spout added; these also are found at Jericho. But in addition there is a considerable number of vessels which are clearly imports, distinguished from the local vessels by being of thin hard ware and by being entirely wheel-made; they are usually dark in colour, with a decoration of straight or wavy lines in a light colour. Unique vessels in the same category are a jug and the goblet (Fig. 36.*9*). Vessels also not found at the other sites are the round-mouthed jugs with strap handles, but they are described as being hand-made and in local ware. Other finds in the tombs included mushroom-headed toggle-pins and a pin with a curled head (Pl. 49).

These finds give a clear indication of the provenance of this group at Megiddo. The teapots are closely paralleled in shape, though not decoration, by forms found at places like Qatna in inland Syria,[8] and sherds with similar decoration have been found in Byblos. The pins point also to Syria, for an identical group has been found at Brak.[9]

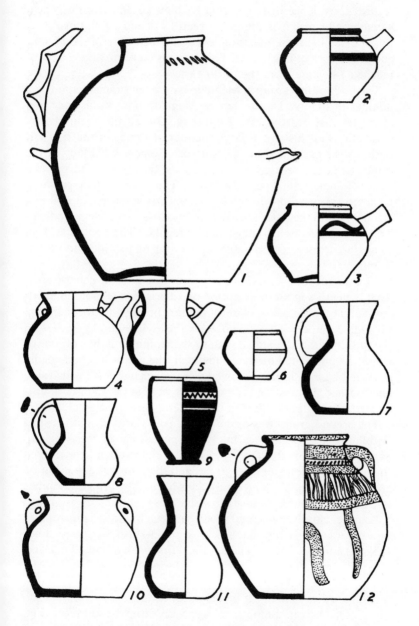

Fig. 36 Pottery of the EB—MB period from the Megiddo Shaft Tombs.

137

The site that provides the greatest amount of, and best-recorded, evidence of this period is Hama on the Orontes, excavated by a Danish expedition between 1931 and 1938. Level J on this site had eight architectural levels in which were found pottery and metalwork of this period. This group is therefore likely to have reached Palestine from the north-east.

The finds of this group at Megiddo have been supplemented by a number of others. The nearest to Megiddo both in distance and characteristics are those at Beth-shan. During the Pennsylvania excavations at this site, a large number of tombs of the EB–MB period were excavated in the Northern Cemetery.[10] Many of the tombs had been re-used in later periods, but there was clear evidence of their original period and plan. The tombs all had rectangular shafts, associated with single, two linearly arranged, or multiple chambers, and the latter are exceedingly close to the Megiddo Shaft Tomb plans, though somewhat less regular. The contents of all tombs are closely comparable with those of the Megiddo Shaft Tombs.[11]

Two similar cemeteries have been found in the same general area. That beneath a modern extension of Tiberias is the more interesting, for not only are the finds similar, but the tomb plans are certainly related.[12] They do not have the architectural precision of the cutting of the Megiddo and Beth-shan tombs, but the only one of which the plan could be traced in detail (the tombs had been badly damaged by a bulldozer) showed a central chamber off which side ones opened. In most tombs, the burials were in the form of disarticulated piles of bones, but in some there were intact skeletons.

The second group was found at Ma'ayan Barukh, south-east of 'Affuleh.[13] The pottery certainly resembles that of the Megiddo Shaft Tombs, though the toggle-pin is of the swollen-headed type found in the other Megiddo group, and there do not appear to be any imported vessels. The tomb plans have only a single chamber opening off the base of a shallow shaft.

Another closely connected group has been found in Transjordan, in a cave south of the modern town of El-Husn, about 13 miles (22km.) north of Jerash. The cave had first been occupied in Early Bronze I, and after a long gap re-used for burials by this EB–MB group. The resemblance of the pottery to that from the Megiddo Shaft Tombs is striking. It includes, for instance, spouted jars (cf. Fig. 36.*2–3*), round-mouthed jugs with strap handles (cf. Fig. 36.*7–8*), decorated jars (cf. Fig. 36.*12*) and ledge-handled jars (cf.

Fig. 36.*1*), and a pin with curled head (cf. Pl. 49c). It does not, however, include any of the imported wares. The group perhaps reached Transjordan via Palestine, which might emphasize the probability of an entry into Palestine from the north.

So far we have only dealt with the tombs of this period. In fact, by far the greater part of our evidence comes from this source. On nearly all sites the evidence within the town itself is of the slightest. At Tell Ajjul no traces of occupation were found on the tell. At Tell Beit Mirsim two strata, I and H, are assigned to this period, but the architectural remains are scanty and there is no town wall; almost all the published pottery comes from a single deposit in a cave. At Tell Duweir there was a settlement site in Area 1500, about 500 metres north-west of the tell. The traces were found in caves and pits, and there was only one poorly built house which might belong to the period. The pottery from this settlement occupation is in a different repertory of forms than that of the cemetery, a curious feature which occurs again at Jericho. At Beth-shan there are a few vessels published from Levels XII and XI which are obviously intrusive in those contexts (the stratification at this level showed clear signs of disturbances), which are an indication of some slight occupation, but again there are no structures.

The clearest evidence comes from Jericho. Immediately over the ruins of the Early Bronze town appears EB–MB pottery, and houses are found of a new type. But it is clear that there was prolonged occupation before the first houses were built. They are found mainly on the slopes of the tell, for the levels of this period on the summit have disappeared in erosion. Halfway down the slope of the tell these houses overlie the ditch of the last Early Bronze Age defences. To the bottom, this silt contained EB–MB pottery, and a depth of 2·50 metres had accumulated before the first house was built. There was thus a prolonged occupation of a camping nature. This occurs not only all over the tell, but on the surrounding hill slopes as well, for in the cemetery area patches of EB–MB domestic pottery are found, without any associated structures. When the first houses appear on the tell, they are slight in character, and entirely different from the preceding houses of the Early Bronze Age town. They are built of rather soft rectangular bricks of a curious green colour. The walls are only one course thick, the rooms small and rather irregular in shape (Pl. 50). One structure may have been a shrine or temple. Beneath its wall was an infant foundation burial, and in two adjacent rooms were solid blocks of brickwork, about a

139

metre cube, which may be altars. The settlement, even after houses began to be built, seems to straggle irregularly down the slopes of the mound, and there is no town wall. The pottery found in the settlement (Figs. 37, 38) is surprisingly different from that in the tombs, even allowing for the fact that many domestic forms, such as cooking-pots, are not ordinarily found in tombs. Even the jar forms are different, many having the high, flaring rim found in the Tell Ajjul and Tell Duweir cemeteries. Bowls and cups are found on the tell, which are very rare in the tombs at Jericho, and a striking feature is that it is only on the tell that vessels are found with an incised or combed decoration in a combination of straight and wavy lines which is a feature of the pottery of the period at Tell Beit Mirsim and Tell Ajjul. This last differentiation also occurs at Tell Duweir. This distinction between tell and tombs constitutes a problem that cannot as yet be answered; as with the problem of the interrelationship of different groups of which the cemeteries provide evidence, further research is required.

There remains the problem of Megiddo. As the material is published, there appears to be an overlap, with pottery of the Early Bronze, EB–MB, and Middle Bronze appearing side by side in Strata XVI, XV, XIV, and XIII. [14] But I have shown [15] that this is due to intrusive burials and other disturbances. No such mixture occurs in the tomb groups, and it is virtually certain that on the tell

Fig. 37. Pottery of the EB–MB period from the tell at Jericho. ⅕

Fig. 38. Pottery of the EB–MB period from the tell at Jericho. $\frac{1}{10}$

the occupation of the three periods is as distinct as it is elsewhere. Owing to these disturbances it is difficult to be certain which, if any, of the structures in these levels belong to the EB–MB period. There is a strong probability that at least one building period does come here. In Area BB of the excavations three adjacent temples are attributed to Stratum XV. It is highly improbable these are all contemporary.[16] The second plan was probably as is shown on Fig. 39, though whether the somewhat monumental approach from the east is contemporary or not cannot be proved. This temple seems to have succeeded two similar ones to the north-west. This one was subsequently rebuilt with a much smaller cella (Fig. 40), and incorporated in the rebuild was an axehead of fenestrated type (Fig. 28.*17*), which can be shown to be typical of the EB–MB period.[17] In the pottery associated with all the successive builds of the temples, there is an appreciable proportion of EB–MB types, and though the

141

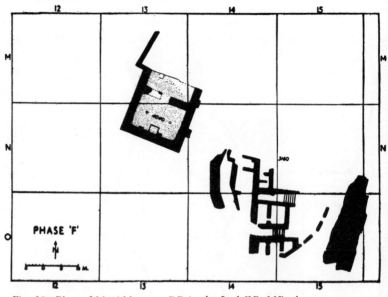

Fig. 39. Plan of Megiddo area BB in the 2nd EB–MB phase

lack of adequate stratification makes it impossible to be certain, it seems quite possible that all three stages belong to the period.

This would obviously be in considerable contrast to the evidence from elsewhere. In support of such an attribution, it may be suggested that in their care for the disposition of the dead the EB–MB people do everywhere show considerable concern for things spiritual, and there is also the possible shrine at Jericho, just described. It is also a fact that in the Shaft-Tomb people at Megiddo we have clearly a much more sophisticated group than elsewhere, with an almost architectural approach to their tomb-digging. Moreover, they would appear to have come from a comparatively civilized area, in which there was a well-developed architectural tradition. The clearest evidence of this comes from Hama.[18] The massive sounding made here by the Danish expedition between 1931 and 1938 revealed the remains of eight building levels, to finds from which the Megiddo pottery and metal objects can certainly be related, though, one must admit, as poor relations. The point of importance is that here at Hama one has the clear evidence of fully urban occupation, which had been suggested at other sites such as Khan Shiekhoun, Qatna, Tell 'As, and others. Increasing know-

142

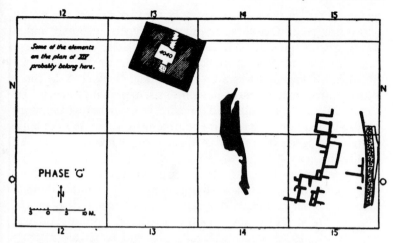

Fig. 40. Plan of Megiddo area BB in the 3rd EB–MB phase

ledge of the history of Syria towards the end of the third millennium B.C. shows that the older cultures were submerged under that of Amorite newcomers. These Amorites in origin and always in part were semi-nomadic, but some part of these newcomers rapidly became urbanized, and from their material culture the fringe of semi-nomads derived much. This must be the source of these post-EB and pre-MB settlers in northern Palestine, who at Megiddo showed a trend to town life.

But in the general picture Megiddo is exceptional. Elsewhere we have a clear picture of a very numerous people, not interested in town life. They were in fact pastoralists and not agriculturists, and many of their dwellings may have been tents or shelters scattered over the hillsides, leaving little trace for the archaeologist other than the occasional potsherd. The concentrated cemeteries may represent tribal burial grounds, to which the dead were brought from a relatively wide area. Such a practice, the relic of more completely nomadic days, has already been suggested as an explanation of the custom of burying skeletalized remains. The very noticeable differences between the possessions and burial practices of all the groups described show that though there were broad similarities, there was no uniform culture in any way comparable with that of the preceding and succeeding periods, and that the groups remained separated and tribal in organization.

In addition to the evidence provided, mainly from tombs in the

143

fertile area of Palestine, notice must be taken of evidence from the desert fringes. Surface surveys both in the Negeb and Sinai[19] and in Transjordan,[20] indefatigably carried out by Nelson Glueck, have shown a wide scatter of occupation sites. The remains consist mainly of potsherds and a few fragmentary walls, and are likely to be camp sites of semi-nomads, seasonal pastoralists, or perhaps traders. This sort of life may have continued for many years, perhaps after more civilized conditions and town life returned elsewhere. It is certainly a great exaggeration to talk of them as evidence of a vanished civilization.

This description has concentrated on groups for which the pottery and other finds suggest basic homogeneity, with slight but definite links with other groups. Forty years ago knowledge of the cultural phase was so slight that it was hardly recognized. Formulation only began in the 1930s when J. H. Iliffe gave the name Intermediate Early Bronze–Middle Bronze to a section of the material he was arranging in the new Palestine Archaeological Museum. Since then both the material and attempts at classification have multiplied enormously. Probably the best definition is that proposed by Mrs Amiran,[21] who uses the term 'families' to define three main groups. In the Family A she includes most of the finds from the hills north of Jerusalem and Jericho southwards, a broadly acceptable grouping, though it is susceptible of further subdivision. B and C are found in the north, with for B an extension south to Jericho. These two, and especially C, show the greatest connection with Syria. Other discussions, classifications, and proposals for derivations have been made by W. G. Dever[22] and P. W. Lapp.[23] Theories of the origins of the newcomers are very various. This may indeed be reflected by the variations shown by the material. Theories of chronology and succession are also numerous and few meet with general agreement. To me it seems that we do not yet have the evidence to produce the full answer. At present, a general derivation of the southern groups as semi-nomadic, with only loose interconnections, from the desert fringes to the north-east, and of the northern groups from an area in closer connection with the north Syrian towns seems probable.

Exact dates for the beginning and end of the period are difficult to fix, but the general period is clear. Professor Albright has shown[24] that the type of waisted bowl or cup, which he calls caliciform, is current in Syria in the last centuries of the third millennium, as is also a type of decoration with combined straight and wavy lines. The imported 'teapots' at Megiddo point to the same date. Associated with the remains of one of the groups of people at Megiddo, that burying their dead in Tomb 1101–1102, was a type of toggle-pin with a swollen or club head. This type of pin is found at Ras Shamra in graves of the Middle Ugarit I period, associated with a cup of waisted profile decorated with straight and wavy incised lines,[25] and with fenestrated axeheads of the type mentioned above. Schaeffer has shown[26] that the type of pin is widespread, and is associated in that area with a group expert in metallurgy. At Ras Shamra the graves are in a fill underlying a temple which was of sufficient importance to receive offerings from Twelfth Dynasty Egypt in the 20th century B.C. A terminal date of *c*. 2000 B.C. is thus indicated in northern Syria. Two other types of pin were found at Megiddo, belonging to the Shaft-Tomb people, a mushroom-headed toggle-pin and a pin with a curled head. As already mentioned, these types are exactly paralleled at Brak, and are associated in a level dated to 2200 B.C.

Palestine thus received a great invasion of nomadic groups in the last centuries of the second millennium, which completely blotted out the preceding urban civilization of the Early Bronze Age. Egypt suffered the same fate. The Sixth Dynasty of Egypt came to an end in 2294 B.C., and Egypt was invaded by barbarians, some at least of them Asiatics. Peaceful conditions were not restored until Egypt was once more reunited under the Twelfth Dynasty, *c*. 1990 B.C.

It seems very likely that Palestine would be affected by barbarian movements at least as early as Egypt, if not earlier, for any Asiatics reaching Egypt would almost certainly have passed through Palestine. For this reason it seems probable that the Intermediate Early Bronze—Middle Bronze period in Palestine began about 2300 B.C., and coincided roughly in period, as it did in effect, with the First Intermediate of Egypt. As we have seen, a late stage in EB III is to be dated *c*. 2600 B.C., and it is difficult to stretch any period of decline even as long as three hundred years, so this seems a minimum date for the beginning of the ensuing period.

The centuries-old Sumerian civilization was also overthrown towards the end of the third millennium. In this case, the agents of destruction are known, and this provides the clue for Palestine.[27] It was the Semitic Amorites, coming from the semi-arid fringes of the Fertile Crescent, who were responsible for the upheavals in northern Syria and Mesopotamia. The Books of Numbers and Joshua record that at the time of the entry of the Israelites into Palestine the Amorites were in the hill country and the Canaanites were on the coast and in the plains (Num. 13:29; Joshua 5:1, 10: 6). Probable evidence for their earlier presence in Palestine comes from the Egyptian Execration Texts. These are very probably to be dated to the Eleventh Dynasty in the 21st century B.C., when the recovery of Egyptian power was beginning, which led to the full Middle Empire of the Twelfth Dynasty. In them a number of Asiatic places are classed as rebels. They can hardly have been actual rebels, since they were not breaking away from a previous sway, for any such sway had disappeared centuries before, but were more likely opposing the spread of Egyptian influence. Some places accused, such as Byblos, can be identified, but most only doubtfully so. Some places have one chief, others two or three, and there is a very slight indication[28] that the coastal towns had a single chief, and therefore a centralized organization, and that inland places had several, and therefore still had a tribal organization. Albright suggests that the names of these places and their chiefs are in the Amorite form of the Semitic language, and that the reason that the places cannot be identified is that they were of districts rather than of the towns which later became known to history. The deductions are based on rather scanty evidence in the texts themselves, but the archaeological evidence which has accumulated since he wrote does seem to present the same picture.

The end of the Intermediate Early Bronze–Middle Bronze period is as sharp cut as its beginning. Materially, the Amorites seem to contribute nothing to the ensuing period. The higher culture of the Middle Bronze, with its reversion to town life, seems completely to submerge and absorb that of the more primitive groups found in the land by the first wave of newcomers who bring the new culture. That the Amorites remained side by side with new groups, whom we can specifically recognize as Canaanites, is established by linguistic and literary evidence. We can deduce that they remained pastoralists from their concentration in the hill country, while the Canaanites occupied the more favourable agricultural land, but they must rapidly have given up their distinctive burial customs and pottery forms. It was a process comparable with the Romanization of Iron Age Britain or the Normanization of Saxon England; a minority of invaders impose their higher culture on the more backward population they find in occupation. The contacts of the newcomers with the Phoenician coastal towns can be clearly established, and at Byblos and elsewhere a Twelfth Dynasty date for the allied culture can be shown. The culture of the Middle Bronze Age was therefore introduced into Palestine not before the 20th century B.C. How early this happened it is difficult to establish, but a conventional date of *c.* 1900 B.C. is unlikely to have a margin of error of more then fifty years either way.

Notes

1. The date ascribed to the end of the Sixth Dynasty in the revised *Cambridge Ancient History*.
2. For instance, R. Amiran in *Ancient Pottery of the Holy Land* (Jerusalem, 1969).
3. ibid.
4. P. W. Lapp, *The Dhahr Mirzbâneh Tombs* (Cambridge, Mass., 1966).
5. P. W. Lapp, *The Dhahr Mirzbâneh Tombs.*
6. *PEQ* (1966).
7. The picture is confused in the publication, *Megiddo Tombs*, pp. 24–7, by all the pottery of the 'Lower' occupation being published as one, whereas the description makes it clear that they were clearly differentiated deposits.
8. *Syria*, XI (1930).
9. *Iraq*, IX (1947).
10. E. D. Oren, *The Northern Cemetery of Beth Shan* (Leiden, 1973).
11. ibid., figs. 18–24.
12. R. Amiran, *Atiqot*, III.
13. V. Tsaferis, *IEJ* 18 (1968).
14. *Megiddo II.*
15. *Eretz Israel* V.
16. *Eretz Israel* V, p. 35.
17. *Eleventh Annual Report of the Institute of Archaeology.*
18. E. Fugmann, *Hama. Fouilles et Recherches de la Fondation Carlsberg*, II.i (Copenhague, 1958).
19. N. Glueck, *Rivers in the Desert* (New York, 1959).
20. *AASOR* XIV, XV, XVIII–XIX.
21. 'The Pottery of the Middle Bronze Age in Palestine', *IEJ* 10, 4 (1960).
22. In J. A. Sanders, ed., *Near Eastern Archaeology in the Twentieth Century* (New York, 1970).
23. *The Dhahr Mirzbâneh Tombs.*
24. *AASOR* XIII, pp. 66–7.
25. C. F. A. Schaeffer, *Stratigraphie Comparée* (Oxford, 1948), Pl. XIII.
26. 'Les Porteurs de Torques', in *Ugaritica*, II (*Mission de Ras Shamra,* tome V (Mission français d'Archéologie de Beyrouth, tome XLVII)).
27. See K. M. Kenyon, 'Amorites and Canaanites', *CAH* (rev. ed.), I, ch. xxi.
28. W. F. Albright, *JPOS* VIII.

7 The Middle Bronze Age and the Hyksos

As was the case with the beginning of the Intermediate Early Bronze–Middle Bronze period, the beginning of the Middle Bronze Age was ushered in by the appearance of a new group of people. This is clearly indicated by the appearance of new pottery, new weapons, new burial customs, and a revival of town life. Unlike their predecessors, they came from an area possessing a developed civilization, for it is with the Phoenician coastal towns that close links were established. In the early stages, there were also links with some of the settled areas of inland Syria, but these grew less as the Middle Bronze Age culture of Palestine developed. With Canaanite Phoenicia, the ties which were established about 1900 B.C. were permanent, and on the evidence of the pottery we can say that the same basic culture grew up in an area stretching from Ras Shamra in the north to the desert fringes of Palestine in the south. Moreover, the culture now introduced into Palestine was to have a very long life. In spite of the fact that a series of events took place of major political importance, there is no cultural break until at least 1200 B.C. These political events we know of on literary evidence, for we are now in a period in which written history can supplement (but by no means replace) archaeology. Archaeology can show a recognizable progression of artifacts such as pottery, and can show that towns suffered a succession of destructions, but after these destructions the old culture was re-established.

This period therefore marks the genesis of the Palestine that we meet in the Old Testament, the Palestine through which the Patriarchs journeyed in their wanderings, and the Palestine in which their descendants subsequently settled. The early Israelites found this Canaanite culture in the land, and much of it they absorbed. In the times of the Hebrew Kingdoms, the reformers amongst the

148

kings and prophets were still struggling against aspects of which they disapproved.

The new pottery (Fig. 41) which appears is in very striking contrast to that of the preceding period. For the first time in Palestine it was entirely made on a fast wheel. Ever since the Proto-Urban period some vessels had been finished on a form of slow wheel. In the EB–MB period the rims were made on what must have been quite an efficient wheel, but the bodies of the vessels are still very obviously hand-made. The new vessels are as well made as at any time in Palestinian history, all on the wheel except for coarse cooking-pots. The old flat-bottomed jars and ledge handles disappear, and a completely new set of forms appears: jars with pointed bases and loop handles, bowls with sharply angular forms, dipper juglets with a single handle and pinched mouth—in fact a whole new repertory.[1] Not a single form can be traced through from one period to the other. It has been claimed that the most domestic vessel of all, the cooking-pot, which at this period has a flat base, upright walls with an applied band, and holes pierced through below the rim, is of Early Bronze Age origin, but there is no certain evidence of this, and much evidence that it does only appear now. Another characteristic of the new pottery is that bowls, jugs, and juglets are usually covered all over with a deep red slip which has been given a highly burnished finish. The vessels have often been finished on the wheel with very fine combing, even in cases of vessels which were subsequently given a red slip and burnished.

This red burnished pottery and the sharply angular forms of the bowls suggest metallic prototypes. No examples of these metal prototypes have been found in Palestine, which is not surprising, for such vessels are frail and corrode easily in the soil. Just such a bowl, in silver, has, however, been found at Byblos, where it was buried in a jar as a foundation deposit, with a quantity of clay sealings which suggest that this type of metal vessel began to be made at Byblos during the EB–MB period.[2]

This is an important pointer both for the date of the new development in Palestine and also for the direction from which the new peoples came. Byblos does in fact provide clear evidence as to date, for in the period of the renewed prosperity of Egypt during the Twelfth Dynasty, relations which had existed with this important Syrian port were resumed and the chieftains of Byblos became clients of Egypt. As a result, the royal tombs at Byblos can be closely dated by Egyptian objects. In tombs of the period of Amenemhet

III and IV (second half 19th–beginning 18th centuries B.C.) there appears pottery which is very close to this new pottery in Palestine. Moreover, on a number of other sites in coastal Syria we find the same kind of pottery, and it is clear that part at least of the new population of Palestine must have come from this area.

The new groups brought with them other new developments in addition to wheel-made pottery. The most important of these was the use of bronze for weapons. The evidence for the first use of bronze is not as clear as it might be, owing to lack of analyses of metal, but at Megiddo the question was systematically investigated, and it is consistently in groups associated with this new kind of pottery that bronze first appears. The forms, moreover, of the weapons are distinctive: a short broad-shouldered dagger with short riveted hilt-plate and elaborate multiple ribs on the blade, a narrow parallel-sided axehead with shaft-hole and nick, presumably to help bind the head to the shaft, and a socketed spear. Arrowheads in metal do not yet appear, as presumably bronze was still too precious to be used on such expendable objects. This identical equipment is found on a number of sites in Palestine at this period, for instance Megiddo, Jericho, Tell Ajjul, and Gezer, and here again the process can be paralleled in Syria.

The MB I sites which, on the evidence of the pottery, show the closest associations with coastal Syria are in southern Palestine. At Tell Ajjul closely similar pottery was found in a number of burials within the area of the subsequent town. These were called by Petrie the Courtyard Cemetery,[3] since they lay beneath the courtyard of the large building he called the Palace, but it is clear that they are in fact earlier than the courtyard. How much occupation there was at the time on the town site is not at present clear. At Tell Beit Mirsim there was, however, undoubtedly a developed town. Two strata, G and F, are ascribed to this period.[4] Only a portion of the town of this period was cleared, but though it was badly mutilated by subsequent buildings, enough remained to show that it was laid out in an orderly manner and was closely built up. It was surrounded by a great wall about 10 feet thick, with solid towers at intervals, and the houses were built closely against the wall at the back. One building was sufficiently preserved to show what a typical dwelling-house of the period may have been. It seems to consist of a large hall with roof supported on a line of pillars, and with a series of smaller rooms opening off it. Within MB I there was apparently a considerable destruction, for the interior buildings of Stratum G were completely

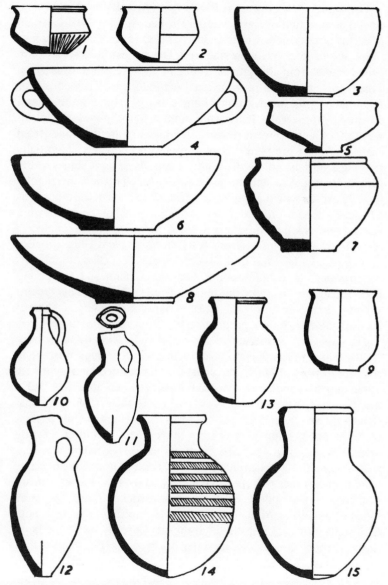

Fig. 41. Pottery of Middle Bronze I from Ras el 'Ain (2–4, 6–10, 13–15) and Tell Ajjul (1, 5, 11–12). ⅕

rebuilt in Stratum F, and the city wall strengthened and thickened.

The same pottery occurs at Ras el'Ain (Aphek) in central Palestine. The first find of Early Middle Bronze Age (my MB I, Israeli MB IIa) pottery here was in industrial excavations, and therefore there was little associated evidence.[5] The richest finds so far published come from the graves found in these earliest soundings. These graves are of a form unusual for Palestine. They consist of rectangular pits lined on the long sides by stone walling, and covered by stone slabs. In the walls of three of the graves (the fourth was that of a child) were recesses in which apparently bones from earlier burials were placed. The graves were, however, essentially for single burials, unlike the multiple burials of later stages of the Middle Bronze Age, and the bodies were placed in them in a slightly flexed position with the head to the east. With each of the adults was a bronze weapon, either a spear or a dagger. Most of the graves were liberally provided with pottery vessels. Many among them closely resemble the MB I vessels from Tell Beit Mirsim and Tell Ajjul. But others are of a type not found there, especially a class of globular, round-mouthed, handleless jar, sometimes plain and sometimes with decoration in encircling bands of red or brown. This type of vessel is characteristic of inland rather than coastal Syria, so some at least of the newcomers probably came from that direction.

The excavations on the site are continuing. Already these have shown that at this important place, which had a strategic position in relation to the *Via Maris*, the coastal route connecting Egypt with Syria and Mesopotamia, was a fully developed town. It had a brick-built town wall, probably subsequent to the first MB I occupation on the site; its relation to the tombs from which the fine pottery comes is not yet apparent. Within this earliest period of the true Middle Bronze Age (my MB I), the urban development was considerable, with a public building that the excavators consider may have been a palace.[6] Types of jar similar to those at Ras el 'Ain are also found at Megiddo. Here they are associated with the same types of angular, carinated bowls and plump dipper juglets, both with well-burnished red slip, as at the sites already mentioned, but there is a much more elaborate repertory of forms (Fig. 42). Particularly characteristic are wide bowls with thickened rims, on which is a band of red wash, jugs with narrow splaying necks and elaborate multiple-strand handles, and plump dipper juglets with decoration in bands of red or red and black. These vessels have been found nowhere else in Palestine, and their ancestry is not as yet apparent.

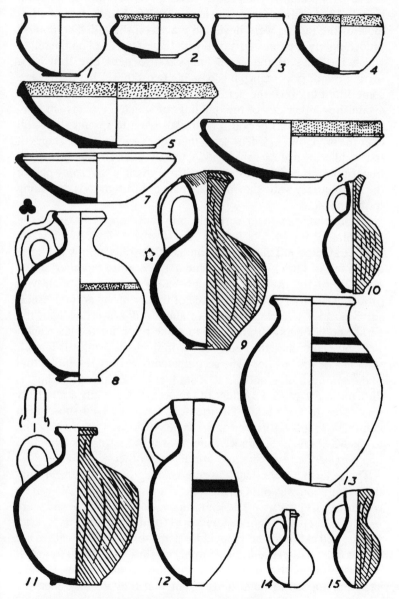

Fig. 42. *Pottery of Middle Bronze I from Megiddo.* ⅕

The great majority of these vessels at Megiddo come from burials. In two cases, these were in re-used EB–MB shaft tombs, but most of the burials were in simple graves on the tell. The pottery unfortunately is published mixed with that of the level on the tell to which the base of the grave happened to penetrate, but by a sorting-out of provenance it is possible to establish that there were some fifty burials of the period in Area BB. It is more difficult to establish whether any of the buildings of which the plans are published belong to this period. The burials seem to spread almost all over the area, but, as will be seen, there does seem, in later stages of the Middle Bronze Age at Megiddo, to have been strange juxtapositions of burials and houses; it is therefore possible that some part of the fragmentary walls shown on the plan of Stratum XIII do belong to this phase.

At Jericho, the town certainly only developed slowly at the beginning of the Middle Bronze Age. In the main cemeteries, no tombs of the period have been found, and the only certain evidence on the tell is a brick-built tomb and a grave, close together on the east side of the mound. The tomb had walls of mud-brick with probably a corbelled roof, but little of that or of the entrance shaft survives. In it were the remains of about a dozen individuals, the earlier bodies being disarranged to make room for the later ones. The grave contained the bodies of two individuals, lying on their left sides in a flexed position. The accompanying pottery resembles that of the southern sites, and not that of Megiddo. Again at Jericho it is difficult to establish the extent of the occupation. Only a relatively small area of the Middle Bronze Age town survived subsequent denudation, and of this area only a small portion has been excavated to the MB I levels. Again we cannot say if there were buildings on one part of the town site and burials in another.

The general picture that does emerge does, however, suggest that the occupation was on a small scale in the first stages. We can be certain of MB I towns at Tell Beit Mirsim and Ras el 'Ain, and there may have been the slight beginnings of town occupation at Jericho, Hazor, Tell el Far'ah, and Megiddo. If any towns on the scale of the MB II ones had existed, they would certainly have been found. It would seem that the newcomers settled on some of the old town sites and started to build houses, but that they did not need the whole area for this purpose; on part of the site they seem, in most cases, to have buried their dead, perhaps wishing to keep the graves close to the settlement to avoid the risk of desecration in an alien land. Ras el 'Ain appears to be an exception as far as urban development is concerned. Here buildings on a considerable scale appear to have been accompanied by burials within the town area. Only further excavation will enable a firm interpretation to be made of this interesting stage, when urban occupation is re-established in Palestine.

The comparatively meagre amount of finds of the period suggests also that it was not of long duration. As was mentioned in the last chapter, it is difficult to give a precise date to the beginning of the Middle Bronze Age. It may begin anywhere between 1950 and 1850 B.C., and the suggested date of 1900 B.C. is only given as a mean between the two. The occurrence of similar pottery at Byblos in tombs and deposits of the period of the Twelfth Egyptian Dynasty gives a general indication of the date. At Byblos, it would seem that this pottery continued in use down to the end of the dynasty and as late as the beginning of the Thirteenth Dynasty, that is to say to the beginning of the 18th century. The MB I period in Palestine is unlikely to have lasted until 1800 B.C. because the material remains of this period are relatively scanty. The individual character of the Middle Bronze II culture in Palestine, especially the pottery which represents a whole series of stages in development, would necessitate a longer period to achieve its remarkably homogeneous character.

A tentative date of 1850 B.C. is therefore suggested for the beginning of MB II. As will be seen, its end may be taken to coincide with the revival of the Egyptian Empire under the Eighteenth Dynasty early in the 16th century B.C. For the intervening period, there is at present no safe means of establishing exact dates. The pottery and other finds can be shown to exhibit characteristic forms at different stages, but to give a term in years to these stages is only hypothetical. In the Jericho tombs five successive characteristic assemblages of pottery and other finds can be recognized,[7] and the finds in the tombs at places like Megiddo, Tell Fara, and Tell Duweir fall into the same categories. Figs. 43–47 show the salient and diagnostic forms in what we will refer to here as phases i, iii, and v of MB II. The characteristics of the successive phases can be briefly summarized.

The pottery of phase i (Fig. 43) is close to that of MB I, and has developed directly from it. At Megiddo a set of tombs showing transitional characteristics can be identified. The chief difference is that the use of a burnished red slip is dying out. The carinated bowls

155

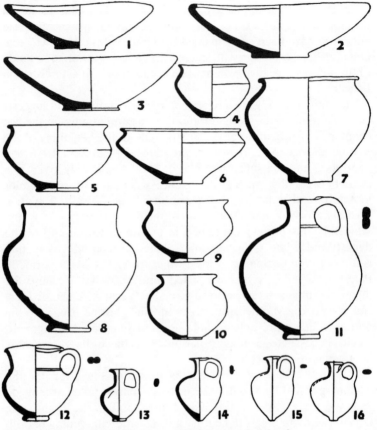

Fig. 43. Pottery of Middle Bronze II phase i at Jericho. ⅕

have a less sharply inclined-in wall, the dipper juglets become less plump, and have a pointed and not a small flat base. A characteristic small bowl has a globular body and short outcurving neck (Fig. 43.*9–10*); it is often finely burnished on a cream slip. Larger bowls with upright necks are also common (Fig. 43.*8*). The characteristic oil flask is the piriform juglet (Fig. 43.*13–16*); in the earlier groups it has a small ring base, but the button base was already found in the phase i groups at Jericho. Allied to this form is the cylindrical juglet (Fig. 45. *3—5*), which is a form occasionally found in MB I, but it is not really adopted in Palestine till phase iii; an occasional isolated example occurs in i and ii, but it is not characteristic. Neither pedestal vases (Fig. 44.*18–20*) nor flaring carinated bowls (Fig.

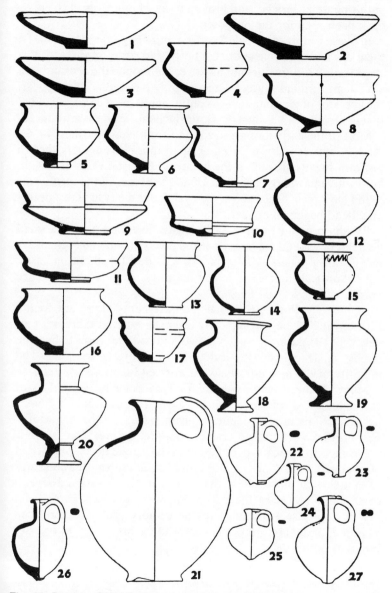

Fig. 44. Pottery of Middle Bronze II phase iii at Jericho. ⅕

157

44.9—*11*) are found. No specially constructed lamps are found in this phase at Jericho, and broken bases of other vessels seem to have been used for the purpose.

In phase ii most of the characteristic forms of phase i continue. To them are added flaring carinated bowls and pedestal vases; at this stage the latter form does not have a cordon round the neck or base. True lamps, round saucers with a slightly pinched nozzle, appear, the ancestor of the lamps which continue into the second half of the first millennium B.C., when the closed Hellenistic type is introduced.

Most of the early forms also continue into phase iii (Figs. 44–5). At this point, cylindrical juglets begin to appear in numbers, though piriform juglets are still in the majority. Pedestal vases are found both with and without cordons. Up to this stage, all the toggle-pins found have plain heads above the eyelet, but the type with a decorated head begins to appear.

By phase iv most of the early forms have died out. The small globular bowls and the larger-necked bowls are no longer found. A few piriform juglets still appear, all with developed button bases, but cylindrical juglets are in the majority. At this stage, faience bottles and flasks first appear.

In phase v (Figs. 46–7) the later elements alone are found. Piriform juglets have completely disappeared, and there is a tendency for the flaring carinated bowls and pedestal vases to become larger. A deep hemispherical bowl is relatively common. The majority of the toggle-pins have decorated heads.

Many of these features have for long been recognized as of chronological significance, but the evidence of the Jericho tombs has enabled more precision to be given to some of the characteristics. Further work will no doubt add a greater precision.

During MB II the towns of Palestine show great development and all the evidence of an eventful history. Each town excavated was rebuilt several times within the period and each suffered several destructions. Most of the excavation was, however, carried out before a precise knowledge of the pottery sequence had been acquired, and therefore the sequence of events can only be established in outline.

In the case of the history of the town of Jericho, the material has not yet been fully worked out, but a broad outline can be given of the sequence in the limited area excavated. The Middle Bronze Age town only survives on the east side of the mound, where throughout its history there was a slope down to the source of the spring. In this

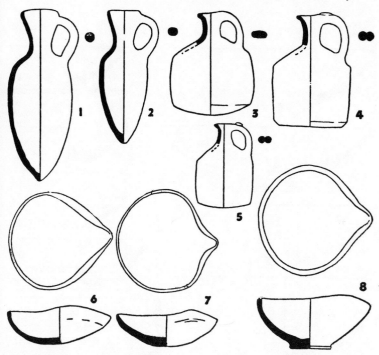

Fig. 45. Pottery of Middle Bronze II phase iii at Jericho. ⅕

area a small section only has been excavated to the base of the MB levels. This section showed that the town was enclosed with a brick wall about 2 metres thick, running along the extreme edge of the present mound, and partly cut into by the modern road. The wall was of the same character as the Early Bronze Age town walls, and the newcomers must have reintroduced this style of defence from the north. Almost certainly the gate lies on the extreme southern edge of the excavated area, for the back of a massive structure, probably a tower guarding an entrance passage, just came within the area cleared. Inside, the buildings climbed the mound in a series of terraces, those immediately within the wall being probably yards or storage enclosures. The town wall has some three building stages, and there was also a complicated series of reconstructions of the internal buildings. The correlation of the pottery from these buildings with that from the tombs has difficulties. One is that the most common vessels from the occupation layers, the cooking-pots, do

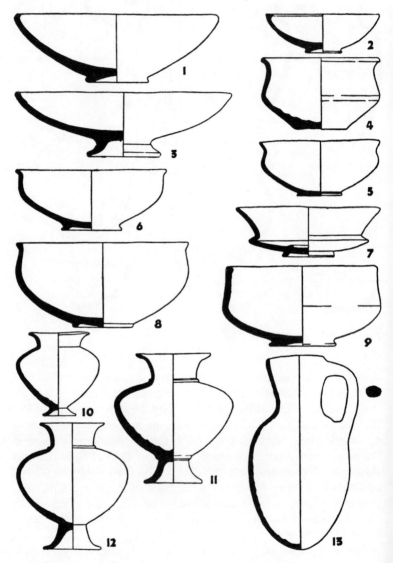

Fig. 46. Pottery of Middle Bronze II phase v at Jericho. $\frac{1}{5}$

not occur in the tombs. Secondly, the finds from the buildings are mostly small sherds, which do not show combinations of features which are diagnostic in the complete vessels from the tombs. In general, this stage in the history of the town roughly covers phases i to iii of the tombs.

At Tell Beit Mirsim it is probable that Stratum E belongs to the same period. The surviving remains were fragmentary, but seem to indicate a spacious layout. The plan of only two houses could be identified. Both were substantial, with a main hall in which the roof was supported by a central line of posts (the old style found already in the Early Bronze Age) with smaller adjoining rooms. The pottery of the period is exceptionally fine, all the better-class vessels being finished with a highly burnished cream slip. Within the life of Stratum E, but overlying pottery of an E type, a town wall was built, but since it is in the style described below, of the next epoch in the history of Palestine, it may be that Stratum E lasted into that epoch.

At Megiddo there is a complicated succession of building periods, which it is very difficult to disentangle owing to uncertainties in the stratification.[8] Early in the sequence comes a very fine town wall, associated in Area AA with a gateway having a sloping ramp which leads up parallel to the line of the wall to a gateway in a court, in which there is a right-angled turn to an inner gate.[9] The wall is characterized by a series of shallow recesses, and is a most impressive example of the town walls of the period. In Area AA the evidence suggests that this may even belong to the end of MB I,[10] though in Area BB it suggests that it is somewhat later, about phase ii of MB II. The house plans in both areas are fragmentary for this stage in MB, but show that there was a succession of substantial buildings.

This phase can be taken as representative of the fully developed culture of Canaanite Palestine, a culture of prosperous city states. On it supervenes another influence. It is represented by an entirely different method of defence, a defence in depth in contrast to the single-wall type of the earlier stages of the Middle Bronze Age and also of the preceding Early Bronze Age.

The importance of this innovation is emphasized by the fact that a number of sites were either founded or greatly extended when the new type of fortification was introduced. Urban occupation of Tell Ajjul and Tell Fara certainly dates from this stage. This may also be the case at Tell Duweir, but not enough of the site has been excavated to this level to be certain. The lower city, or plateau, at Hazor

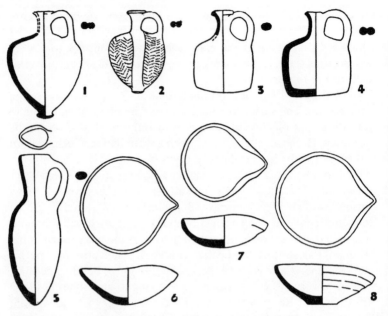

Fig. 47. Pottery of Middle Bronze II phase v at Jericho. ⅕

was certainly only occupied at this stage, and Jericho may have been considerably enlarged.

The evidence for this is especially clear at Jericho. We have seen how on the west side of the tell there had been, during the Early Bronze Age, a succession of town walls crowning the crest of the mound. As the successive walls were built, the layers of débris from their collapse gradually raised the level, but the angle of the slope remained approximately 25 degrees from the horizontal; in the later stages, the foot of this slope was somewhat steepened by a ditch. Above the débris of the final collapse were the remains of the EM–MB houses. In the main area of excavation, the summit of the slope has disappeared in erosion, and therefore there is no trace of the early MB wall which has been found on the east side; at the north-west angle, however, some slight clearance in the area where a trench was cut in earlier excavations has located what are probably the remains of this wall. This wall at the north-west angle, and all the remains in the main area of excavation, were enveloped in a great rampart, consisting of an enormous fill of imported material, faced by a thick layer of plaster, which was keyed by a series of tongues

162

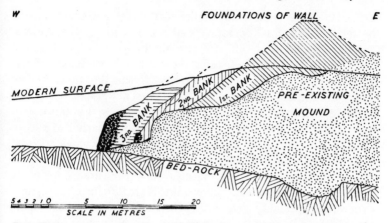

Fig. 48. Reconstructed section of Middle Bronze II rampart at Jericho.

into the fill behind (Pl. 51). The foot of the rampart was revetted by a stone wall; from this the stones of the original line have been removed for subsequent rebuildings, but its character can be deduced from the similar revetment in the final stage (Pl. 52). In the north-west angle the plaster facing can be traced up to the highest surviving point on the tell, where the foundations survive of the town wall which crowned the whole defensive system. Inside the town the great artificial bank sloped down probably some 13 feet (4m.); evidence of this survives in the south-western area. The new defences were therefore 66 feet (20m.) wide from the foot of the revetting wall to the line of the town wall, and the latter was 46 feet (14m.) higher than the ground level at the foot of the defences (Fig. 48).

On the west side of the town, three successive stages of this rampart could be traced, a second plaster-faced bank, with a steeper slope but a less solid plaster facing, and a third bank, of which the plaster facing does not survive, but which provides the best evidence of the revetting wall at the foot of the bank (Pl. 52). This wall was based on bedrock, and the rock outside had been stripped of all earlier deposits, but there was no trace of the ditch which had been presumed to exist. This final revetting wall is the most impressive surviving fragment of the defences of Jericho at any period, but one must remember that it formed a comparatively minor element in the whole defensive system. It is, however, the element in the system which has been traced over the widest area. The plaster facing of the original bank has been traced on the north, west, and south sides of the tell, but the final revetting wall was traced, by the Austro-German expedition of 1907–09, curving round at the north end to the east of the present road, and at the south end extending as far as the line of this road. From this it would appear that there was an appreciable extension of the town to the east in the second stage of the Middle Bronze Age, and there is confirmation that this was so in the excavations of Area H (plan, Fig. 4). The earlier MB town wall had run along the extreme eastern edge of the excavated area. After the abolition of the latest stage of this wall, there are a series of subsequent building levels that cross its top and are truncated by the modern road to the east; they must therefore have run up to a town wall appreciably farther out. This eastern side of the rampart was therefore clear of the town mound, and did not, as elsewhere in its circuit, crown a pre-existing slope. It must therefore have formed a free-standing bank on flat ground, a point which is of importance in relation to similar defences elsewhere. This extension of the defences to the east was presumably intended to enclose the source of the spring, though how the water would be conducted through the ramparts without its channel providing a point very vulnerable to attack is a problem on which we have no evidence.

Most of the material in the bank is derived from earlier deposits, together with a not very enlightening collection of MB sherds. The material from the successive levels in Site H, with the sharp differentiation between those contemporary with the earlier lines of the wall and those passing over their top and running out to the vanished line to the east, suggests that the pottery likely to be contemporary with the new developments should be placed towards the end of phase iii of the tombs.

Jericho, therefore, provides the evidence both of a pottery sequence which can be used to help the chronology of other sites and also of a broad classification based on the methods of defence. After MB I occupation, probably without any defences, the MB II town was at an early stage defended by a free-standing brick wall of a type traditional in the area in the third millennium. After three successive building stages, this type of defence was succeeded by one in which the important element was an artificial bank; at Jericho this again had three stages. At a large number of other important sites, the earliest MB II defences were in the form of free-standing walls. These can be identified at Megiddo, Gezer, Shechem, and Tell el

Far'ah. In most instances, an artificial bank can be traced as succeeding these walls.

This type of defence is widespread in Palestine in the Middle Bronze Age. The best parallel to Jericho comes from Tell Duweir. Here there was a very similar rampart containing material derived from earlier levels, faced by a smooth hard plaster slope (Pl. 53) and probably[11] revetted at its foot by a massive wall. Outside was what is known as the Fosse, but it is not an effective ditch forming part of the defences, for it is flat-bottomed, with the outer edge only a metre high; rather was it a cutting into the slope of the rock in order to give a steeper slope to the inner side. The Duweir evidence points to approximately the same date as Jericho. Sealed beneath the plaster surface were rock-cut tombs belonging to phase iii, which provide a *terminus post* for the construction of the bank, and débris containing 16th-century pottery that accumulated in the Fosse indicates that the defences had ceased to be kept in repair by that date.

A very similar plastered bank has been found at Tell Jeriseh, where the constructional methods are similar to those of Jericho.[12] A similar type of defence is found at Tell Ajjul,[13] where it makes an impressive sweep round the great mound, and at Tell Fara,[14] though in both cases a ditch seems to form part of the system. Both at Tell Beit Mirsim at a late stage in Stratum E,[15] and at Megiddo in Stratum X, there were ramparts of *terre pisée* at the base of the town wall, though their surviving remains were perhaps not so impressive as those already described.

The most impressive site of all to be surrounded by this type of defence is that most recently excavated, Hazor (Pl. 54). Here, to the original Early Bronze Age tell was added a great enclosure of about 178 acres (72·03ha.), surrounded by a bank and, except where the external slope rendered it unnecessary, a ditch. As far as the published evidence goes, the earliest occupation of the area previously used for tombs is contemporary with rampart-type defences, and in date belongs to the period of Jericho phase iii, late 18th century B.C. The 1956–59 excavations have shown without doubt that this plateau, lower-city, area represented a fully urban development, which included temples and a palatial-type building.

Such an entirely new system of defence must certainly have been introduced from outside. It must also reflect new conditions of warfare, for it is axiomatic in military history that new systems of defence are the sequel to the appearance of new methods of attack. It does not seem possible to identify these new methods of attack either as chariot warfare, for there is no satisfactory evidence of the use of chariots in this area until the time of the Eighteenth Dynasty, or of the use of archery, for bronze arrowheads are not found in Palestine until the Late Bronze Age. The most probable explanation is that the bank was intended to impede the use of battering rams, which it would be almost impossible to drag up the steep and slippery slope to reach the town wall, or to operate them when standing on such a slope.

It must, however, be strongly emphasized that though the system of defences was new, the life in the towns within them continued unbroken. As will be seen, there was no break in culture. The type of defensive system was something which was superimposed on the other elements of town life.

The clue to the problem lies in the fact that this type of defence is not confined to Palestine. To the south, at Tell el Yahudiyeh, a little south of Cairo, a great plaster-faced sand bank, still 41 feet (12·50m.) high, surrounds an area of more than 23 acres (9·31ha.), the bank here standing up from the level of the surrounding country like the walls of a Romano-British town. To the north, the ancient tell of Qatna, east of Homs, was surrounded, at a distance of *c*. 400 metres on three sides and 600 metres on the fourth from the foot of the tell, by a similar great free-standing, plaster-faced bank, here associated with a fine inturned entrance with the passage divided by three piers. At each of these places the defences are associated with pottery native to the area. The same types of defence can be traced even farther north, at places like Carchemish. It would seem that the method of defence came south to Palestine and Egypt, and we may with some certainty ascribe its introduction to the Hyksos, who secured control over northern Egypt *c*. 1730 B.C.[16]

The best explanation of the Egyptian word Hyksos is 'rulers of foreign lands', and therefore it is of no help to identify them, though other Egyptian references make it clear that they were Asiatics. The majority of the names identifiable on Hyksos scarabs are Semitic, but there are a number which are not, and the Hyksos must therefore include other ethnic elements as well. Now in Asia in the first half of the second millennium B.C. we have literary and linguistic evidence of a number of groups of people on the move. In the first place there are the Ḫurri, who seem to have established themselves on the middle Euphrates at the beginning of the millennium, and groups of whom certainly reached the Syrian coast and Palestine in the following centuries. At the period of the Amarna Letters, the first half of the 14th century B.C., a number of the chiefs in Palestine bore Hurrian names, and such names are even found in Egypt during the period of the Eighteenth Dynasty. It is therefore now clear that an important new group of people, probably of Indo-European origin, gained control of a key area in the Fertile Crescent at the beginning of the millennium, no doubt thereby causing a considerable upheaval and setting other groups in motion, while bands of this people penetrated farther afield and probably established an alien military aristocracy in a number of towns on the Syrian and Palestine coast.

At the same time we find mention of other alien groups designated as the Ḫabiru. Unlike the Ḫurri, the Ḫabiru, in the opinion of most scholars, cannot be recognized as an ethnic group, since no characteristic names can be associated with them. Nor can they be recognized as following some definite occupation, for sometimes they are apparently professional soldiers, sometimes they are labourers, and sometimes slaves. The only common characteristic is that they are foreigners, and the best explanation would appear to be that they were bands of adventurers and soldiers of fortune, who in times or areas of unrest would appear as raiders of defenceless towns, in times of warfare between strong states would enlist as mercenaries, and in times of peace and strong government might have to sell their services as labourers or slaves. Such groups might be recruited from various sources: from among displaced persons, such as must have been put on the move by the establishment of the Ḫurrian kingdom; from bands of adventurers seeking to conquer new territories, such as the Ḫurrians themselves; from outlaws evicted from their native cities; and above all from that reservoir of groups seeking a richer country, the Semitic Bedouin of the Arabian Desert. Such groups would therefore be of mixed origin, though in any one band there might well be a predominance of one ethnic group, or even homogeneity. Such an explanation accords well with what we know of the Ḫabiru. The majority seem to bear Semitic names, for the Arabian Desert would certainly be the best recruiting ground, but a percentage of the names is non-Semitic, including even Egyptian. The wanderings and settlings of the Ḫabiru were principally in Semitic countries, and therefore they adopted a predominantly Semitic culture. Such an explanation again fits the description of Abraham as a Hebrew (to the equation of Hebrew and Ḫabiru and the Egyptian 'Apiru there is no philological objection), for he is clearly a soldier of fortune and a wanderer, and the general story of the Patriarchs and the area covered by their wanderings is similar to what we know of the Ḫabiru.[17] It is not, however, generally accepted that there is a complete equation of the Ḫabiru of the Amarna texts with the Hebrews of the Bible, but many scholars accept the view that the Hebrews may have formed one element subsumed within the wider Ḫabiric grouping.

Therefore at the period when the Hyksos appear in Palestine and Egypt, we have on the move groups of Ḫurrians and Ḫabiru, and the most probable explanation of the Hyksos is that they were recruited from such bands, and formed a group welded into sufficient cohesion to establish themselves as overlords in these countries.

As regards Palestine, the effect is clear. Strong rule and efficient means of warfare, together with the control of the riches of Egypt, brought prosperity. New ethnic elements were established, as shown by the Hurrian names of some rulers in the succeeding period, in a previously almost pure Semitic area. But the basic culture of the country remained that established in the preceding period, as is so often the case with the superimposition of a ruling aristocracy rather than a complete emigration of peoples.

In addition to the groups reaching Palestine with the initial invasions, other alien groups no doubt settled there on the expulsion of the Hyksos from Egypt, for the Egyptians drove them back across Sinai, but did not systematically pursue them beyond southern Palestine, and the expelled groups must have been left to secure for themselves homes among the allied groups who had settled there earlier and among the pre-existing population. If this interpretation is correct, we thus have by the 16th century B.C. a population in Palestine which is basically Semitic, and of which the Semitic characteristics show a great power of survival and of absorption of other elements, with superimposed on it a number of other groups, some Semitic, some Ḫurrian, and some as yet unidentified, while some of the newcomers had settled direct in Palestine, and others had been in Egypt for a period, and no doubt had acquired elements of Egyptian culture and habits. But some of the Habiru undoubtedly remained in Egypt, where they are recorded as late as the Twentieth Dynasty. On the other hand, others, still nomadic, continued to arrive from the north to a later period, for the Ḫabiru who constitute the menace of the Amarna age represent later groups of similar characteristics and possibly similar mixed origins.

As has already been mentioned, the culture of Palestine

remained basically the same. Of this, the pottery provides undoubted evidence. There are no intrusive elements, and the descendants of the types introduced at the beginning of MB I continue throughout. The finish of some types is less good, and there is a tendency for well-burnished vessels to disappear, but this is the usual course of typological development. Domestic architecture and building methods remain much the same. At Tell Beit Mirsim in Stratum D (Fig. 49), the final MB level, there is a suggestion of rather less prosperity and increasing congestion, for the layout of the town is more cramped and the majority of the houses smaller. There appears, however, to be one house on a very much larger scale than the rest. This suggests that some families were enriching themselves at the expense of the general population. This house, in the upper right centre of the plan, consisted of a large courtyard, into which a wide doorway opened, with, in the centre of it, a basin. Obviously livestock was brought into the courtyard. Along one side was a row of rooms. There is clear evidence that these had an upper storey, which provided the living-rooms, while the lower ones served as store-rooms and possibly stables. In one were in fact found large numbers of the storage jars typical of the period. In the débris above these rooms were found a number of objects fallen from the upper storey. The most interesting is the lower portion of a stela of a serpent-goddess (Pl. 56). The stela had a rounded back, and must have stood in a niche in an upper room. Light is also thrown on the life of the period by the find of the inlay from a gaming board and a set of playing pieces (Pl. 55). The game, which was apparently Mesopotamian in origin, but was widespread in the Orient, was played on a board of three rows, of which the top and bottom were of four squares and the centre of twelve squares. One side played with conical and the other with pyramidal pieces of blue faience. The teetorum or die is numbered from one to four.

At Jericho a considerable portion of the plan of the final Middle Bronze Age town has been recovered (Fig. 50). This plan represents the last of several building stages which followed the construction of the new-style defences farther to the east. Two streets running up the steep slope of the mound have been traced. They are about 6 feet 6 inches (1·98m.) wide, and climb the mound in a succession of wide cobbled steps (Pl. 58). Beneath them are well-built drains (Pl. 57). On to the streets open a series of closely packed houses with small rooms.[18] Many of the features of streets and houses recall those of eastern towns today. The ground-floor

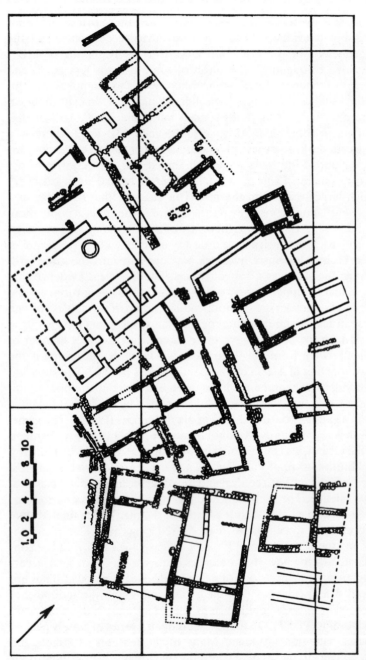

Fig. 49. Plan of Tell Beit Mirsim Stratum D

1 [*above*] The caves in the Wadi Mughara, Mount Carmel (p. 19)

2 [*left*] Mesolithic carving of a young deer, from Mugharet el Wad (p. 20)

3 [*right*] Skull with crown of *dentalia* shells, from Mugharet el Wad (p. 21)

4 Necklace of twin pendants carved from bone, Mugharet el Wad (p. 21)

one sickle-handle, with
al-head end, from
haret Kebara (p. 20)

6 Bone and flint implements of the Lower
Natufian, from Mugharet Kebara (*c*. 5/6) (p. 19)

7 The mound of ancient Jericho, with modern Jericho beyond (p. 22)

8 [*left*] A Mesolithic structure at Jericho (p. 24)

9 A house of Pre-Pottery Neolithic A at Jericho (p. 25)

12 The great stone tower of the Pre-Pottery Neolithic A defences at Jericho (p. 26)

10 [*above left*] A house of Pre-Pottery Neolithic A at Jericho (p. 25)

11 [*left*] Steps leading down into a Pre-Pottery Neolithic house at Jericho (pp. 25–6)

13 The defences of Jericho in the Pre-Pottery Neolithic A period (p. 27)

14 Pre-Pottery Neolithic A flints from Jericho (*c*. 5/6) (p. 26)

15 Bone tools of the Pre-Pottery Neolithic A period from Jericho (*c*. 5/7) (p. 26)

18 Pre-Pottery Neolithic B flints and bone tool from Jericho (c. 2/3) (p. 32)

16 [above left] A house of the Pre-Pottery Neolithic B period at Jericho (p. 31)

17 [left] A typical wall of a Pre-Pottery Neolithic B house at Jericho (p. 31)

19 Pre-Pottery Neolithic B quern, stone bowl, and implements from Jericho (p. 32)

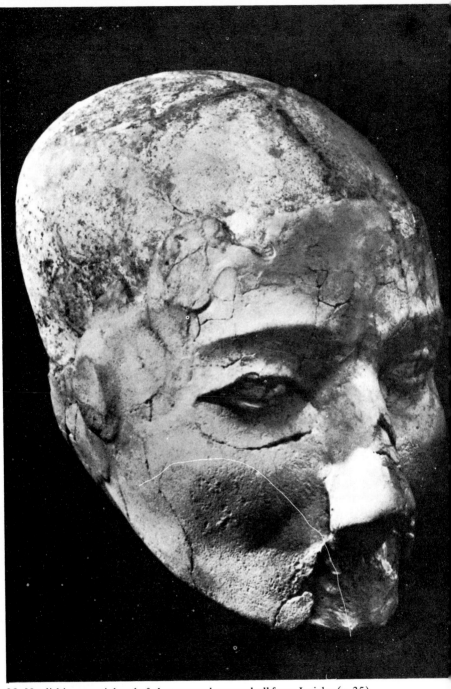

20 Neolithic portrait head of plaster on a human skull from Jericho (p. 35)

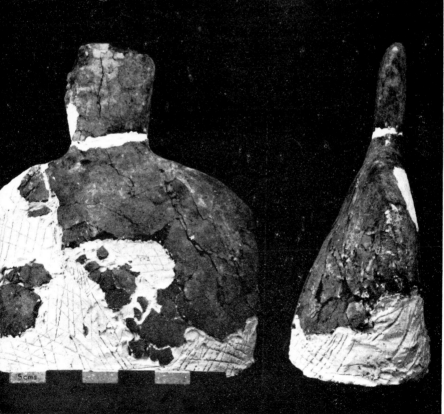

21 [*above*] Three Neolithic portrait heads from Jericho (p. 35)

22 [*below*]Completely stylized human head and bust in plaster from Jericho (p. 36)

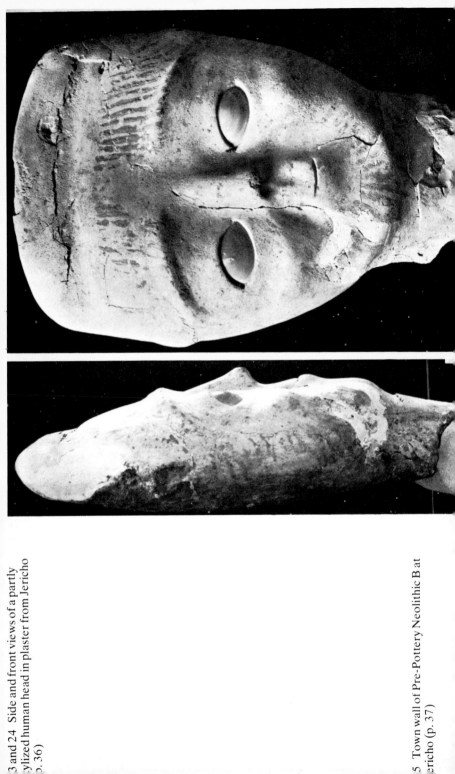

23 and 24 Side and front views of a partly stylized human head in plaster from Jericho (p. 36)

25 Town wall of Pre-Pottery Neolithic B at Jericho (p. 37)

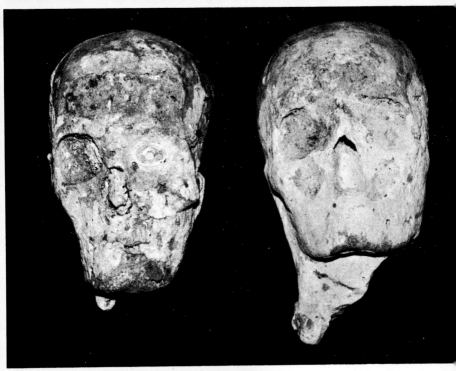

26 Pre-Pottery Neolithic B portrait heads of plaster on human skulls from Tell Ramad in Syria (p. 38)

27 Pre-Pottery Neolithic B portrait head of plaster on a human skull from Beisamun (p. 39)

28 [*above right*] Pre-Pottery Neolithic round houses in Level VI, Beidha (p. 40)

29 [*right*] Pre-Pottery Neolithic rectangular room with plastered floor from Level II, Beidha (p. 40)

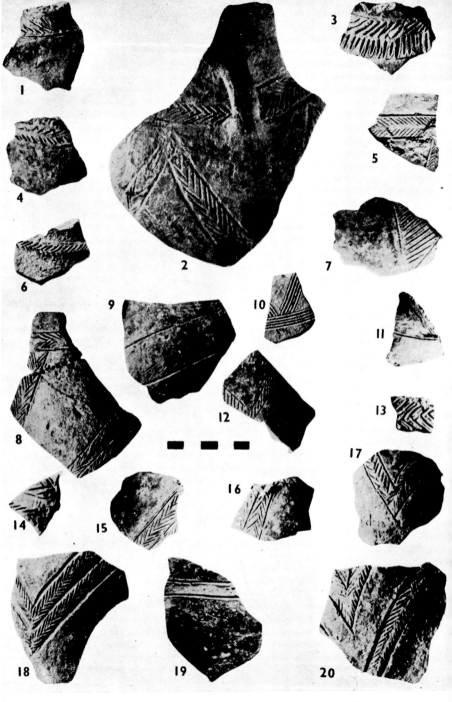

30 Pottery from Sha'ar ha Golan of the Pottery Neolithic B period (p. 48)

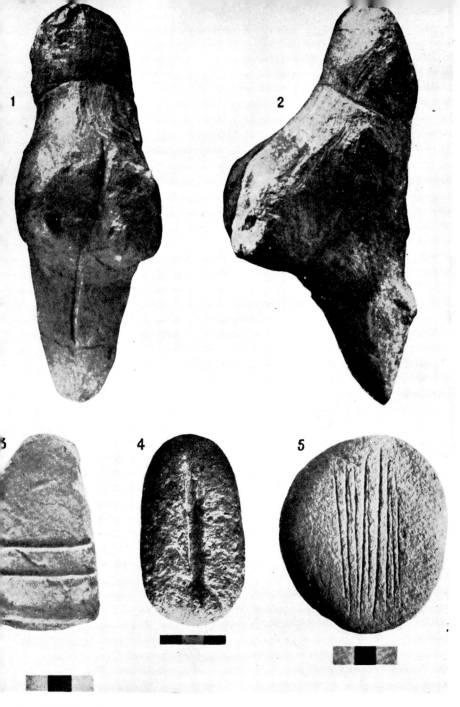

31 Pebble figurines from Sha'ar ha Golan (p. 48)

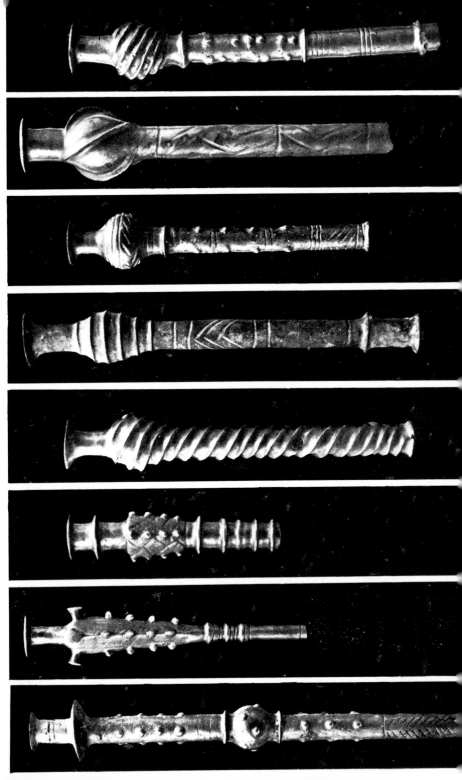

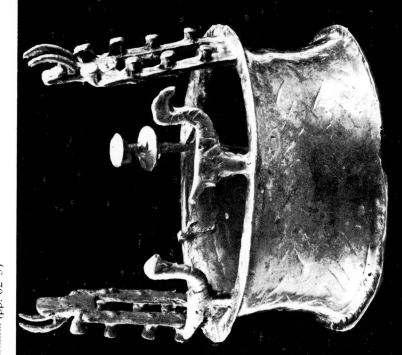

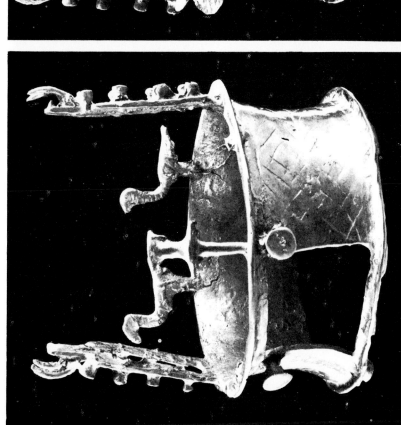

32 Copper wands from Nahal Mishmar (pp. 62–3)

33 Two views of 'Crown' with projecting 'gate' and bird figurine, from Nahal Mishmar (pp. 62–3)

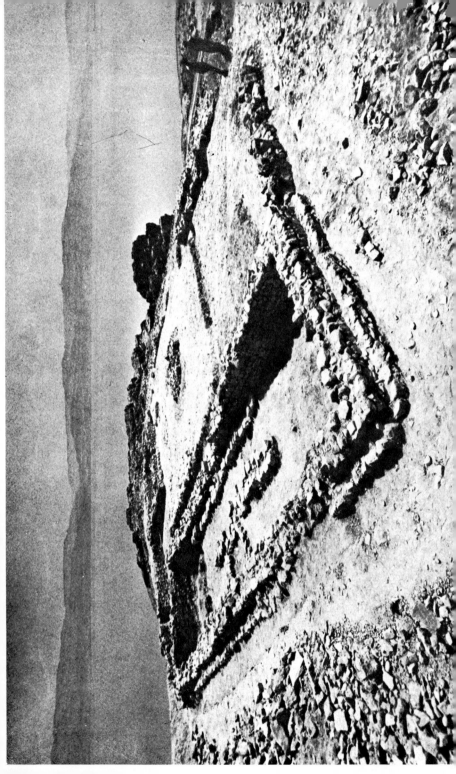

WATER HOLE

BB

CC

N

34 Chalcolithic enclosure, looking north-east at Ein Gedi (p. 88)

35 Air view of Megiddo (pp. 75, 96)

36 Inner side of Early Bronze town walls at Jericho (p. 91)

37 Great pile of ash against Early Bronze Age town Wall of Jericho (p. 92)

38 [*above*] Air view of Tell el Far'ah (p. 94)

39 [*below*] A pottery kiln of the Early Bronze Age at Tell el Far'ah (p. 96)

40 Terrace wall of Stratum XVIII at Megiddo (p. 97)

41 Altar 4017 at Megiddo (p. 97)

42 View of Beth-shan (p. 97)

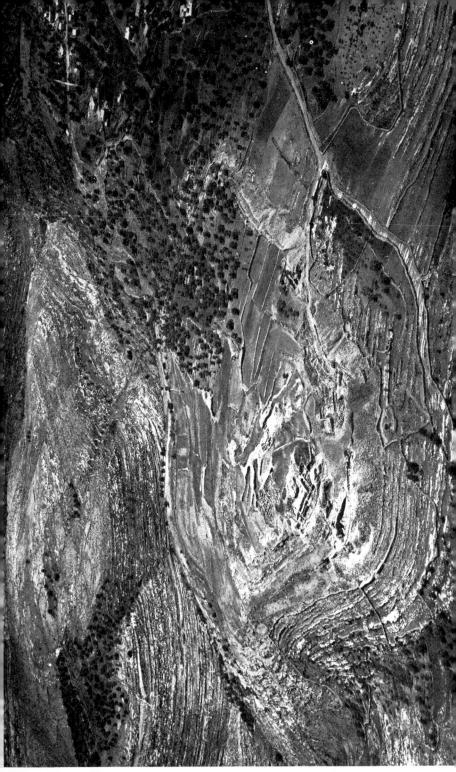

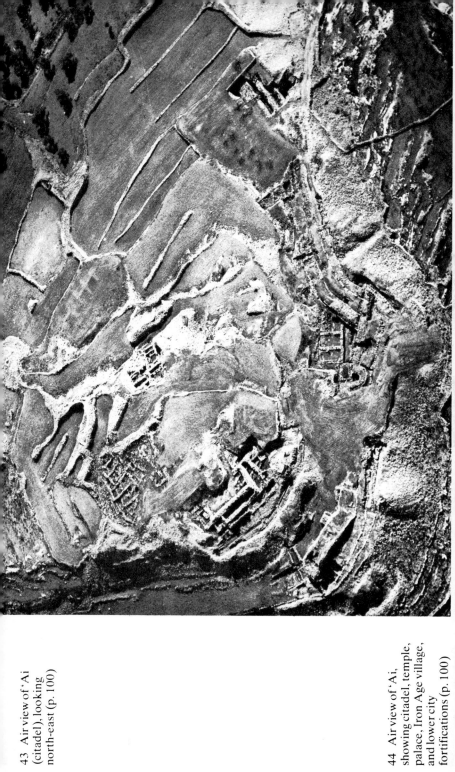

43 Air view of 'Ai (citadel), looking north-east (p. 100)

44 Air view of 'Ai, showing citadel, temple, palace, Iron Age village, and lower city fortifications (p. 100)

45 [*above*] View of Tell Duweir (pp. 102 ff.)

46 [*below*] Dagger-type tomb of the EB–MB period at Jericho (p. 122)

47 Pottery-type tomb of the EB–MB period at Jericho (p. 122)

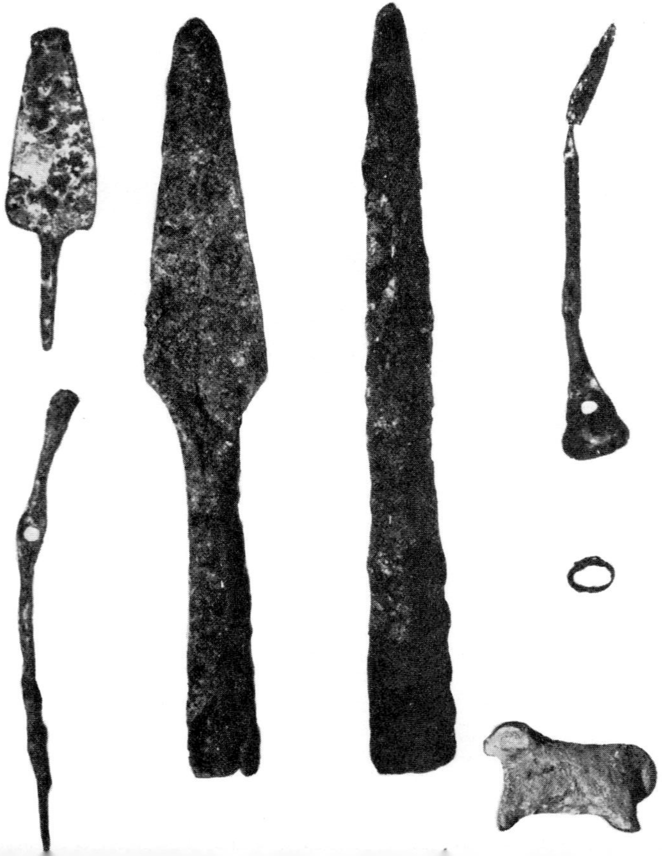

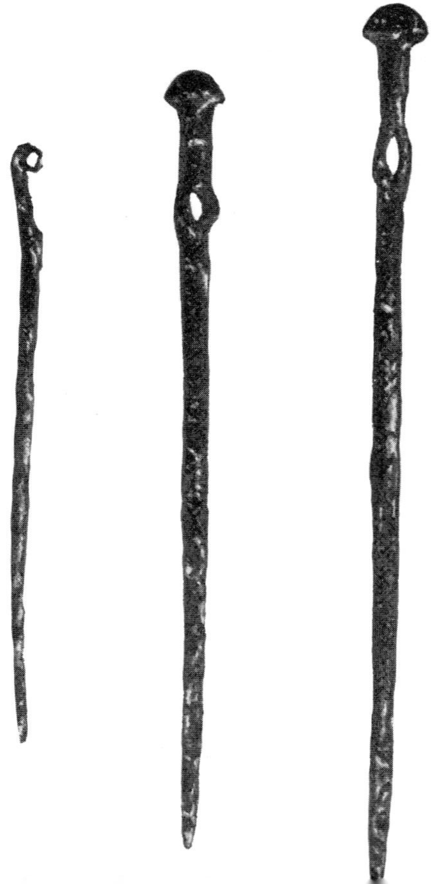

·8 Copper objects from
'omb 1101 B Lower at
Megiddo (p. 133)

·9 [*right*] Pins from
Shaft-Tombs at Megiddo
p. 136)

·0 A house of the
EB–MB period at Jericho,
n Trench II (p. 139)

51 [*above*] Middle Bronze Age plastered rampart at Jericho (pp. 162 ff.)

52 [*right*] Revetment at base of final Middle Bronze Age rampart at Jericho (p. 163)

0   100   200   300 M.

55 Gaming pieces
from Tell Beit Mirsim
(p. 169)

56 Part of stela representing a serpent-god,
from Tell Beit Mirsim (p. 169)

57 [*above*] The lower part of the Jericho street, with drain beneath (p. 169)

59 [*below*] Grain jars in a Middle Bronze Age house at Jericho (p. 171)

58 A street in Middle Bronze Age Jericho (p. 169)

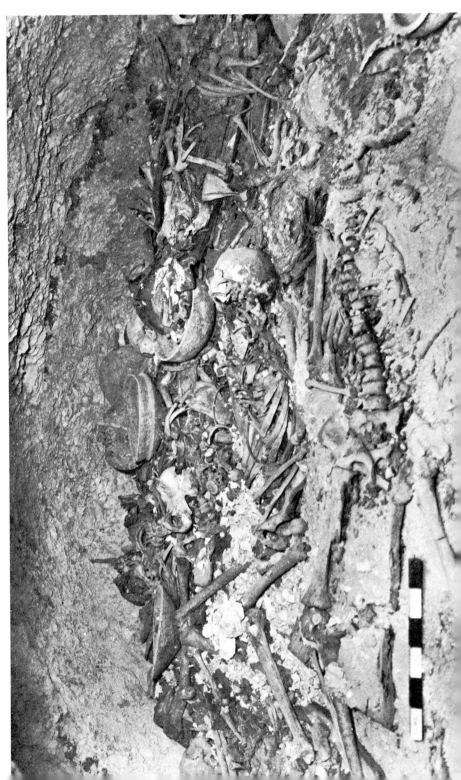

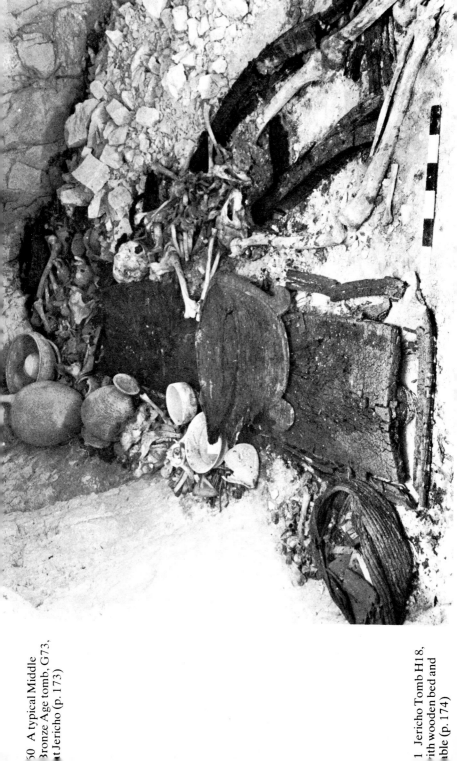

50 A typical Middle
Bronze Age tomb, G73,
at Jericho (p. 173)

51 Jericho Tomb H18,
with wooden bed and
table (p. 174)

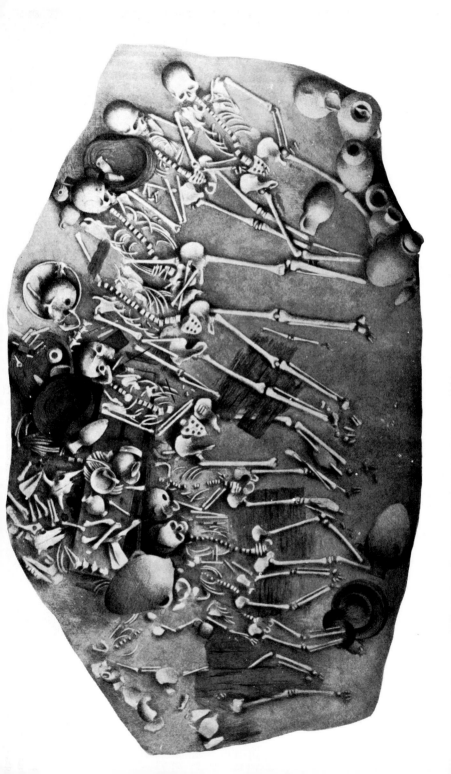

2 Jericho Tomb H22.
th mass simultaneous
rials (p. 173)

3 Reconstruction of a
om in Middle Bronze
ge Jericho (p. 175)

66 [*above*] The niche of the 13th-century B.C. 'Stelae Temple' as found in Area C at Hazor (p. 199)

67 [*below*] Hazor Temple Area H (p. 199)

64 [*above left*] Altar of Fosse Temple I at Tell Duweir (p. 190)

68 [*above left*] Libation tray of limestone from Tell Beit Mirsim (p. 201)

69 [*left*] Fragmentary remains of Late Bronze Age house at Jericho (p. 208)

70 Carved ivory box from Megiddo (p. 201)

71 Ivory plaque with representation of a griffon, from Megiddo (p. 201)

72 Anthropoid
coffin-lid from
Philistine tomb at Tell
Fara (p. 220)

73 Ivory plaque with
representation of a
sphinx, from Megiddo
(p. 201)

74 Looking down the great water-shaft at Megiddo (p. 269)

75 Last wall of the Jebusite and Davidic periods at Jerusalem, looking south-east (p. 235)

76 The eastern slopes of the earliest Jerusalem. The excavation trench extends from the Post-Exilic walls on the crest of the ridge to the position of the Jebusite and Davidic walls at the extreme foot of the trench. The position of the spring which supplied early Jerusalem with its water is indicated by the lower of the two small buildings in the right centre (p. 234)

77 East wall of Haram, showing Herodian and Phoenician-style masonry (p. 240)

78 Phoenician masonry at Ras Shamra (p. 265)

79 [*above right*] Phoenician-type ashlar masonry at Ramat Rahel (p. 243)

80 [*right*] Air view of the Solomonic Gate at Hazor (p. 244)

81 [*above left*]
Unfinished building of early 9th century B.C. at Tell el Far'ah
(p. 259)

82 [*below left*]
Entrance to Stratum IV B palace courtyard at Megiddo (p. 252)

83 Solomonic Gate at Gezer, Field III, looking from rear towards entrance
(p. 251)

84 The outer enclosure wall of Samaria (pp. 243–263)

85 [*left*] The first enclosure wall of the royal quarter at Samaria (pp. 243, 262)

86 The hill of Samaria from the east (p. 260)

87 Ivory plaque from Samaria (p. 264)

88 Ivory plaque representing a palm-tree, from Samaria (p. 264)

90 [*right*] The tunnel from the shaft to the spring at Megiddo (p. 269)

89 Ivory 'bed-head' from room SW7, Fort Shalmanezer, Nimrud (p. 265)

91 [*above*] Wall of later monarchy at Jerusalem (pp. 277, 304)

92 [*below*] Crest-mount of a Syrian helmet from Tell Duweir; on right, reconstruction (p. 290)

93 Street of Level III at Tell Duweir (p. 301)

94 Original rock-cut channel carrying the overflow from the Pool of Siloam (p. 293)

95 The cult centre
outside walls of Jerusalem
(p. 295)

96 Wall of Jerusalem on
western ridge during the

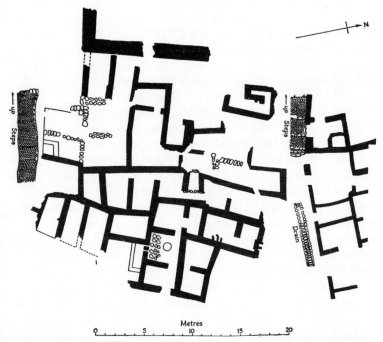

Fig. 50. Plan of Middle Bronze II houses on east slope of tell at Jericho

rooms seem mainly to have been shops and stores. The shops are single-room booths, not connecting with the rest of the building. In many of the stores, belonging either to private houses or to the shops, were found rows of jars full of grain, carbonized in the fire that destroyed the town. This fire caused the collapse into the ground-floor rooms of the upper-storey rooms and their contents. These rooms no doubt, as today, provided the living accommodation. But they seemed to have served for industrial purposes too. Great quantities of clay loom-weights were found, suggesting that weaving had been carried out. In one area, fifty-two saddle-querns and many rubbing stones were found, a number in excess of the requirements of a private house, indicating that a cornmilling business may have been carried on there; to this business perhaps belonged the supply of grain in the ground-floor room (Pl. 59).

Buildings destroyed by fire, such as these, offer particularly favourable opportunities to archaeologists, as usually all the contents of the houses are left in the débris. But many of the details of the equipment of the houses are missing owing to the limitation of

171

archaeology, which can only concern itself with those material remains which have survived. All evidence of everything made of organic matter has disappeared. Thus from the excavation of this town site we can recover no evidence of the wooden furniture, the bedding, clothing, and food. There is fortunately at Jericho another source of information in the finds in the tombs.

There seems to have been some considerable diversity of burial practice, for at Tell Ajjul and Megiddo many burials were certainly in graves containing a single body, dug on the tell. At Megiddo, at least, it does not seem possible that unoccupied parts of the town area were used for burials. The pottery sequence seems to run right through the Middle Bronze, and during that period there are at least five building periods. The graves must therefore have been adjacent to or even underneath the houses. A few of the burials on the tell at Megiddo are in built tombs instead of single graves. These built tombs were obviously to enable successive burials to be made, the tomb being reopened each time; it is probably not the case that these tombs are structurally part of the houses, for in most cases they are not built in connection with the house within which they are situated, but break through it.

The practice of communal burial is the one more generally found, for instance at Tell Fara, Tell Duweir, Tell el Far'ah, and Jericho. The tombs at Jericho are particularly well preserved, both structurally and in the contents, and may be taken as examples of the procedure. The tombs are cut into the soft rock of the lower slopes of the hills which curve round the west and north sides of the tell. They consist of a vertical shaft with the tomb chamber opening off its base. Many of these used in the Middle Bronze Age in the northern cemetery were originally cut in the EB–MB period, and were re-used at this stage; it is not clear whether this was the case in the western cemetery, which was excavated by the earlier expedition. With a single exception, the tombs contained multiple burials, but not on the scale of the Proto-Urban Period or Early Bronze Age. Exceptionally they may contain about forty burials, but the average is about twenty. Apparently the tomb shaft was filled after each burial and re-excavated for the next one. Each dead person was put in the tomb with food and equipment for the after-life, as will be described below. The body was placed on its back with limbs untidily disposed, and often with the knees raised. When the next burial was made, the body and offerings belonging to the earlier ones were pushed roughly towards the back and sides of the tomb chamber. As a result, a jumble of bones and offerings became piled up in the rear of the tomb, while the front was kept comparatively clear, and when excavated would be found occupied by the final burial (Pl. 60). From this description, it will be realized that it is impossible to deduce the relative age of objects from their height within the latest deposit in the tomb, as has been done in the past when the objects have been recorded by their height above the floor of the chamber, for the latest deposits are usually the lowest, and the objects in the pile may have slid into any position. Any deductions as to sequence can only be made from a careful study of an accurately made plan of the deposits.

Such tombs can therefore only give an overall impression of the period within which the tomb was used. It is reasonable to deduce that they were family vaults, and therefore that twenty or so deaths would cover a fairly long time, but probably under a century. The dating evidence is therefore valuable, but not very close.

In the mounding process, too, many of the objects were broken, and further damage was caused by roof fall. But at an early stage in the excavations it became clear that the contents were exceptionally interesting, since some preservative property had prevented the complete decay of organic substances, such as wood, textiles, and flesh. The cause of this is not yet certain, but apparently some gases had accumulated in the tomb chambers which had killed the organisms of decay before they had completed their work. Decay had begun, and the objects had been rendered very fragile, but their form was preserved. But from this fragility the wooden objects had suffered severely in the mounding process, and in the earlier tombs to be excavated only small objects and tantalizing fragments of larger furniture could be recovered.

The full possibilities from the evidence of these tombs did not become apparent until a group of tombs was discovered in which a number of burials had been made simultaneously and not subsequently disturbed. There is little doubt that each represents a family group, with adults, adolescents, and children. The bodies were found laid out side by side, with all the supply of food and the general and individual equipment readily identifiable (Pl. 62). From this we can deduce what was considered to be the necessary equipment for a person of Middle Bronze Age Jericho in the after-life, and it is reasonable to suppose that this had been their equipment during life. In these mass burials, the supply of food is communal, with jars of liquid, drinking-vessels, and platters ranged round the

Fig. 51. Jericho furniture

edge of the tomb, and a liberal supply of meat, usually in the form of roasted sheep, either jointed or entire. In the tombs in which only single burials had been made at a time each burial had probably been accompanied by food. With family groups was placed family furniture (Fig. 51), of which the important item was a long, narrow table, made with two legs at one end and one at the other, in order to stand better on uneven ground. This in fact seems to have been the only universal piece of actual furniture. Most of the dead lay on rush mats, on which they probably slept and sat during life. In about a dozen tombs, additional items of furniture suggest that the family buried in them were more wealthy and that among the persons buried there were individuals of importance. The most striking is the burial shown on (Pl. 61). Here, the body in the centre of the chamber lay on a bed beside the table, which was found laden with joints of meat, removed before this photograph was taken. The legs

174

of both bed and table had collapsed during the early stages of decay. The other members of the family were more simply deposed round the edge of the tomb. Another bed can be identified, in a tomb which has an unusual feature of a platform of mud-bricks upon which one of the bodies was placed. In only three tombs were such platforms found; that important and rich individuals were placed upon them is suggested by the evidence from one of them that the tomb had been ransacked and the bones displaced in the search for objects of value, not generally found in the tombs. Even stools were not common, being found only in a maximum of ten tombs. The individual personal adornments were simple. With most of the bodies was a toggle-pin, usually on the left shoulder, showing that the garment was secured there, and most had a scarab, either on a bronze finger ring or suspended round the neck or from the toggle-pin; bead necklaces were rare. In a number of cases there were carved wooden combs by the heads, and in some cases in positions which suggested they had been in plaits; fragments of plaits were actually found. In most tombs a supply of toilet equipment was placed with each adult, consisting of a cylindrical juglet which probably contained oil, and often a basket holding little wooden boxes decorated with bone carvings, an extra supply of combs, an alabaster juglet for oil or scent, and in some cases a wig. In only a few exceptionally poor tombs was this provision omitted.[19]

The equipment was therefore simple, and we can presume that the equipment of most of the houses of Jericho at this time was simple. The furniture was skilfully made by good carpenters, but with little adornment. All the details are sufficiently well preserved for the reconstruction of a room in Jericho at this period shown on (Pl. 63) to be completely factual, the only exception being the clothes, for only fragments of textile were preserved. The date of the group of tombs which gives this evidence comes at the very end of MB II, in phase v, and the finds in them would therefore represent the furniture of the houses of which the destruction marks the end of Middle Bronze Age Jericho. It may be surmised that there was a serious epidemic which swept off whole families at a date so late in the life of the town that the tombs were never reopened for subsequent burials.

It is probable that the picture of Jericho at about 1600 B.C. is reasonably representative of that of many of the towns of Palestine, though the greater ones may have shown more signs of wealth. Jericho certainly was not wealthy. In all the tombs excavated, only

175

one contained any gold, five scarabs being mounted in this material, with, in addition, a simple gold bracelet. At Tell Ajjul there was much greater wealth, with quite a number of gold bracelets, torcs, pendants, and toggle-pins coming from this period and the beginning of the following one.

The culture of Middle Bronze Age Palestine was largely individually Palestinian. As we have seen, the people who brought it came from Syria and were mainly Canaanites from the Phoenician coast. By the beginning of MB II a distinctively Palestinian version of the culture had grown up, as can be judged from a comparison of the finds with those of Syrian coastal towns such as Ras Shamra; the pottery for instance is related but not identical. With inland Syria the links thereafter were much slighter. There is no doubt an appreciable amount of Egyptian influence. Under the Twelfth Dynasty, Egypt re-established some sort of control over the Syrian coast, as is shown by finds at Byblos and Ras Shamra. Evidence of this in Palestine is slight, a Twelfth Dynasty funerary statuette at Gezer and a few Twelfth Dynasty scarabs, but it is to be presumed that tribute was demanded from the rulers of at least the more important towns. During the Hyksos rule in Egypt, contacts between the Asiatics there and those who had set up a comparable ruling aristocracy in Palestine were probably fairly numerous. Trade and economic contacts no doubt existed, for we learn of this both from Egyptian documents, including the famous Beni Hassan paintings showing Asiatics coming to Egypt, and also from Egyptian influence on local artifacts. The scarab is in origin Egyptian, and a few of Egyptian origin are found in Palestine, but the great majority are of local manufacture, with either simple pattern decoration or else blundered and uncomprehended versions of Egyptian hieroglyphs. The alabaster vessels resemble the Egyptian in form, but they are made out of a local stone. The wooden furniture at Jericho copies Egyptian types, but in much simplified style. But in all this Palestine was undoubtedly the poor relation. To the mixture the coming of the Hyksos chieftains added little. From the material remains one would never deduce the setting-up of a new ruling class, with its alien Hurrian elements, if it were not for the appearance of the new type of fortification.

The picture of Palestine at this time is of especial interest in that it provides the background for the beginning of the biblical story. It is highly probable that the period of the Patriarchs is to be placed in the Middle Bronze Age, and that the Israelites were the descendants of Ḫabiru groups that entered Palestine from northern Syria at this time. The traditional character of the Book of Genesis, built up of long-transmitted oral legend, makes any exact chronology impossible. The suggestion that Amraphel of Genesis is to be identified as Hammurabi of Babylon, whose reign is now dated *c.* 1793–1750 B.C.,[20] has no historical foundation. It is in fact highly improbable that a semi-nomadic tribal chief, which is the aspect given by the Book of Genesis to Abraham, could have taken on a group of kings including the ruler of the most powerful kingdom of Mesopotamia. From the evidence of their customs and laws, it is clear that the groups in question had been in contact with the Ḫurrians, for similar customs appear in the Mari documents of about 1700 B.C. It is certain that one cannot build up a chronology on the spans of years attributed to the Patriarchs, nor regard it as factual that Abraham was seventy-five years old when he left Harran and a hundred when Isaac was born, or that Isaac was sixty when Jacob was born and that Jacob was a hundred and thirty when he went into Egypt, for the evidence from the skeletons in the Jericho tombs shows that the expectation of life at this period was short. Many individuals seem to have died before they were thirty-five, and few seem to have reached the age of fifty. The biblical figures only reflect the veneration felt for the tribal ancestors, to whom tradition came to ascribe great years and wisdom.

But though an exact chronology is impossible, the setting of the period reflects that recorded in the biblical story. The Patriarchs were semi-nomadic pastoralists, moving into the more fertile coastlands, and living in their tents among, but separate from, the Canaanites living in the towns of the type which archaeology reveals. Pastoralists in their tents leave no evidence which archaeology can recover, but we now know something of their surroundings.

A convenient date for the end of the Middle Bronze Age is the rise of the Eighteenth Dynasty in Egypt in 1567 B.C.,[21] when Egypt drove back the Asiatics and began to recover her control over Syria. Punitive campaigns driving back the Hyksos into Palestine are recorded in Egyptian documents. Both Tell Beit Mirsim and Jericho were violently destroyed at about this time, probably by such campaigns, and were not reoccupied for many years. Hazor and Shechem were destroyed, and the succeeding occupation was slight, and there was possibly even a complete gap. Other towns, such as Megiddo, were destroyed, but occupation is immediately resumed. This revived occupation exhibits the same character as the preceding. New foreign elements may have arrived with the mixed Asiatics driven out of Egypt, but there is little material evidence of this. Canaanite culture continues into Late Bronze Age Palestine.

Notes

1. Mrs Amiran does not agree with the sharpness of the division (*IEJ* 10), but I am not convinced by her arguments.
2. Kenyon, *Amorites and Canaanites*, Schweich Lectures, 1963 (London, 1966).
3. F. Petrie, *Ancient Gaza,* II (London, 1932).
4. Called by Albright MB IIa, since he calls the Intermediate Early Bronze–Middle Bronze Period MB I.
5. Since earlier editions of this book were written, excavations have been carried out here under the direction of M. Kochavi by the Institute of Archaeology of the University of Tel Aviv.
6. *IEJ* 22, *IEJ* 23.
7. K. M. Kenyon, *Jericho* I, II (1969, 1965), published by British School of Archaeology in Jerusalem.
8. *Levant* I, pp. 25–60.
9. *Megiddo* II, Fig. 378.
10. With a proviso that this is the lowest level reached in excavations in this area, and it is possible that the gate belongs to the Early Bronze Age.
11. It is probable that the whole of the fill in *Lachish* IV, Pl. 96, from 6 feet in fact represents the MB bank, for in ibid., Fig. 4, it is clear that from that level upwards there is an appreciable quantity of MB material, mixed with earlier sherds from derived deposits. From the section it also appears very probable that the great revetment is the equivalent of the revetment at Jericho, for though the line was used in the Iron Age, it is clear from the account in *Lachish*, III, p. 89, that there must have been patching of an earlier line. The pocket behind this wall in the section may represent an earlier stage, as at Jericho.
12. *QDAP* X.
13. *Ancient Gaza* I, p. 11.
14. F. Petrie, *Beth-Pelet* I (London, 1930), p. 16.
15. *AASOR* XVII, pp. 27 ff.
16. For full description, see Kenyon, *Amorites and Canaanites*, pp. 65–72.
17. Proponents of another school of thought claim that the Ḫabiru did constitute a true ethnic group, and that the reason that non-Semitic names are found among them is that some Ḫabiru adopted the names of the peoples among whom they settled. Moreover, other schools are not satisfied that Ḫabiru and Hebrew are equivalent. There are in fact many uncertainties, but the foregoing explanation appears to be the most satisfactory.
18. Those on the left-hand side of the plan (Fig. 50) were excavated during the 1930–36 excavations, and were called the Palace Store-rooms. Further investigation has shown that they were not associated with the so-called Palace, and were ordinary private houses.
19. For a full classification of burial characteristics see *Jericho* II, pp. 566 ff.

20. S. Smith, *Alalakh and Chronology* (London, 1940). Other scholars hold divergent views as to the exact dates, but nearly all agree as to the general period.
21. In the chronology accepted in the revised edition of the *Cambridge Ancient History*.

8   The Late Bronze Age
and the Coming of the Israelites

In about 1567 B.C. the one hundred and fifty years of domination of Egypt by the Asiatic Hyksos came to an end with their expulsion by the first kings of the Eighteenth Dynasty. This event had a twofold repercussion on Palestine. In the first place, the expelled groups were thrown back on Palestine. Some, or even the majority, must have settled there. In so doing they would add to the mixed racial elements which probably settled there in the preceding period. One would have expected them to have brought a considerable amount of Egyptian culture, for just as in Palestine the invaders, as we have seen, adopted the native Semitic culture, so in Egypt they became to a large extent Egyptianized; but of this there is no great archaeological evidence. Secondly, the Egyptian rulers proceeded to reassert their empire over Palestine and Syria. This probably did not amount to more than punitive campaigns, and did not, any more than under the Twelfth Dynasty, imply a close political control. Archaeology does, however, provide two types of evidence for the new state of affairs, that of the destruction of cities which may reasonably be ascribed to Egyptian campaigns, and the evidence of trade contacts showing the increased connections between Palestine and the rest of the eastern Mediterranean.

There is no direct evidence to show how quickly Egyptian authority in Palestine was reasserted. There may have been a series of campaigns over a period of twenty years or so. A number of Palestinian sites show a break which must, from the pottery chronology, fall within the period 1600–1550 B.C., and which may reasonably be ascribed to conquest by an Egyptian army.

It is, unfortunately, relatively rare for literary evidence from Egyptian records and archaeological evidence from stratification and finds to combine to produce a firm chronology. There has been considerable vagueness in defining the characteristics of Late

Bronze Age pottery in chronological terms, largely owing to the inadequate methods with regard to exact stratigraphy by which many of the most important sites were excavated. One major source of error was in the use of Egyptian objects such as stelae and scarabs without assessing the true significance of the find-spots. Of this, the excavation of Beth-shan was an outstanding example, with derived or displaced objects used to give too early a date to the other associated objects, especially pottery. The second source of error is exemplified by Megiddo, where tombs within the town site were only recognized when the floor of the chamber was reached, and the finds in the tombs were then assigned to the stratum reached by the tombs, instead of to the higher level from which the shaft had been cut. To establish the true chronology of these Late Bronze sites it is necessary to build up a corpus of pottery that form recognizable assemblages. The starting-point for this is sites on which there is an absolute break at the end of the Middle Bronze. This could be due to Egyptian campaigns at the beginning of the Eighteenth Dynasty, of which the first ruler, Amosis (1570–1546 B.C.), captured the Hyksos capital Avaris early in his reign. Probably more far-reaching would be the activities of the Asiatics displaced from Egypt, in efforts to find new homes in western Asia. Evidence of destruction from these causes comes from a number of sites, but those that were not immediately reoccupied provide what is useful, for pottery and other objects not found in the preceding MB levels can be taken as the first group belonging to the succeeding period.

The two sites that provide unequivocal evidence of such a break and abandonment are Tell Beit Mirsim and Jericho. Both were destroyed, and neither was reoccupied for an appreciable period. At the former site the remains of Stratum D were found to be covered by a layer of ashes, and the succeeding town C was laid out on new lines and a changed orientation. The new town can be dated to about the middle of the 15th century B.C.; that is to say, there was a break in occupation of about a hundred years.

At Jericho, the evidence for the destruction is even more dramatic. All the Middle Bronze Age buildings were violently destroyed by fire. The stumps of the walls are buried in the débris collapsed from the upper storeys, and the faces of these stumps and the floors of the rooms are strongly scorched by fire. This destruction covers the whole area, about 52 metres by 22 metres, in which the buildings of this period surviving subsequent denudation have been excavated. That the destruction extended right up the slopes of the

181

mound is shown by the fact that the tops of the wall-stumps are covered by a layer about a metre thick of washed débris, coloured brown, black, and red by the burnt material it contains; this material is clearly derived from burnt buildings farther up the mound. Such a layer represents a long period of erosion, and is typical of the fate of the mound when it was not occupied; material from the ruins on the surface is gradually carried down to the foot of the mound by violent winter rainstorms, after it had been made dry and crumbly by the heat of summer.

The stratigraphical evidence suggests in itself that there was a gap in occupation at Jericho. This is confirmed by a gap in the use of the tombs. Burials cease in all the tombs in the northern cemetery at the end of the Middle Bronze Age. There is a similar break in those in the western cemetery. But in the latter area, five were found to contain deposits belonging to the Late Bronze Age. At the time of their excavation, the pottery of the 16th and 15th centuries B.C. in Palestine was not well known, and it was not realized that this was missing both in the tombs and on the tell.[1] Moreover, the stratification of the tombs was not understood. The process by which earlier deposits were mounded up round the edge, described above, resulted in Middle Bronze Age objects being on the same absolute level as those of the Late Bronze Age inserted in front. Therefore the layers seemed to show an actual intermingling of and transition between the characteristic pottery forms of the two periods. When the material is analysed in the light of our present knowledge, it becomes clear that there is a complete gap both on the tell and in the tombs between *c.* 1560 B.C. and *c.* 1400 B.C.

On the basis of the Tell Beit Mirsim and Jericho evidence, a corpus of pottery groups has been built up which enables general comparisons to be made between sites, so that phases in their histories can be fitted into the general picture. It must of course be accepted that there can be variations and time-lags in the appearance of new pottery types on different sites, so that all that can be claimed is general and not exact contemporaneity.

The first phase of the Late Bronze Age is marked by the appearance of pottery types not found in the Tell Beit Mirsim and Jericho MB groups, notably bichrome ware with elaborate patterns, Cypriot **Black lustrous wheel-made juglets and monochrome vessels,** and truncated dipper juglets,[2] and the continuance of Middle Bronze Age forms such as cylindrical juglets. The assemblage is taken as Group A, with Megiddo Tomb 1100 as the type group.[3]

In Group B, most of the same forms are found, but though vessels with linear bichrome decoration continue, there is a marked decrease in vessels with elaborate patterns in bichrome and in cylindrical juglets, whole Cypriot Basering I ware is common and White Slip I ware appears. The type groups are Megiddo Tombs 77, 1145,[4] 3015, 3018, 3005,[5] and Hazor Cistern 7021 and Cistern 9024 Stratum 3.[6] The importance of the Megiddo tombs is that there can be shown to be a break at Megiddo following the period of these tombs, covering most of the 15th century B.C.[7] The long siege and destruction of Megiddo by Thotmes III in 1470 is one of the best-documented links of a Palestinian site with fixed chronology, and it seems a very reasonable assumption that the break can be fixed at this date. A most valuable point in the dating of pottery groups can thus be suggested.

Group C is taken as the pottery associated with Lachish Temple I.[8] In considering this, only the deposits undoubtedly associated with the earliest temple have been used, the deposit found on the earliest altar[9] and the pits definitely beneath Temple II, and therefore belonging to the lifetime of Temple I. These groups cover a period not long after that of Group B, for many of the same forms continue. There is, however, a complete absence of bowls with elaborate bichrome decoration.[10] New types that appear are White Slip II milkbowls and the Late Bronze type of dipper juglets with pointed base. A terminal date for the group is given by the find of a plaque of Amenophes III (1417–1379 B.C.) above the ruins of a wall of Temple I and beneath a wall of Temple II. The date of Group C is therefore likely to be 1475 or 1450 B.C. to *c.* 1400 B.C.

There is a very distinct break between Group C and Group D, and it is likely that there should be an intervening phase for which there are no satisfactory groups. The representatives of Group D are Hazor Tomb 8144–5[11] and Lachish Tomb 216.[12] In these groups, almost all the forms characteristic of Groups A to C have disappeared, with the exception of Basering I, which is still common in Lachish Tomb 216, possibly first used rather earlier than the Hazor tomb. The Late Bronze Age dipper juglets are exclusively found, with a more round-based type also appearing in Tomb 216. White Slip II milkbowls and Basering II vessels are very common, and also some imitation Basering jugs. Pilgrim flasks appear. The importance of Hazor Tomb 8144–5 is that a considerable number of Mycenaean vessels are found, all Mycenaean III A, and the majority late III A 2.[13] The date of transition between Mycenaean III A and III B is placed *c.* 1300 B.C., and the Hazor tomb, and with it Stratum I B of the lower town, is therefore to be placed in the second half of the 14th century. Yadin suggests[14] that the destruction of the town of Stratum I B is the work of Seti I (1318–1304 B.C.) in his Palestinian campaign at the beginning of his reign.[15] A general date for Group D could be *c.* 1350–1320 B.C.

This group brings us to the end of the period of the Eighteenth Dynasty. Group E consists of Lachish Tomb 1003, Megiddo Tomb 911, and the latest material associated with Lachish Temple II. It may cover the period 1325–1275 B.C. Group F consists of Hazor Cistern 9024 Stratum I; Megiddo Tombs 912 and 877, in both of which were Mycenaean III B vessels, and 989; Tell Fara Tombs 902, 936, both containing scarabs of Rameses II, 905, 914, both containing scarabs of Merneptah, 949, and 939. The date range should therefore be *c.* 1275–1230 B.C. Lachish Temple III probably comes within this period. A group that on pottery is distinctively later consists of Tell Fara tombs 934 and 960, both of which have scarabs of Rameses IV (1166–1160 B.C.). It presumably covers the first half of the 12th century, and includes types of vessels also found in the Tell Fara tombs that have Philistine pottery, so the date is not far from the appearance of that ware.

It is on the basis of the pottery chronology illustrated by this succession of groups that periods of occupation are assigned to the sites described in this chapter. A firm ascription is of course only possible if a reasonable number of vessels are assigned to phases in the history of a site and are adequately illustrated.

There was thus considerable dislocation of life in Palestine in the period following the end of Hyksos domination. Conditions are likely to have remained disturbed until the period of more intensive Egyptian control under Thotmes III after his campaign in 1479 B.C. Owing to the fact that some of the more thoroughly excavated sites have a gap at this period, our information is somewhat scanty. There are a number of other sites at which there was probably a break, such as that at Tell Beit Mirsim, but the evidence is either inadequately published or the levels of the period not yet fully exposed. Such sites are Gibeon (el-Jib), Shiloh, and Bethel. The publication of the recent excavations at Gezer is still in progress, but so far there is no evidence for occupation at the beginning of the Late Bronze Age, pottery from Groups A and B being absent, the earliest probably belonging to Group D. The important site of Shechem, also, has not apparently produced any evidence of the beginning of

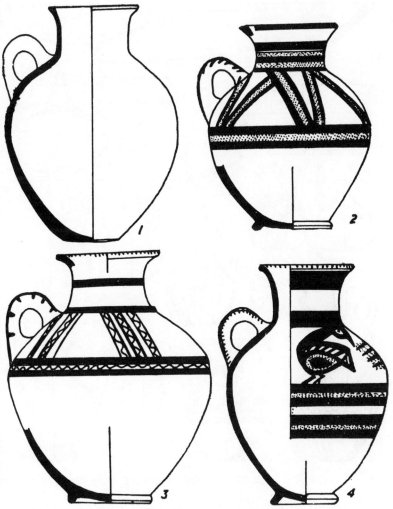

Fig 52. Group A pottery of the 16th century B.C. from Megiddo. ⅕

the Late Bronze Age. The best evidence for the beginning of the Late Bronze Age comes from Megiddo, for though the final Middle Bronze Age town was destroyed in the initial disturbances, it was rebuilt without a break. Associated with this rebuilding was the Group A pottery described above, which is illustrated on Figs. 52 and 53. The Megiddo evidence, however, requires a good deal of untangling. Stratum IX is that assigned to the 16th century, but a

185

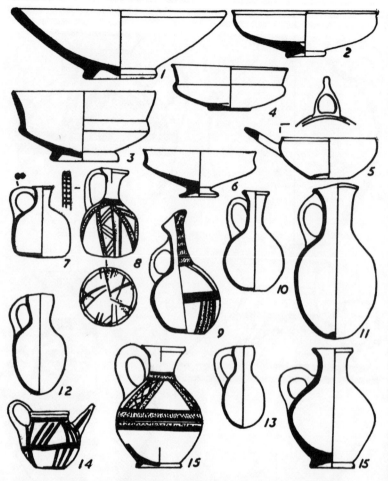

Fig. 53   Group A pottery of the 16th century B.C. from Megiddo. ⅛

good deal of Group A pottery, especially the fine bichrome jars, is published as coming from Stratum X. This is entirely derived from tombs and therefore really belongs to the overlying Stratum IX. Strata IX, VIII, and VII B apparently followed each other in rapid succession, without much change of plan, for it can be shown[16] that Temple 2048 belongs only to Stratum VII A. The pottery from the tombs which give dating evidence for these strata belongs mainly to Group A, but that of Group B begins to appear, with the Basering I juglets which appear first in the 15th century. The evidence there-

186

fore seems to fit nicely the interpretation that the last of the building stages, VII B (without Temple 2048), was destroyed in the campaign of Thotmes III in 1482 B.C. The annals of Thotmes record the long siege and complete destruction of the town.

The next event recorded in the principal excavation area BB was the construction of Temple 2048, of which the 14th-century date is clearly indicated by the pottery on its floor. A similar break is found in Area AA, where the fine gateway and adjacent 'palace' (Fig. 57) ascribed to Stratum VIII can also be dated to the 14th century B.C. Megiddo, therefore, was abandoned for most of the 15th century B.C. The Egyptian rulers may have felt it unwise to allow a town in so strategic a position to be reoccupied.

So far, the pottery types have been discussed only as providing a chronological framework, but they do also provide useful evidence about culture. The most striking point is the appearance of the bichrome painted pottery (Figs. 52 and 53), taken as diagnostic of Group A. The decoration is nearly always red and black, and the most typical vessels have a combination of metopes enclosing a bird or a fish with geometric decoration such as a 'Union Jack' pattern or a Catherine wheel. At Megiddo the first bichrome pottery is attributed to Stratum X, but all the published material comes from tombs intrusive into that level. It is in fact characteristic of Stratum IX. Similar pottery is found in great profusion in southern Palestine, and has even been ascribed to an individual potter working at Tell Ajjul. It may be too much to suggest that an individual potter was responsible for all the vessels found, but they may at least be ascribed to a well-pronounced school of potting. Very similar vessels are also found on the east coast of Cyprus and on coastal Syrian sites as far north as Ras Shamra.

The particular style referred to may be the product of a Palestinian school, but it is part of a larger complex of painted pottery, which started to reach Palestine in the 16th century B.C. It has certain affinities in style to Hurrian decorated pottery, and may be taken as evidence for renewed northern contacts, and probably the continuance of the infiltration of new groups from that direction.[17]

The second point of interest suggested by the pottery is the evidence for the opening-up of the Syrian coast to trade with the eastern Mediterranean. At first this trade was almost entirely with Cyprus. Cypriot imports during the Middle Bronze Age are rare, though they begin to appear towards the end of the period. But in the period covered by Megiddo IX, they become much more numerous, until during the Late Bronze Age almost as much pottery of Cypriot connections is found as that in the native tradition. As described above, there was also traffic in the reverse direction. It is clear that during the period of the strong rule of the Eighteenth Dynasty in Egypt conditions favoured maritime trade.

The third point of general interest shown by the pottery is that though there were the new elements which have just been described, the basic wares and forms continue throughout with only normal development. There is no break in culture, only the addition of new elements. This is probably a true indication of the racial position. From the period in the 20th century B.C. when the big changes in equipment appear that mark the beginning of the Middle Bronze Age, the basic Semitic Canaanite population, like its pottery, remains the same. New groups are absorbed, new rulers with alien names may establish themselves in the various towns, but the culture remains Canaanite though the race is no longer pure.

Megiddo has, as described above, provided the best evidence for a site that recovered rapidly after destruction in the 16th century, only to succumb to Thotmes III in the early 15th century. Its near neighbour, Taʻanach, likewise commanding the plain of Esdraelon, and equally powerful, seems to have had a similar history. Its destruction, like that of Megiddo, is recorded in the annals of Thotmes III, and there is a gap in occupation to late in the 14th century. Tell Ajjul, in southern Palestine, remained a town of importance throughout the 16th century during the currency of Groups A and B pottery, with the imposing public building 'Palace I', laid out when the town was founded towards the end of the Middle Bronze Age, still in use. Eventually it was destroyed and, with the defences, was covered by a thick layer of burning. This was probably the work of Thotmes III. It was probably reoccupied by the end of the 15th century, on the evidence of pottery belonging to Group C.

The evidence concerning Jerusalem is still very scanty. As described (p. 235), the site subsequently to be captured by David was fortified in the Middle Bronze Age. Very few occupation levels within the town have survived erosion and quarrying, and for the Late Bronze Age the only survivals were some terracing late in the period (p. 237). There is, however, evidence of occupation at the beginning of the period in tombs on the Mount of Olives, across the Kedron Valley from the town site. The majority of vessels in the large quantity of pottery found belongs to Groups A and B, but there were also objects belonging to the time of Groups C and D, probably to *c.* 1300 B.C.

There is also a number of sites in which there is evidence of recession in the 16th–early 15th centuries, but not complete abandonment. At Hazor, both the tell and the lower city continued in use into the Late Bronze Age, but apparently with a reduction in population. Only one tomb can be ascribed to Group A. A revival comes within the period of Group B, with more tombs and some important buildings, including a palatial structure on the tell linked with a great cistern, a rebuilding of the Site H temple above a MB predecessor and a shrine in Site C, cut into the rear of the MB rampart. It is, however, probable that Hazor suffered at the hands of Thotmes III, as there is a gap in the evidence so far published covering the period of Group C, down to *c.* 1400 B.C.

At Tell Duweir, there may have been a little occupation in the 16th century, for a fine bichrome crater was found in débris below the earliest of the Fosse Temples. The evidence is only of a slight occupation, the Late Bronze Age levels were barely excavated. Tell Fara was probably not fully reoccupied until the 13th century after the destruction at the end of the Middle Bronze Age, though five tombs containing pottery of Group B types showed that there was some slight occupation early in the 15th century. There is similar evidence of slight occupation in the 16th–15th centuries, but certainly less than in the Middle Bronze Age.

The towns of Palestine thus suffered a severe setback at the end of the Middle Bronze Age. Some took many years to revive after the initial disturbances. Others were severely hit by the campaigns of Thotmes III.

The best evidence of the beginning of a revival in the 15th century comes from Tell Duweir. Here the main clearance of the tell has not yet reached the levels of the period, but deposits and buildings belonging to it have been discovered in the Fosse at the base of the great Hyksos rampart. It would appear that after the end of the Middle Bronze Age, the ramparts ceased to be maintained in repair and the Fosse was allowed to fill with débris. This can be interpreted alternatively as a change of fashion in fortification, as a period of peace in which fortifications were not required, or a period of weakness within the city in which it was not possible to maintain them; only further excavation can show which explanation is likely to be correct.

This period of silting up of the Fosse, which may not necessarily have been a long one, was followed by the erection in it of a most interesting structure, a small temple, the first of three superimposed buildings on the same general plan. The exact foundation date is difficult to fix. The archaeological evidence points to approximately 1500 B.C., and it is possible that it should be placed after 1482 B.C., when the restoration of Egyptian control under Thotmes III would provide the peaceful conditions that an extra-mural building like this would seem to require. The temple continued in use down to about 1400 B.C., since a plaque of Amenhotep III was found in the filling between it and the immediately succeeding Temple II.

The temple was simple in plan (Fig. 54), consisting of an oblong sanctuary with two attached rooms, only one of which was entered from the sanctuary. It is notable that there was no inner room, or Holy of Holies, such as was required by the Hebrew religion, and has been found in much earlier Semitic sanctuaries. The roof had been supported on columns, probably of wood, of which the bases were found in position on the central axis. The entrance was screened by a wall which prevented a view into the sanctuary from the outside. The shrine consisted of a low bench, 1 foot high, from the front of which three rectangular blocks projected (Pl. 64). It is suggested that the cult objects stood on the bench, and that the projecting blocks served as altars. The existence of three projections suggests that a trinity of deities was worshipped. On the central axis in front of the shrine were two jars sunk in the floor, which may have been receptacles into which libations were poured, while against one end of the bench was found a great pile of vessels, abandoned when the temple was rebuilt, which had presumably served as containers of liquid and solid offerings. Outside the temple was found a number of pits used for the disposal of vessels which had served a similar purpose. There was also a low bench along one wall, which, on the analogy of the more numerous benches found in the later structures, may also have served for the deposit of offerings.

Unfortunately, little evidence was recovered to indicate the deity or deities worshipped in this temple or its successors. A statuette of Reshef, the Syrian god of war and storm, may suggest that he was among those worshipped, while one suggestion for the translation of the inscription on the Duweir Ewer found in Temple III (see below, p. 197) includes the name of the goddess Elath, apparently as part of a triad.

UPPER TEMPLE   MIDDLE TEMPLE   LOWEST TEMPLE

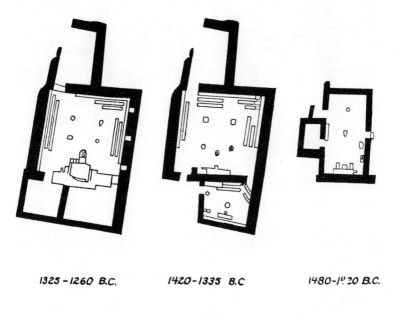

1325 – 1260 B.C.   1420–1335 B.C   1480–1ᵘ20 B.C.

SCALE

Fig. 54   Plans of the three successive temples in the Fosse at Tell Duweir

The main revival of the towns of Palestine must have begun to take place towards the end of the 15th century, for there were towns of importance by the time of the Amarna Letters, between *c.* 1390 and 1365 B.C. It is difficult to establish when these towns developed, for at this point the corpus of pottery which helps to establish chronology may have a gap. Group D is very distinct from Group C, which is based on the finds in the Lachish (Tell Duweir) Fosse Temple I, which certainly goes down to 1400 B.C. The date of Group D and that of later LB pottery is based on the evidence of imported Mycenaean pottery. The elaborate styles of form and decoration of this pottery have been closely studied by experts, who often can give much closer dates than can be claimed for ordinary Palestinian coarse ware. The deposits assigned to Group D contain Mycenaean III A to III A12 vessels and thus go down into the

191

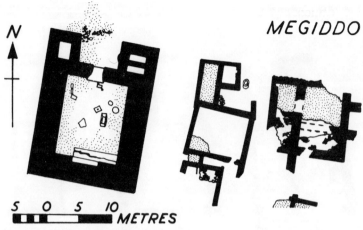

N

MEGIDDO

S   O   S   10
METRES

Fig. 55   Megiddo Temple 2048

second half of the 14th century, probably dating to *c.* 1350 to 1320 B.C. The evidence of Group D therefore cannot be used to pinpoint the levels associated with the towns of the period of the Amarna Letters.

The Amarna Letters are a series of documents discovered at the site of Tell el-Amarna, in the Nile Delta, in the palace of the Pharaoh Akhenaten. They provide contemporary evidence for the break-up of the Asiatic empire re-established by Thotmes III. The Amorite cities of northern Syria were in revolt, largely instigated by the Hittites, and their example was followed by the Canaanite cities of the south. Either as cause or effect, among the revolting cities appear bands of Ḥabiru, a name which, as suggested above (pp. 167 ff.), probably in its broadest sense covers bands of wandering warriors of somewhat mixed origin, who might be expected to take advantage of times of trouble, and who would also stimulate such trouble. The letters are written by the rulers of those towns which remained faithful to Egypt, notably Jerusalem in the case of Palestine, asking for help against the rebels and invaders. As has already been mentioned, it is an interesting reflection of the racial elements which had settled in Palestine in the preceding centuries that some of these rulers have Hurrian names. The help was not forthcoming, and Egyptian control of Palestine was not re-established until early in the reign of Seti I (1318–1304 B.C.), though the Hittites, who took advantage of this weakness in the north, did not advance south of Galilee.

Excavation, as has been said, cannot pinpoint the stages in the history of the towns which are contemporary with the Amarna Letters. Disturbances caused by the Ḥabiru are not observable in the material remains. We have, however, ample evidence of active and flourishing communities for this second half of the Late Bronze Age.

Megiddo is one of the cities mentioned in the Amarna Letters, and the buildings which can be shown archaeologically to exist in the 14th century must belong to a town rebuilt before the time of the letters. The most striking is the temple in Area BB,[18] published as belonging to Stratum VIII, but certainly later than the other buildings ascribed to that stratum.[19] The interpretation of the history of this temple is a matter of considerable difficulty. It occupies almost exactly the position of successive cult centres and temples belonging to the Early Bronze Age, the latest of which was rebuilt in the EB–MB period, and may even have continued into the Middle Bronze Age, when it seems to form a focus round which the MB I tombs were concentrated, and it may also have been in use with a first building stage of the MB II buildings. Thereafter, the published plans show a strange hiatus until Temple 2048 appears on the plan ascribed to Stratum VIII. It is probable that the hiatus is filled by a succession of structures that have almost completely disappeared. In an early stage, these consisted of very irregularly arranged standing stones and rubble pavements, followed by a massive building of which only one wall fragment (4008) survives. The plan of Stratum IX shows the forerunner of Temple 2048, in the form of what are described as successive rubble pavements, of which the outline is that of the walls of 2048. The most probable interpretation is[20] that there was a thorough rooting-out of pre-existing structures in this area, leaving only the amorphous fragments just described. Into the featureless mound of earth so left were sunk the foundations of Temple 2048, consisting of a rubble packing about 1 metre deep (the so-called rubble pavements), then rubble footings, and finally a good ashlar superstructure, published on the plan of Stratum VII B.

The analysis of wall remains that has led to the conclusion that Temple 2048 is later than the buildings shown on the same published plans is confirmed by the pottery finds. Only one floor is firmly associated with the temple. On it was found a group of pottery vessels (Fig. 56) which certainly belongs to the 14th century B.C., comparable with that from Lachish Temple II, certainly later than 1400 B.C. (see p. 187). On the other hand, the buildings into which

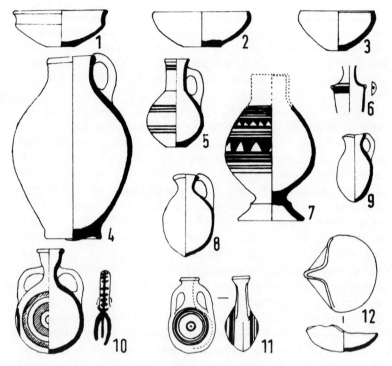

Fig. 56. Pottery on the floor of Megiddo Temple 2048

the temple foundations cut can be shown to belong to a date not later than the early years of the 15th century.

We can thus infer a complete gap in occupation at Megiddo following the Thotmes III destruction in 1482 B.C. It is tempting to make further inferences from the destruction evidence in this area. Very particular care seems to have been taken to root out all the material remains of the pre-existing cult centres, while the succeeding structures recognized the continuance of a sacred area. One can suggest as hypotheses that such a rooting-out was the expression of severe Egyptian reprisals, or that the builders of the reoccupation period disapproved of the deities to whom the area had previously been sacred, and therefore did their best to cleanse it before putting up their own cult centre. There is no evidence, and no adequate parallels to enable a conclusion to be drawn.

To this reoccupation stage belongs also[21] the construction of a gate in the north-west sector of the tell (Area AA), and an adjacent building on a grand scale (Fig. 57), which might justify the title of palace. The gate was approached at an angle by a sloping roadway, and had a triple-buttress plan which has a long history in the Middle Bronze Age. These architectural features are evidence of the stature of Megiddo in the 14th century. Probably to this period also belongs a treasure hoard, with gold-mounted and ivory objects found buried beneath the floor of the palace, but the stratigraphical evidence is inadequate.

Jerusalem, Shechem, Gezer, Lachish, and Hazor are all mentioned in the Amarna Letters. The lack of surviving evidence of the Late Bronze Age at Jerusalem has already been mentioned (p. 188). Excavation at all the other sites confirms the prosperity of these towns in the 14th century B.C.

One of the towns most deeply concerned in the plots and counterplots of the period was Shechem. Its ruler, Lab'ayu, seems to have controlled a large area and to have interfered in the affairs still further afield. He was the subject of many complaints to Pharaoh. Unfortunately in this instance archaeology does not supply supporting evidence. This is mainly because within the town excavations for

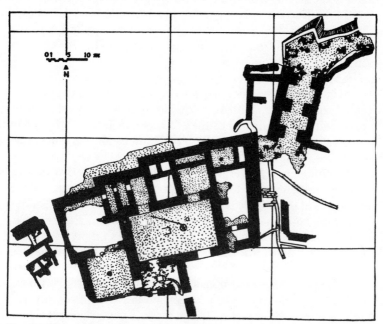

Fig. 57. Plan of Megiddo Area AA Stratum VIII

the most part have not penetrated below the Iron Age levels. It is surprising that there has been no satisfactory identification of defences of the period. A suggestion[22] that the fine orthostat gate on the east side should belong to the Late Bronze Age is not acceptable to the authors on the grounds that it was covered by the destruction débris marking the end of the Middle Bronze Age. This must presumably be accepted, though there are architectural and stratigraphical problems which do not seem to be solved. Further excavation, however, will probably provide Lab'ayu with a satisfactory capital.

These towns mentioned in the Amarna Letters probably reflect the political background in Palestine for much of the Late Bronze Age, with a considerable number of independent towns bickering among themselves. This bickering is probably as important an element in the troubled history of the period as the presence of the warlike Ḥabiru bands. The Ḥabiru no doubt profited a great deal from taking sides with one or other of the town rulers, and provided an excellent excuse for appeals to Pharaoh for help. It could well be that it was only this presence of wandering warlike bands that made this period different from the political history of much of the Bronze Age. In the Early Bronze Age, the time when most of the Palestinian towns originated, the towns were heavily fortified, and the fortifications were frequently destroyed and rebuilt. One can certainly deduce a prolonged period of inter-town tension for nearly a thousand years. There may have been greater centralization of control in the Middle Bronze Age, with a general use of the rampart type of fortification, but even this is not certain. As the towns recovered towards the end of the 15th century from the Egyptian campaigns, culminating with those of Thotmes III, they must certainly have rebuilt their defences.

It does happen, however, that the evidence for Late Bronze Age defences is rather slight. This may be in part due to the re-use of the great banks of the Middle Bronze Age defences, and upper features above these banks have often disappeared in erosion. For example, at Jericho the town probably refounded *c.* 1400 B.C. may have made use of the Middle Bronze Age rampart, but only a tiny fragment of that MB rampart survived subsequent erosion. At Hazor, the MB ramparts that enclosed the area of the Lower Town continued in use when the town revived from its recession in the 15th century B.C. With it was associated a rebuilding of the east gate, which provides a good example of the triple-buttress gateway.[23]

The best example of this type of gateway is found at Megiddo (Fig. 57), though its association with a contemporary town wall is uncertain. There is good evidence that this gate dates to the 14th century B.C.

At Gezer the Middle Bronze Age bank is cut into by a wall with towers that have been traced nearly the whole way round the tell. This the excavators date to the Late Bronze Age, but there are grounds for believing that it really is Hellenistic.[24]

The best evidence for the later part of the Late Bronze Age comes from temples, which provide interesting and important evidence concerning Canaanite religion. The best-known site is Beth-shan where there was a temple of the first half of the 14th century on the highest part of the citadel, which was succeeded by other temples and even eventually by a Christian church. The earliest temple, of Stratum IX, had a rather amorphous plan with a multiplicity of courts and altars and a *mazzebah*, or sacred pillar, which is a Canaanite representation of a deity. The Stratum VII temple, dating to *c.* 1300 to 1150 B.C., was quite different, being a smallish rectangular building with a partly roofed court and a raised sanctuary at the rear. The plan has a close resemblance to small Egyptian shrines of the 14th century B.C., particularly of the Amarna period. There was certainly strong Egyptian influence at Beth-shan, and probably an Egyptian garrison here from the time of Seti I. The finds, however, show that the cult was very mixed. Egyptian influence is shown by figurines of Egyptian goddesses, but the majority of the cult objects belong to Canaanite fertility cults. The deities worshipped included Ashtoreth and a storm god Mekal, probably connected with the Syrian Reshef.

If the plan of the Beth-shan Stratum VII temple is rightly connected with Egypt, it is interesting that temples of very similar plan have been found at Tell el Far'ah[25] and Tell Duweir.[26] There is no obvious reason to expect Egyptian influence at the former site, but it could be possible at the latter. An Egyptian temple within the town might help to provide an explanation for the three successive temples outside the walls, known as the Fosse Temples since they were situated above débris in the so-called Fosse of the Middle Bronze Age defences.

The earliest of these Fosse Temples, dating from *c.* 1480 to 1400 B.C., has already been described. The succeeding ones had the same basic plan, a single room with the roof supported on columns, and an altar at one end (Pl. 65). The main difference is in size, with a gradual

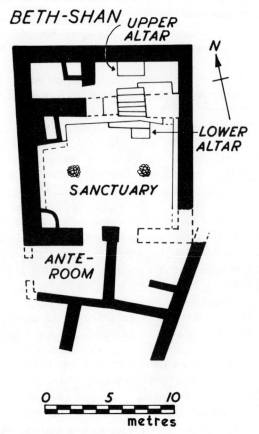

Fig. 58. Stratum VII Temple at Beth-shan

growth suggesting increased prosperity. Clearly here conditions were peaceful enough for an extra-mural temple to flourish. The offerings, too, suggest considerable wealth. They show some Egyptian influence, for instance in the faience, but not as strong as at Beth-shan. On the other hand, there are not so many objects suggestive of a purely fertility rite. The emphasis is certainly on diversity of religion.

This diversity is again accentuated at Hazor. No less than five temples or cult areas were found in the lower city and one on the tell. In some, the first building period belongs to the Middle Bronze Age, with a rebuilding ascribed to LB I; the published pottery, however, suggests strongly that they do not belong to the 16th century B.C., and probably belong to the revival later than the campaign of Thotmes III. Nearly all of them have a LB II reconstruction of 14th-century date. Two of the temples are of particular interest. The first is that in Area C. This is a small chamber, cut back into the rear of the MB rampart. The entrance was in a long side; opposite, backed against the rampart, was a semicircular niche (Pl. 66), on one end of which was a seated basalt statue 40 centimetres high, with adjoining it a row of ten basalt stelae, the tallest 65 centimetres high. The central one had carved on it two arms with hands stretched up towards a crescent beneath a disk. The statue also has a crescent on his chest. There can be little doubt that this was a sanctuary of the moon god.

The temple in Area H (Pl. 67) is more imposing; the structure is solid. The main component was a holy of holies 13·5 metres by 8·9 metres, with a rectangular niche opposite the entrance. In the earlier stages this main chamber was approached through a shallow porch, and outside the porch there was a number of rather irregular subsidiary installations with a great mass of animal bones, derived from the sacrifices, in the surrounding débris. The 14th-century temple was enlarged by the insertion of an inner hall between the porch and the main chamber. On the floor of the main chamber was found a rich collection of cult objects, an incense altar, libation tables, offertory table, kraters, and basins. None was in position, but they provide an excellent illustration of the equipment of a Canaanite temple. There are reasonable grounds for believing that it was dedicated to the storm god Hadad.

The temple on the tell[27] had the massive structure and oblong plan of the Megiddo temple already mentioned. A square temple, built over a double temple of the Middle Bronze Age, which has Assyrian parallels, has a parallel in a temple at Amman, dated to the end of the 14th century B.C. This Amman temple is interesting as showing that the general Late Bronze Age culture of Palestine had now spread across the Jordan, and it is also interesting in the evidence it has provided from the Mycenaean pottery found there of the extent to which trade with the Aegean had developed.

Hazor has thus provided evidence of a multitude of temples within the confines of one town, of the same or overlapping periods, and has shown that they may be of very different plans. The time may come when one can say that one plan is usually associated with a particular deity, but there is not yet enough evidence.

The archaeological picture on the whole suggests that the second half of the Late Bronze Age in Palestine is architecturally, artistically, and sociologically undistinguished. Closely built-up towns, such as Tell Beit Mirsim Stratum C, may show considerable urban vitality. They can of course also suggest that the whole population of a district preferred on security grounds to live within the defences of the local centre, from which the inhabitants issued daily to carry out their agricultural activities.

Archaeological evidence from relatively unimportant sites shows undistinguished town planning associated with undistinguished finds. Tell Beit Mirsim remains the best evidence for such a site. The site recovered *c*. 1450 B.C. from its 16th-century destruction, and

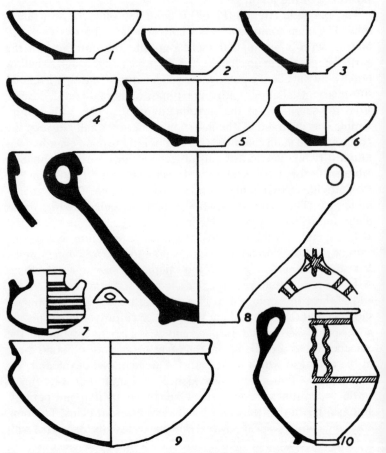

*Fig. 59. Pottery of Late Bronze II from Tell Beit Mirsim.*¼

there are two stages in the Late Bronze Age town. The pottery of the final LB town is illustrated on Fig. 59. All the forms are decadent and dull, and they include derivations of Mycenaean forms which appear in the 14th century B.C. An endearing example of the art of that period is a limestone libation tray from Tell Beit Mirsim (Pl. 68).

Places like Tell Beit Mirsim probably provide illustrations of the ordinary small town of LB II Palestine, but there was more luxury in the bigger towns. The temple offerings at Tell Duweir and Bethshan show many fine objects, some of them imported. Megiddo, as might be expected, had buildings of greater architectural pretensions, and its pottery is not so dull (Figs. 60 and 61). Most striking of all is the collection of ivories found in the ruins of the palace of the second phase in VII, which provide an indication of the cultural tastes at least of the ruling classes. These ivories, specimens of which are illustrated on Pls, 70–1, 73, were found in a small room, which it is suggested was a treasury, broken and disordered possibly when articles in precious metals were looted. They must originally have formed the decoration of furniture, but since the room was too small to have contained the furniture, they must have been stored for their own sake, as a collection of *objets d'art*. A model pen-case carried a cartouche of Rameses III, which shows that the collection was still being added to in the 12th century B.C., while the oldest object may go back to the 14th century B.C. They represent an art of which specimens are found in Egypt, Cyprus, and Phoenicia, and show that Megiddo at least was in contact with the best artistic life of the period. Megiddo, therefore, though it may have had its share in political disturbances, was not submerged in the increasing tide of barbarism.

Beth-shan too may be expected to exhibit a higher degree of civilization, for it too was a very strong city, and was moreover in close contact with Egypt. Here, however, our knowledge from excavations is confined to a more limited area, that occupied by the succession of temples, described above. The contacts of the city with Egypt, and the control exercised there by that country, are indicated by the finds of scarabs and other objects, dating, in the levels examined, from the time of Thotmes III, and of stelae set up there by Seti I (1328–1304 B.C.) and a statue of Rameses III (1198–1166 B.C.). There are also fairly frequent references to the site in Egyptian texts. At Beth-shan there is, within the area excavated, no indication of the destructions which affected other sites. The

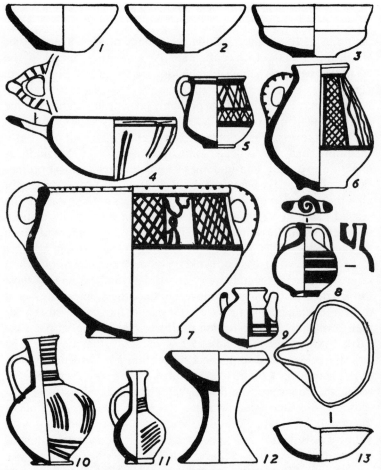

Fig. 60. Pottery of Late Bronze II from Megiddo. ¼

Egyptian garrison apparently maintained here at least from the time of Seti I, must have been sufficient to protect the city from the troubles of the time.

The stelae of Seti I set up at Beth-shan provide an interesting record of what was happening. Seti was the first king to restore Egyptian control in Palestine after the disasters of the Amarna period, and he clearly had to deal with a number of marauding and raiding bands. It is recorded in a stela set up at Beth-shan in the first year of his reign (1318–1317 B.C.) that bands from across the

202

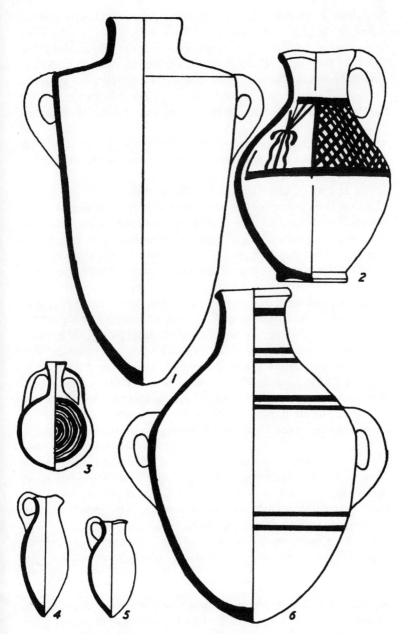

Fig. 61. Pottery of Late Bronze II from Megiddo. ¼

Jordan were attacking Beth-shan and neighbouring towns, and his defeat of them is described. In another stela, unfortunately only partly decipherable, the defeat of 'Apiru from the 'Mountains of the Jordan' (the last word uncertain) is apparently described. As has already been said, the equation 'Apiru-Ḥabiru-Hebrew is accepted by many scholars, and thus we here have evidence of bands allied to the Ḥabiru of the Amarna Letters still causing trouble. Whether we have here the other side of the story of the biblical account that the tribe of Manasseh failed to capture Beth-shan there is not yet sufficient evidence to say, but it is not impossible that there is a connection.

The results of the excavations just described have shown the effect on the country of the nomadic invasions of which we have historical evidence from the 14th century onwards. All but the very strongest cities suffer from one or more waves of destruction, and whether or not the destructions are followed by the settlement of some of the nomads, prosperity and culture inevitably decline. Egyptian control of the great land route was maintained sufficiently to ensure more settled conditions, and a resulting greater degree of civilization in the cities along it, and further evidence that even the backward and disturbed conditions of the interior did not prevent trade connections with the Mediterranean area, is given by the large amount of imported Cypriot and Syrian pottery found on all sites.

This LB II Palestine is the country in which the Israelites settled. Archaeology provides surprisingly little evidence of their entry into Palestine just as it provided little for the events of the Ḥabiru scourge earlier in the 14th century. Though many but not all linguistic scholars accept the equivalence of the words Hebrew and Ḥabiru, few would now claim that the events recorded in the Amarna Letters represent the arrival of the Israelites. All that can be claimed is that they may belong to the same general group and that like the Ḥabiru they consisted of groups which made a nuisance of themselves to the Canaanite occupants.

For the chronology of the entry of the Israelites we are entirely dependent on archaeology, for there is no reflection of the events described in the Book of Exodus in Egyptian records. The only help we can get is a suggestion of a suitable historical setting. In interpreting the biblical account, one must realize how this account was compiled. The early books of the Old Testament were probably not written down in their present form until the 10th or 9th centuries B.C. There may have been some earlier written versions, but basically they were dependent on oral traditions handed down independently in the various tribes and clans. Oral traditions are notoriously unreliable about chronology. To attempt to produce a chronology covering a period of several hundred years by adding together the different spans of thirty or forty years mentioned in the Bible is just waste of time, as is shown by the different results reached to fit in with various theories. There is also the difficulty that the early books of the Bible are a compilation from a number of tribal traditions, in which the editor has tried to mould them all into a consecutive account of the movements of what by that time was thought to have been a whole people. The all-important aspect of this was that this redaction made it appear that all the tribes took part in the Exodus and shared in the great religious experience in Sinai, when Yahweh revealed himself to his people.

It is in fact probable that the tribes that settled in Palestine had a varied background. This is a matter of literary and textual criticism, and this book, concerned with archaeology, is not the place to discuss it. The broad conclusions which seem to me to be the most acceptable (but there is disagreement among scholars) is that there were three main groups of proto-Israelites. The first, found in the north of the country and Transjordan, probably did not go down into Egypt at all. The second and third went down into Egypt, but two separate Exoduses can be inferred, one an expulsion-Exodus, in which rebellious Asiatics were driven out, entering Palestine from the south, and the second or flight-Exodus, in which ill-treated Asiatic slaves escaped from forced labour and journeyed across Sinai and up the desert fringes of Transjordan in the leisurely semi-nomadic way of life of not far-distant ancestors. These tribes would have entered Palestine from the east and it would have been this group that had the great religious experience on Sinai. Such a flight-Exodus fits best in Egyptian history during the reign of Rameses II (1304–1237 B.C.), the only suitable period when the capital was in the Delta, whence the Israelites under Moses could, *c*. 1260 B.C., have fled from the forced labour of building Pi–Ramses.

It is at this point that one must see what archaeological evidence can be found. While one can now discount the simplistic biblical account of immediate and wide invasion, what one might expect to find is the destruction of some towns and villages and either abandonment or a reoccupation showing evidence of the presence of bearers of a new culture.

One must, however, abandon immediately the hope of discovering evidence of the appearance of a new culture. In point of fact at no single moment in the archaeological record can one say that the Israelites have arrived. This must reflect the nature of the culture of the immigrants. Migratory bands, whether of the Ḥabiru of the Amarna Letters or of the Israelites of the Old Testament story, would be most unlikely to have a large equipment of durable material objects. Their containers may well have been mainly of skin, they would lack house furnishings or ornaments or experience in architecture, their places of worship would have been temporary and have had little in the way of fitments. History and archaeology show again and again how such bands, coming amongst a settled population, tend to adopt the material culture (which alone is reflected archaeologically) of the population. This must be the case wherever within this period 1400 to 1200 b.c. one puts the arrival of the Israelites, for there is no complete break within the period. The biggest change does in fact occur at the beginning of the period, with the deterioration in culture, marked for instance in the pottery, of the transition from LB I to II. The situation as described above could reflect the state of affairs during the acclimatization to settled life of wanderers such as the Ḥabiru bands of the Amarna Letters and the Israelites of the Old Testament. It is not, however, possible to deduce on the existing evidence any spread of conquest or, on grounds of material remains, to say that at any one time a certain district fell under the control of invaders.

For the entry from the south, which clearly emerges from a dissection of the literary account, and which, it has been suggested, is associated with an expulsion-Exodus, archaeological corroboration can be claimed from the evidence of the destruction of towns. The best-documented destructions in the second half of the 13th century b.c. are those of Tell Beit Mirsim and Tell Duweir. At the former site, Stratum C is divided into two phases, both ending in a destruction. Stratum C 2, starting about 1350 b.c., was a typical LB II town, with the characteristic uninspiring material culture. It came to an end with a particularly violent destruction which Professor Albright dated to 1230 b.c. At Tell Duweir, the third of the Fosse Temples came to an equally violent end, and soundings on the tell showed that the city met with the same fate. 1230 b.c. is also suggested for this destruction, after which the city lay in ruins for some time.

These destructions could well be the work of Israelites thrown out of Egypt. The presence by this time of groups recognizable as Israelites is indicated by the Merneptah stele. This is dated to 1230 and describes the triumphs of Merneptah's expedition into southern Palestine. Among the lists of conquered towns and people appears the name Israel in a grammatical form which suggests that the reference is to a people not yet settled. There are, however, other historical events which could account for the destruction. They might have taken place in connection with Merneptah's punitive raid itself. About 1190 B.C. there was the incursion of the Peoples of the Sea, and either these newcomers intent on acquiring a foothold in Palestine or Egyptian expeditions under Rameses III aimed at chasing them out could have been responsible.

Whoever was responsible for the destructions, they are an indication of unsettled conditions which would be favourable to the infiltration of new groups. The progress of this infiltration was gradual and the biblical evidence shows that it was halted by the line of strong Canaanite cities of Jerusalem—Ajlun—Gezer. Until David welded all the tribes into the United Monarchy, these tribes entering from the south remained to the south of this line. The archaeological evidence only shows that there was no sudden change in material culture. Tell Beit Mirsim is here again useful. The town of Stratum C is succeeded after the destruction by that of Stratum B with no noticeable changes, and only gradually during the next three hundred years do features in buildings and pottery emerge which were to be characteristic of Iron Age Palestine.

The biblical story of the entry from the east is given much more prominence than that from the south, for to the Israelites the Sinai story was of such outstanding importance that it came to be regarded as part of the history of all the tribes. The Book of Joshua gives an account of the crossing of the Jordan, the capture of Jericho, the destruction of 'Ai and Hazor, and a rapid conquest of the whole country under the leadership of Joshua. Archaeology has much to contribute on this subject, though reconciliation with the biblical record is difficult.

The capture of Jericho might certainly be expected to come early in any penetration with Palestine from the east. The description of the capture in the Book of Joshua is so vivid and dramatic that it is tempting to believe it is the record, committed to writing probably after very many years, of a folk memory of an important event. In the 1930–36 excavations, it was believed that the walls destroyed by

Joshua had been found, and the date suggested was 1400 B.C. The 1952–58 expeditions showed that both these conclusions were wrong. The walls in question were Early Bronze, and pottery believed to be 15th century was in fact 14th century.

Middle Bronze Age Jericho had been destroyed by fire probably *c*. 1560 B.C., and during a subsequent abandonment the houses of the period were covered by a great wash of burnt material. Above this wash there was, in Square H III excavated in 1954, the scanty remains of a house, consisting of a single wall with about a square metre of floor beside it (Pl. 69); on the floor was a small clay oven with a juglet lying beside it. Over the rest of the area excavated the modern surface was below the level of this floor, as a result of continuing erosion. The 'Middle Building' excavated in 1930–36 probably belongs to the same period.

The pottery shows that these buildings are Late Bronze Age, and date to *c*. 1400 B.C. Almost no finds contemporary with the use of these rooms survive erosion. Pottery from the tombs, however, is more helpful. In the 1930–36 excavations, five of the Middle Bronze Age tombs were found to have been re-used in the Late Bronze Age. Among the pottery in them were some Mycenaean vessels that are probably to be dated to LM III A 2, 1375–1300 B.C. This is then probably the span of occupation of LB Jericho. It might have ended earlier, but is unlikely to have continued into the 13th century.

Evidence concerning the defences of this LB town is even more scanty. The paucity of evidence concerning LB defences has already been mentioned (p. 196), and it was suggested that many re-used the great MB ramparts. At Jericho, only a few metres of the wall surmounting the rampart survives, on the highest pinnacle of the tell. Any LB re-use has therefore vanished in erosion.

The evidence from the 1952-58 excavations at Jericho indicates that there was a LB town there in the 14th century which might have been that attacked by Joshua, but nothing survives to illustrate the biblical account. It also suggests that if this destruction, followed by some six hundred years of abandonment, was the work of the Israelite tribes under Joshua, it is not likely to have been later than *c*. 1300 B.C., which is difficult to reconcile with a flight from Egypt *c*. 1260 B.C.

In the Book of Joshua, the capture and destruction of 'Ai follows closely on that of Jericho. The site has long been identified with et-Tell, some 10 miles (15km.) north of Jerusalem. The editors of the account of the entry of the Israelites under Joshua have produced a consecutive story of countrywide conquest out of gradual infiltration and occupation which was only completed in the 11th century. Even if the destruction of 'Ai is to be interpreted as an isolated foray by the band that had captured Jericho, the archaeological evidence does not fit in with the biblical account. 'Ai, as identified with et-Tell, was a powerful city in the Early Bronze Age. It was thereafter abandoned. Excavations have produced only a slight undefended village of the beginning of the Iron Age, with two phases separated by a destruction which could possibly represent the site destroyed by the Israelites. The archaeological remains are unconvincing, and the chronological evidence not very satisfactory. Suggestions have been made that the events recorded really took place at the nearby site of Bethel, or may have been transferred to this prominent ruin for propaganda reasons.

As already mentioned, most of the rest of the spread of conquest as described in the Book of Joshua probably represents an editor's rearrangement of unrelated events into a tidy chronological sequence. The case of Hazor is different. Its geographical position would certainly associate it with an entry into Palestine from the east. Archaeological evidence also suggests a sequence of events similar to those shown by the archaeological evidence at Jericho, and the evidence is much better preserved.

The Late Bronze Age town of Stratum I B described above (p. 184) was violently destroyed somewhere about 1300 B.C., as part of Seti I's restoration of the Egyptian Empire after the troubles of the Amarna period. This seems a very reasonable hypothesis. The buildings, of which most of the evidence comes from the lower town, were then immediately rebuilt in Stratum I A, on the same plan, but with obvious indications of a less prosperous economy. The finds are very similar. An important difference, however, is that whereas in Stratum I B Mycenaean pottery is classified entirely as Mycenaean III A 2, down to *c*. 1300 B.C., the finds in Stratum I A include some late III A 2, but also a little III B. The stratum therefore goes down into the 13th century B.C. It could be as late as 1230 B.C. But the small quantity of this pottery, the closeness of the remains to those of Stratum I B, and the general resemblance of the finds suggest that the end of Stratum I A need not necessarily be later than *c*. 1275 B.C. The end was violent and its effects long-lasting. The whole city was destroyed by fire, which would agree with the biblical account. Thereafter, the whole site was abandoned. The lower city was never reoccupied, and the upper city, the original EB tell, was only a village until the time of Solomon.

The destruction of Hazor and Jericho, therefore, could form part of an entry from the east, but of a more gradual process than suggested by the biblical account, with the two events possibly separated by about twenty-five years. In this case, neither could be associated with the culmination of a flight from Egypt about 1260 B.C. If the destruction of Hazor is as late as 1230 B.C., as Professor Yadin suggests, this episode could fit the chronology that best suits Egyptian history. Jericho would therefore have to belong to a separate tradition, which is perfectly possible, and it would then be necessary to propose that there were three separate exoduses. It is clear that archaeology has not yet produced a full answer.

Notes

1. *PEQ* (1951).
2. K. M. Kenyon, 'The Middle and Late Bronze Age Strata at Megiddo', *Levant* I, pp. 50–1.
3. *Megiddo Tombs*, Pls. 45–48.
4. *Megiddo Tombs*, Pls. 41 and 49–52.
5. *Megiddo* II, all published as Area BB, Stratum VIII; see also Kenyon, 'The Middle and Late Bronze Age Strata of Megiddo', pp. 2–4.
6. Y. Yadin *et al.*, *Hazor* I (Jerusalem, 1958), Pls. CXXV–CXLII, and CXXII–CXXIV.
7. Kenyon, 'The Middle and Late Bronze Strata at Megiddo', pp. 59–60.
8. *Lachish* II.
9. ibid., p. 39.
10. A single elaborate bichrome vessel is published as associated with the temple, *Lachish* II, Pl. XLIX 256, but Miss Tufnell has stated that it really came from under débris beneath the temple.
11. Y. Yadin *et al.*, *Hazor* II (Jerusalem, 1960), Pls. CXXVIII–CXXXVIII.
12. *Lachish* IV, pp. 232–5.
13. V. M. Hankey, 'Mycenaean Pottery in the Middle East: notes on finds since 1951', *BSA* 62 (1967), p. 123.
14. *Hazor* II, p. 159.
15. *CAH* vol. II, ch. xxiii.
16. K. M. Kenyon, 'The Middle and Late Bronze Age Strata at Megiddo', *Levant* I (1969), pp. 25–60.
17. A study of this pottery has been made by C. Epstein in *Palestinian Bichrome Ware* (Leiden, 1966).
18. *Megiddo* II, fig. 402.
19. *CAH*, rev. ed., Vol. II. 1, ch. xi. *Levant* I (1969), pp. 36 ff.
20. *Levant* I, pp. 49–50.
21. *Levant* I, pp. 57 ff.
22. *CAH* II, Part 1, ch xi, p. 542.

23. Y. Yadin, *Hazor,* Schweich Lectures (London, 1972), p. 62, fig. 14.
24. *PEQ* (1977).
25. *RB* LXIV, fig. 8, p. 575.
26. Still (1979) in course of excavation.
27. Y. Yadin, *Hazor,* Schweich Lectures, fig. 26.

9 The Philistines and the Beginning of the Early Iron Age

About the year 1200 B.C. there was a catastrophic interruption in the civilization of the whole of the eastern Mediterranean, producing a Dark Age very like that following the end of the Roman Empire in Europe some sixteen hundred years later, and brought about by similar events, the incursions of barbarian groups. The great empires of the Near East all succumbed to or were severely shaken by these inroads. Palestine did not bear the full brunt, for it was not such a rich prey as the great empires, but its position as part of the land route between Asia Minor, which may have been the home of some of the invaders, and Egypt meant that some of the effects were felt there.

The tale of the attacks of the Peoples of the Sea upon Egypt is graphically described on the monuments of Rameses III. In their final and greatest attack, *c.* 1191 B.C., they came by land and sea. and were thrown back by the Pharaoh after great battles on both elements. Rameses claimed such a complete victory that he was able to drive through Palestine up into the lands of the Hittites in Syria, for their empire had been disrupted by the newcomers' advance. But in spite of this, he allowed the defeated tribes to settle on the Palestinian and Syrian coast, and it may be doubted if this would have been the case if his victory were as thorough as he claimed. At all events, the failure of the raiders to force their way into Egypt led to the settlement of some at least of them in Palestine.

The Egyptian records make it clear that the Peoples of the Sea were a composite group drawn from a number of tribes. The monuments of Rameses III at Medinet Habu (Fig. 62) mention six tribes, the Pulasati or Philistines, the Sherdanu, the Danunu, the Shekelesh, the Zakkala, and the Washasha, while other Egyptian lists add some eight more names. Archaeology has so far thrown little unambiguous light on the origins of these groups. Biblical

Fig. 62. Representation at Medinet Habu of Egyptians fighting the invading Peoples of the Sea

accounts associate the Philistines with Caphtor, which many scholars consider to be the equivalent of the Egyptian Keftiu, and identify as Crete. Philological studies suggest that the homeland of some at least of the groups was in the south-west of Asia Minor, while the equation proposed by some scholars of Danunu with Danaoi and Ekwesh (mentioned in the list of Merneptah) with Achaeans, brings us into contact with the tribes of the Homeric legend. Such archaeological evidence as exists is at least not discordant with such an origin.

It must once more be pointed out that archaeological evidence may in such a case be inadequate, for here again we are dealing with warlike bands. It is true that the Medinet Habu reliefs show the land invaders accompanied by women and children in ox-carts, and they therefore came as intending settlers and not as mere raiders. But even so, their material equipment must have been light, and they would have taken over much from the Canaanites among whom they settled, as indeed archaeological evidence suggests.

There is, however, one class of archaeological material which may reasonably be associated with the newcomers. This is a type of pottery, entirely new to Palestine, decorated with elaborate patterns. The most characteristic elements in the decoration are metopes enclosing stylized birds, very often with back-turned head, friezes of spirals, and groups of interlocking semicircles. The form of the vessels and the elements in the decoration all have their origins in the Late Helladic ceramic art of the Aegean. It has been shown that the closest parallels are in the pottery of Rhodes and Cyprus, but in almost no case are the Palestine vessels exact copies; the same elements are there, but they are differently combined. The originals from which the Palestinian types developed can be dated to the late 13th century B.C., while new fashions which were coming into use about 1200 B.C. are not represented. In the mixture, too, Egyptian elements are represented,[1] which may be accounted for by the fact that for centuries Shardans (Sherdanu) and others of the confederates had been in the habit of serving the Egyptians as mercenaries. The ware of the vessels does not differ from that of the native Palestinian pots. The conclusion which is thus suggested is that the newcomers did not bring this pottery with them, but manufactured it in Palestine in imitation of the vessels to which they were accustomed in their homeland, which they must have left before the new 12th-century style came into use. An exception may be Ashdod.

It cannot of course be accepted without question that this pottery is necessarily associated with the Philistines, but the evidence does seem to be strongly in favour of this ascription. It has just been shown that it must be dated to about 1200 B.C., while the historical date given for the repulse of the invaders by Rameses III is c. 1191 B.C. Secondly, the distribution of the pottery corresponds well with the area occupied by the Philistines. It is concentrated in the coastal plain and the borders of the hill country, which was the area of the primary Philistine conquests, while in the hill country proper it occurs only sporadically. Finally, archaeological evidence shows that it appears suddenly at the end of the Late Bronze Age on the coast, but rather later farther inland.

The archaeological evidence was first well illustrated at Askelon, which was one of the five chief cities of the Philistines. The site is a large one, with important Roman buildings in the later levels, and for the most part excavation did not penetrate below these levels. But a cliff face provided a section through the north edge of the central mound which revealed the strata belonging to earlier periods, and a cut was made through these successive strata. This showed a sharp-cut division at the end of the Late Bronze Age. A continuous layer of ashes, about 50 centimetres thick, indicative of a wholesale destruction, overlay a layer which was typical of the cosmopolitan culture of the period in Palestine, with finds showing Cypriot, Mycenaean, and Egyptian contacts. Above the ash layer these imports cease, and Philistine pottery and local derivatives appear. It thus seems very probable that the ash layer represents the destruction of the Canaanite town by the Peoples of the Sea, some of whom then settled on the site, and built their own city above the ruins. It is only at Askelon that such good stratigraphical evidence of an important Philistine city has been obtained, but in so far as the other cities, Gaza, Gath, Ashdod, and Ekron, have been identified and examined, the evidence produced seems to be similar.

The sequence of events suggested by this very limited investigation at Askelon has been confirmed by extensive excavations at Ashdod, another of the five main Philistine cities. Ashdod had been a flourishing Late Bronze Age town. It was founded late in the Middle Bronze Age, at the end of the 17th century B.C., and a number of references in the Ras Shamra archives show that its inhabitants were active in trade, with an emphasis on textiles, with that town in the Late Bronze Age. Late in the 13th century there was a destruction marked by a thick layer of ash. On several of the

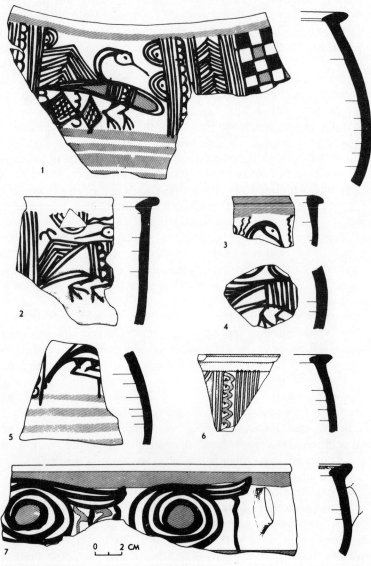

Fig. 63. Philistine pottery from Ashdod

excavated sites the occupation layer that succeeded this destruction remained Canaanite in character, but the foreign imports, Cypriot and Mycenaean, were lacking. The next stratum was fully Philistine. An interesting point is that in a few areas the first groups of new pottery types to appear can be identified as Mycenaean III C 1, *c*. 1200 B.C., of the type found in Cyprus, and some of the earlier settlers may have come direct from that island with their own pottery imports. The sequence, therefore, is close to that of Tell Beit Mirsim, and here again there is emphasis on the fact that a strong basic Canaanite element continued, upon which the Philistine influence was superimposed. The excavators record the continuation of ordinary Late Bronze Age pottery forms, though most of the illustrations are of the rich finds of Philistine pottery.

In most of the Ashdod areas excavated, three or four Philistine layers could be identified, which the excavator, Professor Dothan, suggests covered the period from early in the 12th century to the beginning of the 10th century. A sufficient area of these Philistine levels was excavated to show that it was a well-built town with a generous layout. The excavations did not, however, locate the Temple of Dagon to which the Ark of the Covenant was carried off (with unpleasant results to the inhabitants of the town) after the battle of Ebenezer. One area was identified as a probable cult centre, with a number of altars, but no formal temple plan was found. An attractive figurine type of a seated goddess depicted as merged with her throne could be evidence of the great Mother Goddess of the Aegean world, not yet absorbed into the Canaanite pantheon of Dagon and Ashtoreth which subsequently dominated Philistine religion.

Ashdod provides interesting evidence of the assimilation of the Philistines into the basic Canaanite population. The most obvious evidence is the pottery. By the 10th century B.C., there is a very clear mixture of late Philistine forms with local Canaanite elements, leading to Iron Age types specific to the Philistine areas, especially in vessels with hand-burnished red slip with decoration in black. Equally striking is the evidence concerning language and script. In the early Philistine levels were found seals in Cypro-Minoan script, which was presumably that which was in use among the newcomers. By about the 10th century B.C., the finds suggest that there was a transition to the use of the Hebrew-Phoenician script.

Most of the evidence has suggested that, as at Askelon and Ashdod, the Philistines seized and destroyed Canaanite towns, and

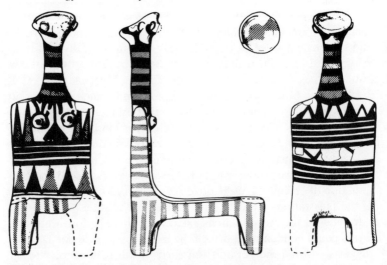

Fig. 64. Philistine Mother-goddess figurine from Ashdod

then built their own towns on the ruins. Excavations at Tell Qasile have, however, provided an illustration of a town founded by the Philistines in the 12th century B.C. which had no Canaanite predecessor. Tell Qasile is situated in the outskirts of the modern city of Tel Aviv, not far from the banks of the river Yarkon. Its period of importance was confined to the Philistine period, and after a destruction ascribed to David the occupation was slighter, though of a similar character. The most important part of the area excavated provided evidence of a succession of temples. Ample finds of cult objects and pottery mixed with layers of ashes and the bones of animal sacrifices show that these temples were Philistine cult centres. The successive buildings were found, in Strata XII, XI, and X (Fig. 65), with an attached smaller sanctuary (Fig. 65D) in Strata XI and X. Though the buildings grow in size and elaboration, the character remains the same. The essential feature is a platform at the end of the main hall, on which presumably the cult image stood. The other characteristic throughout is the lining of the walls with benches for offerings. One can presume that the religious observances allowed worshippers to enter the main hall to deposit their offerings. The practices must have been similar to those in use at Tell Duweir (p. 190). In fact, though the pottery found makes it certain that the inhabitants of Tell Qasile were Philistines, there is nothing that seems very alien to Canaanite Palestine.

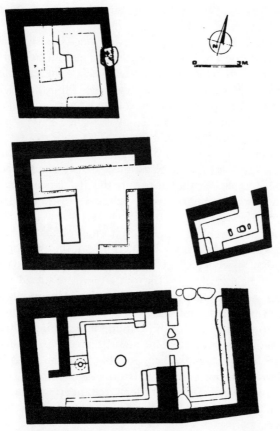

Fig. 65. Plans of temples at Qasile

It is in fact clear that not only did the Philistines usually occupy Canaanite sites, but they seem also to have taken over some part at least of Canaanite culture. The introduction of a distinctive type of pottery has been described. But associated with it in tomb groups and other deposits are other types which have developed directly from the native Late Bronze Age wares. Even the names of their chief gods, Dagon and Ashtoreth, seem to be Canaanite, but it is very possible that there has been assimilation between these and Aegean deities with similar attributes. It must, however, be admitted that archaeology has not yet given us a clear picture of the Philistines, for their important cities have as yet been

219

insufficiently excavated for any generalizations as to Philistine or non-Philistine traits to be made.

Some evidence of their burial customs does exist. At Tell Fara was found a group of five tombs which stand out both in contents and plan from others in the same site.[2] Their contents include some fine pottery vessels with characteristic Philistine decoration, together with many plain vessels of native Late Bronze Age types. There were a number of bronze bowls, while the typical weapons appeared to be daggers and spears. The majority of them was bronze, but there was an iron dagger with a bronze hilt, and a slightly curved iron knife. Such a knife was also found in the Stratum XII Qasile temple. We thus have here the first appearance of iron in Palestine in well-authenticated associations. In plan, the tombs are consistent. They are approached by a long, narrow, stepped passage or dromos, which enters the base of a trapezoidal-shaped chamber with markedly straight sides. In the centre of the chamber is a sunk well or passage, while, round the side, benches are left to receive the burials. At the rear of two of the tombs there are subsidiary, smaller chambers, again slightly trapezoidal in plan. The burials appear to have been extended, lying on their backs. These tombs are in strong contrast to the majority of those found in Palestine, which usually consist of one or more irregular rounded chambers. There is thus a suggestion of foreign influence, possibly from the Philistine homelands. Two of the preceding Late Bronze Age tombs at Tell Fara are the only ones which approach them at all nearly in plan and these again are cases in which there appears to be considerable Aegean influence.

Another interesting suggestion of foreign contacts was the discovery in two of these tombs of pottery coffins with anthropoidal lids (Pl. 72). These coffins are certainly not native to Palestine. They have, however, been also found at Beth-shan, and in Egypt examples are known from a number of sites. At Beth-shan, the dates of the burials of which they formed part appear to belong to Late Bronze II and Early Iron I. In Egypt they range from the time of Thotmes III (1501–1447 B.C.) to as late as 600 B.C. In Palestine one of the most striking finds is a cemetery beneath sand-dunes at Deir el-Balah[3] some 14 kilometres south-west of Gezer. The cemetery was a large one, but no trace has been found of an associated settlement. As well as burials in pottery anthropoid coffins, there are simple burials in graves. The faces of the coffins were exceptionally well moulded, and the offerings of bronze, alabaster,

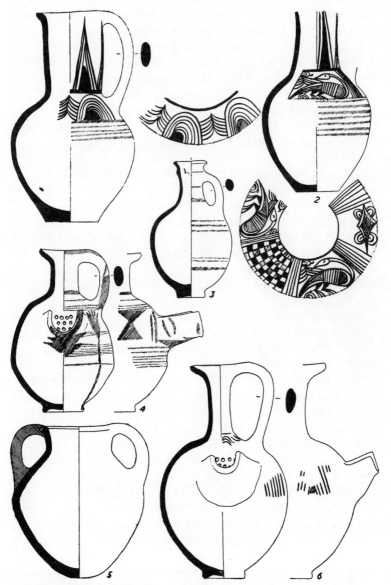

Fig. 66. Pottery from Philistine tombs at Tell Fara. ⅕

jewellery, and pottery are rich. The date is 13th century B.C. These burials, like nearly all with such coffins, both in Egypt and at Beth-shan, have Aegean and Cypriot objects associated with them. It is known on literary evidence that Shardan mercenaries were employed by the Egyptians, and they are specifically mentioned as forming part of the Egyptian garrison in Palestine at the period of the Amarna Letters. As the Shardans also were one of the tribes making up the Peoples of the Sea defeated by Rameses III, they may well have formed part of the group that settled in Palestine to which the name Philistine was applied by the Israelites, while a related group may have formed part of the Egyptian garrison of Beth-shan.

The area initially settled by the Philistines is difficult to assess on archaeological evidence. The appearance of a moderate amount of Philistine pottery on a site cannot of course be accepted as evidence of political control, for it might have been acquired in the course of trade. At Megiddo, for instance, a small number of typical sherds occur in both Strata VII and VI, too few, however, to suggest that the Philistines formed any substantial part of the population, for the importance of Megiddo is such that if it had come under their control, there would certainly be some literary reference to the fact.

Such exact evidence as there is suggests that an initial settlement on the coast was followed by a more gradual conquest of towns farther inland, up to the edge of the central ridge, which they never settled, though in the 11th century B.C. they exercised some degree of suzerainty over the Israelites there. The evidence comes from the relation of the appearance of the Philistine pottery to the termination of the 13th-century Cypriot and Mycenaean imports, which has been described above and which must be ascribed to the disruption of trade caused by the movements of the Peoples of the Sea. At the coastal site of Askelon, as we have seen, the layer in which these Aegean imports occur is separated from that in which Philistine pottery first appears only by a layer of burning. Similarly, at Tell Jemmeh, another site near the coast, the succession again seems to be immediate. In the Shephelah, or low hill country, there seems, on the other hand, to be an intermediate phase. At Tell Beit Mirsim the typical Late Bronze Age imports are found in Level C2, destroyed towards the end of the 13th century. This town was immediately succeeded by another, belonging to Level B1, of which the estimated duration (it is admittedly only an estimate) was between fifty and a hundred years. In this level there were no foreign imports at

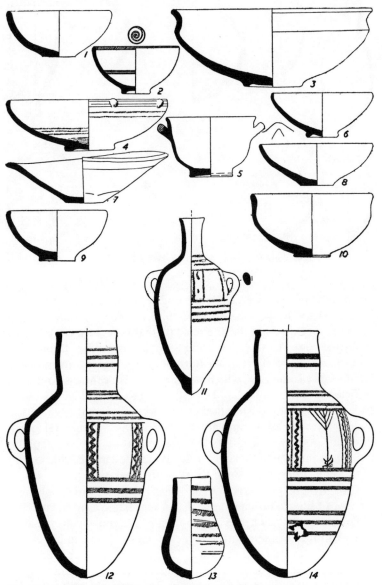

Fig. 67. Pottery from Philistine tombs at Tell Fara. ⅓

223

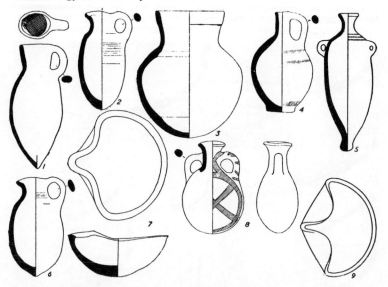

Fig. 68. Pottery from Philistine tombs at Tell Fara. ⅕

all, and the pottery represents the development of the native Late Bronze wares. In the succeeding level, B2, however, there is much Philistine pottery, and the site must by that time have come under Philistine control. At Ashdod the sequence is similar, though the time-span may be shorter. At Beth-Shemesh, again a town of the Shephelah, Stratum IV, which starts in the 15th century, continues sufficiently late to overlap Tell Beit Mirsim B1. This stratum is ended by a general destruction of the city, covering the whole site with a layer of ashes, and in the succeeding Stratum III much Philistine pottery appears. It may thus be that the expansion of the Philistines into the Shephelah, which is included in the biblical land of the Philistines, took some thirty to fifty years.

Though there is not exact archaeological evidence from a sufficient number of sites to provide more than a suggestion as to the process of Philistine expansion, the distribution of sites on which considerable quantities of their pottery appears does provide an indication as to their main area of occupation. The pottery hardly appears at all on the central ridge. It is not found at Jerusalem, Gibeah, or Beth-zur, while there is no more at Tell Nasbeh, some 9 miles (15km.) north of Jerusalem, than could be accounted for by trade. On the coastal plain and in the Shephelah it is found plentifully as far south as the Wadi Ghazzeh, on which are Tell Ajjul, Tell Jemmeh, and Tell Fara, while the distribution extends as far north as the neighbourhood of Jaffa, the ancient Joppa. But even within this area may have been enclaves which held out. No evidence of the Philistines, for instance, has been found at Tell Duweir and very little at the neighbouring Tell Hesi, but too much weight cannot at present be given to this suggestion since it is not quite certain whether either site was occupied at this period. Farther north, there is no trace of the typical pottery at Dor, in spite of the fact that there is literary evidence that it was occupied by the Sakkala, one of the kindred tribes of the Peoples of the Sea. Similarly, there is no trace of it at Tell Abu Hawam, at the foot of Mount Carmel, while, as has already been mentioned, at Megiddo there is a small amount, probably as a result of trade. At Beth-shan, though it was certainly a Philistine city in the 11th century in the time of Saul, there is none at all.

Thus the area of Philistine occupation was a limited one, though ultimately their political control extended considerably beyond this. For a hundred years or so they lived side by side with their Canaanite and Israelite predecessors. As has already been said, there is no archaeological evidence to decide which sites belong to which of these two groups. It is only on historical grounds, for instance the mention of the people Israel by Merneptah, that we know in fact that the Israelites were by now firmly established in the land, in two groups, divided by the Canaanite wedge round Jerusalem.

For this period, roughly from 1200 B.C. to 1000 B.C., Palestine was divided, though in a rather fluid and shifting manner, into three spheres of influence, that of the Philistines, just described, that of the surviving powerful Canaanite towns which for the time being withstood the pressure of Philistines and Israelites alike, and that in which the Israelite tribes were becoming firmly established and coalescing into larger groups.

Jerusalem, Megiddo, Beth-shan, and Gezer can be taken as the most important places which remained Canaanite for the time being. The lack of surviving evidence from Jerusalem has already been described. At Megiddo, the Late Bronze Age Stratum VII town established by the beginning of the 14th century B.C. lasted late enough to receive some Philistine pottery, though there is not enough to suggest a Philistine conquest. A statue base of Rameses IV, mid-12th-century B.C., apparently belonging to Stratum VII, suggests that this town lasted at least to this time, and that there was still Egyptian influence in this area. It was succeeded by the town of Stratum VI B, for which the surviving evidence is slight; all that can be said is that there is an architectural break between it and Stratum VII, and all the wall fragments ascribed by the excavators to this period are of an unimpressive character. The sacred area which had probably existed from the third millennium disappears, and the position of the northern gate is changed. It has been suggested[4] that the break between Strata VII and VI is so great that VI represents the arrival of the Israelites. This is a tempting conclusion, but the capture of this mighty city by the Israelites in the 12th century is improbable.

The succeeding building phase VI A was inadequately differentiated in the original excavations, but the surviving remains suggested a more important town. One of the few destruction details recorded by the original excavators was that all the walls were built of mud-brick on a foundation of stones. The report of the original excavations does not record any evidence of a destruction which abolished the Megiddo Stratum VI A buildings. Professor Yadin, in the interim of his lightning-scale excavations during the 1960s, aimed at the elucidation of certain debatable points, directs attention to the destruction of the VI A town by fire, though this point is not mentioned in the original excavation report. The large quantity of pottery in the destroyed buildings includes vessels classified as belonging to the third, degenerate phase of Philistine pottery, and it is considered to be comparable with Tell Qasile Stratum X. This does not in itself provide an absolute date. Professor Yadin suggests that the destruction may be the work of David early in the 10th century B.C. One can have some hesitation in accepting this suggestion for two reasons. Historically, there is no biblical reference to the capture of Megiddo by the Israelites. It seems improbable that such an imposing town as that revealed by the remains of Megiddo Stratum VI A should not be recorded in the biblical record. Archaeologically, the finds in the destroyed buildings do not suggest a date as late as the 10th century B.C. The ascriptions to strata of the pottery published in *Megiddo II* are not completely reliable, and the picture may be altered when the finds from Professor Yadin's excavations, in which the strata were accurately recognized, are published. As the evidence stands, however, the pottery suggests quite a considerable gap between this period and the Solomonic period to be described in the next chapter. A terminal date of, at latest, 1050 B.C. seems probable.

Thereafter, Megiddo declined. There were two succeeding phases with unimportant little buildings, V B and V A. There is no evidence for any defences; a defenceless town in those unsettled times is perhaps improbable, and the defences may have disappeared in erosion, which an accurate stratigraphic record could establish. The general conclusion is that the mighty Canaanite city of Megiddo, with a history stretching back to the fourth millennium, gradually came under Philistine influence, though it is doubtful whether it became a Philistine town. It was eventually destroyed, probably in the middle of the 11th century B.C., and during the period of succeeding settlements of minor importance it came under the control of the Israelites.

Beth-shan seems to have had something of the same sort of history as Megiddo with, perhaps surprisingly, more evidence of Egyptian control. In Stratum VI there were many fragments of typically Egyptian architecture. An inscription of Ramses Weser-khepesh, a general and important official of Rameses III, shows that this Pharaoh drove right across the plain of Esdraelon in his campaign against the Sea Peoples. On the evidence of the pottery, the town remained basically Canaanite under Egyptian rule, with a rebuilding of the Stratum VII temple. To this period belonged the anthropoid coffins which often have Philistine associations (p. 220). At Beth-shan, however, they have not. Only one sherd of Philistine pottery was found in the course of ten seasons of excavation. The coffins probably represented the burials of Aegean mercenaries in the service of the Egyptians.

This Egyptianizing town of Stratum VI was destroyed, but this did not mark the end of Egyptian control, for the stelae bearing the inscriptions of Seti I, Rameses II, and Rameses III were re-erected in Stratum V (a fact which has for many years confused the chronology of Palestinian pottery). This could suggest a time for the beginning of Stratum V towards the end of the Twentieth Dynasty, perhaps *c.* 1100 B.C.

Beth-shan Stratum V was a major rebuilding, which can be divided into a lower and upper stage. The lower stage shows a flourishing town in which Egyptian architecture still played its part, with at its centre two temples of basilical form. The re-erection of the earlier stelae show the extent of Egyptian influence. This was the city of the time of the battle of Mount Gilboa, upon the walls of which the body of Saul was exposed. The biblical ascription of Beth-shan to the Philistines could be evidence of just confusion or conflation, or could be evidence of a very recent capture of the town by the Philistines.

At Gezer, the Late Bronze Age town was destroyed by fire in the second half of the 13th century B.C. This was probably the work of Merneptah *c.* 1230 B.C., whose inscription specifically refers to the capture of Gezer. This destruction brought to an end the flourishing Late Bronze Age town. Some of the inhabitants may have returned, and the evidence of the next stratum suggests an undistinguished settlement based on the preceding culture, with no Philistine influence, resembling Tell Beit Mirsim B 1.

The succeeding Stratum XIII shows more substantial remains and Philistine pottery appears for the first time; the greater part of the pottery continues the Late Bronze Canaanite tradition. In Strata XII–XI there are again prosperous towns. There was a considerable amount of Philistine pottery, but the underlying indigenous culture, on the pottery evidence, continues. It is in fact difficult to say, on the evidence so far available, whether Gezer became a Philistine town or merely had a close commercial relationship with the neighbouring Philistine coastal towns. It should be noted[5] that painted Philistine pottery can be estimated at less than 5 per cent of the total vessels found. The most probable conclusion is that Gezer remained Canaanite in culture and possibly independent, though a Philistine ruling class would not be impossible.

Beth-shan Stratum VI is certainly Iron Age. The conclusions as to the chronology of the site drawn by the Philadelphia excavators in the 1920s were seriously wrong, for the current archaeological technique in Palestine was unable to identify correctly the successive building strata. The material was, however, meticulously recorded, to the extent that Dr Frances James has been able, by an equally meticulous examination, to establish the chronological succession with a great degree of certainty. In the present context of the competing spheres of influence during the 12th and 11th centuries, the most interesting point is the recognition of the extent to which Egyptian influence penetrated into Palestine. The rulers of Egypt were still interested in the route from the Mediterranean towards north Syria and Mesopotamia. In Stratum VI there was a rebuilding of the Stratum VII temple. The whole architecture, with characteristic details of cornices, thresholds, and door-jambs inscribed in hieroglyphs, was Egyptian, and an inscription of Ramses Weserkhepesh, a general and governor appointed by Rameses III, dates the stratum to early in the 12th century B.C. It is probable that the population was still basically Canaanite. The pottery is differentiated from that of the Late Bronze Age mainly by the disappearance of Aegean and Cypriot imports, leaving a residue of indigenous Late Bronze Age forms.

The presence of Egyptian governors also explains the tombs with anthropoid coffins, which have been mentioned above. The pottery associated with them is that of Stratum VI, and the conclusion is, in the virtual absence (one sherd only) of Philistine pottery at Beth-shan, they belong to Aegean mercenaries who were part of the Egyptian garrison at Beth-shan.

The Stratum VI town was destroyed at a date which, it is suggested, cannot be much later than the first quarter of the 11th century B.C. The grounds for this dating are that the succeeding town, Lower V, is still Egyptian, for the stelae of Seti I and Rameses II and the statue of Rameses III were, as Dr James has shown, carefully rescued from the débris of VI, and set up again in association with the two temples that took the place of the earlier one. The most probable time when Egypt had sufficient power and interest is towards the end of the Twentieth Dynasty. There is no evidence as to who was responsible for the destruction of VI. It could well have been the work of one of the groups of the Sea Peoples, who were thus temporarily challenging the last outposts of Egyptian rule.

The new temples of Stratum V could possibly be the temples of Dagon and Ashtoreth which are mentioned in connection with the battle of Gilboa, *c.* 1030 B.C. The numerous cult objects provide evidence of a mixed Egyptian–Canaanite cult. The plans break with those of the preceding levels. The southern temple, in particular, is of a type new to Palestine but at home in Phoenicia, basically basilical in plan, with storerooms flanking a central hall and a shrine at the rear which is unfortunately destroyed by a Hellenistic reservoir. It therefore has resemblance to the Temple in Jerusalem. The northern temple was a simple oblong hall, with the roof supported by four columns.

All the sites so far described lie outside the area at this period occupied by the Israelites. It must in fact be admitted that we know tantalizingly little about the early Israelite settlements. The reason for this is partly owing to the limitations of archaeological evidence, partly owing to the limitations of the culture of the Israelites themselves.

The archaeological limitations arise from the fact that the area in which these settlements lie is the hill country. Sites in such districts do not present the same thick deposits of successive strata as do the sites in the plains. The buildings are naturally constructed of stone, which is readily available all over the area. As a result, when buildings of one period decay, their walls are apt to be dismantled and the stones re-used in their successors. Thus instead of the ruins being buried intact beneath a mass of collapsed mud-brick, the usual material for the superstructure in the plains, they are disturbed and destroyed to the very base of the walls. The story of the successive phases is thus very much more difficult to deduce.

The character of the settlements is the second factor which limits our information. The period is undoubtedly that in which the national consciousness of the Israelites is developing greatly. The biblical narrative shows how the groups were gradually combining together, with tentative efforts at temporal unification under the Judges and the stronger spiritual link of a national religion, with the high priest at times exercising temporal power. It is during these centuries that the groups allied by race, but differing in the manner and time of the settlement in Palestine, if the course of events suggested in Chapter 8 is the correct one, must have come to combine their ancestral traditions together under the influence of the Yahwehistic religion, and to believe that all their ancestors took part in the Exodus. The nation was thus emerging, but its culture was as yet primitive. Its settlements were villages, its art crude, and the objects of everyday use homely and utilitarian.

For this reason, excavations on sites such as Shiloh, Bethel, and Gibeah, all names famous in biblical history, have produced only the remains of a succession of somewhat rough structure dating to the 13th and 12th centuries B.C. At Bethel, there had been a settlement with well built houses in the Late Bronze Age, which was completely destroyed, and there was then a break in occupation. The succeeding Iron Age structures were much cruder than those of the city destroyed earlier. A second Iron Age level was even more miserable, and it was not until a phase ascribed to the 10th century B.C. that any improvement took place.

Perhaps typical of many villages of the time is the site of Tell el Fûl, lying 5 kilometres north of Jerusalem, and very probably to be identified with the Gibeah which was the home of Saul. Its occupation seems to start at the beginning of the Iron Age, early in the 12th century B.C. It consisted of a village with at its centre a solidly built fortress or tower. The walls of this tower, which was about 15 metres square, were strongly built, but very rough. Much of the superstructure must have been of wood, for when it was destroyed, it was covered with a thick layer of ashes and charred timber. It is interesting that the timber employed was cypress and pine, for coniferous trees subsequently disappeared completely from Palestine until modern times, and may in fact have vanished by the time of Gibeah III in the 9th century B.C., when the wood employed was almond. No doubt as settled life in Israel increased, and villages developed into towns, there was increasing deforestation from the need of timber for building.

Gibeah I was completely destroyed, probably in the second half of the 12th century B.C. It is difficult to be certain whether this is to be associated with any event recorded in the Bible. It may be the work of other Israelites, whose vengeance on Gibeah is recorded in Judges 19-20. On the other hand, warfare with neighbouring tribes was clearly endemic, for the Bible describes 'oppressions' by various eastern neighbours, Moabites, Edomites, Midianites, and others, which must belong to this period.

After an interval, a second fortress was built on the ruins of the first, partially incorporating them. This was better constructed than its predecessor, but nothing survived of any architectural pretensions, and its occupants were certainly not acquainted with luxury, to judge from the simple finds. It may be that this was built by the father of Saul, and it may thus illustrate the humble social status from which the leaders of Israel were drawn.

A site about which a little more is known is that of Beth-Shemesh, but it is not clear whether it formed part of Israel at this time. It is referred to in the Bible as a border city of Dan, before that tribe migrated northward, and subsequently as a border city of Israel. Yet to judge from the pottery, the town, which was built about 1150 B.C., was strongly under Philistine influence. It lies in the Shephelah, and must have been somewhat near the border between the Israelites and the Philistines, and the amount of Philistine pottery certainly suggests that it belonged to them, in spite of the biblical references. The remains recovered suggest a fairly large city, though no buildings of any particular merit were found. A principal industry of the town seems to have been bronze-working, for several smelting ovens and fragments of pottery flowpipes were found. Iron was in fairly common use on the site for weapons and jewellery. It is interesting, however, that flints set in wooden hafts continued to be used for sickles until the 10th century B.C. The city was violently destroyed by fire at the end of the 11th century B.C., possibly in Saul's wars with the Philistines.

Another aspect of the early Israelite settlements is that found in the north of the country, especially in the hills of Galilee. Surveys in this area by Professor Aharoni and others have located a number of small, unwalled villages. The historical position of these villages is shown by the finds at Hazor. As described above (p. 209), the Late Bronze Age town was destroyed and blotted out in the 13th century B.C. The great plateau extension of the Middle Bronze Age was never reoccupied. On the original tell, however, there appears a village occupation of the simplest type, with the foundations of flimsy huts, ovens, and storage pits as the only evidence. The pottery from this village is similar to that from the Galilee villages, and can be interpreted as evidence for the gradual settlement of the newly-arrived, semi-nomadic, Israelite tribes.

For something like a hundred years the Philistines and the Israelites lived side by side, the Philistines in the rich coastal plain, the Israelites in the more barren hill country. About 1080 B.C. the Philistines began trying to extend their control over the hill country, and this is the period of oppression by the Philistines of which the Bible gives such a vivid account. The period was one of oppression, but it was also one that gave a stimulus towards nationhood. Saul, leading a revolt which started about 1030 B.C., became the acknowledged leader of the whole country in the struggle, and though his success was varied, and marred by quarrels with the religious leaders and with David, and terminated by defeat on Mount Gilboa, it was on the foundations of the unity that he achieved that David was able to establish the free and united kingdom of Israel.

Notes

1. T. Dothan, *Antiquity and Survival* (Jerusalem, 1957), II, pp. 151 ff.
2. F. Petrie, *Beth-Pelet* I (London, 1930), pp. 6 ff.
3. T. Dothan, *IEJ* 22.
4. Y. Aharoni. *Near Eastern Archaeology in the Twentieth Century,* ed. J. A. Sanders, pp. 263–5.
5. *Gezer II* (HUCBASJ).

10   The United Monarchy

The united kingdom of Israel had a life span of only three-quarters of a century. It was the only time in which the Jews were an important political power in western Asia. Its glories are triumphantly recorded in the Bible, and the recollection of them profoundly affected Jewish thought and aspirations. Yet the archaeological evidence for the period is meagre in the extreme.

After the disaster on Mount Gilboa, when the bodies of Saul and Jonathan were exhibited as trophies at Beth-shan, the Philistines set up two vassal kingdoms, with David as ruler at Hebron and Ishbaal in the north. In between the two lay Jerusalem, still occupied by the Canaanite tribe of Jebusites. But David, though he had taken refuge with the Philistines when Saul had turned against him, was not prepared to continue as a vassal now that his old leader was dead. He succeeded in defeating Ishbaal, apparently without intervention by the Philistines, thus reuniting the kingdom of Saul, and he threw off the Philistine overlordship. He then achieved the crucial success of capturing Jerusalem.

The control of Jerusalem was essential to the control of a united Palestine, as it lies on the central ridge which is the only convenient route north and south through the hill country. The fact is well illustrated by the dislocation caused by the 1948 frontier between Israel and Jordan, since the natural road between Jerusalem and Bethlehem, 8 kilometres to the south, was cut by a salient of Israel, and the subsequent road connecting the two, in order to keep in Jordanian territory, had to make a detour of incredible steepness and engineering difficulty, owing to the valleys running down abruptly from the watershed. From Jerusalem to the east a road runs down to the Jordan Valley near Jericho, across a ford over the Jordan, and up to the rich plateau of Transjordan; while to the west there is a choice of good routes down to the Shephelah and the coastal plain.

The previous lack of cohesion among the Israelites is well illustrated by the fact that this Canaanite enclave had been allowed to persist in their midst for centuries. Without its possession, political unity was impossible. Once it was secured, the great period of Israelite history begins. But the effect of the long division of the Israelites into two groups, added to that of probable difference of origin between the northern and southern tribes, was permanent and contributed to the renewed division into Israel and Judah at the end of the 10th century B.C.

The problems of the archaeology of Jerusalem have attracted investigators ever since exploration in Palestine began. But all the difficulties inherent in dealing with cities in the hill country described in the last chapter are present to a far greater degree in Jerusalem. Occupation here has been more prolonged and on a greater scale than anywhere else in Palestine. Part of Israelite Jerusalem lies under the modern city, and great rubbish deposits and continuous building operations, all tearing up the walls of earlier structures, have profoundly modified the contours of the ground. In addition, quarrying has removed most of the very rock on which Jerusalem was built.

The original Canaanite town lay on the hill of Ophel, to the south of the present walled city. This forms a spur slightly below the rest of the ridge, but strength is given by the steep valleys on either side, the Kedron to the east and the Tyropoeon to the west. Much of the latter valley is now imperceptible on the surface, but excavation has shown that the original slope here was nearly as steep as that to the east. Some 20 out of 50 feet (6.10m out of 15.10m.) of the filling halfway down the valley dates to the period after the destruction of Jerusalem by Titus in A.D. 70, the rest of the period after the end of Byzantine rule. The two valleys converge, and the ancient site was thus strongly defended by nature except on the neck joining it to the higher ground where modern Jerusalem lies.

It was not only the steep enclosing valleys that caused Ophel to become the site of the original settlement, but the still more important consideration of a perennial water-supply. It was only when lime-mortar came into use (about the end of the second millennium) to provide an impermeable lining for cisterns, that towns could be independent of such a source of water. The source for Jerusalem was the spring Gihon (or the Virgin's Fountain) in the Kedron Valley (Pl. 76).

Excavations in Jerusalem began in 1867, the first venture of the newly founded Palestine Exploration Fund. The ensuing three-quarters of a century of excavations made it clear that there was an older Jerusalem stretching south from the present Old City. A line of town wall was traced that ran from the south-east corner of the Old City along the eastern crest of Ophel, across the mouth of the Tyropoeon, and round the curve of the Hinnom Valley to join the south-west corner of the Old City. It was generally accepted that this line of wall enclosed Israelite Jerusalem, though there were different theories as to the date at which the expansion from the original settlement on the eastern ridge took place.

A portion of the wall along the eastern crest of Ophel was cleared in excavations between 1923 and 1925, including an imposing stone-built tower. This the excavators ascribed to the work of David and Solomon, and considered it to be an addition to the original Jebusite defences. The weakness in this interpretation, and indeed in the whole identification of the defences on the crest of the ridges as those of the original city, was the relation between the supposed city wall and the water-supply in the valley below. The necessity of protected access to water is obvious and the inhabitants of Jerusalem made provision for such access. Details of succession of shafts and tunnels connected with the spring, of which the latest and most famous is the Siloam Tunnel (p. 291), were studied by Père Hugues Vincent during cleaning operations carried out by a British expedition in 1909–11. The earliest was a combination of tunnels and a vertical shaft. It was believed that this provided the Jebusites with their access to the water, and it was also suggested that this was the water channel up which Joab and his men crawled to take the defenders in the rear and to enable David to capture the town that the Jebusites believed to be impregnable. Herein lies the weakness in interpretation referred to, for the shaft comes to the surface well outside the line of defences ascribed to David and the Jebusites.

When excavations were resumed at Jerusalem by the British School of Archaeology in 1961, the investigation of this problem was a major objective. It was in fact found that the defences on the crest were late, Post-Exilic and Maccabean, and that the original town wall was 160 feet farther east and 83 feet (29m.) lower on the slope (Pl. 75). This wall proved to date from *c.* 1800 B.C., and to have continued in use down to the 8th century B.C. It was thus the wall of the Jebusite town and the wall of the City of David. Of the Middle Bronze Age town to which the wall originally belonged, only slight

235

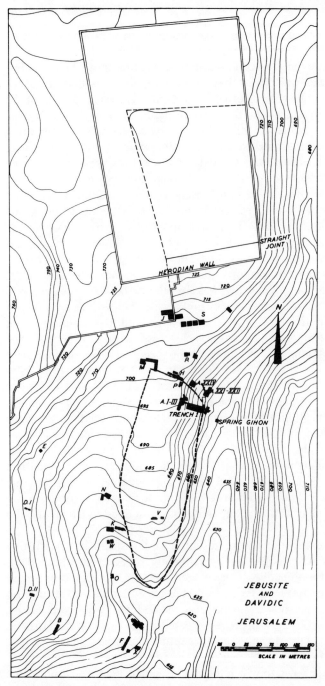

Fig. 69. Plan of Jebusite and Davidic Jerusalem

remains survived the continual process of erosion to which buildings on this steep slope were subjected. There were also some traces of Early Bronze Age occupation and, as already mentioned (p. 102), tombs of the Proto-Urban period have been found in Jerusalem, but there is so far no evidence of a town earlier than 1800 B.C.

The east wall of the Jebusite–Davidic town was therefore well down the east slope, at a point strategically low enough to deny attackers access to the spring, but not so low that it was commanded by an enemy on the other side of the valley. The line from the identified point has not been further traced, but may be presumed to follow about the same contour to the southern tip of the ridge. The west wall seems to run north from this point along the edge of the summit of the ridge, for areas below this line were shown by excavation to be outside the Iron Age town. The northern wall can be shown to have crossed the ridge at a distance c. 200 metres south of the present south wall of the Haram.[1] The area enclosed by the walls was 10·87 acres (4·40ha.).

David not only took over the defences of the town that he captured, but also a very important element in its layout. The Middle Bronze Age town had been built on rock following its steep slope up to the west. In about the 13th century B.C. a great town-planning operation was carried out, in which a series of terraces were constructed as a basis for a much more grandiose town. These terraces were taken over and enlarged, and may in fact be the 'Millo' (or filling) which David and his successors are said to have built or repaired. A town built on such terraces was much better laid out than one on a steep slope, but the terraces were very liable to collapse, and in fact the only structures that survive on them belong to the last years of the Jewish kingdom in the 7th–6th centuries B.C.

The capture of Jerusalem is to be dated c. 995 B.C. By it, David's position was assured. His growing power inevitably aroused the hostility of the Philistines. Their defeats at Baal-Perazim and Rephaim caused their withdrawal once more to the coastal plain, and they ceased to be a permanent menace. But though David now started on a policy of expansion, he never annexed Philistia. It may be conjectured that Egypt, in spite of its weakness at this time, gave sufficient support to deter him. The coastal plain in fact never became part of the Israelite domain,[2] and the Philistines reappear in the 8th and 7th centuries B.C. as an independent group.

David followed up his success against the Philistines by attacking other ancient enemies. The various 'oppressors' were now

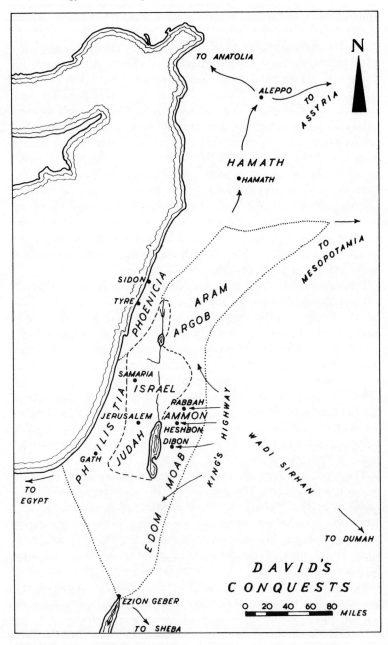

Fig. 70. Map of David's Conquests

oppressed in their turn. Moab, Ammon, Edom, were all subjugated, and the most surprising expansion is the defeat of the Aramaeans and the annexation of Damascus. The Israelites thus controlled a large part of the country from the Euphrates to the borders of Egypt, though the Phoenician towns on the Syrian coast remained independent.

This unification and expansion inevitably brought about a revolution in the culture of the country. The people of simple hill villages, united in reality only by religious ties, became part of an organized kingdom. The transfer of the religious centre to Jerusalem established a combined political and religious focus, and strengthened the monarch at the expense of the priesthood. The international contacts of the Israelites were opened up for the first time. Instead of being circumscribed within their limited area, they were brought into touch with the main currents of civilization of the period. In particular, they were brought into touch with the Phoenicians. Recent archaeological research in Syria and the adjacent countries has shown that Phoenicia at this time had a highly developed civilization, manifesting itself in fine buildings and a distinctive (though eclectic rather than original) art, and a remarkable development in literature, as well as in the trading and colonizing ventures for which they have long been famous. Research in Palestine is beginning to show how strong Phoenician influence was in the process which began under David, in fact the civilizing of Israel.

This process was indeed begun under David, but he only provided the groundwork for the great developments under Solomon. There is little in the record, either literary or archaeological, to show that much progress towards civilization was made during David's reign. For Solomon's reign there is considerable literary evidence, but not much archaeological. Many attempts have been made to reconstruct on paper the Temple Solomon built at Jerusalem on the hill north of Ophel. Finds on other sites make it easier to understand the description and to visualize some of the details, but the area of the Temple and that of the extension of the city under the Israelites lie beneath modern Jerusalem, beyond the reach of the archaeologist's spade.

The site of the Temple lies beneath the Moslem sanctuary, the Haram esh-Sherif, in the centre of which is the Dome of the Rock. It is probable[3] that the axis of the Temple ran east and west, and that the Temple lay to the west of the sacred rock now covered by Abd el Melek's great Dome. The rock may have been the site of the altar of sacrifices. The present enclosure owes its form to Herod's rebuilding of the Temple, begun in 19 B.C. The space for the great courtyard is provided by a terrace supported by massive retaining walls rising in places to at least 130 feet (39·62m.) above rock. The layout of Solomon's Temple must also have involved great terracing operations.

The position of the south-east corner of the platform supporting Solomon's Temple can be identified with considerable probability. Clearance outside the south-east angle of Herod's platform has revealed a straight joint between Herod's masonry to the south and earlier masonry to the north (Pl. 77) 32·72 metres away from the present south-east corner. The style of the earlier stonework suggests comparisons with structures of the Persian period in Syria, especially at Eshmoun,[4] near Sidon, and Byblos.[5] It is very tempting to associate it with the reconstruction of the Temple by Zerubbabel *c.* 516 B.C., when the Persian successors to the Babylonians allowed the exiles to return to Jerusalem, though what is actually visible may be part of later rebuildings in the Persian period. It is very unlikely that Zerubbabel would have enlarged Solomon's Temple, and it is reasonable to suggest that beneath this angle lies the angle of Solomon's platform. No corresponding straight joint is visible on the west side of Herod's platform, where Herodian masonry is visible for a distance of 180 metres from the south-west corner. The original platform is therefore on this side completely encased by that of Herod, and must be farther east. There are grounds for suggesting that the line is that subsequently followed by the present salient of the wall of the Old City. This would confine the Solomonic platform to the eastern ridge, which is in general likely from the plan of Jerusalem at that time.

Though the position of the west wall is hypothetical, there is reasonable certainty about the southern one. The southern wall of the Temple enclosure therefore was at a distance of *c.* 232 metres to the north of the north wall of the Jebusite–Davidic town, and the Solomonic town was therefore extended to include this area. The new wall on the east side was not, however, a continuation north of the original wall low down the slope. Excavations showed that this part of the slope was not included within the town until about the 8th century B.C. The Solomonic extension, of which some slight architectural evidence was found, was thus on the crest of the ridge only.

This additional area, outside the original town, no doubt closely built-up, gave Solomon space for his other public buildings. Of these, his palace is described in detail in I Kings 7:1–2, and it is very probable that it was situated in this new quarter, though it might have been on the platform. The palace for his principal wife, Pharaoh's daughter, would certainly have been outside the Temple precincts, and then accommodation had to be provided for all his wives, and for the officials required for the new organizations established for his kingdom. This new royal quarter is shown on the plan, Fig. 71.

It has become regrettably clear, however, that, though the lines of the enclosure walls can be suggested, virtually nothing has survived of the interior of the city of Solomon or of its predecessor and successors. A considerable part of the surface of the ridge has been excavated during the past fifty years, and it is now clear that these excavations, especially those of R. Weill in 1913–14, must be interpreted as showing that the surface of the rock has been extensively quarried, and the overlying buildings therefore destroyed. Much of this quarrying took place when Aelia Capitolina succeeded Jerusalem, leaving the area of the original city outside the wall, but some quarrying had already taken place in the time of Herod the Great.

But though the site of the Temple itself yields no evidence, it is, however, now clear that Solomon's Temple was wholly Phoenician in character. The most plausible reconstruction makes it a long rectangular building raised on a podium, with a porch leading into an oblong hall lighted by a clerestory, at the back of which a flight of steps led into the Holy of Holies. Surrounding and buttressing the main building were three storeys of small rooms, whose support enabled the walls of the main hall to withstand the thrust of the wide roof. A small temple which reproduces nearly exactly the main features of the central structure has now been excavated at Tell Tainat in Syria, providing valuable evidence of contemporary temple planning in Phoenicia. Archaeological finds, too, supplied illustrations for the decorations. Fragments of ivory carvings found at Megiddo, Samaria, Arslan Tash in Syria, and especially at Nimrud provide many parallels for the carved palm trees, flowers, and gold leaf with which it was adorned, and show that the cherubim were almost certainly winged sphinxes. The building methods also were Phoenician, for walls built 'with three courses of hewn stone and a course of cedar beams' have been found at Ras Shamra in Syria. It can, moreover, be suggested that the masonry of the Temple and its

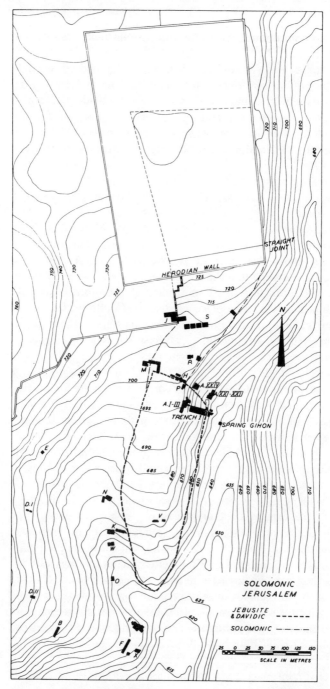

Fig. 71. Plan of Solomonic Jerusalem

platform may have been very similar to that of the buildings of Omri and Ahab at Samaria, the former in the finely jointed ashlar shown on Pl. 85 and the latter in the bossed masonry of Pl. 84. On stylistic grounds it can be shown[6] that the Samaria masonry is Phoenician in character, and Omri, whose son Ahab married the Phoenician princess Jezebel, may have asked for craftsmen just as Solomon did from Hiram king of Tyre. These craftsmen would have built in the same style as did those employed by Omri at Samaria. Bossed stones like those shown in Pl. 84 were in fact found re-used in a later wall, probably *c.* 800 B.C., near the probable line of the enclosure wall of the Solomonic extension between the original north wall and the Temple platform.[7] Thus, though no remains of the Temple have been found, comparative material does now make it possible to interpret intelligibly the written evidence.

Further support for the assumption that Phoenician-type masonry was used in Jerusalem is provided by the excavations at Ramat Rahel, a hill a short distance to the south-west of Jerusalem. In the later years of the kingdom of Judah there was here a citadel or palace of an obviously royal or at least official character. Fragments of walls within this structure, which was of 8th- to 6th-century date, were of superb ashlar masonry (Pl. 79), to which the rest of the walls were completely alien. They must have survived from an earlier structure. The face of the walls closely resembles that of the Samaria Period I walls, but the masonry is in fact better, for the ashlar blocks are rectangularly dressed on all sides, whereas the Samaria blocks are quite irregular in the core of the wall. There can be little doubt that this is Phoenician workmanship of the period of Solomon. Such workmanship in the time of the dual monarchy, when Omri's palace was built, is much less likely. The purpose of such an imposing building, as can be deduced, so close to Jerusalem is conjectural, as the structural details are inadequate. It could be a palace for one of Solomon's multitudinous wives, or a centre for his Civil Service.[8]

Solomon was thus engaged in decorating his capital with all the luxurious equipment to be found in the most civilized countries of his time. At the same time he was of course profoundly modifying every aspect of his country's culture, including that of its religion. He would appear to have been cosmopolitan in every sense, and to have brought strange gods into the country almost as equals to Yahweh. But of this, unfortunately, archaeology so far has told us nothing.

Most of Solomon's material innovations were no doubt concerned with the rebuilding and beautifying of Jerusalem. The rest of the country may even have been impoverished as a result of exactions to support the luxury of the capital. The biblical account, however, gives ground for expecting that three other cities received special attention. In I Kings 9:15, it is stated that the tax (or forced labour) that Solomon levied was used not on building the Temple and his palace and the walls of Jerusalem, but also on building Hazor, Megiddo, and Gezer. These three cities have background features in common at this time. All had been very important Canaanite towns in key strategic positions. All had suffered major destructions and periods of abandonment in the late 13th–12th centuries B.C. The levels that can now be ascribed to Solomon at Hazor and Megiddo represent virtual refoundings of the city. At Gezer an especial emphasis is given by the biblical record (I Kings 9:16) that Pharaoh gave Gezer to Solomon as a dowry for his wife after he had come up and destroyed it. It thus seems reasonable to place these three cities in a special category, and to call them Royal Cities. In them, Solomon could have a free hand in planning the layout, and the key strategic positions of most sites demanded a major consideration of their defences.

The identification of the Solomonic cities is due in the first place to Professor Yadin's excavations at Hazor between 1955 and 1958. The complete destruction of the Late Bronze Age city in the 13th century has been described in Chapter 8. Its successor was a primitive village which formed part of the Israelite spread in Galilee. A succeeding stratum was also small-scale and simple, and may have included a cult centre. Only with Stratum X does a town once more appear, which from the finds is 10th-century and could well fit the time of Solomon. The town of Stratum X was confined to the original tell (Pl. 54) which dates back to the Early Bronze Age, leaving the lower city added in the Middle Bronze permanently outside the walls. The new town in fact occupied only the western half of the tell. In the schematic plan on Fig. 72, the transverse wall was the original east wall. In it was a very fine triple-chambered gateway with externally projecting towers (Pl. 80) which was set in a casemate wall. Very little of the interior of this Stratum X town was excavated. The only exception was a building with small rooms just inside the west wall which, it is suggested, may have been barracks.

The excavation of the gate and wall of Solomon's Hazor has, however, provided the key for the identification of the correspond-

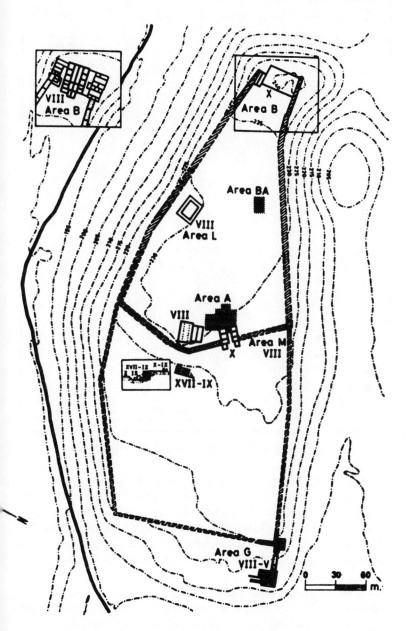

Fig. 72. Schematic plan of Iron Age walls on tell at Hazor

245

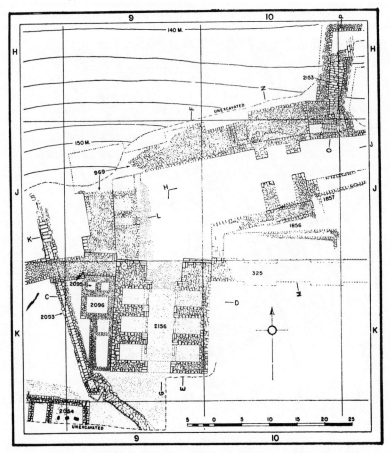

Fig. 73 Gateway of Megiddo, possibly of the Solomonic period

ing Solomonic building activities at Megiddo and Gezer. It was immediately obvious to Professor Yadin that the plan of the gate very closely resembled the Stratum IV gate at Megiddo (Fig. 73).

In the Chicago excavations of 1925 to 1939 Stratum IV was the one that was ascribed to Solomonic Megiddo. The main basis for this was that it included a number of long buildings divided into a nave and two side-aisles by massive stone piers. These buildings were interpreted as stables largely because between the piers were troughs which could have served as mangers, and a number of the piers were pierced by holes which might have been used for tethering ropes. The excavators suggested these buildings were the stables for the horses of Solomon's chariotry, which is mentioned in the Bible. Doubts had already been thrown on the identification of these buildings as stables of the period of Solomon as long ago as the Samaria excavations between 1931 and 1935. Used in them, and in the courtyard of a palace ascribed to the same phase, were ashlar blocks of the two types found at Samaria in the buildings of Omri and Ahab, *c.* 800 B.C. or soon after.[9] The Samaria excavations also established the pottery repertory of the 9th–8th centuries B.C. The stratigraphical methods used in these excavations at Megiddo make it difficult to rely on much of the pottery evidence. However, enough can be identified that can be attributed to the building stage of these Stratum IV buildings to show that they can be linked with phases III and IV at Samaria, and must therefore belong to the second half of the 9th century B.C.

Professor Yadin's approach to the problem was based on military architecture. The gateways of Hazor X and Megiddo IV were identical in plan, though, since only the foundation courses survived at Hazor, the masonry could not be compared. Associated with the Hazor gate was a town wall of casemate plan, but at Megiddo, the wall claimed to be contemporary was a solid wall with a series of shallow external and internal offsets, a type that appeared at Hazor only in Stratum VIII. Professor Yadin's re-examination of the evidence at Megiddo revealed the existence of a casemate wall beneath the offsets-and-insets wall. The junction of the newly discovered wall with the gateway had been destroyed, but there is very little doubt that to the original gate belonged the casemate wall, and that the offsets-and-insets wall belonged to an obvious rebuilding of the gate.

From the area on the north side of the tell where superimposition of the offsets-and-insets wall over the casemate wall was established there also came architectural and stratigraphical evidence to confirm the conclusions based on Samaria which are referred to above. Beneath the building called in the Chicago report the Northern Stables, which was associated with the offsets-and-insets wall, was found a building on an impressive scale, which was designated Palace 6000. The north wall of this building in fact formed part of the defences, with the casemate wall abutting it to east and west. Moreover, the ascription of the offsets-and-insets wall to a period secondary to that of the gate cleared up the position of Palace 1723 on the southern side of the city. This monumental structure built in fine ashlar masonry was abolished by the offsets-and-insets wall, but it could now fall into place as part of the layout that can be ascribed

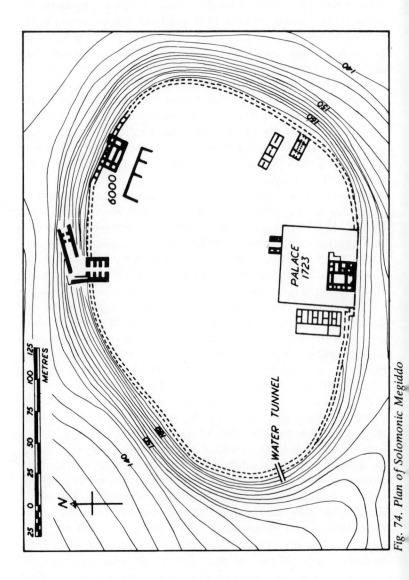

Fig. 74. Plan of Solomonic Megiddo

248

to Solomon. Similarly, the adjacent building 1482, probably administrative, had been truncated by the main stable building, and its original plan can now be accepted as belonging to the period of the casemate wall.

Based on the Hazor and Samaria evidence, the layout of the Solomonic Megiddo has now emerged (Fig. 74). The summit of the mound is encircled by a casemate wall associated with a very fine three-chambered gateway. Incorporated in the circuit of the wall are two imposing buildings or 'palaces'. The plan of these buildings shows clear affinity with contemporary palaces in northern Syria.[10] There is still no certainty about the buildings covering the rest of the fortified area. The plans of the Chicago excavations show beneath the Stratum IV large-scale buildings a Va level with houses of a small scale and undistinguished character. It is conceivable that in Solomon's layout some public buildings were imposed upon a town of ordinary domestic abodes.[11] However, Professor Yadin in his final investigation[12] made the observation that to the south of Palace 6000 walls could be traced by breaks in the well-marked beaten-chalk floors which enabled the plan of the building to be traced by robber trenches. Such methods had been used in the Samaria excavations of 1931–35, but the evidence had not been observed during the Chicago excavations (or indeed subsequently). It is therefore a real possibility that the rest of the fortified area was occupied by public buildings constructed with ashlar blocks, which would be very tempting for subsequent builders, and that the evidence of the robber trenches of these buildings was completely missed by the excavators.

A feature of which the stratigraphical position is again explained by the interpretation of the date of the offsets-and-insets wall is a sloping gallery down to the spring. This approach to the main water-supply of Megiddo precedes that of the great shaft. It was blocked by the offsets-and-insets wall, and on present evidence this could allow it to belong to the Solomonic period. An investigation of its stratigraphy and structure, in typical ashlar, shows this is where it belongs.[13] Another feature belonging to the Solomonic town may be the large number of cult objects found, horned altars, incense stands, braziers, and chalices, which may have come from small shrines or private chapels.

At Gezer the revelation of the Solomonic town has been equally dramatic. After Professor Yadin had shown the resemblance of the gates at Hazor and Megiddo, it was an obvious step to look for a

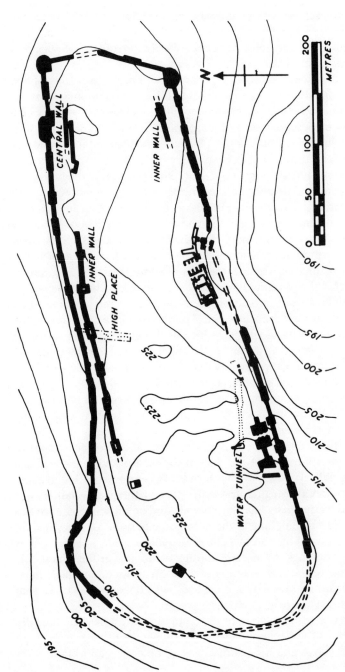

Fig. 75. Plan of Gezer

similar gate at the third site, Gezer. In the plans of Macalister's excavations there in 1902–05 and 1907–09, Yadin identified in the structure ascribed to a Maccabean castle part of the gate with an attached casemate wall identical in plan to those at Hazor, and moreover built-in ashlar masonry (Pl. 83) of the type found at Megiddo.

Between 1964 and 1973, excavations on the site were resumed by the Hebrew Union College in association with the Nelson Glueck School of Biblical Archaeology in Jerusalem, under the direction of Dr W. G. Dever. These excavations revealed the whole plan of the gate (Fig. 75) as postulated by Yadin and an adjacent stretch of casemate wall. Problems, however, remain about the general interpretation. The excavators believe that this fine gateway and the associated casemate wall are to be interpreted as a blocking of a gap in the outer wall, to which they ascribe an unlikely period of use from the Late Bronze Age to the Hellenistic period. It is suggested[14] that this wall dates in fact only from the Hellenistic period, with the re-use in it of ashlar blocks possibly derived from the Solomonic wall. It is difficult to believe that such a fine gateway was not part of a full circuit wall and the existence of such a wall of close-fitting ashlar blocks in the north-west part of the circuit was in fact recorded by Macalister.[15] The disappearance of much of the town wall and of the internal buildings could be accounted for by the re-use of many ashlar blocks in the walls that it is here suggested are Hellenistic. Further clearance might reveal the robber trenches not hitherto recorded.

Beth-shan must have come under Israelite control some time in the 10th century, though there is not precise evidence for this. Dr James has shown from ceramic finds and structural details that the excavators' Stratum V can be divided into lower and upper phases. The lower, Egyptian, phase with its two temples has been described above (pp. 228-9). The Egyptian stelae and statues were destroyed with deliberate violence, and their fragments buried beneath new floors upon which the Egyptian temples were probably converted into administrative buildings. The pottery sealed by the new floors is to be dated to the second half of the 10th century B.C. Also part of this upper Stratum V reconstruction was a gateway, presumably of an acropolis, at the north-west angle of the area excavated, and two blocks of storerooms along the north side of the converted temples. In these new buildings appears ashlar masonry of the type described in connection with Megiddo and Gezer. On the basis of the evidence that Dr James has been able to recover from the original records, it may now be possible to suggest that the upper Stratum V should be yet further divided. Photographs of the gate and the adjacent wall show that it was well built with the heavier, bossed, masonry found at Samaria. On the other hand, in the storerooms to the east of the gate is found the curious use of piers using ashlars which is found in Megiddo IV (Pl. 82). It can therefore be suggested that there was a first Israelite building stage in which ashlars of Phoenician type were employed, followed by a later stage in which they were re-used, as in Megiddo IV. The first stage is likely to be Solomonic. On masonry evidence alone, it could belong to the time of the Omrid dynasty, but the pottery suggests a 10th century B.C. date. Beth-shan can thus probably be added to the list of the towns that Solomon reconstructed.

We have some knowledge of the history of a number of smaller towns at this period. Possibly typical of the layout of such towns is that of Beth-Shemesh II. The preceding town, III, was violently and completely destroyed by fire about 1000 B.C., very probably in David's struggle with the Philistines. Its successor was built on a new plan, and owed little to the earlier layout. The fortifications, in part following the line of the earlier and in part incorporating them, were on the casemate system, found at the three main Solomonic towns of Megiddo, Hazor, and Gezer, which became common in Iron Age Palestine. In this system fairly thin parallel walls are linked by cross-walls, and when the lower part of the casemates was filled up solid, it formed a very thick wall but with a considerable economy of stone. The outer wall at Beth-Shemesh was c. 1·50 metres thick, the inner 1·10 metres, and the space between c. 1·50, so that the total width of the composite was c. 4·10 metres, in places thicker.

Stratum II was divided into three phases, of which the first, IIa, is dated 1000–950 B.C. Not a great deal of this phase was recovered, but apparently many of the later buildings were reconstructions of those of this phase, so that the plan of this second Iron Age town was established now. The layout is a very good example of the two-zone type of plan. At a distance of about 16 metres inside the ramparts was a ring road. The space between this road and the walls was thickly built up with houses arranged radially to the rampart. Inside the ring road the planning is somewhat irregular, but the buildings tend to be orientated north and south.

A number of features characteristic of Iron Age sites in Palestine appear at this stage. One of them is a house plan in which the main block is divided longitudinally by two walls, forming three parallel and approximately equal divisions, while across one end is a room the whole width of the building. It is usually taken that the division formed a four-roomed house, but in none of the examples so far published does there seem to be clear evidence that the longitudinal walls were carried up above ground level; they may therefore be sleeper walls supporting a row of pillars, and the main block may be an aisled hall. Another feature introduced at this time was the use of upright stones up to 1 metre in height. Some of these were incorporated in rubble walls, some free-standing. From the published evidence it is not possible to ascertain where the floor level was in relation to them, and it seems probable that they were at least partially sunk in the ground, and formed bases for wooden pillars supporting the roof. A feature which makes its last appearance at this stage is the presence of round storage silos, stone-linked pits sunk in the ground. Such a method had been in use since the Late Bronze Age, but is not found in Early Iron II.

Stratum IIa is marked by the disappearance of Philistine wares. No doubt, with the driving-back of the Philistines to the coastal plain, their cultural influence diminished, but at this period, even in Philistia, the typical pottery dies out, and its place is taken by derivative forms in a new technique. The new technique, which appears early in the 11th century B.C. and becomes dominant in the 10th, is the use of a dark red haematite slip, almost invariably hand-burnished. The effect is often really beautiful. It is a curious reversion to a practice of the Middle Bronze Age, which had died out completely in the interval.

The Early Iron I town at Tell Beit Mirsim duplicates many of the features of Beth-Shemesh. This stratum, B, was divided into three phases, of which the third, B3, is dated *c*. 1000–930 B.C., and therefore corresponds to Beth-Shemesh IIa. Here again the wall, apparently built in B3, is of the casemated form, of which the overall width was 3·75 metres. There is the same band of radial buildings round the walls, separated by a road from the differently orientated ones in the centre of the town. Round silos continue in use, but disappear in Stratum A. The pottery is the same red hand-burnished ware. Here, as at Beth-Shemesh, there was nothing to suggest any high degree of civilization. The few moulded, carved, or painted fragments illustrate only a very crude art. The most interesting objects are the fertility figurines. These are plaques, like the Astarte plaques of the Late Bronze Age, but represent a pregnant woman. The type is confined to Stratum B, but cannot be more closely dated within that phase. They indicate, however, the strength of the old fertility rites, in spite of the precepts of the religion of Israel.

A site which has provided unusually good evidence of house plans of the 10th century B.C. is Tell el Far'ah. Occupation here was continuous from Middle Bronze II down to the Iron Age, but little of the layout of the earlier periods survived. That of Early Iron I was well preserved in all areas excavated, and showed unusually regularly planned houses. The walls are thin, usually only one course of stones in width, sometimes with a strengthening of masonry filling with rough stones in between. The houses are grouped back to back, opening into parallel streets. The plan of the individual house is essentially tripartite (Fig. 76). The door from the street leads into a courtyard flanked by subsidiary compartments, in part divided from it by pillars and in part by walls. At the end of the courtyard are one or more other rooms. In the courtyard are ovens and other domestic installations. All the houses have a similar plan and roughly the same dimensions. There was obviously very little social inequality.

Archaeology has therefore provided us with little direct evidence of the glories of Solomon's court, and has shown that, apart from the capital and the principal towns, the civilization was not of a very high order, nor are there striking signs of economic prosperity. The country was still one of peasant cultivators, in spite of the cosmopolitan civilization of the court. The national religion still had as its rival the long-established native fertility rites, stimulated, no doubt, by the acceptance, at the court, of the worship of deities from allied Canaanite cultures.

Solomon's wealth must have been derived mainly from his skilful use of the geographical situation of Palestine to build up his position as a merchant prince. It has for long been believed that he gained much from the exploitation of the copper mines in the Wadi Arabah, near the head of the Gulf of Aqaba. An examination of the mines and associated camps and smelting installations has, however, shown there is no evidence of activity at that time. The mines had been worked under Egyptian control in the time of the Nineteenth Dynasty and by Midianites and Edomites into the 12th and 11th centuries, but not later. The well-fortified building at Eilat, at Tell Kheleifeh, thought by Glueck to be a smelting installation, is now considered to have been a storehouse or granary. One can, however, accept the implications of the biblical account that Solomon, in association with Hiram King of Tyre, controlled a harbour at the head of the Gulf of Aqaba, whence expeditions sailed

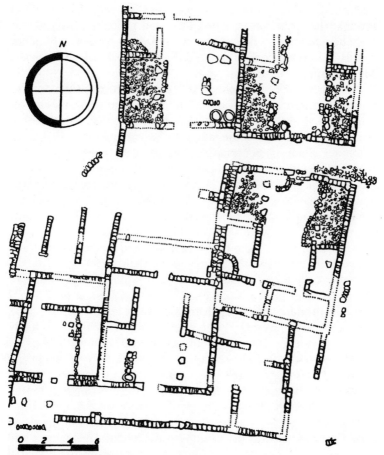

Fig. 76. Plan of Tell el Far'ah Level III

to collect precious eastern products such as spices and gold. It is
possible that this harbour was on the island of Jezirat Fara'un, but
the strong fortifications there have not been dated. The defended
building at Tell Kheleifeh could have been associated with this
trade. The first settlement was not a large one, but it was defended
by a very strong wall. It was built as a planned whole on virgin soil,
and the first stratum was dated by the excavators, the American
School of Oriental Research in Jerusalem under the direction of
Professor Nelson Glueck, to the 10th century B.C. on the evidence
of the pottery. It was very reasonable that there should be a

255

massively defended storehouse in connection with the trade that brought the 'gold, silver, ivory, apes and peacocks' from Ophir. Near here Solomon's fleet of trading ships must have been built, for it must be remembered that he did not control any ports on the Mediterranean coast.

After the time of Solomon, the Israelites controlled the Arabah only intermittently, for it was only during the United Monarchy, or, after the division, when Judah was especially strong, that the Edomites could be kept in subjugation. But whether under Israelites or Edomites, Ezion-Geber remained important as a centre of trade for five centuries. Three rebuildings of the settlement were identified. In the third level was found a jar on which were incised letters of the south Arabian Minaean script, a reminder of the part the port must have played in the trade northwards of south Arabian spices, while in the surface soil were sherds of black-figured Attic ware of the mid-5th century B.C., showing that it also had a place in the trade between the west and the Arabian hinterland.

In the Arabah we thus have evidence of Solomon's position as a great merchant prince which excavations in Palestine have so far failed to produce. It seems clear that his material splendour was concentrated at Jerusalem, where little trace of the period is likely ever to be found. There, Phoenician civilization must have been firmly established. In lesser towns much of the old simplicity remained. It is true that the remains indicate comparatively orderly towns with a homogeneous type of layout and architecture; for the first time since the Middle Bronze Age there was an appreciable number of true towns, instead of straggling villages, but there can have been few with any pretensions to architectural distinction, and we have no evidence of any particular luxury outside the principal towns.

The contrast between the luxury of the capital and the comparative poverty of other districts, to which no doubt exactions to support the royal ambitions contributed materially, was one of the underlying causes of the disintegration of Solomon's kingdom. There is no doubt that the economic basis of the kingdom was unsound, an unsoundness greatly accentuated when Edom was lost, which apparently happened before the end of Solomon's reign. The other cause, which is the one emphasized in the biblical account, was religious. Solomon's heterodoxy and tolerance of foreign gods aroused fierce opposition from the faithful adherents to the austere religion of Yahweh, and it was they who stimulated the revolt of the

northern tribes against Jerusalem. Solomon died *c*. 935 B.C., and by
930 B.C. Jeroboam had led the northern tribes in revolt against his
successor Rehoboam, and the short period of the United Monarchy
was at an end.

Notes

1. *PEQ* (1969).
2. With perhaps a partial exception during the reign of Josiah in the 7th century B.C.
3. L.-H. Vincent et A.-M. Stève, *Jérusalem de l'Ancien Testament* (Paris, 1954, 1956).
4. M Dunand, 'Nouvelles inscriptions phéniciennes du temple d'Echmoun à Bostan ech-Cheikh, près Sidon', *Bulletin du Musée de Beyrouth*, XVIII (1965), pp. 105–9.
5. M. Dunand, 'Rapport préliminaire sur les fouilles de Sidon en 1964', *Bulletin du Musée de Beyrouth*, XIX (1966), pp. 105–15.
6. J. W. Crowfoot, K. M. Kenyon, E. L. Sukenik, *Samaria Sebaste I. The Buildings at Samaria* (London, PEF, 1942), pp. 6–9.
7. K. M. Kenyon, *Royal Cities of the Old Testament* (London and New York, 1971).
8. Cf. Mettinger's thesis on the theory of 'royal estates'. T. N. D. Mettinger, *Solomonic State Officials* (Lund, 1971), p. 95.
9. *Samaria Sebaste I*, pp. 2–15, 93–100. J. W. Crowfoot, G. M. Crowfoot, K. M. Kenyon, *Samaria Sebaste III. The Objects from Samaria* (London, PEF, 1957), pp. 198–204. K. M. Kenyon, 'Megiddo, Hazor, Samaria and Chronology', *Bulletin of the Institute of Archaeology* 4, pp. 149–51.
10. D. Ussishkin, 'King Solomon's Palace and Building 1723 in Megiddo', *IEJ* 16 (1966), pp. 174–86.
11. As is suggested in 'Megiddo, Hazor, Samaria and Chronology', pp. 150–2.
12. *Biblical Archaeologist* XXXIII, 3, pp. 75 ff.
13. ibid., pp. 90–1.
14. K. M. Kenyon, *PEQ* (1977), Reviews and Notices, pp. 57–8.
15. R. A. Stewart Macalister, *The Excavation of Gezer*, I (London, 1912), p. 245, Fig. 127.

11 The Kingdoms of Israel and Judah

Though it was the revolt of the northern tribes against the luxuries and the religious misdoings of Jerusalem that broke up the United Monarchy, the northern kingdom of Israel was in fact the heir of the civilization first brought into Palestine by Solomon, while Judah, reacting against the former luxuries of Jerusalem in an attempt to counteract the effects of the schism, regained much of the simplicity and even barbarism of the earlier period.

This was in fact inevitable. Israel was in close geographical contact with Phoenicia and the other civilized countries to the north; Judah was shut in between Israel, with whom she was usually at war, the backward and warlike kingdoms of Transjordan to the east, and the desert to the south.

Fortunately, archaeology has supplied evidence of what is probably the last expression in Palestine of the Phoenician civilization introduced by Solomon. The evidence for this comes from the site which ultimately became the permanent capital of the Northern Kingdom—Samaria.

In the first years of the divided monarchy, the kings of Israel had no fixed abode. After having been at Shechem the capital was transferred to Tirzah, at least by the time of Baasha, the third king, and possibly earlier. About 885 B.C. Omri laid siege to Tirzah and captured it, and the usurper Zimri perished in the flames of his palace. The excavations of the École Biblique make it as certain as archaeological evidence can that Tirzah is to be identified as Tell el Far'ah. The 10th-century town at Tell el Far'ah was described in the last chapter. This town was violently destroyed, and the contents of the houses were buried in the débris of the superstructures. In the area excavated, the simple private houses were succeeded by something quite different, a building on a much larger scale and with much more massive walls. But this building was never finished. Its foundations were started from the level of débris within the earlier buildings, above which the stumps of the earlier walls protruded. On the level rested dressed stones intended for the superstructure, but these were never placed in position, and the floor levels which would have buried the tops of the older walls were never laid (Pl. 81).

In I Kings 16:23–24 it is recorded

> In the thirty and first year of Asa king of Judah began Omri to reign over Israel twelve years: six years reigned he in Tirzah. And he bought the hill of Samaria of Shemer for two talents of silver, and built on the hill, and called the name of the city which he built, after the name of Shemer, owner of the hill, Samaria.

This accords remarkably well with the evidence at Tell el Far'ah. Omri's first four years were occupied with struggles with his rival, Tibni. Only then was he free to concentrate on his capital. He began to build, but abandoned his work. On pottery evidence, where Tell el Far'ah stops, Samaria begins. In the pottery of Tell el Far'ah there is a complete absence of the types found in the first two periods at Samaria, while at Samaria the pottery of the preceding stage at Tell el Far'ah is not found. When Omri decided to move to Samaria, he took with him his court, and probably most of the inhabitants of Tirzah. Only at the time of Samaria Period III does some slight occupation reappear at Tell el Far'ah, and only in the time of Samaria Period IV does it become a flourishing town once more.

The reasons for Omri's transfer of the capital were twofold. As the description of his buildings at Samaria will show, he had grandiose ideas about the layout of his capital. For such, an unencumbered site such as Samaria gave him much greater scope. But more important was its strategic position. Though the communications of Tell el Far'ah are good, it looks primarily towards the east. Samaria lies athwart the main north–south route, watchful of any advance up from Judah and in easy contact with Phoenicia, and as the history of Samaria shows, Omri desired intercourse with the cosmopolitan towns of Phoenicia; further evidence of this is his marriage of his son Ahab to Jezebel of Tyre. It was equally important for him to have easy communication to the west, where lay the richest lands of his kingdom. On all counts, Samaria was a much better focus than Tell el Far'ah.

Samaria has the unique interest that it is the only major town founded by the Israelites. Archaeologically it has the importance that, as we have a fixed date for its foundation, we can establish very closely the chronology of the pottery and other objects found associated with its first phase. Culturally it has the importance that we can see how the Israelites, when not hampered by buildings of an earlier stage, set about laying out a city.

The site itself is not a commanding one, but nevertheless has a number of advantages to recommend it. The hill of Samaria (Pl. 86) is an isolated one, standing in a basin surrounded by higher hills, not, however, sufficiently close to command it, and it rises fairly steeply from the surrounding valleys. The most important fact is that it commands, as does Jerusalem, the great north–south road along the watershed. The modern road passes along its western foot, and the ancient one must have followed approximately the same line. There are reasonably good tracks leading down towards the Jordan on the east, while to the west it looks out towards the coastal plain and the Mediterranean.

Excavation confirms the biblical account that Omri founded his town on a virgin site. A little Proto-Urban pottery was found in pockets in the rock, together with a number of rock-cut pits belonging to the same period. The site was then deserted from at least early in the third millennium until Omri's building operations began. The floor levels associated with his buildings rest directly upon rock. The layout of the town took advantage of the natural shape of the hill. This slopes down from a summit plateau at about 430 metres above sea level to 350 metres at the point enclosed by the city at its greatest extent, in the Roman period, which is still well above the level of the surrounding valleys. The slope from the summit is steep on all sides except to the east. The size of the summit plateau today is *c.* 250 metres from east to west and 160 metres from north to south. A considerable part of this area is, however, due to ancient structures, starting with those of Omri, and the original width from north to south was only about 90 metres.

The whole of this summit plateau was laid out as a royal quarter (Fig. 77). This is a new conception in Palestinian town-planning. No doubt there was a similar layout in Solomon's Jerusalem, but the first concrete evidence for it comes from Samaria. To some extent it corresponds to the acropolis almost invariably associated with Greek towns, but its significance is rather different. The Greek acropolis is the defensible civic centre of a democratic community. The royal quarter at Samaria may have been defensible, for at least

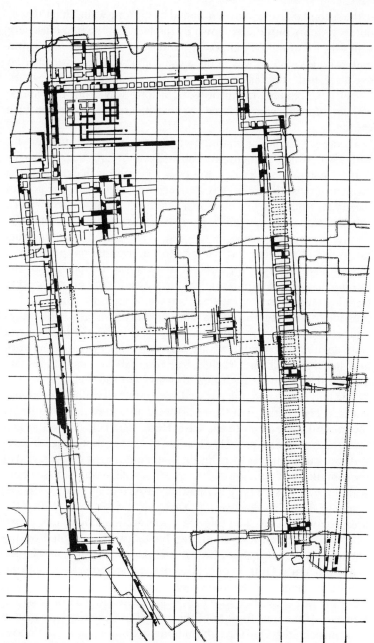

Fig. 77. Plan of the Omri–Ahab Royal Quarter at Samaria

in the second phase it was surrounded by a strong wall. That this was not its primary purpose is shown by the fact that the first enclosure wall was not of military character, and what we know of its layout makes it clear that it was in no sense a civic centre, but rather an exclusive enclosure reserved for an autocratic king and his servants. Social development has proceeded a long way from the simple warrior peasants who became the first kings of Israel in the 11th century.

To the first building phase belongs the enclosure of the summit with a wall which, as mentioned above, cannot have been primarily defensive in purpose, since it was only 1·60 metres thick. As well as an enclosure wall, it served as a terrace wall to increase the area of the summit plateau. On the north side it was built where the rock starts to drop steeply, against a prepared scarp about 2 metres high, and the floor level inside the enclosure (destroyed by later structures) must have been at least 4 metres above that on the outside. The wall was everywhere robbed too low for any portion of the interior face to survive, but a few stretches of the outer face were found. Fragmentary as they are, they enable us to obtain an impression of the magnificent masonry of Omri's Samaria. The face is a superb example of the stonemason's art (Pl. 85). On the rock is a course with the irregular bosses characteristic of foundation work and heavier walls in Israelite Samaria. Above, the stones are dressed flat, and fitted with quite beautiful exactitude.

The line of this magnificent wall was traced all round the summit plateau. The entrance to the enclosure must, from the contours of the ground, have been to the east. Here, the enclosure wall turns forward in a salient, probably leading towards a monumental gateway, but further traces were lost in a later quarry. At the west end of the summit was a building of the same first-rate masonry. Elsewhere within the enclosure only foundations survived, but they were sufficient to show that the layout was regular and spacious. Within the area excavated a considerable space was occupied by a great courtyard with a beaten lime floor; the buildings were aligned on the enclosure wall, but set back from it, and the rooms were fairly large.

Such then was Omri's conception of the layout of a royal quarter. To this original plan additions were made within a short period. They might be ascribed to Ahab, who succeeded his father within six years of the transference of the capital to Samaria. One may in fact consider the Omri–Ahab building operations as a continuous process. The principal addition consisted of the extension of the summit plateau by some 15 metres on the north side and some 30 metres on the west. The wall which supported this extension was at the same time clearly defensive in purpose, thus converting the royal quarter into an inner fortress. It was built on the casemate plan which has been shown to be typical of the Iron Age in Palestine. On the north sides the overall width was 10 metres while on the other sides it was 5 metres. Like the earlier enclosure wall, the casemate wall turns outwards at the east end towards the presumed entrance. On the north and west sides, the earlier wall continued in use, though partially buried by the fill of the additional terrace, but on the other sides the new wall was built right up against it, and incorporated it.

In addition to the new wall on the summit, there are walls enclosing the middle terraces of the hill which probably belong to this stage, though they replace others presumably belonging to the first stage. They illustrate the other very fine style of Israelite masonry in which the casemates were also built, that with smooth-dressed margins and attractively irregular bosses (Pl. 84).

These walls, however, do not represent the city walls, and unfortunately little of these has been traced. In the Harvard excavations of 1908–10 walls in Israelite-style masonry were found beneath the Roman west gate, while in the 1931–35 excavations wall fragments of this period were found 45 metres farther east. Small-scale excavations in 1968, however, showed that the Israelite town to the west of the royal quarters on the summit can at the most have been no more than a narrow spur, probably to protect the main road coming up from that direction. The excavations provided clear evidence that on the next main terrace to the north-west of the summit there was no occupation until the 6th–5th centuries. The main town in the Omri–Ahab period must lie to the east of the summit, beneath the modern village of Sebaste.

Of actual architectural fragments of this period disappointingly little survives. The exception is a number of capitals of pilasters in the Proto-Ionic style. These were all found re-used in later walls, but their find-spots at the east end of the summit plateau suggest that they may have formed part of the entrance structure. Similar capitals have been found at Jerusalem, Ramat Rahel, Hazor, and Megiddo. It has been suggested that they crowned door-jambs and piers supporting the lintels of doorways.

An important indication of the fittings of the buildings survives in the fragments of ivory carvings. Ahab's 'house of ivory' is referred to in the Bible, and there can be no doubt that these fragments came from its furniture, though they were mostly recovered from the débris of the destruction caused by the Assyrians in 720 B.C. There was, however, evidence that ivory carvings were in use in the original buildings. In these ivories we have striking material evidence, which has hardly survived in any other form, of the artistic tastes of the kings of Israel. The original objects were small in themselves, and many of them much broken, and though some hundreds of fragments were found, few of them could be completely restored. This may not seem much from which to deduce the style of decoration of the palace. But it must be remembered that what was recovered was probably only the residue after the palace was looted by the Assyrians. It is therefore fair to suppose that the original decoration must have been very rich, and the use of ivory profuse.

The bulk of the fragments is of plaques, in low or high relief or in openwork (Pls. 87, 88). Very few objects carved in the round were included. The carvings were enriched by gold-foil and glass and paste insets set in cloisonné work. The majority of the plaques are Egyptian in subject and basic treatment. But not one is truly Egyptian; they are the work of men who had seen the Egyptian originals, but copied them in their own national style. That the ivories were not made by Egyptians is also shown by the fact that a number of them had letters in the Hebrew-Phoenician alphabet carved on their backs. These letters, moreover, provide one of the grounds for assigning the carvings to the period of Omri and Ahab, for the form of the letters is that used in the 9th century B.C. The style of the ivories is in fact Phoenician, an art derivative in its inspiration but with sufficient life and feeling to make it one of the finest products of a period not notable for great artistic inspiration.

Further evidence of the origin and date of the ivories comes from other finds of similar material. There are numerous references to the use of ivory for decorative purposes in Syria. There are, moreover, two great collections which contain material very comparable to the Samaria ivories. One was discovered in 1928 by a French expedition at Arslan Tash in northern Syria. Many of the objects are almost identical with those from Samaria, but the class with the strongest Egyptian influence is less common. This collection provided important chronological evidence, in that a bed, which was one of the furnishings decorated by the carvings, was inscribed with the name of Hazael of Damascus, who came to the throne in *c*. 842 B.C. The second collection was found by Layard in

1849 in a palace at Nimrud in Assyria. The palace had been restored by Sargon II and most of the objects in it belong to this period. The ivories are completely un-Assyrian in style. Many of them might have come from the same workshop as those at Samaria, and since they were probably loot or tribute, they may well have come from Samaria itself, which was sacked by Sargon in 722 B.C. More recently, enormous collections of ivories have been recovered by Professor Sir Max Mallowan in renewed excavations at Nimrud. They include some close in style to those from Samaria, but their range is very much greater, and is indicative of the rich artistic resources of the lands ruled by the Assyrian kings (Pl. 89).

The decoration of the palace of Omri and Ahab was thus Phoenician in style. There is little doubt that from the same source came the technique in building already described. Phoenicia has provided an excellent parentage of the style. At Ras Shamra, there are beautiful Late Bronze Age walls of the fine ashlar masonry (Pl. 78) of the first enclosure wall at Samaria. In the harbour works of Tyre, close parallels of the bossed masonry have been found, mainly below water level and without dating evidence, but the architectural tradition is clear. It is reasonable to conclude that Omri imported Phoenician masons, for the closeness of his relations with Tyre is shown by the marriage of his son Ahab to Jezebel of Tyre. This is an echo of Solomon's connections with Hiram king of Tyre eighty years earlier. It is on this basis that an extrapolation can be made for the Solomonic building style at Jerusalem, and that elements in the surviving remains at Megiddo and Gezer can be ascribed to the Solomonic period.

Samaria thus was laid out as a new city, dominated by a royal quarter which was beautified by the skill of Phoenician craftsmen. Archaeology has given us tantalizingly brief glimpses of this, for subsequent buildings have destroyed almost everything, but we can in imagination reconstruct some of the setting of the court of Ahab and Jezebel, of which the luxury and evil-doings aroused such wrath in the prophets. Elsewhere on the hill the rest of the inhabitants of Samaria must have lived, seven thousand of 'all the children of Israel', according to the census of Ahab, and possibly many foreigners as well. A hundred and fifty years later, Sargon deported 27,290 persons from the city. So far, the living quarters of the common people have not been excavated, so we cannot tell whether they shared in the greater degree of civilization of the royal quarter or whether their abodes and their equipment were still simple.

The division of Solomon's kingdom into two cut off the northern kingdom from the Temple in Jerusalem. To emphasize this separateness, Jeroboam I set up cult centres at the northern and southern limits of his kingdom, at Dan and Bethel. Excavations have shown that Dan, at least, shared in the new-style architecture of Samaria. A grandiose gateway and ceremonial road led up to the summit of the mound created by the Bronze Age town, These elements probably belonged to the time of Jeroboam I. On the summit was a rectangular platform, a *bamah* (or high place), approached by a flight of steps. The masonry of the platform closely resembled that of Periods I and II at Samaria, and it is thus likely that it was the work of Omri or Ahab.

In the northern kingdom of Israel, the concept of a royal quarter, administrative in character, was based on the planning of Samaria. The summit of the site, and its most favourable position, was allocated to public buildings. At Megiddo, this may have been the case in the Solomic period (p. 248). There is no doubt that this is the position in the following Megiddo Stratum IV. The pottery evidence[1] shows that the large-scale public buildings belong to the second half of the 9th century B.C., either late in the reign of Ahab or in that of Jeroboam II.

The most striking of these buildings are what the excavators called Solomon's stables. Four sets of these buildings were found. Each consisted of groups of units, three of them of five and one of two. Each unit was divided into three by rows of stone piers, the two side-aisles being floored with cobbles and the central nave with lime plaster. Between the piers were stone troughs. Some of the piers had an angle pierced by a hole. It was therefore a very reasonable suggestion that the buildings were stables, the side-aisles being stalls and the central nave a service passage, with the troughs serving as mangers and the holes in the piers used for tethering. Subsequently this interpretation has been queried, for buildings at Hazor and, especially, Beersheba (pp. 279–80) have been interpreted as storehouses. From the point of view of stable management, there can certainly be some objections. High-spirited horses, probably mostly stallions, not confined in true stalls (for which there is no evidence) could create chaos. The layout, with mangers blocking the gaps between the piers, meant that the horses could only be led out in fixed succession; there was no access to a sick or vicious animal as an individual. But there remain arguments on the side of identifying these buildings as stables. It might be a reasonable conclusion that a basic public-building plan current in the 9th century B.C. could be used for various purposes.[2] We can at least be certain that they were public buildings.

The pottery evidence is clear that these buildings cannot be earlier than the second half of the 9th century B.C. The structural evidence is also clear that they belonged to a period when buildings which used the Phoenician-style ashlar blocks were being pillaged for re-use. In the wall of the courtyard of one of the stables, and in other instances, especially the 'palace' enclosure which is discussed below, there was a very curious style of building, in which narrow (and unstable) piers of ashlar blocks were set at intervals in walls of rough rubble. A study of the published evidence[3] makes it certain that the ashlars were in secondary use. They must have been derived from the Solomonic walls of which Professor Yadin observed the robber trenches.[4]

There was therefore at Megiddo a period of large-scale public buildings, which on pottery and structural evidence must belong to the second half of the 9th century B.C. To this layout must belong the offsets-and-insets solid wall that succeeded the casemate wall, but which continued to use the Solomonic gateway.[5] Fig. 78 shows its relationship to the other Stratum IV structures.

The important Building 1728, called the Southern Palace, was set in a courtyard in which this same style of piers of re-used ashlars was combined with rubble, and this enclosure wall must belong to the 9th-century rebuilding. The entrance into the courtyard was constructed of correctly used, bossed ashlar blocks.[6] Of Building 1728 itself, only a few blocks above the foundations survive, but they were apparently of the original ashlars. 1728 was in any case destroyed by the offsets-and-insets wall, a fact which caused the original excavators great trouble since they wished to ascribe all of this to Solomon, or in wider terms to David and Solomon. The new interpretation here described makes things much easier. The architectural analysis here proposed of ascribing the ashlar pier-rubble combination to a definitely secondary period in the layout of the summit means that one must infer a successor to 1728 farther north in the courtyard. There is nothing in the excavation record to cause difficulty, and it is clear that all the layers here were much disturbed.

To these important and extensive public buildings was added the very major undertaking of the water-shaft, which provided direct access to the spring from the interior of the town (Fig. 79). It

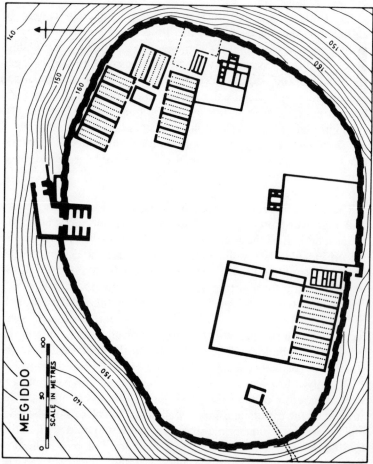

Fig. 78. Plan of Megiddo Stratum IV

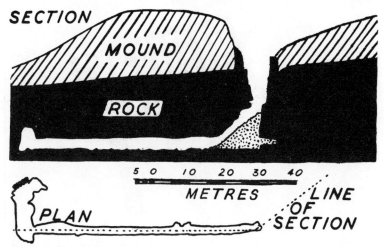

Fig. 79. Plan and section of the Megiddo water system

consists of a vertical shaft 35 metres deep sunk from the surface of the mound; the upper part, through the accumulated occupation layers, was lined with masonry and the lower part was cut through solid rock (Pl. 74). From the foot of the shaft a horizontal gallery 63 metres long led to the spring (Pl. 90), being cut with remarkable accuracy. Access to the water from outside was then blocked by an enclosing wall. The planning and surveying skill demanded was very great, and the task of cutting through and removing the débris and the solid rock with contemporary tools and tackle must have been formidable.

The original excavators assigned this great undertaking to Stratum VI, probably 12th-century B.C., a dating which made the achievement all the more remarkable. The main reason for this dating was that in the guard-chamber which existed before the outside access was blocked was 12th-century pottery, together with the skeleton of a man presumed to be a guard. The guard-chamber was presumed to be associated with the access to the spring provided by gallery 629. This had been put out of action by the offsets-and-insets wall, which was ascribed to Solomon, so the whole sequence was pushed backwards. Once Professor Yadin had shown that the gallery was Solomonic (p. 248), and the offsets-and-insets wall mid-9th-century, the great water-shaft could be assigned to the town of the period of Ahab or Jeroboam II, and thus conforms with the dating of the similar system at Hazor.

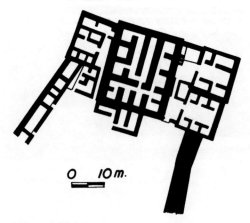

O   10 m.

Fig. 80. Plan of Hazor citadel

The Megiddo water-shaft shows several structural phases. As originally designed, the part of the shaft cut in the solid rock was for nearly half its depth vertical. Below that point there were rock-cut steps leading down to the tunnel. In the second phase, the steps were cut out and an effort was made to get water to run to the foot of the vertical shaft, presumably with the idea of making it possible to haul the water to the top in buckets. The ladies of Megiddo must have objected to the labour of walking down and up the steps. This innovation was apparently not a success. In the third phase, the steps at the base were rebuilt in masonry. The date of these secondary phases was not precisely established, but they all probably fall within the period of the kingdom of Israel, 9th–8th century B.C.

Like Megiddo, Hazor was in the northern part, the kingdom of Israel, of the divided monarchy. There was a similar rebuilding of a royal or administrative quarter. In the first place the area of the town ascribed to Ahab, Stratum VIII, was double that ascribed to Solomon and covered the whole of the original tell; the extension is shown on Fig. 80. The new wall is solid, with offsets-and-insets on its outer face, in contrast with the casemate wall of the Solomonic period; to the west of the junction with the extension, the original casemate wall was converted into the new style. Within the rebuilt defences were a number of important new public buildings. The most important was a massively built citadel at the western end, where the original tell narrowed almost to a point. In the citadel buildings were employed Proto-Ionic pilaster capitals of the type

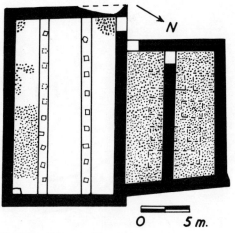

81. Plan of pillared building at Hazor

already mentioned in connection with Samaria (p. 263). Another building which was certainly public was a pillared hall and two adjacent halls (Fig. 81). The plan of the pillared hall is closely similar to that of the stables at Megiddo. It is differentiated from them by the fact that there is just the one unit, instead of groups, mainly of five. Still more important for the identification of the purpose of the building are the finds. Between the pillars were stone-built shelves or cells, in which were found storage-jars and kraters. Other pottery vessels were found adjacent. In the adjacent halls and the other buildings in the neighbourhood the large amount of pottery found shows that this was in fact a storage area and that this particular pillared building was used for this purpose.

A further major official undertaking was the construction of a great water-shaft. This is a direct parallel to the Stratum IV water-shaft at Megiddo, and Professor Yadin deliberately searched for it in view of the parallelism between the two sites at this period. In the Late Bronze Age, the site seemed to have been supplied with water by an immense cistern on the tell collecting surface water,[7] and by other cisterns in the lower city. There is an enigmatic circular depression visible in the air-photograph Pl. 54, at the south-west junction of the defences of the lower city with the tell, which very probably marks a shaft, but it has not been excavated, so the purpose and date are uncertain.

There is, fortunately, clear evidence for ascribing the new water-

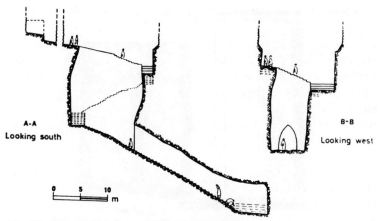

Fig. 82. Plan and section of Hazor water-shaft

shaft to Stratum VIII, for the lack of clear stratigraphical evidence at Megiddo emphasized to Professor Yadin the necessity of establishing firmly at Hazor the town level from which the shaft was dug. Clear evidence was found that the top of the shaft cut structures of the Stratum X Solomonic period, and an administrative building associated with the top of the shaft belonged to Stratum VIII. The water-shaft, therefore, was part of the great reconstruction of the summit with a fortified citadel belonging to the mid-9th century.

The overall depth from the summit to water-level was *c*. 40 metres. The upper part was of ramps, then steps, cut through earlier strata, lined by massive revetment walls. The lower part of the steps were cut into solid rock, with the 6-metre width of the steps suggesting that provision was made for pack-animals, a concession to human labour not found at Megiddo. At the base of the vertical shaft, a sloping tunnel led down with steps to the water-level. It was a surprise to the excavators that the direction of the tunnel was to the west and not out to the south of the tell where the springs in the Wadi Waggas would have provided visible evidence of the presence of water. Access to the water was thus completely within the town, instead of allowing the weakness of a blocked external access. Those planning the system must have had a sound geological knowledge of water tables. This is a second instance of the superiority of the Hazor planning over that of Megiddo.

In this recognition of the form and importance of public administration buildings, there is inherent important sociological evidence.

The king of Israel had in a number of important towns centres in which provision was made for buildings that included storage halls (or warehouses) in which the product of the taxes, collected in kind, could be stored. The ostraca, records written on potsherds, found at Samaria are probably to be interpreted as the documentary record, or receipts, of the tax-products received there, though recognizable storehouses have not survived there. The king would therefore have within his storerooms the wherewithal to support his administrative servants and his army, and perhaps in time of stress to feed the populace.

There is some slight evidence of a similar administrative centre at Beth-shan. The research of Dr Frances James has produced from the evidence of the earlier excavations examples of structures in which ashlar blocks, derived from the probably early 9th-century buildings (pp.251–2), were re-used in the form of piers, such as those in the strange building technique of Megiddo IV. At Beth-shan, the infilling between the piers of ashlar was in mud-bricks rather than stone, but the idea is the same. This can be construed as evidence of some official building activities at Beth-shan, contemporary with those of Megiddo IV. At this point, it would appear, the temple buildings of Stratum V were converted to other uses, possibly storehouses.[8]

At Tell el Far'ah an important town again grew up about 800 B.C., with pottery closely similar to that of the Period IV pottery of Samaria. Here, there was not a royal quarter, though an important building immediately inside the gate may have been an administrative centre or governor's residence. In the rest of the town, however, there does seem to have been a marked distinction between a rich quarter and a poor quarter. A group of excellent private houses, built in the same plan as those of the 10th century B.C., with a courtyard flanked on three sides by rooms, is divided by a long straight wall from a quarter in which smaller houses are closely huddled together. This evidence of the growth of social inequality reflects the denunciations of the prophets on the rich for trampling upon the poor.

The other towns excavated show a much simpler plan, and one much closer to those of the preceding period. It so happens that most of our information comes from cities of Judah. Of the sites excavated in the northern kingdom, at Beth-shan clearance was confined almost completely to the summit area. Here, analysis of evidence suggests that public buildings dominated the town in the area excavated.

On a number of sites a phase of occupation dating from about the beginning of the dual monarchy can be identified. These succeed a violent destruction which may probably be ascribed to the campaign of Shishak I of the Twenty-second Dynasty of Egypt, under whom there was a renaissance of Egyptian power. He appears to have taken advantage of the weakness caused by the secession of the northern tribes to carry out an extensive raid as far north as the Plain of Esdraelon about 926 B.C., and in the process many of the smaller towns no doubt suffered severely. At the foot of Mount Carmel, for instance, Tell Abu Hawam was destroyed and left deserted for several centuries.

It is to Shishak that is ascribed the destruction of the town of Tell Beit Mirsim Stratum B. This destruction was very severe. The earlier town was completely obliterated, and its place taken by buildings which owe little in plan to their predecessors. The city wall in the main continued in use, but the casemates were at least partly rebuilt. About one-fifth of the area of the town was excavated. The plan was that which we have already seen established in Iron Age Palestine, including the preceding level of this site, with a ring road separating radially planned houses round the rampart from the central area of the town. The houses are small and irregularly planned. One of the chief interests of the site is the evidence it provides for the great increase in town life compared with the preceding period. In Stratum B, occupation had been comparatively sparse. At least by the end of A, to which most of the structures recovered belong, the town was closely built up, and soundings outside the walls showed that it has spread well beyond them.

Little can be deduced from the plans of the houses, for the space was too cramped in this phase for any regular plan to be followed; any individual house had to accommodate itself to the exigencies of the site available. One characteristic feature was the extensive use of upright stones, already noted as an Iron Age feature (see p. 253). Explanations of the function of these stones are not completely satisfactory, but one suggestion is that in part the free-standing ones were used as uprights for vertical looms. The evidence certainly does suggest that Tell Beit Mirsim was the centre of a textile industry. Many hundreds of loom-weights were found, and scattered all over the area excavated was a surprisingly large number of dyeing plants. It is estimated that there must have been twenty or thirty in the whole town, which was only a small one with a population of two or three thousand persons. Another characteristic of the period is the disappearance of the sunk storage silos, their place being taken by bins on the floors of the houses.

Another site which was violently destroyed in the second half of the 10th century B.C. was Beth-Shemesh, where the buildings of Stratum IIa were covered with a level of ashes from a very fierce fire. The excavators suggest that this occurred about 950 B.C. If so, it must have been due to a chance conflagration, for a destruction by an enemy is improbable at the height of Solomon's power; a destruction by Shishak about 926 B.C. is historically more probable, and the chronological evidence is not so precise as to make this impossible. The rebuilt town of Stratum IIb followed the main lines of that of IIa, described above (p. 252), but here again there is evidence for a considerable growth of town population.

A third town of which the remains of this period have been excavated is at Tell Nasbeh. The site may be that of the biblical Mizpah. After occupation in the Early Bronze Age, it was left deserted until the beginning of the Iron Age. The occupation before the end of the 10th century appears to have been slight. It is possible that an early, rather slight, fortification wall may belong to this period. If it is the site of Mizpah, it would seem that in the time of Samuel it was little more than a village, but that would not be out of keeping with what we know of sites mentioned in the records of the time. Mizpah first becomes important with the division into two kingdoms, for it then becomes a frontier post of Judah, and was fortified by Asa of Judah in his struggle with Baasha of Israel. To this period may well belong the very strong defences which succeeded the earlier wall. Unfortunately, the complexity of the stratification resulted in the excavators being unable to establish accurately the date of the walls or that of individual buildings. It is clear, however, that the layout as a whole belongs to the period of the divided monarchy.

The town wall is extremely strong, and illustrates a second type which was in use in the Iron Age in addition to the casemate type. The wall itself was 4 metres thick and was built of heavy rubble. It is interesting that here, as in all the other smaller towns excavated, there is no sign of the Phoenician type of stonedressing. Projecting from the wall was a series of rectangular towers, irregularly spaced and of varying sizes. The base of the towers and of the walls on the east and west sides of the town was protected by a massive, stone-faced glacis, the base of which was in places as much as 8 metres thick in front of the footings of the wall. The whole constitutes a most formidable defensive system. The single gate was formed by the overlapping for a distance of 14 metres of the two ends of the wall, the outer being strengthened by a massive tower; the gate itself, consisting of double buttresses, with intervening guard-chambers, projecting from the walls, lay at the inner end of the passage so formed.

Inside the walls, the layout shows many of the characteristics of towns of this period. The buildings nearest the walls are radially arranged, with a ring road about 26 metres inside the walls. They are not, however, built right up against the wall; for the most part there is a gap of about 10 metres, in which was a large number of storage silos. Little of the layout of the centre of the town was recovered, owing to the closeness of the rock to the surface. The use of upright stones, in the walls or free-standing, is common, and there are a number of examples of the house plan with one room across the end of the main block divided either into three rooms or three aisles (see p. 254).

Another site connected with the defences of the southern king-dom against the northern is that of Tell el Fûl, identified as Gibeah (Geba). The original fort here, which had been an acropolis for the surrounding village in the period of Saul, had been allowed to fall into ruins in the period of the United Kingdom. It was rebuilt as a fortress serving as an outpost in the defences of Jerusalem at the end of the 10th century B.C. The plan was square, with a massive wall, of which the foot was protected by a thinner wall with an earth filling between the two, and an external stone glacis. The total width of the base of this composite defensive wall was 9 metres. Little of the internal arrangements of the fortress, which enclosed a space *c.* 13 metres square, could be made out, but the internal superstructure was supported on a series of massive piers. If the identifications of Tell el Fûl with Gibeah and Tell Nasbeh with Mizpah are correct, the two sites may have been fortified at the same time, for it is recorded in I Kings 15 that when Asa of Judah had persuaded the king of Damascus to attack Baasha of Israel from the north, thus forcing the latter to suspend his campaign against the southern kingdom, Asa destroyed the fort Baasha had built at Ramah, and used the material for the fortification of Gibeah and Mizpah. The association of the fortification of the two sites with this incident is supported by the similarity of the method employed, with the use of the enveloping glacis, and by the employment at Tell el Fûl of re-used stones in the walls.

The fortress at Tell el Fûl did not form part of a town or village, as did its predecessors. It is in fact an example of a fortified tower or *migdal* of which representations appear on Egyptian monuments recording campaigns in Palestine. Such towers may have formed a characteristic part of the defences of Judah at this period, for a number of similar contemporary structures have been identified on the southern borders of the kingdom in the Negeb.

At Jerusalem itself all the collapses and quarrying which have been described in connection with the earlier periods have removed any evidence that can be associated with recorded historical events. Excavation evidence has, however, shown that there were two expansions of the Solomonic city within the period of the kingdom of Judah. That on the east comes almost certainly in the 8th century B.C. That on the west side may be 7th century, and is discussed below (pp. 293 ff.). The original east wall had a long life, from its construction in the 18th century B.C., and there is evidence of rebuilding. Plate 91 shows that it was succeeded by a later one, to the west of the main section uncovered, but crossing the latter's angle to the north-east. This wall was in fact not the first to supersede the original wall, for there is stratigraphical evidence of an intermediate wall which has completely vanished. The wall seen in the photograph was itself rebuilt on a number of occasions.

This new line, or lines, of wall indicates a considerable expansion of the town. The siting of the original east wall far down the slope was dictated by the need to control access to the Spring Gihon. Beyond the vicinity of the spring, there was no need to include this uninviting steep slope within the city, and the town wall therefore ran obliquely up the ridge to the north-west. The same reasoning dictated the Solomonic extension, which was limited to the crest of the ridge. The new line of wall ignored the uphill turn of its predecessor and continued north at the same height, midway down the slope of the Kedron Valley. The full dating evidence has not yet been worked out. The crucial point is provided by Square A XXIV. This is only *c*. 26 metres from the area in which the Jebusite terrace walls repaired by the Israelites (see p. 294) were found. In A XXIV there is no trace of these structures, and the earlier building, based on rock, could be about the 8th century B.C. (again fuller assessment of the evidence is required). This first building had substantial stone walls, and in the corner of the excavated area had a staircase with good ashlar treads leading to a higher terrace. In a small niche or cupboard was a nest of bronze vessels, two buckets and a jug. Overlying the first building was a second, circular in plan, which had had a floor of wooden beams, and was probably a storehouse.

These buildings are, therefore, evidence that by the 8th century, or thereabouts, the area of the city had been enlarged to take in the lower slopes towards the north-east. From the surviving remains, the new wall may have run to the south-east corner of Solomon's Temple platform. This is an important piece of evidence for the history of Jerusalem.

The recent excavations of Arad show that the site performed a function on the southern frontiers of Judah somewhat similar to that of Tell el Fûl on the north. The extensive town of the Early Bronze Age has already been described. The north-east corner of the site stands up as a tell high above the level of the rest of the site, for on it was constructed a citadel, founded directly on the final Early Bronze II remains. It was certainly a citadel throughout the life of the kingdom of Judah, with later stages in the Hellenistic, Roman, and Arab periods. Its earliest stage may even belong to the time of Solomon, though the evidence for this has still to be presented. The plan throughout the Iron Age was basically the same, with enclosing walls about 50 metres on each side, the earliest of casemate form, the later built on the offsets-and-insets plan, and a central courtyard surrounded by buildings on three sides. Some were certainly administrative, for a number of ostraca almost certainly belonging to official archives have been found. One complex is of especial interest, since it was certainly a sanctuary. In a large courtyard was a massive altar 2·5 metres square, standing high above the floor level, and built of mud and undressed stones. At the west end of the courtyard was a wide room, entered on one of its long sides, with the entrance flanked by two pillars that recall the pillars Jachin and Boaz of Solomon's Temple. Against the wall of this sanctuary were two benches. In the long side opposite the entrance a very small room projects to the west, plausibly identified as a Holy of Holies. In or near it were found in various strata two small stone altars and a *mazzebah* (or cult stone). The excavators' claim that this is certainly a sanctuary of Yahweh, on the grounds that it complies with biblical ritual laws and that it was part of an official citadel, is not completely convincing. The plan certainly bears no relation to that of Solomon's Temple, for it is planned on a broad and not longitudinal axis, and it can only be called tripartite if part of the courtyard is arbitrarily divided off and called a porch. The impossibility of an unorthodox sanctuary being included within a distant official frontier post is not supported by the evidence of considerable heterodoxy in the highest circles. Moreover, it does not now seem likely that the sanctuary was abolished during Josiah's reforms, for the later citadel wall that destroyed it probably belongs to the Hellenistic period.[9] Even if the implications of evidence of official cult centres of Yahweh outside Jerusalem are not accepted, the site remains of very great interest for the organization of the kingdom of Judah.

Another important southern town of Judah was Beersheba, forming one of the frontier posts facing the desert to the south. It was excavated by the late Professor Y. Aharoni from 1969 to 1972. There was some slight occupation in the 12th–11th centuries, but the first town is ascribed to the period of the United Monarchy, though it is difficult to assess the evidence for this since each stratum is described as comprising the fill beneath the floor, the floors, the débris on the floor, and the subsequent accumulation of soil, and therefore the significance of pottery ascribed to a stratum is ambiguous.[10] The first town wall was solid, with offsets-and-insets. Above it, belonging to Stratum II, was a casemate wall, with its external base protected by a plastered bank. The associated gateway was boldly planned, with two guard-chambers on each side and external towers. The plan of Stratum II, probably 8th century, was the only one of which a considerable area was exposed, though there were indications that the underlying towns had similar plans. The plan (Fig. 83) had much in common with that of Tell Beit Mirsim A and other towns of Iron Age II. Some 15 metres inside the town wall was a ring road. Between the wall and the road were radially planned buildings, which were connected with, and made use of, the casemate chambers. Inside the ring road, the buildings were in separately planned blocks, though not so regularly oriented north and south as at Tell Beit Mirsim. Most of these buildings were domestic, of the standard Iron Age four-room plan. To the right of the gateway there was, however, an interesting exception. In this group there were three blocks divided by stone piers into a nave and two side-aisles, closely resembling those found at Megiddo and Hazor. The side-aisles were cobbled, and were *c.* 0·50 metres below the beaten earth floor of the central nave. Between the piers were walls of rough stones revetting the higher floor in the central nave;

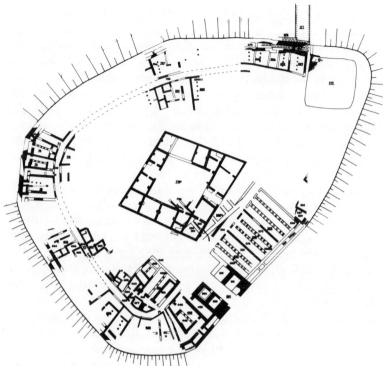

Fig. 83. Plan of Beersheba

the upper part of these walls formed rough compartments which the excavators call shelves, but which could more exactly be described as shallow sunk basins or storage compartments. In the side-aisles were found a very great quantity of pottery vessels. It is convincingly concluded that these buildings were used as storehouses. They could well have been the royal stores to which the taxes in kind, grain, wine, oil, and so on, were taken, and they would thus be evidence that Beersheba was an administrative centre of the region. Other public buildings may have been an imposing residence adjoining the square inside the south-east gate, and a water-collection pit (rather than an access shaft to a spring, which is improbable because of the low level of the water table) in the north-east corner. The further suggestion of the excavators that the whole town was a royal citadel is not supported by convincing arguments.

The two greatest towns of Judah, apart from Jerusalem, were

Gezer and Lachish (Tell Duweir). Gezer was first excavated at the beginning of the century, when excavation technique had not developed to the stage of the interpretation of difficult stratigraphy, though the excavations were in many ways a model of a conscientious attempt to make use of all evidence. The Hebrew Union College excavations between 1964 and 1973 have already been referred to in the case of the Solomonic town. The excavations identified levels with pottery datable to the 8th to 6th centuries B.C. So far there is little evidence of the layout and character of the town, but the publication is still in progress.

The excavation of Tell Duweir, which must be identified as Lachish since there is no other site of sufficient importance in the neighbourhood, had to be suspended before clearance on the hill itself had done more than touch the levels of this period. Work on the site was resumed in 1973 by Tel Aviv University Institute of Archaeology under the direction of Dr David Ussishkin, and in due course more definite evidence should be provided. Lachish is one of the towns included in the biblical list of those fortified by Rehoboam at the time when the division of Solomon's kingdom and the reappearance on the scene of Egypt as a military power under Shishak I again made defence an urgent problem. It is very possible that to Rehoboam should be attributed the fortifications which encircle the site, and which remained in use down to the end of the Israelite period. The method of construction of this wall is interesting. The lowest portion was built of stones on a pronounced batter, forming in fact another example of glacis-type defence. Above this there was a section of vertical stone wall and above this again a section of mud-brick. This illustrates the way in which stone and mud-brick were combined even on sites where stone was relatively plentiful. Within the fortifications a large palace-fortress was identified, with a great open courtyard in front of it. There may thus have been something in the nature of an official quarter here, but not enough of the summit was cleared to determine how it was related to other parts of the town. The existence of a fairly large official quarter may account for the fact that the population seems to have overflowed the walls, for remains of houses of the period were found on the slopes outside.

Excavation has thus shown us that town life was flourishing in the period of the dual monarchy. The towns were well populated, and there seems to have been a certain amount of specialization in crafts; at Tell Beit Mirsim there were many textile workers and at

Beth-Shemesh there was a concentration on the olive-oil and wine industries. There are clearly two types of town, those which are dominated by a large and exclusive official quarter, and those which seem to be occupied entirely by private buildings, in the layout and house plan of which there are many common characteristics. The towns are all walled, and there appear to be two main types of fortification, the casemate type and the type with glacis at the foot.

The great cities at Samaria and Megiddo allow us to get some glimpse of royal and official luxury. The finds at other sites suggest fairly general prosperity but little luxury. Very little has been found that suggests any high degree of artistic skill or taste. Ornaments, consisting of brooches, rings, ear-rings, beads, and other pendants, are simple, the majority of the metal objects being in bronze, with a few in silver. Little gold of this period has been found. Iron is in common use for all types of tools and weapons; for instance iron sickles displace flint ones about 1000 b.c., and iron arrowheads come into common use about the same time. Enough examples have been found of all types of iron tools, woodworking and agricultural, such as ploughshares, to show that the metal was readily available to everyone. The pottery in use is well made and plentiful, though very little really fine ware has been found. An interesting type of toilet object, suggestive of the fineries of Jezebel and her ladies, is a small limestone palette probably used for mixing cosmetics; examples are found in many sites, so its use was not confined to court circles. Not many cult objects belonging to this period have been found, showing that the religion of Israel had not to face so much competition as previously. An exception, however, is the fertility figurines which are found on many sites in the southern but not the northern kingdom. These are of a type, moulded in the round and not as plaques, which appear first in Early Iron II.

At Samaria the layout of the city with its royal quarter lasted throughout the Israelite period. There is, however, a marked decline in building standards. Within the royal quarter new buildings were put up, to give place to which the earliest very fine enclosed wall was abolished. The new buildings were substantial but the masonry very rough. Later buildings, of irregular plan and alignment, were constructed against the casemated enclosure wall, thus spoiling the original symmetry of the layout. The earliest of these inferior buildings must be dated still within the 9th century b.c., perhaps when Jehu drove out the dynasty of Omri in 841 b.c. About 800 b.c. the casemate enclosure wall had to be at least in part

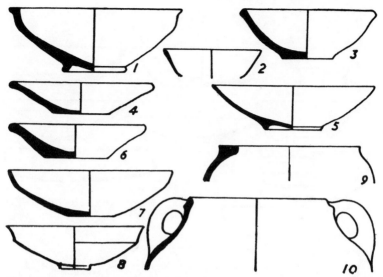

Fig. 84. Pottery of Samaria Period IV. ⅕

rebuilt after some disaster, and the rebuilt wall, with broken and ill-laid stones, shows none of the fine skill so apparent in the early wall. It is clear that when the Phoenician craftsmen imported by Omri and Ahab were no longer responsible for the work, the Israelites reverted to their old, rough, building technique.

In one of the new buildings in the courtyard was found a large number of ostraca—documents written on potsherds. They represent receipts of taxes collected in kind. The building which contained them may have been a government storehouse. The structural evidence, and that of the ware of the sherds, suggest a date towards 800 B.C. The receipts range in date from the ninth to the seventeenth year of some king. The political conditions which would best suit are those of the reign of Jehoiahaz, who reigned for seventeen years from 813 to 796 B.C., but during the first eight years of his reign Hazael and Benhadad of Damascus were oppressing Israel. When the Aramaean threat was ended by the invasion of that country by Adadnirari III of Assyria, Jehoiahaz would have been once more in control of the whole kingdom, and able to collect the taxes, thus accounting for the fact that the receipts start only in the ninth year. Archaeological evidence and historical records thus agree well in the dating, and provide an important fixed point in the chronology of Hebrew scripts.[11]

283

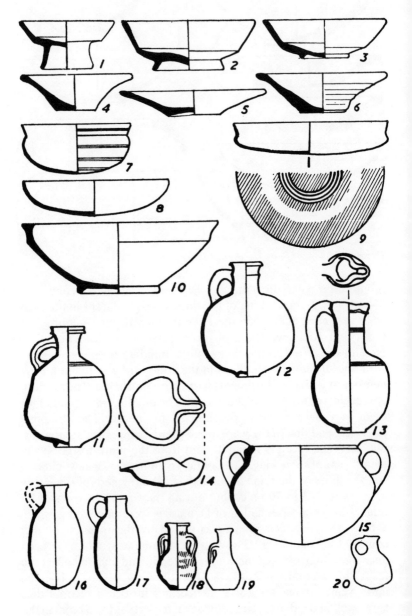

Fig. 85. Pottery of Samaria Period VI. ⅕

At Megiddo, as at Samaria, the Phoenician building style was short lived. The succeeding great official quarter of Stratum IV, in which Phoenician-style ashlars were re-used, may have been destroyed when the town was captured by the Assyrians in 734 B.C. In the new layout which succeeded it, the official quarter was abolished, and its place taken by an ordinary town of private houses. This was fairly regularly laid out in insulae divided by well-planned streets, and the buildings were comparatively spacious; it is in this respect quite unlike the earlier towns of this period, and there is no trace of the ring of buildings round the walls. The building style reverted to the old rubble-wall technique, and ashlars were no longer employed.

Notes

1. *Samaria Sebaste III*, pp. 200 ff; Kenyon, 'Megiddo, Hazor, Samaria and Chronology'. Institute of Archaeology Bulletin 4 (1964), 143–57.
2. The problem is discussed by J. B. Pritchard in *Near Eastern Archaeology in the Twentieth Century,* ed. J. A. Sanders (New York, 1970), and by Y. Yadin in *Magnalia Dei: The Mighty Acts of God,* ed. F. M. Cross *et al.* (Garden City, N.Y., 1976).
3. Kenyon, 'Megiddo, Hazor, Samaria and Chronology', pp. 144–50.
4. *Biblical Archaeologist* XXXIIII, 3.
5. The use of the three-chamber gateway with the offsets-and-insets town wall is clear on plan; the case for its original use is argued on pp. 247 ff.
6. *Megiddo I*, p. 12, fig. 15.
7. Yadin, *Hazor*, Schweich Lectures, pp. 127–8.
8. Frances W. James, *The Iron Age at Beth-shan* (Philadephia, 1966, pp. 43 ff.
9. *IEJ* 15.
10. Y. Aharoni, ed. *Beer-Sheba* I. *Excavations at Tel Beer-Sheba. 1969–1971 Seasons* (Tel Aviv University Institute of Archaeology, 1973).
11. Many alternative proposals for the dates have, however, been suggested.

12 The Fall of the Hebrew Kingdoms and the Post-Exilic Period

Little has been said in the previous chapter of the political events affecting the kingdoms of Judah and Israel. The biblical record, supplemented ьy our present knowledge of the written history of the Near East, makes it clear that peaceful conditions existed only for very short stretches of time throughout the whole period of the dual monarchy. The archaeological record supports that of history. For instance, the fortification of the royal quarter of Samaria may have been caused by the siege of the city by Benhadad II of Damascus at Ahab's accession. The destruction of the fine enclosure wall and its replacement by rougher buildings may have been due to the ravages of Jehu when he exterminated the dynasty of Omri. Rebuildings about the middle of the 8th century B.C. may have been needed after the anarchy that followed the death of Jeroboam II. The end of Stratum IV at Megiddo may have been due to the Assyrian attack on Israel c. 734 B.C., in which most of the northern part of the kingdom was lost. The violent destruction of Stratum V at Hazor is certainly to be ascribed to the same cause. On most sites there is in fact evidence for violent events during this period, but as a rule the archaeological evidence does not provide a sufficiently exact chronology to enable a positive correlation of archaeological and historical events to be made. The general picture is similar, however, and the exact correlation often immaterial.

We know now that behind all the political events in the biblical account lie the vicissitudes in the history of the Assyrian Empire. After some three centuries in which her history is almost a blank, Assyria became a potent factor again under Ashur-nasi-pal (884–859 B.C.). For the next two and a half centuries she adopted a policy of expansion and conquest, spasmodically interrupted by revolts of the subject peoples, usually at the accession of a new king. Between the Hebrew kingdoms and Assyria lay the Aramaic kingdom of Damascus. When Assyria was weak, Damascus was apt to be a thorn in the flesh of Israel. When Assyria was threatening Damascus, Israel was freed from pressure, and could recover her lost possessions. When Israel was at grips with Damascus, Judah would free herself from Israelite control. When Judah was suffering at the hands of Israel, Edom could revolt from her, and when Israel in turn was weak, the other kingdoms east of the Jordan could likewise break away, or attack in their turn. And so the train of events went on, with now one country and now another in the ascendant.

But with each wave of aggression, the Assyrians pressed farther and farther towards the Mediterranean and to the south. In 734 B.C. Tiglath-pileser III marched right into Palestine. So little did the Hebrews realize the perils involved in dealing with the cruel Mesopotamian power that Ahaz of Judah had appealed to him for help against Israel, and he attacked both Israel and the Philistine cities, which after a long period of quiescence were once more taking advantage of the weakness of Judah. Philistia was annexed by Assyria, and Hosea of Israel was left with only the southern half of his kingdom. Galilee and the territory east of the Jordan were annexed, and the tribes of Reuben, Gad, and Manasseh were carried away into captivity. This was in fact the ruthless policy of the Assyrians to control captured territory; whole populations were deported and their place taken by exiles from other parts of the empire. This policy has a singularly modern ring.

This was the beginning of the end for the northern kingdom. In the last stages a new factor appears, the revival of Egypt, which had not intervened in Syrian politics since the time of Shishak I, two centuries earlier. The surviving Syrian kingdoms, relying on help from Egypt, attempted to free themselves from tribute to the Assyrians, but the only result was to hasten the end. In 724 B.C. Shalmaneser V besieged Samaria, which resisted for two years, but fell to his successor Sargon II in 722 B.C. Sargon then advanced right to the Egyptian border and defeated the Egyptians and the Philistines and their other Syrian allies. On his way back in 720 B.C. he carried off the rest of the tribes of Israel into captivity. In their place he settled in Samaria men of Babylon and other foreign cities.

Judah and Phoenicia were the only Syrian kingdoms that survived the great thrust, but future advances were to come. In 705 B.C. Sennacherib once more led the Assyrians south, and much of Judah was ravaged. Lachish was captured and sacked, as were many lesser towns. Jerusalem was besieged, and, though it held out, Hezekiah of Judah had to buy off the Assyrians by paying tribute. Judah survived for another century, but only as a semi-independent vassal. How unreal the independence was is shown in the Assyrian records, where reference is made to a garrison of Philistine mercenaries maintained at Lachish.

On a number of sites archaeological evidence has been found of these events, for their effect was so cataclysmic that there is seldom much doubt in the correlation of the archaeological and historical evidence.

At Samaria the Israelite royal quarter was completely destroyed. In every place where undisturbed levels of the latest Israelite buildings were found, there were thick layers of burnt material. In this débris were found many fragments from the ivory decorations of the palace of Omri and Ahab, and the best were found in similar débris that had been disturbed in later building operations. Many of the ivories were found completely blackened by fire. Those that were not were found embedded in sticky light-coloured deposits, which clearly represented the mud-brick superstructure of the buildings that had fallen on them in the destruction and thus saved them from being burnt. A period of looting no doubt preceded the firing of the building, and it is tempting to regard the almost identical ivories found in Sargon's palace at Nimrud as the proceeds of this looting. Hardly a wall belonging to the period survives above ground level. It is not always clear how much of this destruction of walls took place at this time, or how much at later periods, when the foundations were dug out for building stone. It is certain that none of the interior buildings survived to any appreciable extent, for their lines are completely ignored by subsequent buildings. The casemate wall round the summit may partly have survived, for its line was followed by the 2nd-century Hellenistic fort wall, and it may even have been itself repaired earlier in the Hellenistic period, while the wall on the Middle Terrace certainly was sufficiently intact in the 3rd century B.C. to be strengthened by the great Hellenistic towers. It seems quite reasonable to suppose that the defensive walls were retained and repaired, for Samaria was made the centre of an administrative district under the Assyrians, while the internal buildings were obliterated. The remnants of the population and the strangers settled there must have lived as best they could in the ruins. Least of all would they have required the great royal buildings of the summit, where no doubt the destruction would have been especially concentrated. The living quarters of the ordinary people, about which we have no evidence, may have suffered less damage, and the inhabitants in their reduced numbers may have lived there.

The evidence for a break in the culture of the site is most striking. From Period I to Period VI of the phases identified in the excavations there is a steady development in the pottery and other finds, but no sudden change and no outside influence. In the layer overlying the destruction, a little of the latest Israelite pottery continues, but together with it appear completely new wares. Noticeable among these are a number of bowls with high flaring rims of very thin fine ware which are quite unlike anything found on the site before, and which have no developments in Palestine. It is in fact Assyrian and the very fine vessels belong to the class of fine Palace Ware which has been found at Nimrud.[1] Clearly we have here the pottery imported by some of the new settlers, which dies out after a comparatively short space of time, as the settlers come to use the local pottery.

At Tell el Far'ah an exactly similar course of events can be traced. The buildings of that town which had grown up *c.* 800 B.C. were destroyed by fire. The subsequent occupation is very much poorer and in it appear the same imported types of pottery as at Samaria.*

Megiddo was no doubt lost to Israel earlier than Samaria, in the annexation of the northern territory in 734 B.C. As has been already suggested, it may have been at this stage that the buildings of Stratum IV were destroyed. The pottery in Stratum III does not show such a sharp break as that at Samaria, but a certain number of new forms, with no obvious local ancestry, do appear. But it may well be that the new layout of Stratum III is due to the Assyrians or to their settlers. The plan with its large, regular, rectangular insulae is quite un-Palestinian. Unfortunately, nothing is known of the Assyrian town sites of the period (only the palaces have been excavated), so one cannot say whether the plan owes anything to direct Assyrian influence, but foreign influence of some sort is strongly suggested.

Though only the northern kingdom was annexed, the towns of the southern kingdom suffered severely in the later Assyrian campaigns. It was probably now that Beth-Shemesh IIb was destroyed by fire. The fortress at Gibeah was destroyed by fire at about the same period. Tell Jemmeh, near Gaza, may have suffered the same fate, and it is interesting that here too foreign pottery appears.

* At Shechem there is the same evidence and the same pottery.

There are a few vessels very like those found at Samaria, already mentioned, but most striking of all was a great deposit found together in one pit, which Sir Flinders Petrie called the Dinner Service of the Assyrian governor. A few of the vessels are undoubtedly Assyrian of the late 8th century B.C., small cups of eggshell fineness with high flaring rims, ridiculously small bases, and dimples in the walls. The rest can certainly be called a dinner service; it is not actually Assyrian, but is a copy of the types found in Assyria in the late 8th century B.C. referred to above. It consists of scores of plates with peculiar stepped profiles near the base and ridges below the short everted rim. Some are much finer than others, and of a different ware. They may have been imported by some officer in the Assyrian army and the rest copied locally to his direction in imitation of his own native ware.

That Lachish was captured we know from both the biblical and the Assyrian records. Reliefs found at Nineveh show the siege in progress. The clearest evidence of this destruction came from the débris in the lower roadway on which was found the crest of a bronze helmet identical with those worn by the soldiers depicted attacking Lachish on the Assyrian reliefs (Pl. 92). Fragments of some armour and Assyrian weapons were also found. The identification of the destruction layer on the summit of the mound is a matter of debate, and is discussed below (pp. 297 ff.).

Jerusalem did not fall to the Assyrians, but it was put to desperate straits. In the face of the Assyrian menace, Hezekiah repaired the town walls, and one of the stages of the wall superseding the old line (p. 277) is probably to be ascribed to him. Only when the pottery from the 1961–67 excavations has been fully assessed will it be possible to say which stage comes here. In addition he strengthened the city by carrying out another of those remarkable feats of engineering in connection with the water-supply, of which examples have already been given. The earlier secret access to the spring now known as the Virgin's Fountain, described in Chapter 10, had long been abandoned, and the spring subsequently used to irrigate gardens on the slopes of Ophel. The older tunnel was not restored, for the geography of the city had now changed. Instead, a tunnel was carried right through the hill of Ophel from the north-east to the south-west slopes, which were at that time within the walls of the city, and the waters of the spring were thereby conducted into a pool, the Pool of Siloam of the New Testament, into which they still run.

The achievements of Hezekiah who 'stopped the upper spring of the waters of Gihon and brought them straight down on the west side of the city of David' are referred to several times in 2 Kings and 2 Chronicles. The Siloam Tunnel has long been known, and in 1880 an inscription was discovered on its wall recording the excitement of the workmen when the two parties working from each end met in the heart of the hill. In the excavations of 1909–11 the whole tunnel was cleared out. Archaeological evidence, though it did not provide close confirmation, agreed well with the traditional ascription of this work to Hezekiah, and the meticulous examination carried out at the time by Père Vincent showed how the work was done. The line of the tunnel follows a most curiously sinuous course, for which there is no really satisfactory explanation, though it is suggested that it was in part to avoid disturbing ancient royal tombs. The point of junction of the two sections, with frenzied changes of direction hither and thither, gives eloquent illustration to the triumph shown in the inscription. The level of the tunnel was maintained with much more accuracy than was its line, though it too required some adjustment. Père Vincent has shown that this explains why the height of the tunnel varies from as much as 5 metres, at the southern end, to as little as 1·60 metres. Close examination showed that the tunnel as first pierced was in the neighbourhood of 1·60 metres to 2 metres high, but the slope of the floor was not quite regular. This was adjusted by lowering the floor where necessary, thus forming the higher parts of the tunnel. The resultant level secures a perfect flow from the spring to the pool, with a drop of 2·18 metres in a distance of 512·5 metres. Even though some adjustments were required, it represents an amazing piece of engineering with primitive surveying instruments.

The interpretation of the Pool of Siloam has, however, been complicated by the discovery in the 1961–67 excavations that the inclusion of at least the eastern side of the western of the two ridges, into which the southern part of ancient Jerusalem is divided, comes only in the 1st century A.D. When it was believed, on the basis of the Bliss and Dickie plan,[2] that at least by the time of the later monarchy the whole of the western ridge was enclosed by a wall running round to the southern tip of the eastern ridge, the channelling of the waters of the Spring Gihon to the Pool of Siloam in the central valley which bounds the eastern ridge to the west seemed satisfactorily to meet Hezekiah's requirements of making the water unavailable to the enemy. On the plan, Fig. 86, are shown the sites excavated on the

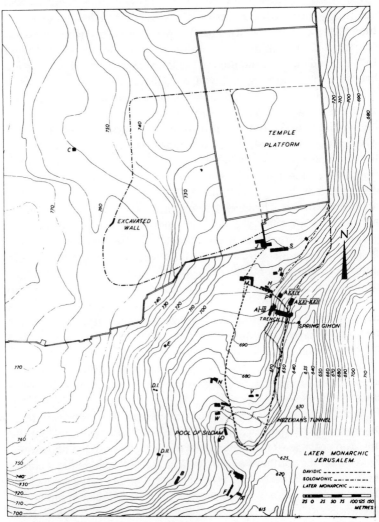

Fig. 86. *Plan of Jerusalem during later monarchy*

western slope of the eastern ridge and the eastern slope of the western ridge. The evidence is conclusive. None of the sites on the slopes of the western ridge gave any evidence of occupation earlier than the 1st century A.D. The sites on the eastern side of the central valley are equally emphatic that there was no spread across the valley during the period of the monarchy. Some of the individual soundings that provided this evidence may be small, but the cumulative area and the evidence therefrom is considerable and cannot be brushed aside to fit in with other theories.

The position of the Pool of Siloam, therefore, suggests at first sight that Hezekiah's major work in bringing the water through the hill to the west side did not achieve very much. The central valley was slightly less exposed than the eastern valley, but the position of the Pool was still outside the walls, and entirely commanded by an enemy occupying the western ridge. Attempts made to find an enclosing wall were fruitless, and in fact any wall enclosing the Pool at the base of the valley would have been impossibly vulnerable to attack from the steep slopes to the west.

The explanation came from the observation that the overflow from the Pool was carried in a rock-cut channel whose, outer (Pl. 94) edge had been truncated by quarrying. If care was thus taken to disguise the line of the overflow, instead of letting it run down the normal route of the centre of the valley, the position of the Pool itself must have been disguised. It must in fact have been a rock-cut, roofed, cistern, accessible by a staircase or shaft from within the city, but invisible from the outside.

The discussion of the evidence concerning the Pool of Siloam has an important bearing on the problem of the expansion of the city, during the period of the later monarchy, on to the western ridge. Excavations within the Old City by Professor N. Avigad have produced evidence[3] of a massive wall (Pl. 96), certainly a town wall, midway up the slope to the summit of the western ridge (see Fig. 86). This is certain evidence that the city had expanded into the western ridge at this time. The further course of the wall has not been established. Professor Avigad's view that it continued south to enclose the Pool of Siloam before curving round to the east to rejoin the tip of the eastern ridge cannot be accepted on the evidence from the sites shown on the plan, Fig. 86. On this plan is suggested the outline of this expansion of the city. It can in the present lack of evidence be very much varied by prolonging the southern bulge to the south, on the summit of the ridge, an area inaccessible to the

1961–67 excavators because it was in no-man's land. The only fixed point is that the extension must have rejoined the original city north of Site M, of which the western end was certainly outside the built-up area of the Iron Age city.

It has been suggested[4] that this expansion onto the western hill was caused by the influx into Jerusalem of refugees from the northern kingdom of Israel after the completion of the Assyrian conquest in 720 B.C. This is an attractive idea, but the full publication of the pottery evidence must be awaited before the matter can be settled. It is, for the time being, the reason why this expansion is dealt with separately from that on the eastern slope, which would appear to have come earlier.

The kingdom of Judah was not brought to a final end until more than a century after the fall of Israel. From Jerusalem there is some slight evidence for this final century. To it belong the few surviving domestic buildings in Jerusalem found by the 1961–67 expedition. They survive at the summit of the eastern slope above the Spring Gihon. They are constructed directly on the terraces that were the Jebusite contribution to the planning of Jerusalem (see p. 277), and that were repaired by David and his successors. The terraces were precarious structures, dependent on retaining walls, each bounding a terrace and each supported by terraces lower down the hill. The frequent catastrophes, from natural agencies or human destruction, are proved by the fact that though the original terraces were certainly Jebusite, and some repairs can be attributed to the early stages of the monarchy, the only houses actually to survive on them belong to the 7th century B.C. They consist of domestic buildings of unimpressive character. The walls are of very roughly dressed stones, only roughly coursed, set in mud-mortar and originally faced with a covering of mud-mortar. Most of the rooms were small, and the planning was only roughly rectangular. Only one room was larger than those at Tell Nasbeh which belonged to the tripartite houses which have a central area divided from two side areas by rows of monolithic piers. Only one of these rows was found, as the easternmost had collapsed down the hill in the erosion following the Babylonian destruction. The basically domestic use is shown by the plan and by the find of a characteristic domed clay oven. In one area, the find of forty-one stone weights, some of them inscribed with their denomination, suggests the abode of a shopkeeper or craftsman.

To a period that may just precede this final century in the history of Monarchic Jerusalem or may belong to the beginning of this century, belongs one of the most interesting finds of the 1961–67 excavations; the question of whether it is to be ascribed to the end of the 8th century or the early part of the 7th has still to be established by an analysis of the finds. It consisted of structures (Pl. 95) low on the eastern slope, outside the contemporary walls. One complex consisted of a shallow cave surrounded by massive walls, in which there was a large deposit of pottery. Adjoining it was a small room in which there were two standing stones, certainly to be interpreted as *mazzeboth*, or cult symbols. On the rock scarp above was a small rectangular structure that could well be an altar. It is reasonably certain that the complex is to be interpreted as a sanctuary, in which the cave served the function of a *favissa*, a repository of vessels offered in the sanctuary, which would not thereafter be returned to profane use. Ten metres to the south was a larger cave, containing a much larger deposit of objects, mainly pottery vessels, but including a fine incense-burner and a large number of figurines, female figures of the fertility-goddess type, and animals including horses with disks on their foreheads, possibly associated with the 'horses of the sun'.[5] This cave must also have been a *favissa* of the same or an adjacent sanctuary. The complex must be interpreted as an extramural sanctuary of an unorthodox cult. The denunciation of the prophets prepare one for such sanctuaries, but it is a surprise to find this evidence within *c.* 300 metres of the boundary of the Temple of Yahweh. It is tempting to see in the great accumulation of objects, some 1,300 in all in the larger cave, evidence of the cleansing of all unorthodox sanctuaries by Josiah *c.* 750 B.C. The stratification makes it difficult to accept a date as late as this, and full interpretation must wait until the analysis of the finds has been completed. Elsewhere archaeology has not produced much evidence. Towns which had been destroyed were in some cases rebuilt. At Beth-Shemesh, for instance, the town of Stratum IIc was built on the ruins of IIb, on approximately the same plan.

It is to this period that Level III of Lachish is probably to be attributed. The problem of the precise identification of pottery types from deposits of the 7th century B.C. is crucial to the interpretation of the archaeological evidence. Following the campaign of Sennacherib, Judah enjoyed a century of nominal independence, though it was in fact a vassal of Assyria. In 621 B.C. the Assyrian empire gave place to the Babylonian in Mesopotamia, and the Babylonians became heirs to the Assyrian dominions and power.

The respite for Palestine was only temporary, and Nebuchadnezzar, in campaigns in 598 and 589–587 B.C., finally annexed Judah. The archaeological problem is to identify the evidence of the destructions ranging from that of Sennacherib in 701 B.C. to those of Nebuchadnezzar in the early 6th century.

Certainly within this period most towns in Judah suffered violent destruction. The excavations of Tell Beit Mirsim in the 1920s were the first to provide detailed evidence. The site was completely destroyed and never reoccupied. The abundant pottery found in the ruins of the destroyed town has been taken to be typical of the late 7th–early 6th centuries B.C. At Beth-Shemesh there was a similar destruction and abandonment. Beersheba suffered a similar fate. But here the excavator, Professor Aharoni, claimed that the destruction was the result of the campaign of Sennacherib. To account for the resemblance of the pottery in the destruction level to that from Tell Beit Mirsim A, he suggests that the greater part of the destroyed town of Tell Beit Mirsim A was 8th century, and that only a small rebuilding near the gate belonged to the final town destroyed by Nebuchadnezzar. This may be a perceptive analysis of published evidence, or special pleading. Only further evidence will provide the answer. Involved in this discussion is the date of the destruction of Lachish III, which in preliminary reports J. L. Starkey ascribed to the first Babylonian campaign, but in the final report of Miss Tufnell ascribed to Sennacherib.

The major problem must concentrate on exactitude in dating the pottery of the 7th century B.C. In the Samaria report[6] it was argued that the published pottery ascribed to Lachish III, of which the analysis excluded areas of uncertain stratification, was completely different from that of Samaria VI, destroyed by the Assyrians only twenty years earlier, while the Lachish group was very close to that of Tell Beit Mirsim A, ascribed to the Babylonian destruction.

The town of Beersheba Stratum II was likewise completely destroyed, and Professor Aharoni argued that this destruction was the work of Sennacherib's campaign, though this involved some special pleading to account for later biblical references, which, it is suggested, referred to dependent villages beneath the modern town of Beersheba. In this argument, which is weak, the date of Lachish III is involved, and Aharoni would wish to return to the Assyrian dating. A detailed pottery analysis of the Beersheba deposits,[7] those of the *favissa* caves at Jerusalem,[8] and those of Lachish Level III,[9] suggests[10] that the deposits can be differentiated, with the suggestion that the destruction of Beersheba II comes somewhere in the middle of the 7th century, and is not the work of either Sennacherib or Nebuchadnezzar.

A crucial point in the problem is the evidence from Tell Duweir (Lachish), now being excavated by Dr David Ussishkin. These excavations—carrying on from the point at which those of the Wellcome–Marston excavation, under the direction of J. L. Starkey, had to be suspended, have made the evidence concerning the last stage of Iron Age Lachish much more clear.[11] The excavations were concerned mainly with Levels IV and III. Both levels used the same substantial brick-built town wall, to which is considered to belong the excellent three-chambered gateway, and stages in the podium of the palace or fort on the summit could be assigned to each of the two stages. Between the south end of the podium and the gateway, private houses of Level IV underlay those of III. All the structures of Level III were destroyed by fire, the débris from which was in some places very deep. Level IV also ended in destruction but not by fire. It is on these grounds that Ussishkin assigns the destruction of III to Sennacherib in 701 B.C. This capture of Lachish by Sennacherib is particularly vivid to us, since it is illustrated dramatically in the reliefs from his palace at Nineveh, reliefs now in the British Museum. The reliefs decorated what was apparently a ceremonial suite, and it may be concluded that the capture of Lachish was considered of great importance. The military action up to the storming of the city and the carrying-off of captives and families going into exile is vividly portrayed. The accompanying text[12] describes the besieging and conquest of '46 of the strong cities, walled forts', of 'Hezekiah the Jew', and the driving-out of the population and the taking as booty their flocks and herds. It does not mention the razing or burning of Lachish (or the other cities). This Ussishkin notes, but reasonably concludes that it was probable. Against this it could be argued that Hezekiah's towns which Sennacherib had plundered were given over to some of the local princes, which could suggest that they were not wiped out.

This argument that the heavily burnt level must represent the Sennacherib destruction has therefore a weak link. It could be that the destruction recorded by Ussishkin as ending Level IV but without evidence of burning is really that of the Assyrian attack. It is difficult to accept the earlier date for the Level III destruction because of the problem of the pottery. The reasons why in *Samaria-Sebaste III* the suggestion was made that Lachish III was destroyed in 597 B.C. have already been given. This conclusion was accepted by many but not all archaeologists. Not only is there considerable difficulty in putting the III pottery into the 8th century, but it leaves almost nothing for the 7th century. It is not impossible, though improbable, that it will prove to have been a century of very slow change. When the pottery from the Jerusalem excavations has been studied in detail, it will be possible to be more precise. The comparison of the pottery from the Jerusalem cult centre referred to above (p. 295) already suggests that differentiation will be possible.

The argument is also used that in the Level III destruction are found royal Judaean stamped jars. For long these jars, or at any rate most of them, have been dated to the 7th century B.C. The raising of their date has been on the grounds of the associated pottery, for paleography cannot yet of itself produce form dating. The argument is therefore a circular one.

Another difficulty in accepting the Level III ascription to 701 B.C. is that it means that for the next century the very important town of Lachish was an unwalled town with a squatter occupation, which seems improbable.

This element of doubt concerning the dating of Lachish Level III effects conclusions about the rest of the towns and villages of Judah. To fit his conclusions about Beersheba, Professor Aharoni had to transfer almost all the remains of the flourishing little town of Tell Beit Mirsim A, which he claimed was destroyed by the Assyrians, to the 8th century, leaving only some very poor fragments to cover the 7th century. Building periods in many other towns have been dated by comparison with Tell Beit Mirsim, of which the excavation by Professor Albright in the 1920s first provided a good stratified sequence of pottery (admittedly by methods which did not produce complete reliability). It is difficult to accept that the kingdom of Judah was left almost completely unpopulated, and until there is conclusive evidence to the contrary, one is tempted to retain the previous picture of the 7th century, the last century of the kingdom of Judah, and this is the view followed in the next paragraph.

Other towns, which had escaped destruction by the Assyrians, continued on the same lines as before. At Tell Beit Mirsim there is no major disturbance to be traced between *c*. 930 and 588 B.C. At Tell Nasbeh, likewise, there is continuous occupation. No doubt the position was the same in many other small towns. The culture remains the same, with perhaps even less to suggest artistic taste than before. Seventh-century pottery can be distinguished from that of the 8th century, but it is a development of it and there is no sharp dividing line. The development is in the direction of dullness and mass production; the pottery of the period is in fact ugly and uninteresting, though technically quite well made. It seems to reflect the low ebb in the political life of the kingdom.

Archaeology fully supports the biblical evidence of the disastrous effect of the Babylonian campaigns which brought this period to a close. Large numbers of towns were destroyed and never occupied again. Of these, Tell Beit Mirsim and Beth-Shemesh are typical examples. There had been periods of intermission of occupation of sites previously, but at no other time had large numbers of sites ceased permanently to be towns. This shows clearly how disastrous an effect the Babylonian policy had on the economy of the country. Probably only a proportion, possibly a quarter, of the population was actually carried into captivity, but the captives included all the leaders, and with it the organization and trade of the country was broken up. Its economy would no longer support the thickly populated towns of the period of the Jewish kingdoms.

The problem of the date of the destruction of Lachish Level III has just been discussed, and for the moment it is here ascribed to the first Babylonian destruction, in 598 B.C., with the destruction of Level II ascribed to the second campaign in 588 B.C. In the first campaign, the town of Level III was utterly destroyed in the view accepted here. Perhaps a last effort to prepare the town to withstand the coming assault was the excavation of an enormous rock-cut shaft, rectangular in plan with sides of 80 feet (24·38m.) and 70 feet (21·34m.) in depth. This colossal undertaking was never finished. The floor was completely irregular, and much lower on the south than on the north. There is no conclusive evidence of its purpose, but it was probably connected with the water-supply, either as a shaft to a spring or as a reservoir. But the Babylonian onslaught must have come before it could be brought into use. Right at the base of the filling are sherds of 6th-century pottery, and the hole was left open to fill up gradually in the course of the succeeding centuries.

The débris which overlies the remains of the town of Level III shows the violence and completeness of the destruction. In the gateway, 8 feet (2·43m.) of burnt débris separated the floors of this period from their successors. The palace-citadel was completely ruined, and a mass of calcined bricks overlay its stone foundations.

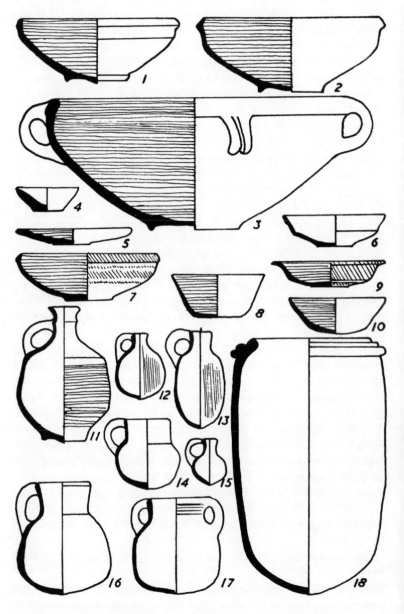

Fig. 87. Pottery of Tell Duweir Level III. $\frac{1}{5}$

Near the palace a row of shops was excavated (Pl. 93), one of the few portions of the interior of the city yet cleared. The rooms were found filled with the objects in use at the time of the destruction, which the inhabitants did not have time to rescue, great storage jars for corn, and a weaving establishment, representative of the industries and trade typical of a Palestinian town of the time. Outside the city was found a most extraordinary deposit of some two thousand bodies thrown into an old tomb through a hole in the roof. Some of the bones had been partly calcined, and the bodies must thus have been salvaged from the burnt buildings. J. L. Starkey believed that the remains represent the clearing-up of the city after savage slaughter by the Babylonians. Some of the skulls show battle injuries, but the most curious discovery was three skulls which had been trephined. In two cases, a square of bone had been removed by saw cuts. The surgery was very crude, and the patients did not survive. Does this represent experiments carried out by the conquerors on prisoners, in the manner of the Nazis, or the desperate attempts of survivors to save the life of a man injured in battle? Perhaps the second explanation is the more probable, in that in the third case, in which a hole had been made by scraping, the patient had apparently lived long enough for the bone to heal; it must therefore have been an old operation and not the immediate cause of death. Trephining may thus have been a recognized Israelite surgical practice, employed in the other instances on battle casualties.

Above the débris of destruction, the town was rebuilt with a few miserable houses. The incompleted great shaft was left open, to be filled in by gradual accumulation. Only the defences show some thoroughness in rebuilding, with a new gate built on top of the 8 feet of débris covering the ruins of its predecessor. In the final assault of Babylon against Judah, Lachish is listed by Jeremiah together with Jerusalem and Azekah as one of the last strongholds of Judah 'for these fenced cities remained of the cities of Judah' (Jer. 34:7).

But these 'fenced cities' soon fell before the Babylonian might. Excavation showed that the restored Lachish was once more destroyed by fire. In a guardroom between the outer and inner gate of the city, in the layer of ashes representing this fire, was found a collection of ostraca, or potsherds used for writing messages. Eighteen ostraca in all were found, of which seven are sufficiently legible to make connected sense, while on the others only isolated sentences and words can be read. The interpretation of the documents is difficult, partly because readings are in places uncertain, and partly because they allude to events and other documents that can only be conjectured. Experts differ both as to the readings and interpretation. But if the interpretation of Professor Torczyner, who was responsible for the full publication, is accepted, the documents are of extraordinary interest from their connection with the biblical account of the last days of the Hebrew kingdom.

The documents are all letters. A number are from a certain Hosha'yahu to his lord Ya'ush, and it is very possible that the less legible ones are part of the same correspondence. Hosha'yahu is apparently the commander of a fortified post and Ya'ush the governor of Lachish. The correspondence may come to a climax in Letter IV, in which Hosha'yahu says 'for the signal-stations of Lachish we are watching, according to all the signs which my lord gives, because we do not see [the signals of] Azekah'. The mention in Jeremiah of Lachish and Azekah as two of the last surviving cities of Judah has already been quoted. This sentence is most suggestive of impending tragedy; Azekah would appear to have fallen, and Hosha'yahu was dependent on orders getting through to him from the more distant Lachish.

But the documents do not appear to represent a collection of the latest letters received before Lachish fell, as it were the letters in the office filing-basket. In the first place, they seem to deal with events over an appreciable period of time. Secondly, they seem all to be from the same person, being in some cases written on pieces of the same pot, and it would be odd if while one correspondent wrote eighteen letters, no one else wrote any at all. There is, moreover, a theme running through all the intelligible letters, for in each Hosha'yahu seems to be trying to excuse himself and to deny he has committed some crime, which seems to be connected with having read some letters. Professor Torczyner has suggested a most ingenious interpretation, based on another passage, in Letter III, which seems to refer to events recorded in Jeremiah.

The efforts of the military leaders in Jerusalem at the time to oppose the power of Babylon were being greatly hampered by the prophet Jeremiah, who preached submission to Babylon and threatened with the wrath of Yahweh all who fought against its power. Another prophet who preached in the same vein was Urijah. Jeremiah, though often threatened and in peril, managed to escape death as a fifth-columnist. But Urijah was less fortunate. He was warned of impending arrest and fled to Egypt, but 'Jehoiakim the king sent men into Egypt, namely Elnathan the son of Achbor, and certain men with him'. Urijah was brought back and executed. In Lachish Letter III, in which an unnamed prophet is mentioned, there occurs the passage 'Down went the commander of the army [Yi]khbaryahu the son of Elnathan to come to Egypt and . . . his men he sent to take from here', and Professor Torczyner interprets the continuation of the letter to imply that the prophet had written a letter to warn a friend. He considers that the two accounts refer to the same incident, in one of which the general's name and that of his father have been transposed. He suggests that here in fact is the basis of at least one of the charges against Hosha'yahu, that he had improperly read confidential letters entrusted to him to forward, and had betrayed to the king or his officers that Urijah had fled to Egypt. This would imply, of course, that Ya'ush belonged to the party supporting the prophets Jeremiah and Urijah, and not that of the court circles. Such an interpretation would also provide an explanation for the presence of this particular collection of documents in the guard-chamber. A room at the gate of the city is traditionally the position of courts of justice in eastern countries. A court-martial may have been held on Hosha'yahu, to answer a charge of betraying Urijah, and there are hints in other letters that military charges may be involved too; the ostraca may have formed part of the files supplying evidence for the case, the rest of which may have been on papyrus and thus have been destroyed in the subsequent fire.

An intelligible explanation of such ancient documents is always difficult and must be in part conjectural. But whether Professor Torczyner's deductions are right in every respect or not, the names used, the language, and many small details reflect the conditions prevailing at the time at which Jeremiah wrote. They have also a very human interest. Most of the ancient documents which have survived are official, religious, or business documents. These are letters dealing with the doings of individuals. Their association with the last days of the Jewish kingdom is firmly fixed, for the ashes which covered them represent the final destruction of Lachish, never again to be occupied as a town, though it subsequently served as an administrative centre.

The climax of the Babylonian campaign was the capture of Jerusalem. The disappearance of Azekah is inferred; for the destruction of Lachish there is archaeological evidence. Of the 'fenced cities' of Judah, therefore, only Jerusalem remained. The strength of the fortifications of the capital is shown by the fact that the siege which started in 588 B.C. lasted for eighteen months, somewhat aided by a temporary intervention from Egypt, which may have allowed the inhabitants a breathing-space for revictualling. The final capitulation was due to famine, not to any breaching of the defences. One can infer that Nebuchadnezzar, having bottled up the intransigent rebels against Babylonian suzerainty, was content to leave a small besieging force, and did not bother to bring his full military might to bear.

Of this final stage of monarchical Jerusalem, the last rebuilding of the east wall (Pl. 91), low on the eastern slope above the Kedron Valley, is the most important evidence. The wall has a considerable number of rebuildings, of which the final one was pretty certainly the wall of Jerusalem at the time of the Babylonian siege in 588–587 B.C.

For the century between Hezekiah's rescue of Jerusalem from the Assyrians, through the somewhat dim period in which Judah was virtually an Assyrian tributary, one has, in fact, slightly more evidence of domestic occupation there for the earlier period. The destructive agencies of quarrying on the summit of the eastern ridge and of collapse of terraces on the slope has already been described (pp. 234, 237). The main area of excavation of the 1961–67 expedition was at the head of Trench I, running up to the walls and tower, completely erroneously ascribed to David and the Jebusites. The whole succession in fact belongs to the Post-Exilic and Maccabean period.

The houses here were very clearly, on visual and stratigraphical evidence, earlier than the so-called (unfortunately by the tourist guides *still* called) Tower of David. The pottery evidence, still to be worked over in detail, dated them to the 7th century B.C. The destruction of this period in the history of Jerusalem has been shown by the 1961–67 excavations to be very clear.

The houses on the crest of the eastern slope show the violence of the destruction. The surviving floors are covered with great piles of stones from the collapsed upper parts of the walls. More disastrous still was the collapse of the retaining walls that supported the terraces on which the houses on the eastern slope were built. The whole structure on the slope was an interlocking one, each terrace being partly supported by that lower down the slope, with the lowest supported by the town wall. When the lowest walls were breached, as must clearly have been the case in the Babylonian destruction, the next terraces up the hill would be weakened, and the collapse would have spread cumulatively back up the hill behind each breach in the town wall. The effect would not be instantaneous, but a single hard winter's rains would complete it. The surviving remains on the eastern slope show the result. Low down the slope only substructures and what are probably to be interpreted as basements survive. At the summit there are the remains of houses already described. Their outer edge has, however, collapsed, with the retaining wall that supported them. This is clearest in the large room, originally tripartite with the plan, that can be presumed from parallels, of a central hall divided from side-aisles by two lines of monolithic piers. At just the point at which the easternmost line should have been found, steep lines of erosion cut down across the floor, and the rest of the building has disappeared. The cumulative collapse created the tumble of stones that confronted the excavators in 1961–67, and which had also confronted Nehemiah when he came to rebuild the city walls.

The evidence of the destruction in the main town area on the eastern ridge has been destroyed by quarrying. The destruction of the buildings on the western ridge enclosed by the second wall (p. 293) and the occupied area which had gradually been expanding up towards the summit of the ridge was, however, complete, and this area was thereafter abandoned for several centuries. Much of the city was destroyed by fire, at any rate 'every great house', and the extent of the looting is described in II Kings 25:13–14. All the important inhabitants were carried away captive to an exile in Babylon.

The low ebb of civilization in Palestine, which lasts for the next three centuries or so, makes it very difficult for archaeology to recover any evidence. Town life suffered a severe setback, and such reduced settlements as there were, with little in the way of substantial buildings, were mostly obliterated by later building operations.

With the sack of Jerusalem, the administrative centre of the district, now a Babylonian province, was moved to Mizpah. If this place is to be identified with Tell Nasbeh, we can perhaps see what a very serious blow had been struck at town life in Palestine. A certain number of objects, notably jar-stamps, have been found, which must be Post-Exilic in date, but there is almost nothing in the way of buildings that can be attributed to this period. This is in fact the position on all sites in Palestine which were not completely abandoned. The remnants of the population must have continued to live in such villages as had survived destruction, but contributed little towards their structural history. One reason, no doubt, is that it was mainly the unprogressive peasantry that escaped deportation. Another is that mixed with these Jewish survivors were immigrants from many other lands, brought thither by the Assyrians and Babylonians, The homogeneous Israelite culture was thus broken up, and there was no unifying power to build up a new one in its place.

In 540 B.C. the Babylonian empire was annexed by the Persians under Cyrus. The Persian policy of toleration for the national cultures and religions of their subject races brought about some amelioration in the position of the Jews. During the next hundred years, under successive leaders inspired by religious zeal, parties of Jews returned from Babylonia and attempted to restore Jerusalem. In 520 B.C. Zerubbabel rebuilt the Temple, and in 444 B.C. Nehemiah restored the walls of the city. But the homogeneity of the Jewish people had been too severely disrupted for a new kingdom to grow up round it, even if the Persians would have allowed it. Many Jews preferred to remain among the comforts of civilization in Babylonia. Those who returned were at continual enmity with the 'peoples of the land', whom they despised as being of mixed blood, and each successive group from Babylon made the same accusation against those who had preceded them, whom they denounced as having intermarried with the other inhabitants. These inhabitants in their turn resented the claim of the returned refugees and their descendants to be the only true Jews and the only true followers of the Jewish faith. Quarrels such as these led in time to the Samaritan schism, when Manasseh, the grandson of the High Priest Eliashib, was driven out by Nehemiah, on the grounds of the intermarriage of his family with those of mixed race. Sanballat, governor of Samaria, built for him a temple, as a rival to that of Jerusalem, on Mount Gerizim, and thus to enmity on racial grounds was added a conflict of religious centres, which has continued to modern times.

The 1961–67 excavations at Jerusalem have revealed dramatic evidence of the contrast between Jerusalem of the period of the Kingdom of Judah and that of the Post-Exilic period. Of the Temple rebuilt by Zerubbabel no trace of the actual Temple building survives. Reference has already been made (p. 240) to the identification of the south-east corner of Zerubbabel's Temple platform. The straight joint 32·72 metres north of the Herodian south-east corner is certain evidence of an earlier, smaller platform. This corner must therefore be at least as early as the pre-Herodian Maccabean

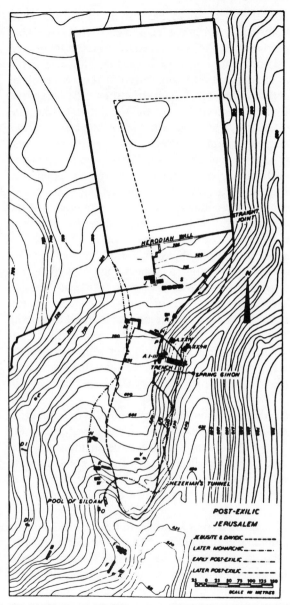

Fig. 88. Plan of Jerusalem in the Maccabean period. The plan of the Solomonic Temple is presumed to have continued throughout the Maccabean period. In the Herodian period, the earlier Temple platform was enveloped by its larger successor

period. There is visual evidence of at least three reconstructions in the surviving masonry, and this in itself could carry the first visible stage back to the time when Zerubbabel completed the rebuilding of the Temple *c.* 516 B.C. under the aegis of the Persian successors to the Babylonians. This ascription is supported by a comparison of the masonry with that of known Persian structures in Syria, that of the great temples of Eshmoun[13] near Sidon, dated to the late 6th–early 5th centuries B.C. and the rather later Persian structures at Byblos. The suggestion that this Persian-style platform corresponds in outline with that of the Solomonic period is discussed above. But the outlines of Nehemiah's town are now beginning to take shape. In the area excavated on the eastern slopes of Ophel, the evidence was clear of a collapse overlying the buildings of the 7th–early 6th centuries B.C., and of the great denudation on the slope that followed the collapse of the terraces on which the houses were built. These were the ruins that confronted Nehemiah in his survey of the city when, wishing to inspect the walls along the eastern valley, he says 'But there was no room for the beast that was under me to pass' (Nehemiah 2.14). Not only were the ruins daunting, but the town needed for the poor remnant returned from exile was much smaller than that of the period of the monarchy. It was now that the wall on the crest of the hill, for long erroneously ascribed to an earlier period, was constructed, and the excavations proved that against its foot tailed up midden-tips of the 5th–4th centuries B.C.

Post-Exilic Jerusalem had therefore shrunk back to the summit of the eastern ridge, and there it remained, for the tower previously ascribed to the time of David is now known to be an addition of the Maccabean period, when the Hasmonean rulers were striving to create a new Jewish kingdom, to the walls of Nehemiah. The position of the defences on the western side of the ridge is probably indicated by the massive gateway found in the 1927 excavations, which was certainly in use during Maccabean times. The 1961–67 excavations have made it quite clear that the wall enclosing the two ridges (p. 235) did not exist either in the period of the monarchy or in the Post-Exilic period. It dates only to the period of Herod Agrippa (*c.* A.D. 40–44), and no occupation on the southern end of the western ridge has been found earlier than this date. The northern end of the western ridge was, however, included within the city during the Maccabean period.

Over the rest of the country, all that we have is a few buildings connected with the administration of the region by the Babylonians and Persians. Presumably only such buildings were sufficiently substantial to survive subsequent disturbances.

The best preserved of such buildings is at Lachish. It was built above the ruins of the palace-fort of the Jewish period; the earlier building had itself been raised on a podium above the contemporary level, and this elevated position was accentuated by the later structure, which was surrounded by an earth ramp. The plan is symptomatic of the new influences in Palestine, for it is quite unlike previous official buildings in that country. It consists of a great courtyard, surrounded on two sides by rows of rooms and on the other two by porticoes. The deeper of these porticoes, raised above the level of the court, leads to a great hall stretching across the width of the courtyard, at the rear of which doorways lead to private rooms and domestic offices. The great hall no doubt served for public audiences, the rooms round the court may have been administrative offices, and those at the rear of the hall the living quarters of the governor. One interesting structural feature is that the rooms were vaulted, in contrast to the pre-Exilic buildings, in which, as far as our evidence goes, the ceilings were flat. In some rooms portions of the fallen roof were recovered as they had fallen, showing that the vaults had been formed by voussoirs laid diagonally. The best parallel to this type of building comes from Arslan Tash in northern Syria. It is an illustration of the cosmopolitan character of the Persian empire.

The history of Lachish is probably representative of that of Palestinian towns. For a century or so after its destruction by the Babylonians it had lain in ruins. Then the fortifications were repaired, and it was made an administrative centre, with the necessary official buildings, but apparently little in the way of houses for the ordinary people. Moreover, it was an administrative centre not in Judah, but in the new province of Idumaea, an illustration of the way the Edomites and other semi-nomadic peoples had pushed into Palestine during its weakness.

A possibly similar building, though not identical in plan, of the same general Post-Exilic period, has been found at Tell Jemmeh, where the latest building is a very massive structure on three sides of a long narrow court. Again there appear to be no contemporary private houses.

In the northern province of Samaria, the successor of the Kingdom of Israel, a building at Megiddo very similar to that at Tell

Jemmeh is attributed to Strata II and I. Unfortunately, the upper-most levels were very much denuded, and their exact dating is uncertain. But it is probable that associated with this fortress or residency was a town, covering only part of the area of the old city, of small and ill-built houses. The regularly laid-out insulae which have been attributed to the Assyrian period have disappeared, and the site is in fact a village rather than a town. Its occupation may have lasted down to the middle of the 4th century B.C., but before the beginning of the Hellenistic period even this occupation had ceased, and the history of Megiddo had come to an end.

At Samaria, too, the decline of town life is well illustrated. The site remained an administrative centre, but no official buildings of the period have been discovered in the area excavated. There are traces of a few insignificant buildings on the summit, which must be dated to the 7th and 6th centuries, and more may have been destroyed by subsequent building operations. The clearest evidence that the site was not closely built up comes from probably early in the 5th century, when an area of about 50 metres by 45 metres on the summit was apparently converted into an elaborate garden. Over this area all earlier walls were systematically rooted out and their contemporary floor levels pulled into the resultant holes and levelled over. On top of this make-up, thus carefully cleared of stones and débris, was laid a band, 25 centimetres thick, of sticky chocolate-coloured soil. This type of soil is found in crevices in the rock at Samaria and on the surrounding hills, and must have been especially collected for this purpose. It was recognized by the workmen employed on the excavations as extremely fertile, and was carried away by them for their own gardens. The only explanation for this enclosure seems to be that it was for use as a garden or orchard, which may have been associated with a residence of a Persian governor, lying in the unexcavated area to the east.

Traces of occupation for the whole pre-Hellenistic period at Samaria are very scanty. Only nine coins prior to 300 B.C. were recovered in seven seasons of excavation. Pottery and other finds of the period were equally rare, and only a few isolated groups of buildings could be attributed to it. The finds were sufficient to show that the site was occupied, but their proportion compared with those of earlier and later periods emphasizes how slight this occupation was.

The great cities of the Israelite period therefore play little part in the life of the country under the Babylonians and the succeeding

Persian empire. The slight glimpses we get of the culture of Palestine come largely from unimportant sites. It is perhaps significant that most of them come from the coastal belt. The Persian empire had reunited the eastern Mediterranean lands to a degree unknown since the Late Bronze Age, and once more one finds in Palestine and Syria pottery and other objects identical with finds in Egypt, Cyprus, and Greece. Coastal Palestine thus once more was in the current of eastern Mediterranean trade, while the hill country was a backwater.

Tell Abu Hawam at the foot of Carmel, abandoned since its destruction in the late 10th century B.C., was once more occupied. The architectural remains are unimpressive, and it was nothing more than a village, yet in it appear Corinthian and Attic vases dated from the 6th to the early 4th century. Some of the coarse pottery has Phoenician affinities, and these Greek and Phoenician finds emphasize two of the elements found in the cosmopolitan culture of the period.

At 'Athlit, near Haifa, beneath the Crusader castle, have been found tombs dating to the 5th and 4th centuries B.C. In them were Phoenician coins and scarabs, and much Greek pottery, but there was a predominance of the third element in contemporary culture, namely scarabs and ornaments of Egyptian type. At Tell Jemmeh, Greek pottery of the 6th and 5th centuries B.C. has been found in sufficient quantities to suggest a Greek colony, and other fragments have been found at Askelon and Tanturah on the coast.

At Tell Fara a tomb was discovered which throws interesting light on the contacts with other parts of the Persian empire, and has also produced objects of artistic merit.[14] These consist of the framework of a bronze couch and stool, and a silver bowl and dipper. Representations of similar couches and stools appear on Greek vases of the 6th and 5th centuries. The fact that they were manufactured for the Syrian market is apparent because as a guide to their assembly the different components are marked with Hebrew letters of 5th-century script. The dipper is Syrian in style, and close parallels for the bowl have been found in the Egyptian Delta and at Susa in Mesopotamia. Tombs belonging to this same period, and producing objects illustrating the same cultural affinities, have also been found at Gezer.

The preceding paragraphs will have shown something of the character of the culture of Post-Exilic and pre-Hellenistic Palestine. The Jewish civilization, of no great artistic merit, but homogeneous and with a vigorous town life, has been completely disrupted. The only architectural remains belong to official buildings presumably associated with the Persian administration, and the few rich burials probably belong to members of the official hierarchy. The administrative centres seem to have no large towns associated with them. The few town and village sites which can be ascribed to this period have only mean structures. But nevertheless in the coastal area we have evidence that Palestine was once more in trade relations with the adjacent Mediterranean countries. In particular, we see the increasing contacts with Greece, which paved the way for the inclusion of western Asia in the Hellenistic empire, under which once again town life begins to prosper.

Notes

1. *Iraq* XVI, 164–7; *Iraq* XXI, 130–47.
2. F. J. Bliss and A. C. Dickie, *Excavations at Jerusalem 1894—1897* (London, 1898), key map.
3. N. Avigad, 'Excavations in the Jewish Quarter of the Old City of Jerusalem, 1970 (Second Preliminary Report)', *IEJ* 20, 3–4 (1970), pp. 129–40.
4. By recent Israeli excavations in Jerusalem.
5. T. A. Holland, 'A Study of Palestinian Iron Age Baked Clay Figurines with special reference to Jerusalem: Cave I', *Levant* IX (1977), 121–55.
6. *Samaria Sebaste III*, pp. 204–8.
7. *Beersheba* I.
8. Not yet published.
9. *Lachish* III.
10. *PEQ* (1976).
11. *Tel Aviv* 4. 1–2.
12. *Ancient Near Eastern Texts*, J. B. Pritchard, ed. (Princeton, 1969).
13. *Bulletin du Musée de Beyrouth,* XVIII, XIX.
14. The tomb, No 650, was dated by the excavator to 850 B.C., but has been shown by J. H. Iliffe (*QDAP* IV) to belong to the 5th or 4th century B.C.

Appendix:
Excavated Sites and Bibliography

The majority of sites to which reference is made in the body of the text have produced evidence concerning the remains of several or many different periods. A brief description of the various excavations can therefore best be given as an appendix. In the main, only excavations subsequent to 1920 are described, since from them most of the evidence is derived.

Abbreviations

AJSLL	*American Journal of Semitic Languages and Literature.*
AASOR	*Annual of the American Schools of Oriental Research.*
ADAJ	*Annual of the Department of Antiquities of Jordan.* Amman.
AJA	*American Journal of Archaeology.*
APEF	*Annual of the Palestine Exploration Fund.* London.
Archaeology	Archaeological Institute of America, Cambridge, Mass.
Atiqot	Journal of the Israel Department of Antiquities, Jerusalem, Israel.
BA	*The Biblical Archaeologist.* American Schools of Oriental Research, Cambridge, Mass.
BASOR	*Bulletin of the American Schools of Oriental Research.* New Haven, Connecticut.
CAH	*Cambridge Ancient History.* Revised edition.
Eretz Israel	Annual of the Israel Exploration Society. Jerusalem, Israel.
HUCBASJ	Hebrew Union College Biblical and Archaeological School in Jerusalem.
IEJ	*Israel Exploration Journal.* Jerusalem, Israel.
JPOS	*Journal of the Palestine Oriental Society.* Jerusalem, Palestine.
LAAA	*Liverpool Annals of Art and Archaeology.* University of Liverpool.
Levant	*Journal of the British School of Archaeology in Jerusalem.*
OIP	*Oriental Institute Publications.* University of Chicago.
PEFQS	*Palestine Exploration Fund Quarterly Statement.* London.

PEQ	*Palestine Exploration Quarterly.* London.
QDAP	*Quarterly of the Department of Antiquities of Palestine.* Jerusalem.
Qedem	Monographs of the Institute of Archaeology. The Hebrew University of Jerusalem.
RB	*Revue Biblique.* École Biblique et Archéologique de Saint Étienne, Jerusalem, Jordan.
SAOC	*Studies in Ancient Oriental Civilization.* University of Chicago.
Tel Aviv	Journal of the Tel Aviv University of Archaeology.

(*Note: Tell* and *Wadi* are ignored in the alphabetic order.)

Tell Abu Hawam

The site is a small mound on the coastal plain, at the foot of Mount Carmel. It was excavated in 1932–33 by Mr R. W. Hamilton of the Palestine Department of Antiquities. The earliest occupation dated to Late Bronze II, and lasted without any long break until the end of the 10th century B.C. After an interval, it was reoccupied from the 7th to the 5th centuries B.C.

Bibliography
QDAP IV.

Tell Abu Matar

The site lies 1·5 kilometres south-east of Beersheba, occupying a mound of loess covered by alluvial loam. It was excavated in 1954 by M. Jean Perrot. The remains belong to one cultural phase only, the Chalcolithic, and consist of dwellings which in the earlier stages were subterranean, cut into the loam and sometimes into the underlying rock to varying depths. Four main phases could be identified, in the last of which the subterranean dwellings were succeeded by surface structures. The culture of the inhabitants can be linked with that of Ghassul.

Bibliography
IEJ 5, 6.

'Ai

Excavations at 'Ai were carried out by Mme Judith Marquet-Krause between 1933 and 1935 with funds provided by Baron Edmond de Rothschild. The main circuit of the Early Bronze Age walls was traced, and within the town work was concentrated on the area adjoining a great tower on the walls, a large building which may be a palace or temple, a sanctuary showing a triple succession of rooms, and a small area of houses. Tombs show that the site was already occupied in the Proto-Urban phase. Mme Marquet-Krause died in 1936, when only preliminary reports had been issued, and the material has been published from her records by her husband, but consists of only her preliminary reports and a transcription of her field register.

Excavations were resumed in 1964 by a joint expedition headed by the American Schools of Oriental Research, under the direction of Professor J. A. Callaway. Work continued until 1972. Remains of a village of the Proto-Urban period were found on the summit. The history of the Early Bronze Age town was established in considerable detail. The first walled city belonged to Early Bronze IC, *c*. 3000 to 2860 B.C., and there was a succession of reconstructions. The city was dominated by an acropolis, on which, at least in the later stages, was a temple. In the Early Bronze III stage at 'Ai there was considerable evidence of Egyptian influence, which was overlaid by northern influence in the final stage. The Early Bronze city came to an end *c*. 2400 B.C., and the site was abandoned until the end of the 13th century B.C.

Early in the Iron Age there were two successive villages on the site, but attempts to relate them to the biblical account of the capture of the town by Joshua are not very convincing.

Bibliography

Les Fouilles de 'Ay (et-Tell), 1933–35, 2 vols. J. Marquet-Krause. Institut Français d'Archéologie de Beyrouth. 1949.

BASOR 178, 183, 196, 198.

Pottery from the Tombs at 'Ai (et-Tell). J. A. Callaway. London, Colt Archaeological Institute Monograph Series 2. 1964.

The Early Bronze Age Sanctuaries at 'Ai (et-Tell). J. A. Callaway. London, 1972.

PEQ (1974). 'A re-examination of the Lower City at 'Ai (et-Tell) in 1971, 1972'. J. A. Callaway and N. E. Wagner.

Tell Ajjul

Tell el 'Ajjul was excavated by the British School of Archaeology in Egypt under Sir Flinders Petrie between 1930 and 1934. It lies at the mouth of the Wadi Ghazzeh, some 6 miles (9·65km.) south of the modern town of Gaza. The earliest remains excavated on the tell consisted of a cemetery belonging to Middle Bronze I. This lay beneath a large building, called by Petrie a palace, belonging to Middle Bronze II, which was succeeded in turn by four other large buildings, the latest dating probably to the beginning of the Iron Age. Portions of the dwelling-houses of corresponding periods were also excavated. The maximum expansion of the town was apparently in the Middle Bronze Age, when it was defended by a great fosse of the type ascribed to the Hyksos. Occupation of the site must, however, date from an earlier period than that of the town levels excavated, for tombs with the typical pottery and weapons of the Intermediate Early Bronze–Middle Bronze phase were found.

Bibliography

Ancient Gaza, I–IV. Flinders Petrie. British School of Archaeology in Egypt and Bernard Quaritch, London 1931–34.

ADAJ III. 'Tombs of the Intermediate Early Bronze–Middle Bronze Age at Tell Ajjul'. K. M. Kenyon.

AJSLL (1938) 'The Chronology of a South Palestinian City'. W. J. Albright.

Bulletin of the Institute of Archaeology (University of London) III (1962). 'The Courtyard Cemetery at Tell el-Ajjul'. O. Tufnell.

Arad

The site lies in the Negeb, 30 kilometres east-north–east of Beersheba. Excavations were carried out here between 1962 and 1971 under the direction of Professor Y. Aharoni and Mrs Ruth Amiran. After a stage in which there was evidence of Chalcolithic settlement, there were two quite separate periods of occupation. The earliest was a town of 22 acres (8·90ha.), at first unwalled, and then surrounded by a wall with projecting semicircular bastions. It belonged entirely to Early Bronze I and II, and was contemporary with the First Dynasty of Egypt. There was clearly a close trading connection with Egypt.

The second period of occupation was confined to a citadel on the highest part of the Early Bronze Age town. It starts with a settlement in the 12th–11th centuries, and from the time of Solomon to the end of the kingdom of Judah there was a citadel which must have formed part of the southern frontier of Judah. An important find was a sanctuary associated with the worship of Yahweh.

There were similar frontier posts here in the Hellenistic and Roman periods and an Arab *Khan*.

Bibliography

IEJ 12, 14, 16, 17.

·Catalogue of the Israel Museum, 1967. *Ancient Arad*. R. Amiran and Y. Aharoni.

Archaeology 17 (1964), 43–53.

Ashdod

The site lies about 4 kilometres inland from the coast, 14·5 kilometres north-east of ancient Askelon. This part is probably represented by Tell

Mor. It consists of a higher mound, or acropolis, and a lower city. Excavations were carried out between 1962 and 1972, mainly under the direction of Professor M. Dothan. Some Chalcolithic and Early Bronze Age sherds indicated a slight occupation in the fourth–third millennia. The earliest fortified town, resting on bedrock, belongs to late in the 17th century B.C. This was followed by a Late Bronze I phase. The most flourishing stage belongs to LB II, when Ashdod merchants selling textiles are noted in the Ugaritic records.

This LB II town was buried beneath a thick destruction layer of ash. This may well have been the work of the Sea Peoples, but there are succeeding levels which are basically still late LB, in which there is no evidence of Philistine influence. These belong to the first quarter of the 12th century, and are followed by three main strata belonging to the time when Ashdod was one of the five cities of the Philistines. To the beginning of this period belongs a cult centre of a Mycenaean-type mother goddess. By the beginning of the 10th century the culture of the Philistines, on the evidence of the pottery, began to merge with that of the neighbouring Canaanite Iron Age inhabitants. Only for a very brief period was Ashdod an Israelite town.

The town was destroyed by the Assyrians under Sargon II late in the 8th century B.C. and destroyed again in the late 7th century. There was some occupation in the Persian period, but the next important town was Hellenistic with a well laid-out town plan, lasting into the Roman period.

Bibliography

Ashdod I. Atiqot VII. M. Dothan D. N. Freedman. Jerusalem, 1967.
Ashdod II–III. Atiqot IX–X. M. Dothan. Jerusalem, 1971.

Askelon

Excavations at the coastal site of Askelon were carried out on behalf of the Palestine Exploration Fund by Professor Garstang in 1920 and 1921. Excavations on the summit cleared only remains of the Roman period, but sections were cut in the face of the mound, which revealed the succession break between the end of the Late Bronze Age and the beginning of the Early Iron Age, which can probably be attributed to the Philistine invasion.

Bibliography

PEFQS (1921, 1923).
IEJ 17 (1967), 125–6. V. Tsaferis.

Azor, Tell

Tell Azor is located 6 kilometres from Jaffa, on the modern road from Jaffa to Jerusalem. Although the mound, revealing traces of settlement from the

Archaeology in the Holy Land

Chalcolithic onward, has not been excavated, many tombs have been found in the surrounding *Kurkar* hills with remains trom the Chalcolithic period to medieval times. The Chalcolithic ossuary tombs were extensively excavated by J. Perrot and those belonging to the Bronze and Iron Ages by M. Dothan. Two burial caves of the Proto-Urban period, located about 200 metres south of the highway, were excavated by A. Ben-Tor in April 1971. The contents of these two burial caves are dated to the transition period between the Chalcolithic and the Early Bronze Age.

Bibliography

Atiqot III (1961), 1–83. 'Une tombe à ossuaires du IVe millenaire à Azor, près de Tel-Aviv'. J. Perrot.

Qedem 1, Monograph of the Institute of Archaeology, Jerusalem (1975), 1–83. 'Two Burial Caves of the Proto-Urban Period at Azor 1971'. A. Ben-Tor.

Bab edh-Dhra'

Attention was attracted to the area of Bab edh-Dhra', to the east of the Dead Sea adjoiniug the Lisan, the tongue of land that projects into the Dead Sea (the position is given in the *Oxford Bible Atlas,* p. 96), by the rich finds appearing in the hands of antiquities dealers in Jerusalem. Excavations were conducted there by Dr Paul Lapp on behalf of the American School of Oriental Research in 1965. The large Early Bronze Age town apparently came to an end with the arrival of the EB–MB invaders, but hardly any investigation of the town has taken place. Adjacent to it was a most imposing and important cemetery. The earliest tombs belonged to the Proto-Urban period, and were shaft tombs in which a number of chambers opened out of a single shaft. It was calculated that there may be as many as 20,000 chambers in the whole cemetery. The bodies in the tombs excavated were mostly disarticulated and were accompanied by a lavish number of pottery vessels. In the Early Bronze Age there were some shaft tombs, but most of the bodies were deposited in a disarticulated mass in charnel houses, which at least in some instances had an upper storey. There were also tombs of the EB–MB period, in which intact bodies were buried in a narrow grave, above which was a small tumulus of stones.

Bibliography

RB, LXXIII.

Liber Anuus 15 (1964–65), 137–219. 'Bab Edh-Dhra''. S. Saller.

P. W. Lapp, *Archaeology* 19 (1966), pp. 104–11

BASOR 189 (1968), 12–41. 'Bab Edh-Dhra' Tomb A 76 and Early Bronze I in Palestine'. P. W. Lapp.

Tell Beersheba

This site is well summarized by the author's article listed below.

Bibliography

Beer-Sheba I. Excavations at Tel Beer-Sheba. 1969–1971 Seasons. Tel-Aviv University Institute of Archaeology, 1973. Y. Aharoni, ed.
PEQ (1978), 63-4. 'The Date of the Destruction of Iron Age Beer-Sheba'. K. M. Kenyon.

Beidha

The prehistoric site known as Beidha is located at Seyl Aqlat, situated in the Wadi Beidha, 6 kilometres north of Petra in the Hashemite Kingdom of Jordan. The site was discovered in 1956 by Diana Kirkbride who conducted excavations there from 1958 to 1965 on behalf of the British School of Archaeology in Jerusalem and with assistance from the Department of Antiquities in Jordan.

The earliest, Natufian, occupation has only been excavated in two trial trenches to date, but on the bases of finds made at Mugharet el-Wad and recent excavations at 'Eynan, the excavator dates the assemblage of finds to the early Natufian. The Pre-Pottery Neolithic B settlement consists of six phases, the earliest being Level VI. The great importance of Beidha is that the finds provide much information concerning the wide distribution of the Pre-Pottery Neolithic B industries, especially as they relate to the PPNB settlement at Jericho.

Bibliography

PEQ (1960), 136 ff., (1965), 5–13, (1966), 8–72; *ADAJ* VI (1962), 7–12); *Revue Biblique* 69 (1962), 88–91; 71 (1964), 246–50; 72 (1965), 248–52 D. Kirkbride.

Tell Beit Mirsim

For four seasons between 1926 and 1932 excavations were carried out at Tell Beit Mirsim by the American School of Oriental Research in Jerusalem, under the direction of Professor W. F. Albright. The tell, for which the identification with Kirjath-sepher has been suggested, is a comparatively small mound in the low hill country south-west of Hebron. The importance of the excavations is derived not from the intrinsic merits of the remains revealed, but in the successive layers of occupation dating from late in the third millennium to 6th century B.C., and in the thoroughness with which the objects recovered, especially the pottery, were studied and published. The earliest occupation belongs to a late and decadent phase of Early Bronze III, followed by the Intermediate Early Bronze–Middle stage (designated Middle Bronze I by Professor Albright), and a series of Middle Bronze Age levels. At the end of the Middle Bronze Age there is a destruction followed by abandonment, and occupation is resumed in the second half of the 15th century B.C. Between the Late Bronze Age and Early Iron Age levels is a destruction, but no appreciable interval in the occupation. The site was finally abandoned after the Babylonian destruction in 588 B.C.

Bibliography

The Archaeology of Palestine and the Bible. W. F. Albright. New York, 3rd ed., 1935.
Tell Beit Mirsim I: *The Pottery of the First Three Campaigns. AASOR* XII.
Tell Beit Mirsim Ia: *The Bronze Age Pottery of the Fourth Campaign. AASOR* XIII.
Tell Beit Mirsim II: *The Bronze Age. AASOR* XVII.
Tell Beit Mirsim III: *The Iron Age. AASOR* XXI–XXII.

Bethel

The site of Bethel has been identified as the modern village of Beitin, a little north-east of Ramullah. A small area was excavated by Professor W. F. Albright in 1934 on behalf of the American School of Oriental Research in Jerusalem. Occupation of the site seems to begin in the Early Bronze–Middle Bronze Age. Professor Albright suggests that the occupation of Bethel was complementary to that of 'Ai, 2 miles away, for the two sites seem rarely to have been occupied at the same time. The town of the Late Bronze Age was particularly well built. The period comes to an end with a great destruction by fire, probably early in the 13th century B.C., and Professor Albright considers that the destruction was the work of the Israelites. When occupation was renewed, there was a complete break, with a much poorer culture. The site was finally destroyed in the 6th century B.C.

Bibliography
BASOR 56, 57.

Beth-shan

Like that of Megiddo, the excavation of Beth-shan by the University of Pennsylvania was planned on a large scale, which likewise could not be carried out. The work was under the direction of Mr Alan Rowe. The lowest level to be reached on the summit was IX, dating probably from the 14th century B.C. Most of the work was concentrated in an area in which there was a series of superimposed temples, lasting from that date well into the Early Iron Age, and succeeded by a Hellenistic temple and a Byzantine church. The lowest levels were penetrated in a sounding; the dwellings seemed to be in pits comparable to those of Tell Abu Matar, and to be of the Chalcolithic period, succeeded by phases belonging to the Proto-Urban period and the Early Bronze Age. A large number of tombs of all periods from the Early Bronze Age to the Byzantine period were also excavated. The material has been only partially published. Interim reports described the progress of the excavations, and Mr G. M. Fitzgerald described in detail the pottery of the Chalcolithic to Early Bronze Age, but the final report only deals with the later periods, the Temple buildings from Level IX onwards and the pottery from Level VIII. It is generally agreed that the dates assigned to the levels by the excavators must be drastically lowered; it seems probable that the chronology is approximately: Level VIII, 1350 B.C.; Level VII, 1300 B.C.; Level VI, 1150 B.C.; Level V, 1000 B.C.

Bibliography

Beth-shan I: *The Topography and History of Beth-shan.* A. Rowe. 1930.
Beth-shan II.i: *The Four Canaanite Temples of Beth-shan.* A. Rowe, 1940.
Beth-Shan II.ii: *The Four Canaanite Temples of Beth-Shan.* G. M. Fitz-gerald. 1930.
Beth-shan III: *Beth-shan Excavations 1921–23. The Arab and Byzantine Levels.* G. M. Fitzgerald. 1931.
Beth-shan IV: *A Sixth Century Monastery at Beth-shan.* G. M. Fitzgerald. 1931.
   (All published for the University Museum by the University of Pennsylvania Press.)
PEFQS (1927, 1928, 1929, 1931, 1932, 1934).
Museum Journal, Philadelphia, XXIV. 'The Earliest Pottery of Beth-shan'. G. M. Fitzgerald.
The Iron Age at Beth-shan. Frances W. James. Museum Monograph of the University Museum, Philadelphia, Pennsylvania, 1966.
The Northern Cemetery of Beth Shan. E. D. Oren. Leiden, 1973.

Beth-Shemesh

The tell of 'Ain Shems, lying almost due west of Jerusalem, where the important Wadi Sorek emerges from the hill country of Judah into the Shephelah, was first excavated for the Palestine Exploration Fund in 1911–12. Between 1928 and 1931, extensive excavations were carried out there by the Pacific School of Religion and the American School of Oriental Research in Jerusalem, under Professor Elihu Grant. The earliest remains belong to the Middle Bronze Age. A good succession of levels from the late Bronze Age to the end of Early Iron II were uncovered. The evidence of a typical town plan in the Iron Age is particularly useful.

Bibliography

APEF I and II. 'The Excavations at Ain Shems'. Duncan Mackenzie. 1911 and 1912–13.
Ain Shems I: *Ain Shems Excavations.* E. Grant. 1931.

Archaeology in the Holy Land

Ain Shems II: *Ain Shems Excavations.* E. Grant. 1932.
Ain Shems III: *Rumeilah.* E. Grant. 1934.
Ain Shems IV: *Ain Shems Excavations* (*Pottery*). Text. E. Grant and G. E.
Wright. 1939.

(All published at Haverford.)

Dan

Tell el-Qadi is a mound of about 5 acres (2·02ha.) at the foot of Mount
Hermon on the headwaters of the Jordan. It has long been accepted that it
represents the Israelite town of Dan and its predecessor, the Canaanite
Laish. Evidence of the importance of Laish is provided by mention in the
18th-century B.C. Execration Texts and the Mari Letters, and in the records
of Thotmes III.

Excavation of the site by the Israel Department of Antiquities under the
direction of Dr A. Biran began in 1966 and is still (1979) in progress. Levels
of the Early Bronze Age exist, but have not yet been excavated to any
extent. There was also occupation in Middle Bronze I, but the earliest
defences located belong to Middle Bronze II, in the second half of the 18th
century B.C. They consist of a massive earth bank sloping down both to the
exterior and interior of the town, piled against a stone core, and faced with
plaster. A brick wall was built on top of the stone core. These defences
apparently continued in use down to the 12th century B.C. Laish was
destroyed by Thotmes III in 1481 B.C. and may thereafter have been
abandoned for a time. A rich tomb within the town with Mycenaean pottery
is evidence of occupation in the 14th–13th centuries B.C.

Laish was captured by the Israelite tribe of Dan probably in the 12th
century B.C., who gave their name to the town. The earliest substantial
remains consisted of an excellent entrance comprising an outer and an inner
gate, with between them a spacious courtyard. Both the courtyard and the
roadway were excellently paved, with large stones, and the roadway continued up the mound as a ceremonial way to the summit. The dating
evidence suggests that the gate was built by Jeroboam I in the last quarter of
the 10th century B.C., when the north broke away from Jerusalem to form
the northern kingdom of Israel and Jeroboam set up his rival cult centres at
Dan and Bethel.

An important cult centre was in fact found on the summit. It consisted of
a rectangular podium, or *bamah, c.* 18 metres square, approached by a
flight of steps. This is likely to be the successor to that of Jeroboam, since it
was built of finely dressed bossed ashlars laid on alternate headers and
stretchers, a style typical of the Omri–Ahab buildings at Samaria in the first
half of the 9th century B.C.Though Dan was destroyed by Ben-Hadad of
Damascus in 855 B.C. and again by the Assyrians in 732 B.C., it would
appear that it remained a cult centre down to Roman times.

Bibliography

IEJ 16.2, 19.2, 19.4 Notes and News.
BA 37.2. 'Tel Dan'. A. Biran.

Tell Deir 'Alla

The tell is situated in the Jordan Valley, at the foot of the eastern hills and a little north of the junction of the Jabbok and the Jordan.

The earliest occupation was in the Chalcolithic period. This settlement was largely obliterated by the Late Bronze Age occupation. At this stage, the site was an undefended sanctuary, probably frequented by nomadic tribes. Inscribed clay tablets may suggest contact with the Aegean area. The settlement was destroyed by earthquake and fire at the beginning of the 12th century B.C. There was subsequent evidence of occupation by semi-nomadic metal-workers in the 12th to 10th centuries B.C. In the next stage the settlement was walled by newcomers of Syrian Aramean culture. It was only in the 8th century that there is any evidence of contact with Palestine.

Bibliography

Excavations at Tell Deir 'Alla I. H. J. Franken. Leiden, E. J. Brill, 1969.

Deir El-Balah

This cemetery site contains anthropoid clay coffins in Egyptian style. The burials date from the 14th century B.C. until the end of the Late Bronze Age.

Bibliography

IEJ 22 (1972), 65–72; 23 (1973), 129–51. T. Dothan.

Dhahr Mirzbâneh

In 1963, a cemetery of the EB–MB period was located in the neighbour-hood of 'Ain es-Samiyeh, about 7 miles north-east of Beitin, and was excavated by Dr Paul Lapp. There was evidence of an adjacent camping site, and it is suggested that it was occupied seasonally by a group of 50 to 100 individuals.

Bibliography

The Dhahr Mirzbâneh Tombs. P. W. Lapp. American Schools of Oriental Research. Cambridge, Mass., 1966.

Tell Duweir

The great mound of Tell ed Duweir lies in the low hills west of Hebron. Its identification as the site of Lachish is generally accepted. The excavations were initiated by Sir Henry Wellcome, and subsequently supported by Sir Charles Marston. Work began in 1932, and it was intended to excavate the whole mound through all the stages of occupation, but the work was brought to an end by the political troubles, in 1937–38, in which the

Director, Mr J. L. Starkey, was tragically murdered by bandits. The excavation of the town levels, of which the latest belonged to the Hellenistic and Persian periods, only reached the town of Early Iron II. Evidence for occupation at earlier periods comes from caves and tombs, from a section cut in the edge of the mound, and from clearance of areas for dumping. The earliest occupation, in caves in the neighbourhood of the later tell, belongs to the Chalcolithic period. Caves were still used as habitations during the Early Bronze Age, but towards the end of the period occupation of the town site began, and the caves were used for burials. Numerous tombs belonging to the Early Bronze–Middle Bronze period and to the Middle and Late Bronze Ages were found. A massive Middle Bronze Age bank was traced round the town. After it went out of use, a temple was built at its foot, of which the three structural phases lasted from early in the 15th century to the end of the 13th century B.C. The main period of occupation of the town came to an end with its destruction by the Babylonians in 588 B.C., and in the débris of the destruction were found potsherds on which letters had been written during the last months of the existence of the Jewish Kingdom.

Excavations at the site were resumed in 1973 by the Institute of Archaeology of Tel Aviv University and the Israel Exploration Society under the direction of Dr David Ussishkin. The aim is to examine the earlier levels on the summit which had not been reached in the earlier excavations and to provide more evidence concerning the disputed chronology of the Iron II town. The most interesting find concerning the earlier levels is a Late Bronze Age Temple on the summit, partly beneath the Iron Age palace podium. In plan this resembles the LB temple at Beth-shan. As regards the Iron Age chronology, carefully recorded stratigraphy has made it clear that the only destruction by fire is that of Level III, and the excavators therefore revert to the Lachish III dating of this to the Assyrian campaign of 701 B.C. This creates great difficulties in long-accepted pottery chronology, and since there is no proof that Sennacherib burnt the town, the problem should be regarded as being in suspense.

Bibliography

Lachish I: *The Lachish Letters*. H. Torczyner, G. L. Harding, A. Lewis, J. L. Starkey. Oxford University Press, 1938.

Lachish II: *The Fosse Temple*. O. Tufnell, C. H. Inge, G. L. Harding. Oxford University Press, 1940.

Lachish III: *The Iron Age*. O. Tufnell, with contributions by Margaret A. Murray and David Diringer. Oxford University Press, 1953.

Lachish IV: *The Bronze Age*. O. Tufnell. Oxford University Press, 1957.

Tel Aviv 4, 1–2 (1977). 'The Destruction of Lachish by Sennacherib and the dating of the Royal Judean Storage Jars'. D. Ussishkin.

'Lachish'. D. Ussishkin in *Bible et Terre Sainte*, No. 194 (1977).

'Les Documents paleo-Hebreux de Lakish'. A. Lemaire in ibid.

In *Samaria-Sebaste III* (q.v.), pp. 204–8, it is suggested that the destruction of Level III should be dated to 596 B.C. rather than 700 B.C. For a reply to this, see *PEQ* (1960).

Ein Gedi (En-Gedi)

Between 1961 and 1965 an expedition directed by B. Mazar and I. Dunayevsky on behalf of the Hebrew University and the Israel Exploration Society excavated a Chalcolithic cult centre in the oasis of Ein Gedi on the west side of the Dead Sea. The main building was a long narrow rectangular structure with a door in the centre of one long side. Opposite the door was a horseshoe-shaped platform which was presumably an altar flanked by benches, as was the door. Joining the corners of this building were walls of a large courtyard, in which was another rectangular building and a gatehouse. In this courtyard was a circular pile of stones, presumably a *bamah*. The pottery found was Ghassulian.

Bibliography

Atiqot (English series) VI. B. Mazar, T. Dothan, I. Dunayevsky.
BA XXXIV. D. Ussishkin.

Tell Fara

Tell el Fara lies some 14 miles above Tell el 'Ajjul on the Wadi Ghazzeh, at the point where the wadi debouches into the coastal plain. Like Tell el 'Ajjul, it was excavated by Sir Flinders Petrie for the British School of Archaeology in Egypt, between 1928 and 1930. City levels from Middle Bronze II down to the Iron Age were excavated, and a great wealth of material of the same periods was also recovered from tombs. Among the most important of these were five tombs with rich Philistine pottery. Excavations were also carried out in a number of prehistoric occupation sites in the neighbourhood of the tell. The majority of these belonged to the Chalcolithic period, and pottery, stone artifacts, and other objects similar to those from Ghassul were found; other sites belonged to the Early Bronze Age.

Bibliography

Beth-Pelet (Tell Fara), I–II. Flinders Petrie. British School of Archaeology in Egypt and Bernard Quaritch, London, 1930 and 1932.
The Tombs of the Middle Bronze Age II Period from the '500' Cemetery at Tell Fara (South). D. Price Williams. London, 1977.

Archaeology in the Holy Land

Tell el Far'ah

The northern Tell el Far'ah is situated near the head of the important Wadi Far'ah, which provides a highway from the Jordan Valley into hill country. Excavations have been in progress there since 1946, directed, until his death in 1971, by Père R. de Vaux on behalf of the Dominican École Biblique de St. Étienne. Occupation on the site had been traced back to the Chalcolithic, though no structures of this period have been found. The succeeding Proto-Urban period is represented by a number of large tomb groups, of which the pottery shows a mingling of Proto-Urban A and C. The first structures on the town site belong to early in the Early Bronze Age. In EB II, massive town walls were built and five successive phases within the Early Bronze Age have been so far identified. Occupation of the site, however, seems to come to an end in EB II. From that period there was a gap in occupation until Middle Bronze II. The site continued to be important until early in the 9th century B.C. A break then, with an unfinished building, confirms the identification of the site with Tirzah, the capital of Omri before he moved to Samaria. Occupation begins again on a small scale in the second half of the 9th century, and continues until the town was destroyed by the Assyrians in 722 B.C. Some occupation continued till 600 B.C., when the site was abandoned.

Bibliography

RB LIV, LV, LVI, LVIII, LIX, LXII, LXIV, LXVII, LXIX.
PEQ (1956).
Tell el Far'ah: l'installation du Moyen Bronze antérieure au rempart. J. Mallet. Cahiers de la Revue Biblique 14. Paris, 1973.

Gezer

Gezer is one of the most important sites on the western fringes of the hill country. It was excavated for the Palestine Exploration Fund in 1902–05 and 1907–09 by Professor R. A. S. Macalister. Though the material was studied and published with the most exemplary care, the excavation methods and lack of knowledge of the pottery at the time rendered the very complicated history of the site difficult of interpretation. Some small-scale excavations were also carried out by Mr Alan Rowe in 1934. The published material shows that the site was continuously occupied from the Chalcolithic to the Early Iron Age, and perhaps on into Roman and Byzantine times.

Excavations between 1964 and 1973 have provided a scientific basis for the interpretation of the sites. They were carried out on behalf of the Hebrew Union College Biblical and Archaeological School, mainly under the direction of Dr W. G. Dever. The excavations provided no new evidence concerning the Chalcolithic and Early Bronze Age periods, which were obviously unimportant, and which were separated from the period of the first fortified town by a considerable gap. This town belonged to the Middle Bronze Age, about mid-17th century B.C. The first wall, with a three-entry gate and massive stone tower, was originally free-standing. Subsequently a plaster-faced bank, with at least two phases, was added against its outer face. To the Middle Bronze Age belonged a High Place consisting of a row of ten monoliths up to 3 metres high.

The Middle Bronze Age town was covered by a thick layer of burnt débris. This destruction was probably the work of Thotmes III in 1481 B.C., and was followed by a period of desertion. The city only fully recovered during the 14th century. To this period the latest excavators assign a wall with numerous towers traced round the whole circuit; this dating can be doubted, and it is possible that the Middle Bronze Age wall was re-used. A marked level of destruction separated the LB levels from the next period, in which Philistine pottery appears, in combination with degenerate LB wares. The pottery sequence gives most useful evidence of the gradual absorption of these elements to produce the pottery characteristic of the Iron Age. This phase ends in a destruction, which might be that of the Pharaoh who gave the city to Solomon.

The evidence of the Solomonic period is provided by the excellent gateway on the same plan as those found at Megiddo and Hazor. The latest excavators suggest that this gate and the associated casemate wall plugged a gap in the wall ascribed to the Late Bronze Age. This seems most improbable, and traces of a wall in Solomonic-type masonry can be found elsewhere; it is probable that this wall enclosed the whole circuit, and that its excellent ashlars were robbed for re-use in the Hellenistic period.

The succeeding Iron Age levels are unimpressive. There was evidence of 8th-century Assyrian and early 6th-century Babylonian destruction. The city once more became important in Hellenistic times, to which period the most completely-traced circuit of walls should probably still be ascribed.

Bibliography

The Excavations of Gezer. Vols. I-III. R. A. S. Macalister. London, 1912.
PEQ (1935).
PEQ (1962). *BA* XXX. 'The Gezer Crematorium Re-examined'. J. A. Callaway.
IEJ 8. 'Solomon's City Wall and Gate at Gezer'. Y. Yadin.
Gezer I (HUCBASJ). W. G. Dever *et al.*
Gezer II (HUCBASJ). W. G. Dever *et al.*
    Both Annuals of the Hebrew Union College/Nelson Glueck School of Biblical Archaeology.
PEQ (1977). Review of *Gezer II* (HUCBASJ). K. M. Kenyon.

Ghassul

The excavations at Teleilat Ghassul were carried out between 1930 and 1938 by the Pontifical Biblical Institute. The site consisted of a group of very low mounds in the Jordan Valley, on two of which excavations were carried out. It was ascertained that there were four main levels of occupation, but most of the work was confined to the top Stratum IV, which was subdivided into two stages. The whole range of occupation appeared to lie within the Chalcolithic period.

Excavations at Ghassul were resumed in 1960 by the Pontificial Biblical Institute, under the direction of Father Robert North, and in 1967 by the British School of Archaeology in Jerusalem, under the direction of Dr J. B. Hennessy. An interesting result of the latter excavations was to show that the group of mounds had originally been a single mound, subsequently cut into by erosion. A complete succession of levels down to natural was established. At the base there was a level linking with Pottery Neolithic at Jericho, with above it a long and homogeneous succession of the Chalcolithic Ghassulian.

Bibliography

Teleilat Ghassul I. A. Mallon, R. Koeppel, R. Neuville. 1934.
Teleilat Ghassul II. R. Koeppel. 1940.
      (Published at Rome, by the Pontifical Biblical Institute.)
Analecta Biblica (Rome, 1960). R. North.
Levant I. 'Preliminary Report on a First Season of Excavations at Teleilat Ghassul'. J. B. Hennessy.
Teleilat Ghassul. Interim Report. J. B. Hennessy. University of Sydney. 1977.

Gibeah

The site of Tell el Fûl, 3 miles north of Jerusalem, was excavated in 1922 by the American School of Oriental Research in Jerusalem, under Professor W. F. Albright. The site was dominated by a fort-like building, in which four stages, all belonging to the Early Iron Age, were identified. The earlier were surrounded by a small village, but the latest was apparently an isolated watch tower.

Bibliography
AASOR IV.

Gibeon

The site of el-Jib, convincingly identified with the biblical Gibeon, was excavated between 1956 and 1962 by the University of Pennsylvania under the direction of Dr J. B. Pritchard. Tombs proved occupation in the Proto-Urban period, providing material comparable with that at Tell Nasbeh, and the Early Bronze–Middle Bronze period, with material comparable with Dhahr-Mirzbâneh. The earliest occupation found on the tell belongs to Middle Bronze II, and the relatively rich material of this period from tombs is comparable with that of Jericho phases ii and iii; no tombs seem as late as Jericho iv and v, suggesting that the Middle Bronze town may have come to an end earlier than that of Jericho. Only a few tombs provide evidence for the Late Bronze Age, and the bigger groups certainly come late in the period, possibly 13th century B.C. The earliest town wall is dated to the 12th century and the later one to the 10th, but there is not much evidence. The most striking remains of Iron Age date are the water systems. One is an enormous shaft, with steps circling down round its wall, comparable with the shaft at Megiddo, but not associated with a tunnel at its base, and it is therefore considered as a pool. The filling showed that it went out of use in the 7th–6th centuries B.C. A staircase and tunnel to a spring outside the town are considered to be later, but there was no dating evidence. A very large number of stamped jar-handles of 7th–early 6th-century dates and a number of rock cuttings are considered as evidence of a wine-making industry.

Bibliography

Museum Monographs of the University of Pennsylvania Museum:
   Hebrew Inscriptions and Stamps from Gibeon. J. B. Pritchard, 1959.
   The Water System of Gibeon. J. B. Pritchard, 1961.
   The Bronze Age Cemetery at Gibeon. J. B. Pritchard, 1963.
   Winery, Defenses and Soundings at Gibeon. J. B. Pritchard, 1964.
   Gibeon. Where the Sun Stood Still: the Discovery of the Biblical City. J. B. Pritchard. Princeton, 1962.

Hazor

The very large and important site of Hazor lies in the Jordan Valley between Lake Huleh and the Sea of Galilee. It was excavated by the Israel Exploration Society between 1955 and 1958, under the direction of Dr Y. Yadin. It consists of two parts, a tell at the south-west corner and a great defended plateau to the north. Occupations on the tell began in the Early Bronze Age, and lasted down to the Hellenistic period. The plateau area, defended by a massive bank, was added in Middle Bronze II, and continued to be occupied down to the early 13th century B.C., when the site was probably captured by the Israelites. The tell was an important place in the Early Iron Age, and was probably fortified by Solomon. It was destroyed by the Assyrians in 730 B.C., but the citadel continued to be used down to the Hellenistic period.

Bibliography

Hazor. I and II; III and IV. Y. Yadin *et al.* Jerusalem, 1958, 1960; 1961.
IEJ 6, 7, 8, 9.
Hazor. The Schweich Lectures, 1970. Y. Yadin. London, 1972
Hazor. The Rediscovery of a Great Citadel of the Bible. Y. Yadin. London and Jerusalem, 1975.

Ḥederah

The site lies in the Plain of Sharon. The finds were made in a cave excavated by Professor E. L. Sukenik. They were of the Chalcolithic period, with affinities to finds of Ghassul. The most interesting were unique pottery ossuaries made in the form of houses.

Bibliography
JPOS XVII.

Tell Hesi

Tell el Hesi lies on the edge of the coastal plain, due west of Hebron. It was first excavated by Sir Flinders Petrie in 1890 and at this site Petrie made the first beginnings of stratigraphical excavation in Palestine and the first beginnings of linking strata with pottery. He recorded his finds in feet above sea level and observed the changing pottery types in the different levels. By observing the levels at which recognizable Egyptian objects were found, he made a start in establishing the chronology of Palestinian sites by linking them with Egypt; upon this link with Egypt Palestinian chronology is mainly dependent. Since his dating of the earlier Egyptian dynasties was too high, the actual chronology he suggested for Tell Hesi has had to be revised, and his identification of the site as Lachish is not now accepted, but his work here was revolutionary in its importance.

The excavations were continued in 1892 by F. J. Bliss, by tne same methods. In the lowest level of occupation was found an important group of copper weapons. A crescentic axehead is almost exactly paralleled by one found in an Early Bronze III tomb at Jericho, thus dating the first occupation of the site to *c.* 2600 B.C.

Excavations were resumed in 1970 by an American expedition under the leadership of J. E. Worrell and L. E. Toombs. These excavations have done much to explain the finds of the earlier excavators and to revise the dates ascribed by them to the successive levels. The most important clearances here have been of the Persian and Hellenistic levels, with some probing of the Iron terracings and defences.

Bibliography
Tell el Hesy (Lachish). W. Flinders Petrie. London, 1891.

A Mound of Many Cities. F. J. Bliss. London, 1894.
Eleventh Annual Report of the Institute of Archaeology, University of London. 'A Crescentic Axehead from Jericho, and a Group of Weapons from Tell el Hesi'. K. M. Kenyon.
IEJ Notes and News 21, 24.
PEQ (1974). 'Tell el-Hesi 1970–71'. L. E. Toombs.

El Ḥuṣn

The material designated from El Ḥuṣn comes from a cave dwelling with a late secondary burial near the town of El Ḥuṣn in Gilead, approximately 1 kilometre south of Tell el-Ḥuṣn and 22 kilometres north of modern Jerash in Jordan. The finds within the cave belong to two different periods; the occupation remains are dated to the Early Bronze Age and the burial remains to the Early Bronze–Middle Bronze Period. The EB–MB pottery has close analogies with pottery of the same period from Megiddo and Ma'ayan Barukh.

Bibliography

PEF Annual (1953), 1–13, G. L. Harding and J. B. S. Isserlin.
IEJ 10 (1960), 209–13. R. Amiran.

Tell Jemmeh

Tell Jemmeh was the first site to be excavated, in 1926–27, by Sir Flinders Petrie, after the transference to Palestine of the activities of the British School of Archaeology in Egypt. The importance of the excavations lies not in the remains uncovered, but in the continuous succession of strata from the 13th to the 15th century B.C.

A new campaign of excavations was begun in 1970 by the Smithsonian Institution, under the direction of Dr G. Van Beek. The evidence from Petrie's excavation has been studied and re-dated. The most interesting remains examined in detail so far belong to the Persian and Hellenistic periods.

Bibliography

Gerar. Flinders Petrie. British School of Archaeology in Egypt and Bernard Quaritch, London, 1928.
IEJ Notes and News 20, 22, 24.

Jericho

Jericho was first investigated by the Palestine Exploration Fund in 1873, but on a small scale. The first major excavations were those carried out between 1907 and 1909 by a joint Austrian-German mission under Sellin and Watzinger. These excavations showed the great potentialities of the site, but the developments made in the study of Palestinian pottery after the First War made a revision of the suggested datings essential. Further excavations were therefore undertaken by Professor John Garstang between 1930 and 1936, with an expedition sponsored by the Institute of Archaeology of the University of Liverpool, and financed by a number of museums and individuals, chief among the latter being Sir Charles Marston and Lord Melchett. Further excavations were undertaken between 1952 and 1958 by an expedition sponsored by the British School of Archaeology in Jerusalem, the Palestine Exploration Fund, and the British Academy, in collaboration with the American School of Oriental Research in Jerusalem and the Royal Ontario Museum, under the direction of the author. The last expedition showed that almost all traces of the Late Bronze Age town of the time of Joshua had been destroyed by erosion, and that the identification of one of the lines of town walls as belonging to this period was mistaken. Occupation of the site started in the Mesolithic, *c.* 9000 B.C., and there was a continuous development from that stage into a town of the Pre-Pottery Neolithic period, *c.* 8000 B.C., successively occupied by two different groups of people. Thereafter there was a very much lesser occupation by Neolithic people with pottery, but it is not yet clear whether there was a gap before these arrived, and again before the arrival of the Proto-Urban groups. From that time, late in the fourth millennium, there was continuous occupation until the town was destroyed *c.* 1580 B.C. It was probably reoccupied *c.* 1400 B.C., but of the town of this period almost nothing remains.

Bibliography

Jericho. E. Sellin and C. Watzinger. Leipzig, 1913.
LAAA XIX, XX, XXI, XXII.
PEFQS (1930, 1931, 1935, 1936).
The Story of Jericho. J. Garstang and J. B. E. Garstang. London, 1948.
PEQ (1951, 1952, 1953, 1955, 1956, 1957).
Excavations at Jericho, Vols. I and II. K. M. Kenyon. London, 1960 and 1965.
Digging up Jericho. K. M. Kenyon. London, 1957.
Advancement of Science (December 1969). 'The Origins of the Neolithic'. K. M. Kenyon.
In Search of the Jericho Potters. Ceramics from the Iron Age and from the Neolithicum. H. J. Franken. Amsterdam and Oxford, 1974.

Jerusalem

Innumerable expeditions have investigated the problems of the archaeology of Jerusalem, but the continuous occupation of the site for thousands of years has rendered excavation very difficult and most of the results have been inconclusive. Much of the site lies beneath the present walled city and in those parts which are outside the walls successive phases of occupation have made the earlier remains very fragmentary. The first major excavations were undertaken on behalf of the Palestine Exploration Fund by Captain (later Sir Charles) Warren in 1864–67; Warren accomplished an amazing amount in investigating the walls of the Temple area, and his results were beautifully recorded. Between 1894 and 1897 F. J. Bliss and A. C. Dickie carried out widespread excavations in the area to the south of the walled city, again on behalf of the Fund. Both these excavations were admirably carried out for their period, and excellently recorded, but at that stage stratigraphical methods and pottery chronology had not been developed to assist in dating strata, so ascriptions of structures to periods could only be theories, and these theories have since been proved to be wrong. In 1909 and 1911 the Parker Mission carried out many soundings and tunnellings on Ophel, the south-eastern spur of Jerusalem, generally accepted as the site of the original settlement, in search of David's tomb. The main result was to uncover a series of water channels in connection with the Virgin's Fountain. In 1913–14, R. Weill, on behalf of Baron Edmond de Rothschild, conducted excavations on the southern tip of Ophel, in which fragments of a complicated series of fortifications were uncovered. The interpretation of the results of both these expeditions owes much to the constant interest of Père Hugues Vincent of the Dominican École Biblique. In 1923 the Palestine Exploration Fund renewed its attack on the problems of the history of the city, with excavations on the hill of Ophel, outside the walls of medieval and modern Jerusalem. From 1923 to 1925 they were directed by Professor R. A. S. Macalister, and in 1927 by Mr J. W. Crowfoot. The site was very much disturbed, and only fragmentary remains were recovered. Attention was mainly directed to the recovery of evidence concerning the Jebusite and early Israelite defences. In the 1927 excavations an imposing gateway was found well up in the inner side of the Ophel ridge, which was in use in the Maccabean period, and evidence was provided that the southern end of the Tyropoeon Valley dividing Ophel from the western ridge was not occupied until that period. In excavations carried out at the present citadel between 1934 and 1948 on behalf of the Department of Antiquities of Palestine, Mr C. N. Johns was able to date stratigraphically the older lines of wall there (at the north-west corner of the early city) and to show that the earliest line of wall crossing the Tyropoeon Valley and connecting the points of western and eastern ridges was not earlier than the Hellenistic period. Further excavations on behalf of the Department by Mr R. W. Hamilton against the north wall of the present city provided dating for the expanion of the town to the north in Herodian and Roman times, which falls outside the scope of the present volume. In 1961 the British School of Archaeology, in collaboration with the École Biblique and the Royal Ontario Museum, began a large-scale excavation completed in 1967 in all areas of ancient Jerusalem.

Since 1967 a very large number of excavations have been carried out within the Old City and in adjacent areas. Those on the largest scale were at the south-western corner of the Herodian Temple platform, and along its southern boundary, under the direction of Professor B. Mazar. Other excavations, mainly in the old Jewish Quarter, have made valuable contributions concerning the extent of Jerusalem during the period of the Monarchy.

The outline of the history of the city emerging from these excavations may be given briefly. The original settlement was on the eastern of the two ridges included within the maximum extent of the site. There was some occupation in the fourth millennium, but the remains are fragmentary. The earliest town wall found is Middle Bronze Age, but little survives of the town of the period. In the Late Bronze Age, it was a Jebusite stronghold, so strong that it long defied Israelite capture, of which the surviving structures consist of terraces to support houses on the steep eastern slope. About 1000 B.C. Jerusalem was at last captured by the Israelites under David. His city was that of the preceding Jebusites, whose walls he rebuilt. Under Solomon, the Temple was built on the northern part of the eastern ridge, and presumably the town was extended to the north to join the site of the Temple. The area between the Jebusite–Davidic north wall and the Temple platform was probably used for official buildings, perhaps including Solomon's palace. The levels of this period here and along the length of the summit of the ridge have been destroyed by quarrying. There is in fact no evidence of the internal structures of the city and indeed very little to indicate the culture of the inhabitants.

The 1961–67 excavations made it clear that the south-eastern part of the western ridge was not included within the town until the time of Herod Agrippa, A.D. 40–44. There were, however, two additions to the Solomonic town. The last wall of the Jebusite and Davidic city was superseded in the 8th century B.C. by one which continued north to enclose an additional area of the lower eastern slopes, perhaps running gradually up to join the Temple platform. Excavations within the Old City directed by Professor N. Avigad between 1969 and 1971 located a massive wall midway up the slope of the western ridge, showing that the lower part of this ridge was included within the walls by the 8th–7th centuries B.C. There is disagreement as to how this new wall linked with those of Solomonic Jerusalem. The firm evidence of the 1961–67 excavations that there was no occupation at this time in the central valley or on the lower slopes of the western ridge makes it impossible to accept the proposal that the newly-found wall continued south to enclose the Pool of Siloam. The plan that seems best to accord with existing evidence is that given on Fig. 86.

In 587 B.C., the city fell to the Babylonians and was destroyed and depopulated. When it revived, it shrank back to the summit of the eastern ridge. In 538 B.C. Cyrus allowed some of the exiles to return and to rebuild the Temple. The walls, however, were not rebuilt until the governorship of Nehemiah, probably 445–433 B.C. in his rebuilding, the lower slopes of the eastern ridge were abandoned, and the wall followed the crest. The position of the west wall at this period, just below the western crest of the eastern ridge, is indicated by the gate found in 1927. During the Maccabean period, the town expanded once more on to the western ridge, probably sufficiently far south to prevent the eastern ridge being dominated from that direction by the new Hellenistic type of siege weapons. The 1961–67 excavations showed that the full enclosure of the western ridge with a wall joining the southern tip of the eastern ridge belonged to the period of Herod Agrippa.

Bibliography

The Survey of Western Palestine. Jerusalem. C. Warren and E. R. Conder. London, 1884.

Excavations at Jerusalem 1894–1897. F. J. Bliss and A. C. Dickie. London, 1898.

Jérusalem sous Terre. H. Vincent. London, 1911.

La Cité de David, I and II. R. Weill. Paris, 1902 and 1947.

APEF IV. *Excavations on the Hill of Ophel, Jerusalem, 1923–5.* R. A. S. Macalister and J. G. Duncan. London, 1926.

APEF V. *Excavations in the Tyropoeon Valley, Jerusalem, 1927.* J. W. Crowfoot. London, 1929.

PEQ (1962, 1963, 1964, 1965, 1966, 1967, 1968). Interim reports on Excavations 1961–67. K. M. Kenyon.

Jerusalem. Excavating 3000 years of History. K. M. Kenyon. London and New York, 1967.

Digging Up Jerusalem. K. M. Kenyon. London and New York, 1974.

Jerusalem Revealed. ed. Y. Yadin. Jerusalem, 1975.

IEJ 20, 21, 22.

Megiddo

The prime instigator of the great excavations carried out at Megiddo between 1925 and 1939 by the Oriental Institute of Chicago was Professor James Breasted. The work was directed in turn by Dr C. S. Fisher (1925–27), Mr P. L. O. Guy (1927–35), and Mr G. Loud (1935–39). The excavations were on the most monumental scale of any carried out in Palestine. The whole mound was acquired by the Oriental Institute, and the original intention was to excavate it layer by layer in its entirety. Such a scheme proved beyond the resources even of the Oriental Institute. Strata I to V (numbering from the top downwards), dating from approximately 350 B.C. to 1000 B.C. (excavators' date 1060 B.C.), were completely cleared.

Excavation on the tell itself was carried beyond that stage only in four areas and only in one was bedrock reached, in an area approximately 40 metres by 25 metres. In addition to work on the tell itself, a large area was cleared on the lower slopes of the hill, for the purpose of freeing space for dumping. In this was found a further sequence of the earliest periods of occupation, dating from the beginning of the Early Bronze Age to the end of the third millennium, and also a large number of tombs of all periods.

This enormous enterprise of the Oriental Institute was a pioneer work in every sense. It is inevitable that over the years improved excavation techniques and the build-up of knowledge of pottery and other objects have resulted in the modification of some of the conclusions and chronological identifications of the Chicago excavations.

The evidence from the Samaria excavations in 1930–35 threw doubts on the ascription of the Megiddo Stratum IV buildings to the period of Solomon. Professor Yadin's excavations at Hazor emphasized the probability that the Stratum V gate was Solomonic on the basis of the similarity of its plan with the Solomonic gate at Hazor. Some small-scale excavations at Megiddo showed that a casemate wall belonged to this early stage in the Iron Age town of Megiddo, and there is strong, but not conclusive, evidence that this was the original wall to which the Stratum V gates belonged. With this casemate wall was associated a palatial building on the north side of the mound, and the evidence that there was this earlier system of fortification makes it certain that Palace 1723 can be firmly identified as a palatial building which existed before the new wall, the 'offsets-and-insets' wall, was built. The earlier gate was re-used with the new wall. There was evidence that other Solomonic buildings survived only as robber trenches. To this period belonged a covered gallery to the spring at the foot of the mound.

The Solomonic town was probably destroyed in Shishak's raid in 922 B.C. The Stratum IV rebuilding is probably mid-9th century B.C. To it belonged the offsets-and-insets wall, the great series of public buildings known as the Solomonic stables, a rebuilding of the enclosure wall of Palace 1723, with the palace itself succeeded by a replacement which has completely disappeared, and the construction of the water shaft and tunnel. This town was destroyed at the end of the 8th century, and the succeeding Strata III to I are on a completely different plan. The site ceased to have any importance before the Hellenistic period.

Bibliography

Megiddo I: 'Seasons of 1925–34. Strata I–V'. R. S. Lamon and G. M. Shipton. 1939. *OIP* XLII.

Megiddo II: 'Seasons of 1935–39' (1 vol. text, 1 plates). G. Loud. 1948. *OIP* LXII.

The Megiddo Water System. R. S. Lamon. 1935. *OIP* XXXII.

Material Remains of the Megiddo Cult. H. G. May. 1935. *OIP* XXVI.

Megiddo Tombs. P. L. O. Guy and R. M. Engberg. 1938. *OIP* XXXIII.
Notes on the Chalcolithic and Early Bronze Age Pottery of Megiddo. R. M.
  Engberg and G. M. Shipton. 1934. *SAOC* 10.
The Pottery of Megiddo Strata VI to XX. G. M. Shipton. *SAOC* 17. (All
  published by the University of Chicago Press).
Eretz Israel V. 'Some notes on the Early and Middle Bronze Age strata of
  Megiddo'. K. M. Kenyon.
Levant I. 'The Middle and Late Bronze Age strata at Megiddo'. K. M.
  Kenyon.
Bulletin of the Institute of Archaeology 4. 'Megiddo, Hazor, Samaria and
  Chronology'. K. M. Kenyon.
Biblical Archaeologist XXIII. 'New Light on Solomon's Megiddo'. Y.
  Yadin.
Biblical Archaeologist XXXIII. 'Megiddo of the Kings of Israel'. Y. Yadin.
IEJ 16.4, pp. 278–80. Notes and News. Y. Yadin.
Journal of Near Eastern Studies 31.4. 'The Stratification of Israelite
  Megiddo'. Y. Aharoni.
IEJ 16.3. 'King Solomon's Palace and Building 1723 in Megiddo'. D.
  Ussishkin.
Zeitschrift des Deutschen Palästina-Vereins 89. 'The Megiddo Temples'. I.
  Dunayevsky and A. Kempinski.
IEJ 15.4. 'An interpretation of the Megiddo Sacred Area during Middle
  Bronze II'. C. Epstein.

Wadi el Mughara

In the Wadi el Mughara, running from the Carmel ridge down to the
Mediterranean, are a number of caves that were excavated between 1929
and 1934 by Professor Dorothy Garrod, on behalf of the American School
of Prehistoric Research and the British School of Archaeology in
Jerusalem. The caves provided overlapping sequences of deposits from the
Middle Palaeolithic to the Mesolithic. For the period covered by the present volume, the important part of the series is the Mesolithic. A rich series
of deposits, with accompanying burials, belonged to the Lower Natufian,
the Mesolithic of Palestine. They indicated the possibility that incipient
agriculture was being practised. They were succeeded by Middle and Upper
Natufian deposits; in the Middle Natufian there was evidence that the dog
had been domesticated. The Natufian deposits link with the Mesolithic of
Jericho.

Bibliography

The Stone Age of Mount Carmel, I. D. A. E. Garrod and D. N. A. Bate,
  Clarendon Press, Oxford. 1937.
Proceedings of the British Academy XLIII. 'The Natufian Culture'. D. A. E.
  Garrod.

Archaeology in the Holy Land

Tell Nasbeh

Tell en Nasbeh lies beside the main route between Judah and Israel, near the boundary between the two kingdoms, some 8 miles (13km.) north of Jerusalem. It was completely excavated between 1926 and 1935 by Dr W. F. Badé for the Palestine Institute of the Pacific School of Religion, Berkeley, California. Structural remains earlier than the Early Iron Age were scanty, but tombs belonging to the Proto-Urban period were found. The main occupation of the site does not start until the 11th century B.C., and continued throughout the period of the Jewish Kingdom, with remains of decreasing importance in the Post-Exilic period.

Bibliography
Tell en Nasbeh I: *Archaeological and Historical Results.* C. C. McCown.
Tell en Nasbeh II: *The Pottery.* J. C. Wampler. Palestine Institute of the Pacific School of Religion and American Schools of Oriental Research, Berkeley and New Haven.

Tell Qasile

The tell is situated on the outskirts of Tel Aviv to the north of the River Yarkon. Excavations were begun in 1949, and were continued at intervals up to 1974, the later stages being under the direction of A. Mazar. The chief importance of the site lay in the evidence concerning the Iron Age, especially in the Philistine period. The lowest stratum, XII, was Philistine, and there was no evidence of Late Bronze Age occupation. To it belonged the first of a series of temples. They all had a simple rectangular plan, with a platform, approached by steps, jutting out from the north wall, behind which was a small room or cell, either for storage or an inner sanctum. The walls of the main chamber were lined by benches, and in Stratum X there was an antechamber with an entrance at right-angles to the main axis. At this period, the roof was supported by wooden columns. The successive temples were set in a courtyard, in which a second small temple was added in Stratum XI. A rich collection of cult objects was recovered, especially from Stratum X.

Stratum X was destroyed by fire, possibly by David. The subsequent rebuilding of the temple suggested that the occupants of the site were unchanged. Subsequent occupation was slight.

Bibliography
IEJ 1. Interim report. B. Maisler (Mazar).
IEJ 23.2, 25. 2–3. Interim reports. A. Mazar.

Ramat Rahel

The site lies a short distance to the south-west of Jerusalem. It was excavated by Professor Y. Aharoni between 1959 and 1962. The main Iron Age structure consisted of an imposing citadel or palace. The inner citadel consisted of a rectangular enclosure of about three-quarters of an acre (0·30ha.) surrounded by a casemate wall on three sides and a massive building along the west side, of which the outer wall was apparently integral with that of the casemates. Within the enclosure was a courtyard paved with rammed chalk and a number of buildings. All buildings were badly mutilated by the structures of the Roman and Byzantine periods. Joined to the north-east angle of this complex was a wall enclosing an outer area of 4 acres (1·62ha.) and apparently encircling the whole inner citadel except the north-east corner, though there are ambiguities in the published plan. This outer area was also surfaced with rammed chalk over a thick levelling fill, 1 metre to the east, 3 metres to the west, retained by the outer wall.

Professor Aharoni suggests that the citadel was built by Jehoiakim, 608–597 B.C., for which good support is provided by the biblical record, and which fits the evidence of the pottery vessels, late 7th–6th centuries, found beneath the destruction level.

It is, however, clear from the building styles that there were probably at least three periods of use, or at least of construction. The excavators recognized that there was an earlier phase on the site, for a fragment of another row of casemates was found to the south of the inner citadel. To it may belong the fragments of beautiful ashlar work found in patches in the inner citadel. The face of these sections has all the excellence of dressing of Samaria Period I, and the ashlar blocks are even better, since they are rectangularly dressed on all faces, whereas in the Samaria walls the rest of the blocks are irregular. It is true Phoenician-type masonry, and it seems highly probable that it belongs to the time of Solomon. In places, courses of walls in this masonry are buried beneath the later floor, and there is an example of the upper part of a wall in which the finely dressed ashlars are re-used. These stretches of excellent walls were fitted into the greater part of the inner citadel structure which was built also of ashlars, laid as headers which made the width of the wall. The faces of these walls lacked the fine dressing of the earlier walls. They must belong to a stage when the fine artistry of the Phoenician-dressed masonry had been lost, but in which a tradition of using ashlar blocks survived. This stage was not found at Samaria. It could perhaps be 8th-century.

A final stage of deterioration is found in the building in the north-east angle of the inner citadel, in which the walls are entirely of undressed stone, as in the later periods at Samaria and in the late 7th-century domestic houses in Jerusalem. In this building was found much of the 7th–6th century pottery.

Bibliography

IEJ 6.

Excavations at Ramat Rahel. 'Seasons of 1959 and 1960'. Y. Aharoni. Centro di Studi Semitici. University of Rome, 1962.

Excavations at Ramat Rahel. 'Seasons of 1961 and 1962'. Y. Aharoni. Centro di Studi Semitici. University of Rome, 1964.

Ras el-'Ain (Aphek-Antipatris)

The archaeological importance of the site first became apparent when in 1936 work in connection with a new water-supply for Jerusalem uncovered burials of the beginning of the Middle Bronze Age and remains belonging to the Early Bronze Age. These were recorded by members of the Department of Antiquities of Palestine. In 1972, large-scale excavations at the site were begun, under the aegis of the Institute of Archaeology of Tel Aviv University with the support of a large number of American institutions, and directed by M. Kochavi.

The mound is an imposing one, covering an area of about 30 acres (12·14ha.). It is situated near the head-waters of the Yarkon river on the fringe of the coastal plain and on the major route from Egypt to Syria and Mesopotamia, the Via Maris. It can with great probability be identified as Aphek, mentioned in the Egyptian Execration texts and down to the Eighteenth Dynasty, and again in the Bible when it was a border town of Philistia. It also seems to be the town rebuilt by Herod and named Antipatris. Excavation has shown that it was a fortified town in the Early Bronze Age. The evidence so far published does not suggest any EB–MB occupation. Tomb groups of MB I provide some of the best examples of the very characteristic and beautiful pottery of the period, when the town was once more walled. A building of this period of considerable size and importance has been excavated. Full occupation continued throughout the Middle Bronze Age. There may have been a gap after the Thotmes III destruction, and only slight evidence of Late Bronze II–Iron Age occupation has survived, though this may be partly due to erosion. There was some occupation in the Hellenistic period, but full revival only came in the Herodian period. The town had some importance throughout the Byzantine period, and the mound is crowned by an impressive Ottoman fort, within which is a 16th-century mosque.

Bibliography

QDAP V, VI.
IEJ 12, 22.
Excavations of Aphek-Antipatris. M. Kochavi. Tel Aviv University, 1978.

Samaria

The town of Samaria lies on a low hill beside the main north–south route through Palestine, some 10 miles north-west of the pass between Mount Gerizim and Mount Ebal, and overlooking the broad Wadi esh Sha'ir running down to the coastal plain. The first excavations were carried out on behalf of Harvard University by Professor G. A. Reisner from 1908 to 1910. From 1931 to 1935 further excavations were directed by Mr J. W. Crowfoot on behalf of a joint expedition sponsored by Harvard University, the Hebrew University in Jerusalem, the Palestine Exploration Fund, the

British Academy, and the British School of Archaeology in Jerusalem. The results of the work of the two expeditions provided good evidence for the complete history of the site. Although some sporadic occupation had existed on the hill in the Proto-Urban period, the foundation of the city dated only from the 9th century B.C., but it had a continuous existence thereafter until the Byzantine period. The history of the royal quarter of the Israelite city was traced in detail, and also that of the Hellenistic fort and Roman temple which succeeded it on the summit of the hill. The most important finds were a group of ostraca of the time of Jeroboam II and a collection of ivory carvings probably from the palace of Ahab.

In 1967 The British School of Archaeology in Jerusalem recommended excavations at Samaria under the direction of Dr J. B. Hennessy. The purpose of the excavation was to investigate the occupation of the lower slopes of the hill around the area of the royal quarter. The results so far have had the surprising result of showing that to the north-west of the summit plateau immediately outside the royal quarter, there was no occupation until, at earliest, the 5th century B.C. It is very probable that this conclusion involves the whole of the western slopes of the hill. If there was a lower town, occupied by the ordinary population, it is likely to lie to the east, and this still remains to be investigated.

Bibliography

Harvard Excavations at Samaria. G. A. Reisner, C. S. Fisher, D. G. Lyon. Cambridge, Mass., 1924.

Samaria-Sebaste I: The Buildings. J. W. Crowfoot, K. M. Kenyon, E. L. Sukenik. Palestine Exploration Fund, 1942.

Samaria-Sebaste II: Early Ivories from Samaria. J. W. and G. M. Crowfoot. Palestine Exploration Fund, 1938.

Samaria-Sebaste III: The Objects. J. W. Crowfoot, G. M. Crowfoot, K. M. Kenyon. Palestine Exploration Fund, 1957.

Levant II. 'Excavations at Samaria-Sebaste 1968'. J. B. Hennessy.

Shechem

The site of the biblical Shechem can be identified at Balata, at the northern end of the pass between Mount Gerizim and Mount Ebal. The site was excavated between 1913 and 1934 by Dr E. Sellin and, in the later seasons, Dr G. Welter. Very little has been published concerning the results of these excavations. Work was resumed between 1956 and 1964 by the Drew–McCormick Expedition under the direction of Dr G. E. Wright. There was some occupation in the Pre-Pottery Neolithic period, but the first town belongs only to the Middle Bronze Age, MB I to early MB II. A free-standing town wall was succeeded by an earth rampart of the usual type, which was in turn succeeded by a wall of cyclopean masonry associated with a fine triple-buttress gateway. On the fill behind the wall was a building interpreted as a temple. The town was destroyed at the end of the Middle Bronze Age, and deserted till at least the end of the 16th century B.C. Shechem appears prominently in the Amarna Letters. Little of the interior of the Late Bronze Age town has been excavated. It seems probable that a gateway built with magnificent orthostats belongs to this period, though this was not the opinion of the excavators. The Late Bronze town was destroyed in the 12th century B.C., and the site was only reoccupied in the 10th century B.C. Like Samaria and Tell el Far'ah, Israelite Shechem was destroyed by the Assyrians *c.* 720 B.C., and in the slight occupation of the succeeding period imported Assyrian pottery appears. There was a gap in occupation between *c.* 475 B.C. and *c.* 331 B.C., when the Samaritans reoccupied it down to its final destruction in 101 B.C.

Bibliography

Shechem. The Biography of a Biblical City. G. E. Wright. New York, 1964.

Taanach

The city is mentioned in the Bible and in Egyptian records. It lies at the southern edge of the Plain of Esdraelon, about 5 miles south-east of Megiddo. Excavations were conducted here by E. Sellin between 1902 and 1904, and a new campaign was carried out by the American Schools of Oriental Research under the direction of Paul Lapp between 1963 and 1968. The site was first occupied in the Early Bronze Age, when it was surrounded by a stone-built town wall. During the course of EB III it was abandoned and not reoccupied until late in the Middle Bronze Age. Evidence suggests that newcomers from Anatolia were responsible, possibly to be identified as Hyksos. Its defences at this period were of the characteristic plaster-faced rampart type; at one stage apparently capped as a casemate wall. Though the town was destroyed at the end of the Middle Bronze Age, occupation continued into the 15th century, when it was probably destroyed by Thotmes III in 1482 B.C., and abandoned until late in the 14th century. The most interesting feature in the LB I occupation was an abortive water-shaft, which was then plastered and used as a reservoir. This is evidence that waterproof plaster was not an invention of the Iron Age. Occupation in the 13th–12th centuries B.C. was slight, and came to an end *c.* 1125 B.C. To the succeeding period belonged only a slight occupation, of which the most interesting remains belonged to a cult centre. The succeeding violent destruction may have been the work of Shishak. Thereafter the site sinks into insignificance.

Bibliography

BASOR 185. 'The 1966 Excavations at Tell Ta'annek'. P. W. Lapp.
BASOR 195. 'The 1968 Excavations at Tell Ta'annek'. P. W. Lapp.
BA XXX, 1. 'Taanach by the Waters of Megiddo.' P. W. Lapp.

Timna

King Solomon's Mines are part of a tradition that spreads far beyond historical and archaeological evidence. Finds from some excavations have been claimed as evidence of industrial activities at the head of the Gulf of Aqaba, but the most recent assessment concentrated on Timna is that there was during the reign of Solomon no mining activity in this particular area; those searching for a Solomonic mining area must look elsewhere.

The history of the area centred on Timna is fascinating. Excavations there were carried out from 1959 by Dr Beno Rothenberg. They revealed mine pits and shafts of amazing complexity during the Chalcolithic period, with associated working sites. The next stage of exploration belonged to the Late Bronze Age, during which there were close contacts with Egypt. To this period belonged a sanctuary dedicated to the Egyptian goddess Hathor, of which there were most interesting remains. Therefore the area came under the control of the Kenites and Midianites at the time of the entry of the Israelite tribes into Palestine, but it does not seem to have lasted longer than the 12th century B.C. The next period of use was Roman.

Bibliography

Timna. B. Rothenberg. London, 1972.

Brief General Bibliography

Amiran, R., *Ancient Pottery of the Holy Land*. Jerusalem, English edition, 1969.

Avi-Yonah, M. (ed.), *Encyclopedia of Archaeological Excavations in the Holy Land*. English edition, I, 1975, II, 1976. London and Jerusalem.

Avi-Yonah, M., and E. Stern (eds.), *Encyclopedia of Archaeological Excavations in the Holy Land*. English edition, III, 1977 IV, 1978. London and Jerusalem.

Baly, D., and A. D. Tushingham, *Atlas of the Biblical World*. New York, 1971.

Engberg, R. M., *The Hyksos Reconsidered. SAOC*. Chicago, 1939.

Epstein, C. M., *Palestinian Bichrome Ware*. Leiden, 1966.

Hennessy, J. B., *The Foreign Relations of Palestine during the Early Bronze Age*. Colt Archaeological Institute Publications. London, 1967.

Kenyon, K. M., *Amorites and Canaanites*. Schweich Lectures, British Academy, 1966; *The Bible and Recent Archaeology*. London, 1978.

Macalister, R. A. S., *The Philistines*. Schweich Lectures, British Academy, 1911.

May, H. G., R. W. Hamilton and G. N. S. Hunt, *Oxford Bible Atlas*, London, 2nd edition, 1974.

Moorey, P. R. S., *Biblical Lands*. Making of the Past Series. Oxford, 1975.

Moorey, R., and P. Parr (eds.), *Archaeology in the Levant, Essays for Kathleen Kenyon*. Warminster, 1978.

Negev, A., *Archaeological Encyclopedia of the Holy Land*. London and Jerusalem, 1972.

Noth, M., *History of Israel*. London, 2nd English edition, 1960.

Paul, S. M., and W. G. Dever, *Biblical Archaeology*. Library of Jewish Knowledge. Jerusalem, 1973.

Pritchard, J. B. (ed.), *Ancient Near Eastern Texts Relating to the Old Testament*. Princeton, 3rd edition, 1960.

Rowley, H. H., *From Joseph to Joshua*. Schweich Lectures, British Academy, 1948.

de Vaux, R., *Histoire Ancienne d'Israel*. Paris, 1971; *Ancient Israel. Its Life and Institutions*. London, English version, 1961.

Wright, G. E., *The Pottery of Palestine from the Earliest Times to the End of the Early Bronze Age*. New Haven, 1937.

Articles

QDAP VI. 'Phoenician Tombs'. C. N. Johns.
PEQ (1940). 'New Light on the Habiru–Hebrew Question'. J. W. Jack.
PEQ (1942). 'Habiru and Hebrew'. H. H. Rowley.
PEQ (1946). 'The Habiru, the Hebrews and the Arabs'. A. Guillaume.
PEQ (1948). 'King Solomon's Temple and other buildings and works of Art'. J. L. Myres.
AJA (1937). 'Tell Tainat'. C. C. McCown.
RB LXXIV. 'Les Hurrites de l'Histoire et les Horites de la Bible'. R. de Vaux.
Advancement of Science (December 1969). 'The Origins of the Neolithic'. K. M. Kenyon.

Index